MINDS on MATH ▶7

ONTARIO EDITION

Robert Alexander
Formerly with the
Toronto Board of Education
Toronto, Ontario

Katie Pallos-Haden
Memorial Composite High School
Stony Plain, Alberta

Ron Lancaster
St. Mildred's Lightbourn School
Oakville, Ontario

Fred Crouse
Kings County District School Board
Kentville, Nova Scotia

David DeCoste
Dr. J.H. Gillis Regional High School
Antigonish, Nova Scotia

Brendan Kelly
University of Toronto
Toronto, Ontario

Florence Glanfield
Consultant
Edmonton, Alberta

Paul Atkinson
Waterloo County Board of Education
Kitchener, Ontario

Jane Forbes
E.C. Drury High School
Milton, Ontario

Addison-Wesley

An imprint of Addison Wesley Longman Ltd.

Don Mills, Ontario • Reading, Massachusetts
Harlow, England • Glenview, Illinois
Melbourne, Australia

DEVELOPMENTAL EDITORS

Lynda Cowan

Sarah Mawson

Lesley Haynes

EDITORS

Maurice Barry

Mei Lin Cheung

Santo D'Agostino

Anna-Maria Garnham

Lee Geller

Lynne Gulliver

Helen Nolan

Rajshree Shankar

Anita Smale

RESEARCHER

Louise MacKenzie

DESIGN/PRODUCTION

Pronk&Associates

ART DIRECTION

Pronk&Associates/Joe Lepiano

ELECTRONIC ASSEMBLY & TECHNICAL ART

Pronk&Associates/Linda Stephenson, Steve Doinidis, Aleksandar Janicijevic, Craig Swistun, Stanley Tran

COVER DESIGN

Pronk&Associates

Acknowledgments appear on pages 482 and 483.

Canadian Cataloguing in Publication Data

Main entry under title:
    Minds on math 7
Ontario ed.
Includes index.
ISBN 0-201-51269-6

1. Mathematics — Juvenile literature.
I. Alexander, Bob, 1941 —

QA107.M54 1998a   510   C98-931780-3

Copyright © 1998 Addison Wesley Longman Ltd.

ISBN 0-201-51269-6
This book contains recycled product and is acid free.
Printed and bound in Canada.

C D E F – BP – 01 00 99 98

REVIEWERS/CONSULTANTS

Professor Andrew Adler
Department of Mathematics
University of British Columbia

Anne Boyd
Curriculum Consultant
School District 72
Campbell River, British Columbia

Edna M. Dach
Supervisor, Programs
Instructional Services
Elk Island Public Schools
Sherwood Park, Alberta

Liliane Gauthier
Educational Consultant – Instructions
Mathematics & Science - K-8
Saskatoon Board of Education, Saskatchewan

Rita C. Janes
Mathematics Coordinator
St. John's Roman Catholic School Board
St. John's, Newfoundland

Dr. Arthur Jorgensen
Education Consultant
Edson, Alberta

Richard J. Kopan
Coordinator
Calgary Board of Education, Alberta

Peter Saarimaki
Coordinator of Mathematics
Toronto Board of Education, Toronto

Elaine Simmt
University of Alberta
Edmonton, Alberta

Elizabeth Wood
National Sport School
Calgary, Alberta

CONTENTS

CHAPTER 1: TWO-DIMENSIONAL GEOMETRY

CHAPTER 2: FRACTIONS AND DECIMALS

CHAPTER 3: PERCENT AND PROBABILITY

CHAPTER 4: DATA MANAGEMENT

CHAPTER 5: INTEGERS

CHAPTER 6: MEASUREMENT

CHAPTER 9: TRANSFORMATIONS

WELCOME TO *MINDS ON MATH 7*

We hope that this book helps you see that mathematics can be useful, interesting, and enjoyable. We wish you every success.

This book is about…

…Problem Solving
Learning to solve problems is the main reason for studying mathematics. You will find that all the parts of this book are designed to help you improve your problem-solving skills.

…Math in the Real World
This book describes many new ways you can use mathematics to understand your everyday world. You'll also learn about how people use mathematics in their careers.

…Calculators and Computers
Technology is a tool you will be using often in your life, and in your study of mathematics. You'll need a calculator to complete some of the activities and exercises in this book. You'll also want to use a computer and some popular software to work with Draw programs, spreadsheets, and databases. This book will help you add these tools to the paper and pencil you already use every day.

Take a few moments to read the following pages. They explain how this book is organized and how you will be using it.

CHAPTER CONTENTS

Each chapter begins with a magazine-style Contents. This gives you an idea of what you will be studying and what problems the mathematics can help you solve.

WHAT'S COMING UP?

This is a list of the mathematics topics that are covered in the chapter.

DEPARTMENTS

Most chapters contain five departments. You'll get to know the departments as you use the book. For example, a Quest always offers you an interesting opportunity to build your problem-solving skills — and to discover something new.

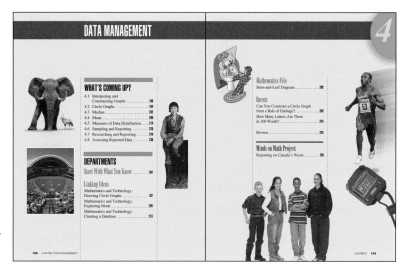

START WITH WHAT YOU KNOW

Each chapter begins with Start With What You Know. These questions and activities give you a chance to review so that you can be successful with the new material.

For example, this Start With What You Know describes how the African elephant is facing extinction because of the ivory trade. The questions help you recall what you know about different types of graphs.

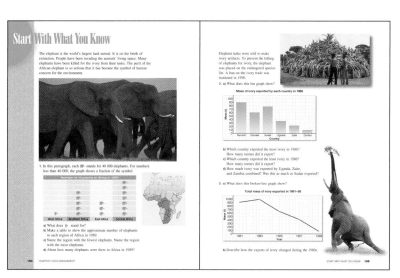

DEVELOPING THE IDEAS

The mathematics in this book is developed in a variety of ways.
Two or more of these ways are often used in the same lesson.

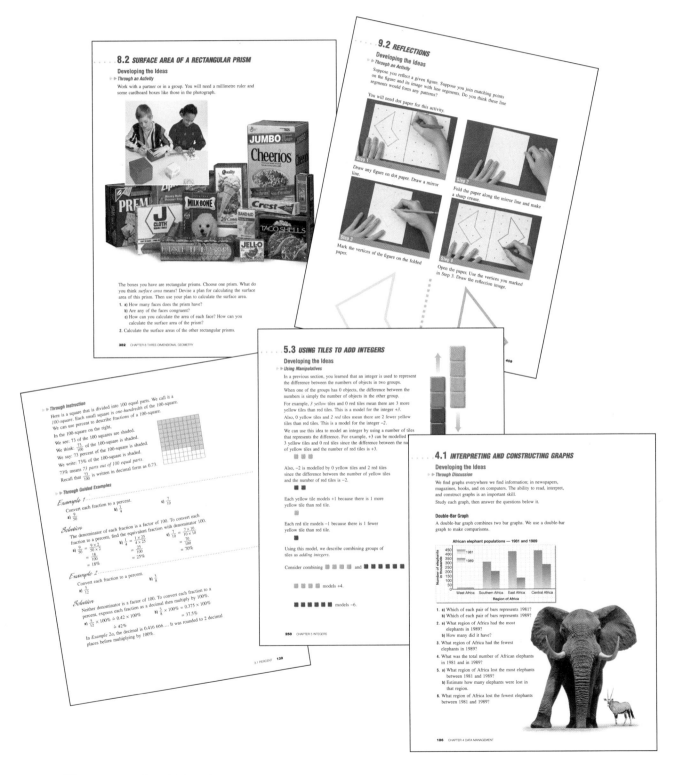

Through Activities

I hear and I forget
I see and I remember
I do and I understand

One of the best ways to learn anything new is to become actively involved with it. This is true whether you are learning to play a musical instrument, learning a new sport, or learning to use a computer.

The same is also true of mathematics. When you use this book you will be actively doing mathematics. Many ideas are developed through activities you can do with a partner or in a small group.

Using Manipulatives

Some ideas are best understood using concrete materials, called manipulatives. They are used to develop understanding in areas such as algebra, fractions, and integers.

Through Discussion

New ideas are often introduced through discussion with a partner, in a small group, or as a class.

Through Instruction

Some Through Instruction sections help you consolidate the ideas you learned through activities or discussion. In other cases, ideas are easiest to understand when you can read a straightforward explanation of the concepts involved.

Through Guided Examples

After you have learned some new ideas through activity or discussion, it helps to see examples showing how to use the ideas. The examples in this book are called guided examples because they usually contain explanations of the steps in the solution.

Using a Computer

A computer can be used to do many calculations in a short time.

WORKING WITH MATHEMATICS

There are five different kinds of exercises in the lessons in this book.

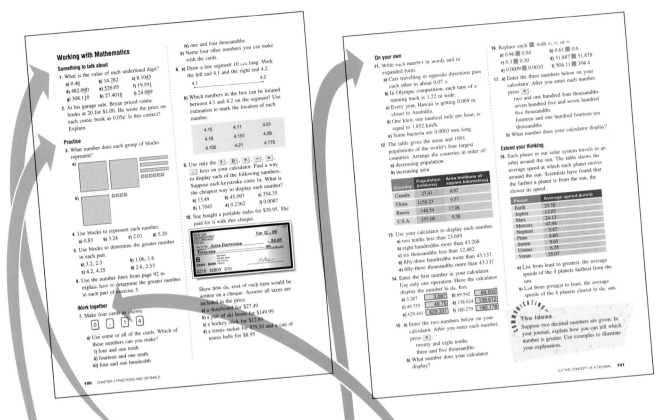

Something to talk about
These exercises will get you talking. They give you and your classmates a chance to check your understanding together before you begin to solve problems on your own.

Practice
Learning anything new requires practice. These exercises let you practise the new skills you have learned.

On your own
After you have gained confidence working with a partner, these exercises should be completed on your own.

Work together
You will probably want to complete these exercises with a partner or in a group. Talking with other students helps you learn because you see how they make connections between the new ideas and what they already know. There are two more advantages:

- Other students can sometimes explain new ideas to you in ways that make sense.
- Explaining something you understand to someone else can help you to understand it better.

Technology

The computer is a tool for learning and doing mathematics in ways that weren't possible just a few years ago. Some of the computer exercises give you a chance to work with popular computer applications, such as spreadsheets and Draw programs. These exercises are labelled with logos. The *Minds on Math 7 Template Disk* lets you get started right away.

For other computer activities, you'll need to use a computer database. The *Minds on Math 7 Data Disk* provides a vast amount of data that you can use to answer questions and to understand and present information.

Using ClarisWorks® or Microsoft Works™ for your applications software will make it easiest for you to do the spreadsheet and Draw program exercises in this book. You will need one of these programs to use the *Minds on Math 7 Template Disk* and the *Minds on Math 7 Data Disk*.

Extend your thinking

These exercises are extensions of the ideas in the lesson. Some of these exercises may require you to think about what you have been doing and to apply your thinking to related ideas. Others may be more challenging than the previous exercises.

DATA DISK   TEMPLATE DISK

Be sure you have correct solutions in your notebook for the exercises in the **Work together** and **On your own** sections of each lesson. To study for a test or examination, try these exercises again. If you have difficulty, refer to the solutions in your notebook.

That's all there is to it!

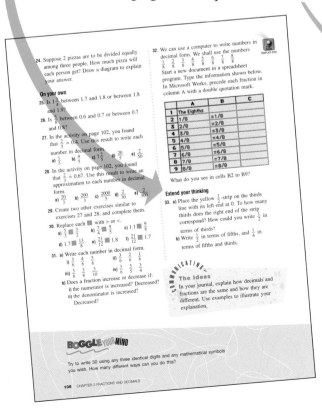

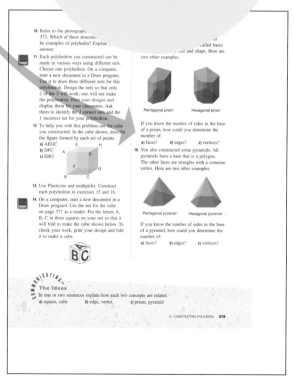

COMMUNICATING THE IDEAS

Communicating your knowledge about a concept or skill can help you learn mathematics. Also, when you learn something interesting or puzzling or exciting, it makes sense to talk about it! In this book you will be asked to communicate your ideas in a variety of ways, such as:

- writing in your journal
- explaining to a friend
- writing a report
- designing a poster

MiNDS ON MATH *PROJECT*

ACTIVITY 2

A geometric figure that resembles an addition sign is called a *Greek cross*. An example is shown on the right. Arrange the pieces of the puzzle to form a Greek cross. Trace the outline of the figure. Record your solution by tracing each piece.

ACTIVITY 3

A quadrilateral that has no parallel sides is called a *trapezium*. Draw two examples of trapeziums to prove that such figures exist. Arrange the pieces of the puzzle to form a trapezium. Trace the outline of the figure. Record your solution by tracing each piece.

ACTIVITY 4

After rearranging the pieces to form the figures in *Activities 1* through *3*, it is easy to forget how the original parallelogram was pieced together. Without looking at the diagram on page 78, arrange the puzzle pieces to form a parallelogram. Trace the outline of the figure and record your solution by tracing each piece.

ACTIVITY 5

While you were working on the previous activities, you may have created an arrangement you thought was interesting and which was different from those described here. If not, try to create such a figure now. If you wish, name your figure. Make one sketch showing only the outline of your figure. Make another sketch showing the five pieces that make up your figure.

COMMUNICATING The Ideas

Prepare your solutions manual. Draw a title page and write an introduction. Include your drawings of the different figures people can make and the solutions you created in each activity. You may wish to order the problems according to difficulty—from easiest to most difficult.

Package your manual in a bag with a set of puzzle pieces. Make the package available to your famil', friends, or classmates who have not completed this project.

MATH PROJECT **79**

Colour a 100-square to show these data in a box graph.
a) What season is the most popular?
b) What season is the least popular?
c) What percent of students chose winter as their favourite season?
d) Is it correct to say that about one-quarter of the students chose winter as their favourite season?
e) What percent of students did not choose summer as their favourite season?

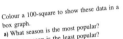

17. Start a new document in a Draw program. Create a small circle. Duplicate the circle and place it next to the first circle. Continue to duplicate until you have a row of 10 circles. Select the whole row and duplicate the row. Place this below the first row. Continue to duplicate until you have 10 rows of 10 circles.
a) Suppose each pattern below is continued. What percent of the circles will be shaded?

i)

ii)

b) Create a pattern in which 80% of the circles are shaded.
c) Create a pattern in which 75% of the circles are unshaded.

18. You know that you breathe in oxygen; an you use carbon, as charcoal, in a barbecu but did you know that your body is mad of these elements, along with others list below?

Element	Percent by mas
Oxygen	65%
Carbon	18%
Hydrogen	10%
Nitrogen	3%
Calcium	2%
Other elements	2%

a) Colour a 100-square to show these elements in a box graph.
b) What percent of your body's mass contributed by the three elements, hydrogen, and oxygen?
c) Make up a question about the box Ask a classmate to answer your q

Extend your thinking

19. The mass of an animal's lungs is a of the mass of its body. The mass animal's heart is about 50% of the its lungs. What is the mass of the each animal?
a) a 6000-kg elephant **b)** a 6-kg c
c) a 600-g hamster **d)** a 60-kg

COMMUNICATING The Ideas

The word *percent* derives from the Latin words *per centum*, meaning "out of 100." How many pennies are there in a dollar? What fraction of a dollar is a penny? What percent of a dollar is a penny? In your journal, use the answers to these questions to explain why we refer to a penny as a cent.

3.1 PERCENT **143**

Keep a Journal.

A journal helps you explore ideas and keep a record of what you have learned. This book gives you many suggestions for what to write about in your journal. If you keep your journal up to date, you'll discover that it can help you review your thinking when you're studying for tests or exams.

QUESTS

Each chapter contains one or two Quests. Each Quest is a significant problem for you to solve.

You'll want to approach Quest problems in a thoughtful way. You can use the four-step problem solving plan built into each Quest to help you. As you work, you'll be finding interesting answers to meaningful questions and learning how to be a successful problem solver.

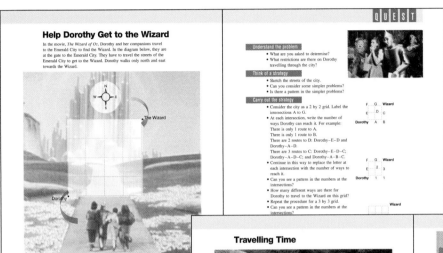

Many Quests contain problems from the world around you.

- Designing a bookcase
- How many letters are there in 100 words?
- What does 2% mean in 2% milk?

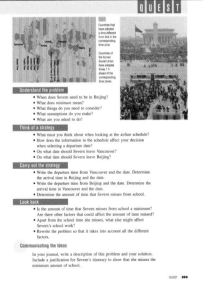

Other Quests involve patterns in arithmetic or geometry.

- The *One Million* book
- Dividing a square into quarters
- Identifying Transformations

LINKING IDEAS

In the Linking Ideas department, you'll find activities that help you explore connections between mathematics and other subject areas, or between strands in mathematics.

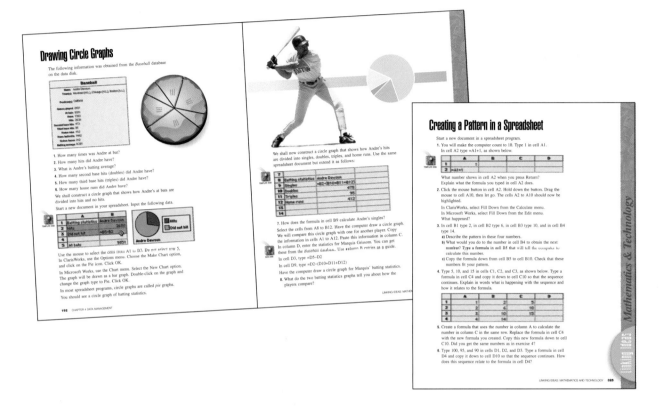

Links with Technology

The computer lets you investigate problems that would be too difficult or involve too much computation to solve with paper and pencil, or even with a calculator. You can also use a computer to explore geometry in a dynamic way that is impossible without a computer.

Other examples of links with technology

- Making Constructions Using a Draw Program
- Creating a Database
- Investigating Patterns Using a Spreadsheet

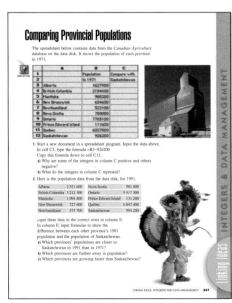

Links with Science

A link feature shows mathematics at work in the field of science.

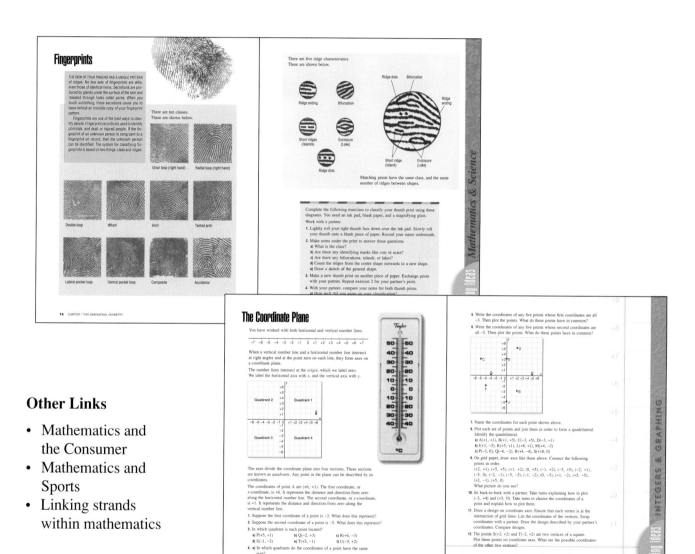

Other Links

- Mathematics and the Consumer
- Mathematics and Sports
- Linking strands within mathematics

MATHEMATICS FILES

Mathematics Files provide opportunities for you to develop your mathematical understanding. These pages may help you see why many people believe mathematics is a fascinating and even beautiful field of study all on its own, with no need for "uses" or "connections" to make it important.

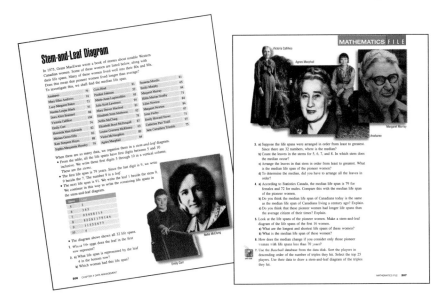

Other examples of Mathematics Files
- Regular Polygons
- Time Zones
- Powers of Ten

BOGGLE YOUR MIND

Many problems involving interesting facts and questions occur throughout the text. These give you more opportunities to practise your problem-solving skills. Often the answers you reach will boggle your mind.

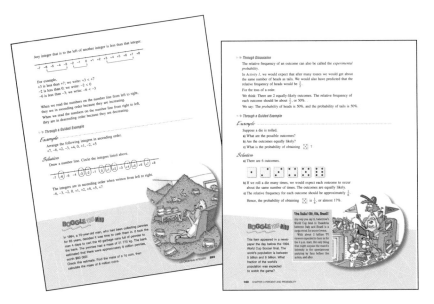

Other Boggle Your Mind topics

- The number of earthworms in $1m^2$ of lawn
- The cost of raising a child in Canada
- The area of the largest iceberg ever recorded

MINDS ON MATH PROJECT

Each chapter ends with a project or investigation that gives you freedom to use and develop mathematics in your own way. You'll need to plan, research, experiment, and make choices and decisions. Probably your project will take a few weeks to complete.

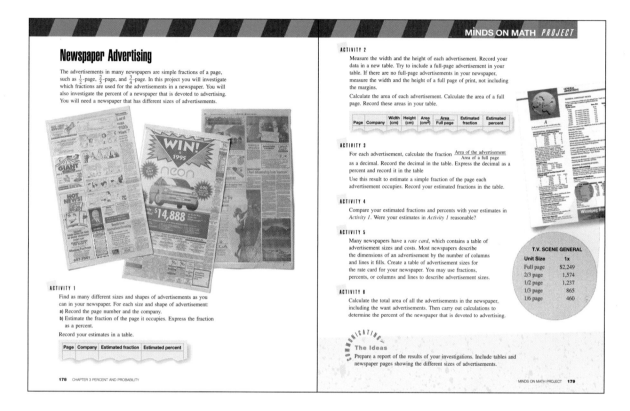

- Each project contains several related activities for you to do over a period of time.
- You can work alone or with a partner.
- The projects are open-ended. This means that there may be more than one answer, or that students doing the same project may get different results.
- You will be asked to write a report or to make a presentation so that you can share your thinking and results with others.

Other topics to explore in Minds on Math

- Reporting on Canada's Waste
- Codes
- Measurement Tools in the Community

PATTERN

Patterns occur everywhere in mathematics. In this introductory section, you will find activities involving patterns. These activities will help you review concepts and skills you learned in previous grades. You will need to use these skills as you work through the chapters in this book.

WHAT'S COMING UP?

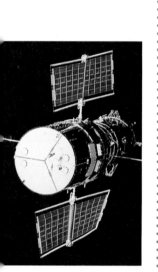

DEPARTMENTS

Minds on Math Project

Start With What You Know

Work in a group or with a partner.

1. a) Identify the object shown in each photograph, on these two pages.

    b) Describe the clues in each photograph that helped you to identify it.

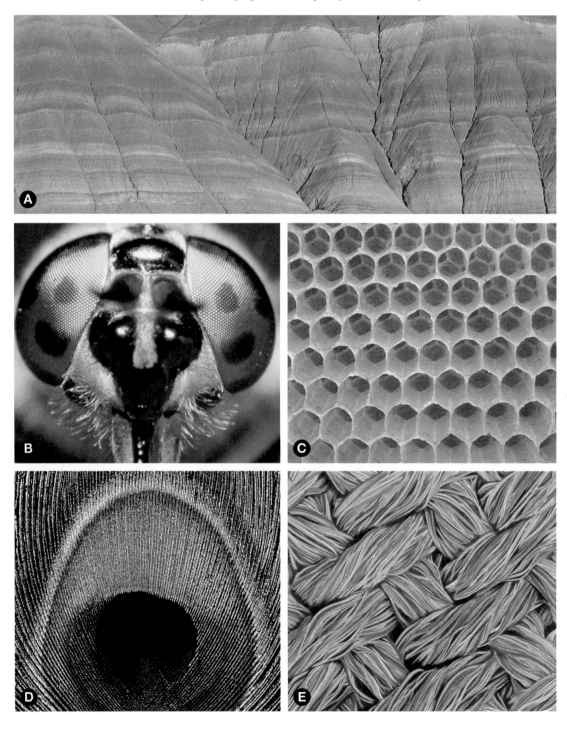

F   G

H   I

2. a) What information does each newspaper clipping contain?

4-6, 6-3, 6-2, 6-7, 7-5
6-0, 6-1, 6-1
3-6, 6-1, 7-5, 6-4
6-2, 6-3, 4-6, 1-6, 0-6
2-6, 3-6, 4-6

110 000 000   2 6 1
000 000 000   0 5 0

8 10   7   7 – 32
4   8 14 14 – 40

70-73-73-68 284
73-68-71-72 284
73-70-68-73 284
72-70-75-68 285
71-71-74-69 285
71-67-74-74 286

b) Describe the clues in each clipping that helped you to identify it.
c) Do you think it is possible that all four clippings were taken from the same newspaper? Explain your answer.

Developing the Ideas

▶ ▶ *Through an Activity*

Work in a group or with a partner.

1. In this advertisement, all the prices are the same. Make up a shopping list of items from the advertisement. How could you use the fact that the prices are the same to calculate the total cost of your items? Use your method to calculate the total cost.

2. Why do you think a store would have all the prices the same?

Working with Mathematics

Something to talk about

1. For the sign below, what is the cost of each set of items?
   a) 2 cassettes   **b)** 3 CDs
   c) 4 videos
   d) 1 cassette, 1 CD, and 1 video

Cassettes... $ $ **2.⁹⁹**
CDs... $ $ **9.⁹⁹**
Videos... $ **11.⁹⁹**

2. Why do you think stores use prices that are 1¢ less than a whole number of dollars?

Practice

3. Multiply.
   a) $5.4 \times 10\ 000$ **b)** 5.4×1000
   c) 5.4×100 **d)** 5.4×10
   e) 5.4×1 **f)** 5.4×0.1
   g) 5.4×0.01 **h)** 5.4×0.001

4. What pattern do you see in the expressions and answers in exercise 3?

5. Divide.
   a) $3500 \div 1000$ **b)** $3500 \div 100$
   c) $3500 \div 10$ **d)** $3500 \div 1$
   e) $3500 \div 0.1$ **f)** $3500 \div 0.01$

6. What pattern do you see in the expressions and answers in exercise 5?

7. Determine each product or quotient. Predict what the next line should be. Check your prediction with your calculator.

   a) $8 \div 4 = \blacksquare$ **b)** $9 \div 3 = \blacksquare$
   $80 \div 4 = \blacksquare$ $99 \div 3 = \blacksquare$
   $800 \div 4 = \blacksquare$ $999 \div 3 = \blacksquare$

   c) $3 \times 2 = \blacksquare$ **d)** $5 \times 11 = \blacksquare$
   $30 \times 20 = \blacksquare$ $5 \times 101 = \blacksquare$
   $300 \times 200 = \blacksquare$ $5 \times 1001 = \blacksquare$

   e) $91 \times 11 = \blacksquare$ **f)** $7 \times 7 = \blacksquare$
   $91 \times 22 = \blacksquare$ $67 \times 67 = \blacksquare$
   $91 \times 33 = \blacksquare$ $667 \times 667 = \blacksquare$

Work together

When you learned multiplication in previous grades, you used a table like this. The next five exercises all involve patterns in the multiplication table.

×	1	2	3	4	5	6	7	8	9	10
	1	2	3	4	5	6	7	8	9	10
	2	4	6	8	10	12	14	16	18	20
	3	6	9	12	15	18	21	24	27	30
	4	8	12	16	20	24	28	32	36	40
	5	10	15	20	25	30	35	40	45	50
	6	12	18	24	30	36	42	48	54	60
	7	14	21	28	35	42	49	56	63	70
	8	16	24	32	40	48	56	64	72	80
	9	18	27	36	45	54	63	72	81	90
	10	20	30	40	50	60	70	80	90	100

8. **a)** Choose any row in the multiplication table.
   i) How do the numbers in this row compare with the numbers in the row above it?
   ii) How do they compare with the numbers in the row below it? Explain why this pattern occurs.
   b) Explain why a similar pattern occurs in the columns.

9. In the multiplication table, the main diagonal goes from the upper left to the lower right.
   a) What patterns can you find in the numbers in this diagonal?
   b) What patterns can you find in some of the other diagonals?

10. In the multiplication table, is there the same number of even numbers as odd numbers, or is there more of one kind than the other? Explain why.

11. The numbers in the ninth row of the multiplication table are called *multiples of 9*.
    a) Determine the sum of the digits for each number in this row. What do you notice?
    b) Choose 5 multiples of 9 that are greater than those in the table. What do you notice about the sums of their digits?

c) Compare your results with those of other groups. Do you think your observation is true for all multiples of 9?

12. The numbers in the third row of the multiplication table are called *multiples of 3*. The final digits of the multiples of 3 are 3, 6, 9, 2, 5, 8, 1, 4, 7, and 0.

a) Write the numbers 1, 2, 3, 4, 5, 6, 7, 8, 9, 0 around a circle. Join them in the order of the final digits in the column showing multiples of 3. Then join 0 to 3. You will get this pattern.

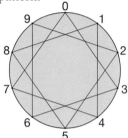

b) Do you think you will get the same pattern if you did this with the final digits of the numbers in the other rows?

c) Check your answer to part b by drawing patterns like the one above using some of the other rows.

On your own

13. Determine each product. Then predict what the next line should be. Check your prediction with your calculator.

a) $6 \times 4 = \blacksquare$
    $66 \times 34 = \blacksquare$
    $666 \times 334 = \blacksquare$

b) $9 \times 9 = \blacksquare$
    $99 \times 99 = \blacksquare$
    $999 \times 999 = \blacksquare$

c) $5 \times 5 = \blacksquare$
    $65 \times 65 = \blacksquare$
    $665 \times 665 = \blacksquare$

d) $101 \times 101 = \blacksquare$
   $202 \times 202 = \blacksquare$
   $303 \times 303 = \blacksquare$

e) $1 \times 9 + 2 = \blacksquare$
    $12 \times 9 + 3 = \blacksquare$
    $123 \times 9 + 4 = \blacksquare$

f) $1 \times 1 = \blacksquare$
    $11 \times 11 = \blacksquare$
    $111 \times 111 = \blacksquare$

14. Write down any 3-digit number with different hundreds and ones digits. Write another number by reversing its digits. Determine their difference:

Reverse the digits of the result, and add:

$$249$$
$$942$$
$$942$$
$$-\ 249$$
$$\overline{693}$$
$$+\ 396$$
$$\overline{1089}$$

a) Do this a few times using your own examples. What do you notice?

b) Why do the hundreds and ones digits of the original number have to be different?

Extend your thinking

15. a) The three number patterns below all start with the numbers 1, 2, 4. Predict the next three numbers in each pattern.
   i) 1, 2, 4, 8, 16, …
   ii) 1, 2, 4, 7, 11, …
   iii) 1, 2, 4, 5, 7, 8, 10, …

b) Write three different number patterns that start with 1, 2, 3.

16. In exercise 13, some of the patterns continue forever and some do not. Identify those that do not continue forever and explain why they don't.

COMMUNICATING
The Ideas

Look up the word *pattern* in a dictionary. In your journal, write some examples that illustrate different meanings of this word.

Number Patterns on a Spreadsheet

We shall use a spreadsheet to generate number patterns.
Start a new document in a spreadsheet program.

Method 1

EMPLATE DISK

Enter the information shown below left; that is, type 2 in cell A1 and the formula =A1+2 in cell A2.

	A	B
1	2	
2	=A1+2	
3		
4		
5		
6		

	A	B
1	2	
2	4	
3	6	
4	8	
5	10	
6	12	

Put the mouse in cell A2. Hold down the button and drag the mouse to cell A6. With the cells from A2 to A6 highlighted:

- in ClarisWorks®, choose Fill Down from the Calculate menu.
- in Microsoft Works™, choose Fill Down from the Edit menu.

(Other spreadsheet programs may have different commands.)

You should see the display of even numbers shown above right.

1. In Method 1, what did the formula in cell A2 do?

2. Start a new spreadsheet document. Use Method 1 to show the first 6 odd numbers.

3. Change just one cell in Method 1. Have the spreadsheet show these even numbers: 48, 50, 52, 54, 56, …

4. Adapt Method 1 to show these numbers: 1, 4, 7, 10, 13, 16, …

Method 2

MPLATE DISK

Enter the information shown below left; that is, type 1 in cell A1 and the formula =A1+1 in cell A2. As described for Method 1, copy the formula to cell A6. Type =A1*2 in cell B1 and copy the formula to cell B6.

	A	B
1	1	=A1*2
2	=A1+1	
3		
4		
5		
6		

	A	B
1	1	2
2	2	4
3	3	6
4	4	8
5	5	10
6	6	12

You should see the display of even numbers shown above right.

5. In Method 2, what did the formula in each cell do?
  a) cell A2   **b)** cell B1

6. Adapt Method 2 to show the first 6 odd numbers.

Mathematics & Technology

Linking Ideas

Powers of Ten

Each photograph shows about 10 times as many people as the one before it.
Observe that the numbers in the photographs form a pattern.

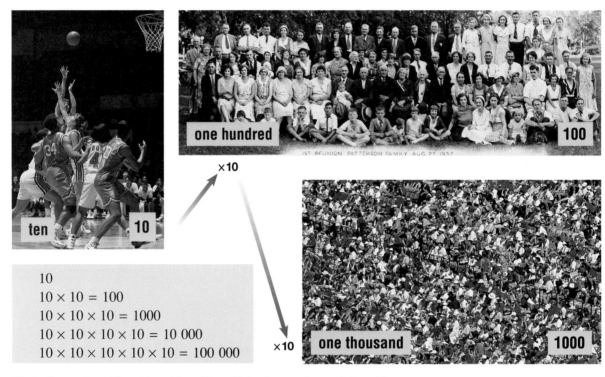

$$10$$
$$10 \times 10 = 100$$
$$10 \times 10 \times 10 = 1000$$
$$10 \times 10 \times 10 \times 10 = 10\ 000$$
$$10 \times 10 \times 10 \times 10 \times 10 = 100\ 000$$

To indicate that $10 \times 10 \times 10 \times 10 \times 10$ is the product of five 10s,
we write:

Exponent

$$10 \times 10 \times 10 \times 10 \times 10 = 10^5$$

10^5 is a *power of ten*. We say: "ten to the fifth."

The exponent 5 tells how many 10s are multiplied together.

The names of very large powers of 10 form a pattern.

Million	10^6	$= 1\ 000\ 000$
Billion	10^9	$= 1\ 000\ 000\ 000$
Trillion	10^{12}	$= 1\ 000\ 000\ 000\ 000$
Quadrillion	10^{15}	$= 1\ 000\ 000\ 000\ 000\ 000$
Quintillion	10^{18}	$= 1\ 000\ 000\ 000\ 000\ 000\ 000$
Sextillion	10^{21}	$= 1\ 000\ 000\ 000\ 000\ 000\ 000\ 000$
Septillion	10^{24}	$= 1\ 000\ 000\ 000\ 000\ 000\ 000\ 000\ 000$
Octillion	10^{27}	$= 1\ 000\ 000\ 000\ 000\ 000\ 000\ 000\ 000\ 000$
Nonillion	10^{30}	$= 1\ 000\ 000\ 000\ 000\ 000\ 000\ 000\ 000\ 000\ 000$
Decillion	10^{33}	$= 1\ 000\ 000\ 000\ 000\ 000\ 000\ 000\ 000\ 000\ 000\ 000$

10 000

×10

ten thousand

×10

one hundred thousand   100 000

1. Write each number as a power of 10.
   a) The average person's nose can distinguish among more than 10 000 different odours.
   b) The human eye can distinguish about 10 million different shades of colours.
   c) A human brain has 100 billion nerve cells, with perhaps 100 trillion connections among them.

2. Write the power of 10 that is closest to each number. Then state each number in words.
   a) In the Lotto 649 lottery there are almost 14 000 000 possible combinations of numbers.
   b) In 1991 the total value of all the Canadian paper money in circulation was approximately $24 500 000 000.
   c) The solar system is part of the Milky Way galaxy, which contains approximately 200 000 000 000 stars.
   d) In 1987 a Canadian astronomer became the first person to discover a supernova (exploding star) since the telescope was invented. This star is about 10 000 000 years old, and about 1 500 000 000 000 000 000 km from Earth.
   e) The Hubble Space Telescope was designed to detect objects as far away as 130 000 000 000 000 000 000 000 km.

3. Estimate the power of 10 that is closest to each number.
   a) the number of broomball players on the ice during a game
   b) the number of countries in the world
   c) the number of students in your school
   d) the total attendance at two Vancouver Canucks hockey games

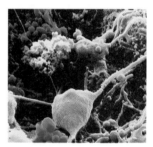

This brain cell shows three dendrites that connect to other cells.

Hubble Space Telescope

The *One Million* Book

The *One Million* book was written to help people visualize one million. There are 200 pages in the book, and each page contains 5000 dots. So, the book contains one million dots.

Each page contains a few items of interest related to some of the numbers represented by the dots on that page. For example, this item appears on page 51 of the *One Million* book:

—People added to the world's population every day

Estimate how many people are added to the world's population every day.

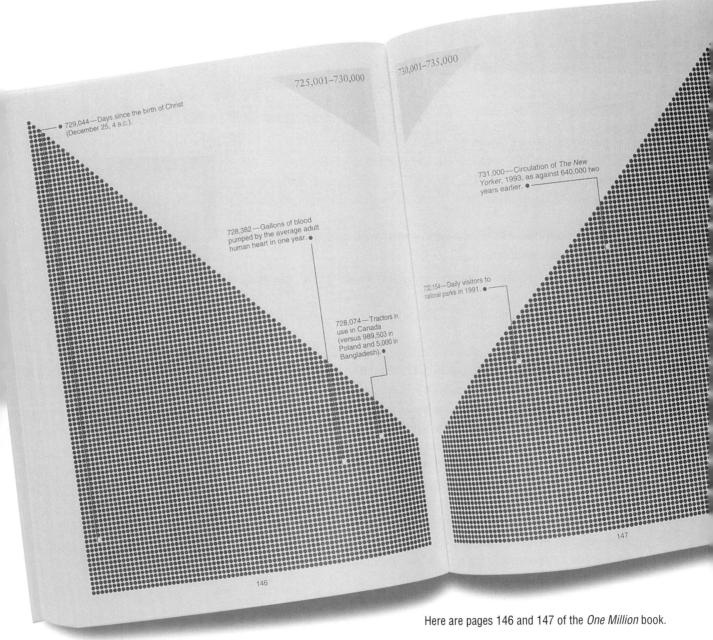

725,001–730,000

730,001–735,000

729,044—Days since the birth of Christ (December 25, 4 B.C.).

728,382—Gallons of blood pumped by the average adult human heart in one year.

728,074—Tractors in use in Canada (versus 989,503 in Poland and 5,000 in Bangladesh).

731,000—Circulation of *The New Yorker*, 1993, as against 640,000 two years earlier.

732,154—Daily visitors to national parks in 1991.

146

147

Here are pages 146 and 147 of the *One Million* book.

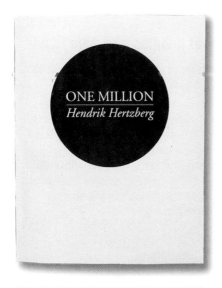

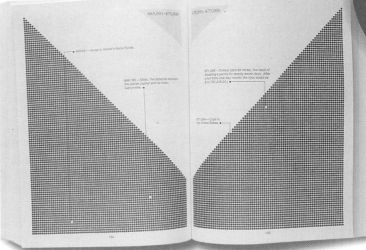

Understand the problem

- How many dots are there on each page?
- On what page does the item about the number of people added to the world's population every day appear?
- What are you asked to do?

Think of a strategy

- You could calculate the total number of dots on the first 51 pages.

Carry out the strategy

- Since every page contains 5000 dots, how many dots are there on the first 51 pages?
- What does this tell you about the number of people added to the world's population every day?
- How many dots are there on the first 50 pages?
- What does this tell you about the number of people added to the world's population every day?

Look back

- Check that if there are 200 pages with 5000 dots on each page, the total number of dots in the book is 1 000 000.
- On which page do these items appear?
  99 336 — Hairs on the average human scalp
  699 122 — Leaves may grow on a large oak tree
- An item on page 68 states that a penny doubled every day for 26 days would amount to $335 544.32. Use your calculator to check this claim.

Communicating the Ideas

In your journal, write a description of this problem and your solution.

Developing the Ideas
▶ ▶ *Through an Activity*

Chef Makes 3 km of Noodles with Bare Hands

Chi Yiu-Yuet is a chef. He says he can make over 3 km of noodles from one lump of dough using only his hands.

He stretches the dough as far as he can between his hands. Then he makes a fold by bringing the ends of the dough together. This makes 2 strands which he stretches to the same length as before. He makes a second fold the same way, by bringing the ends together and stretching. This forms 4 strands. After making a third fold he has 8 strands. Chi Yiu-Yuet continues folding and stretching, until he has made 11 folds in all. By this time the strands have become finer than string.

Is Chi Yiu-Yuet's claim reasonable?

You can check by completing the activity on the following page.

Fold 0, 1 strand

Fold 1, 2 strands

Fold 2, 4 strands

1. Make a table like this. Then complete the pattern in the second column of the table.

Fold	Number of strands	Total length of noodles
0	1	
1	2	
2	4	
3	8	
4		
5		
6		
7		
8		
9		
10		
11		

2. a) Ask someone to measure the distance between your outstretched hands, in metres. Enter the result at the top of the third column in the table.

b) Suppose each strand of the noodles has this length. Complete the third column of the table.

c) Is the total length after 11 folds about 3 km? Do you think the claim that Chi Yiu-Yuet can make over 3 km of noodles from one lump of dough is reasonable?

3. a) Suppose you had measured the distance between your outstretched hands in centimetres instead of in metres. How would the numbers in the third column of the table change?

b) Suppose the numbers in the third column of the table were in kilometres instead of in metres. How would the numbers in this column change?

Working with Mathematics

Something to talk about

1. Suppose the chef on page 34 could make one more fold.
   a) How many strands would there be?
   b) What would the total length of the noodles be?

2. In each pair, which is the larger unit?
   a) millimetre, metre
   b) centimetre, metre
   c) kilometre, metre
   d) millimetre, centimetre
   e) kilometre, centimetre

3. Would you multiply or divide to convert between each pair of units?
   a) centimetres to metres
   b) centimetres to millimetres
   c) metres to kilometres
   d) kilometres to metres

Practice

4. What units would you use to measure each item?
   a) the length of a pencil
   b) the depth of a lake
   c) the distance around a classroom
   d) the length of a caterpillar
   e) the height of the CN Tower
   f) the width of a toothpick

5. Change each measurement to metres.
   a) 2 km   b) 37 cm
   c) 164 mm   d) 683 cm
   e) 2649 mm   f) 0.5 km

6. Change each measurement to centimetres.
   a) 5 m   b) 84 mm
   c) 2.3 km   d) 153 mm
   e) 0.46 km   f) 36.2 m

7. Copy and complete.
   a) 25 cm = ▪ m   b) 1.4 km = ▪ m
   c) 84 mm = ▪ cm   d) 285 mm = ▪ m
   e) 12.6 m = ▪ cm   f) 584 m = ▪ km
   g) 0.5 cm = ▪ mm   h) 2.05 km = ▪ m

8. The tallest living tree in the world is a redwood in California. The tree is 111.6 m tall.
   a) Express the height of the tree in kilometres.
   b) Express the height of the tree in centimetres.

9. The highest mountain in Canada is Mount Logan in the Yukon Territory. It is 5951 m high.
   a) Express this height in kilometres.
   b) Express this height in centimetres.

Work together

10. Work with a partner. Stand with your arms fully outstretched sideways. The distance from the fingertips of one hand to those of the other is your *arm span*. Measure each other's height and arm span in centimetres. Compare the two measurements. How similar are they? Compare your results with other groups.

11. The distance from your elbow to the tip of your longest finger is your *cubit*. When the palm of your hand is stretched, the distance from the tip of your thumb to the tip of your little finger is your hand span.
    a) Work with a partner. Measure each other's cubit and hand span in millimetres.
    b) Divide your cubit by your hand span. The result is called the *ratio of elegance*.
    c) If your answer to part b is about 2 you are elegant. Are you elegant?

12. a) Ask someone to measure the length of your stride (length of one step).
    b) About how far would you go if you walked 1000 steps?
    c) If everyone in your class walked 1000 steps, about what total distance would be covered?

13. In 1994, a group of 1537 students in England formed a human centipede. They lined up and tied their ankles together. They walked 30 m without falling over.
   a) Express the distance they walked in centimetres and kilometres.
   b) Use your measurement from exercise 12a to estimate how many steps the students took.
   c) Take some measurements to help you estimate how long a line of 1537 people would be.

14. Felicia built a fence around a rectangular yard. The posts are 2 m apart. There are 8 posts along the length and 4 posts along the width.
   a) How many posts did Felicia need?
   b) What are the dimensions of the yard?

On your own

15. There is a line of dots in the middle of this page.
   a) Estimate the length of this line in centimetres and in millimetres.
   b) Check your estimates by measuring.

16. a) The height of the CN Tower is 533 m. Express this measurement in millimetres.
   b) Measure the thickness and the diameter of a loonie in millimetres.
   c) Suppose you balanced loonies on top of one another on their edges. How many loonies would you need to reach the top of the CN Tower?

   d) Suppose you stacked loonies on their flat sides. How many loonies would you need to reach the top of the CN Tower?

17. Measure the length and the width of the first small photograph of the chef on page 34.
   a) Write each measurement in centimetres and in millimetres. How do the measurements in millimetres compare with the measurements in centimetres?
   b) Calculate the area of the photograph in square centimetres and in square millimetres. How does the area in square millimetres compare with the area in square centimetres?

18. A contractor charged $500 to lay tiles in a rectangular room. How much should she charge to lay the same kind of tiles in a room that is twice as long and twice as wide? Explain your answer.

Extend your thinking

19. In the diagram below, A is a square and B, C, and D are all rectangles. The areas of A, B, and C are shown. Calculate the length and the width of rectangle D.

B 24 cm²	C 32 cm²
A 36 cm²	D

COMMUNICATING
The Ideas

In your journal, write a sentence or two to explain how the units in each pair are related.
   a) metre, centimetre   b) metre, kilometre
   c) metre, millimetre   d) millimetre, kilometre

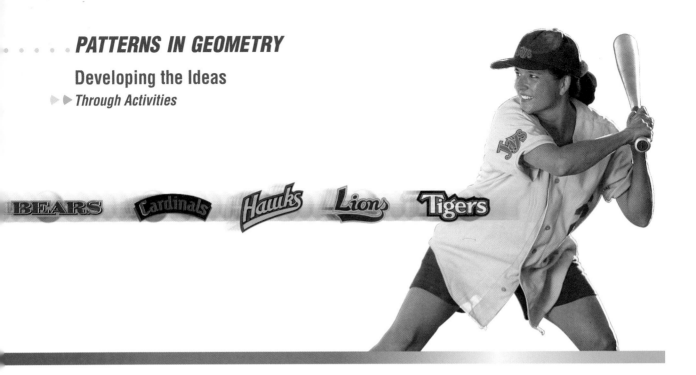

PATTERNS IN GEOMETRY

Developing the Ideas

▶▶▶ *Through Activities*

ACTIVITY 1

Work in a group or with a partner.

In an intramural baseball tournament, each team plays all the other teams once.

1. Suppose there are 3 teams: Bears, Cardinals, Hawks.
   a) Make a list of the games to be played, identifying the two teams for each game.
   b) How many games must be played?

2. Suppose there are 4 teams: Bears, Cardinals, Hawks, Jays. Repeat exercise 1a and b.

3. Suppose there are 5 teams: Bears, Cardinals, Hawks, Jays, Lions. Repeat exercise 1a and b.

4. Suppose there are 6 teams: Bears, Cardinals, Hawks, Jays, Lions, Tigers. Repeat exercise 1a and b.

5. Record the above results in a table.

Number of teams	Number of games
3	
4	
5	
6	

6. Use the pattern in the table to predict the number of games to be played for each number of teams.
   a) 7 teams   b) 8 teams

ACTIVITY 2

The designs below were made by a computer. Each design contains
some dots that were joined in all possible ways.

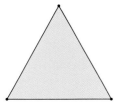 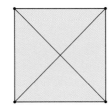 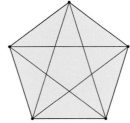

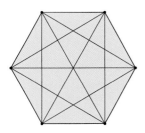 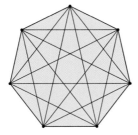 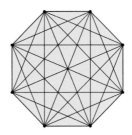

1. Count the number of dots and lines in each design above.
   Record your results in a table.

Dots	Lines
3	
4	
5	
6	
7	
8	

2. How many lines would there be in a similar
   design with each number of dots?

   a) 9 dots **b)** 10 dots

ACTIVITY 3

Compare the results of *Activity 1* and *Activity 2*.
Explain why they are the same.

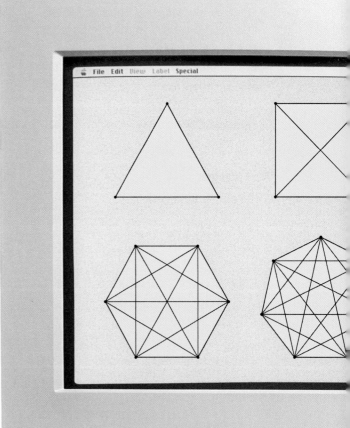

Working with Mathematics

Something to talk about

1. Many businesses use special symbols called *logos* to identify their products and services.

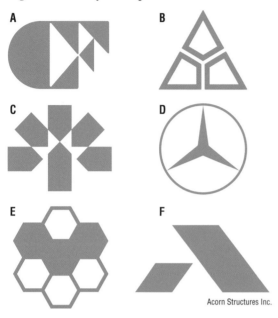

A   B

C   D

E   F

Acorn Structures Inc.

Identify a logo containing each figure.
a) a triangle with two equal sides
b) a quadrilateral with two right angles
c) a parallelogram
d) a pentagon
e) a hexagon that has all sides equal and all angles equal
f) a hexagon that has all sides equal, but not all angles equal

Work together

2. Reema made this design.

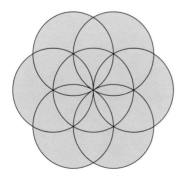

a) Discuss with your partner how you think the design was made.
b) Construct a similar design. Try to include more circles than there are in this one.
c) Look at the points where the circles intersect. Find examples of points that form each figure.
  i) a triangle with three equal sides
  ii) a triangle with a right angle
  iii) a parallelogram
  iv) a trapezoid
  v) a rectangle
  vi) a hexagon

3. How many lines are there in this design?

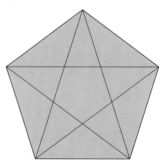

On your own

4. One of the first logos ever designed is shown below. This was used over 2000 years ago as the symbol of the Pythagorean Society of ancient Greece. The design is called a *pentagram*.

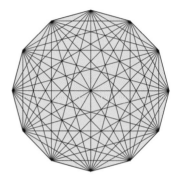

a) In the pentagram, identify as many different figures as you can.
b) How many different triangles can you find in the pentagram? To be different, they must have different sizes or shapes.

c) Use a protractor to measure some of the angles in the pentagram. How many different angle measures are there? What pattern is formed by the measures of the angles?

d) Use the measures of the angles in part c to name each different triangle you found in part b.

e) Measure the lengths of the sides of each different triangle. Use these measures to name the triangle another way.

5. These figures were made using a Draw program on a computer.

1 and 4   2 and 8   3 and 12

a) Look at the pattern of squares. Sketch the 6th figure if this pattern were continued. What pair of numbers would be beneath the 6th figure?

b) Suppose we used the number pairs: 1 and 3, 2 and 6, 3 and 9 to describe the three figures. What number pair would we use to describe the 6th figure?

c) Start a new Draw program document. Create your own pattern of 3 figures that could be described by these number pairs: 2 and 5, 4 and 10, 6 and 15. Extend your pattern to 6 figures.

d) Is there another pattern of number pairs that could describe your figures?

e) Create your own pattern of number pairs. Draw 3 figures that could be described by your number pairs.

6. How many triangles are there in this design?

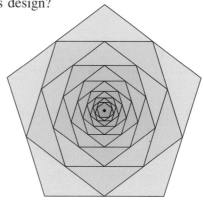

Extend your thinking

7. The black and white squares in crossword puzzles form attractive patterns. Crossword puzzles are designed so that these patterns all have a common property. Obtain a crossword puzzle from a newspaper or a magazine. Compare the pattern of black and white squares with the pattern at the right. What property do the patterns have in common?

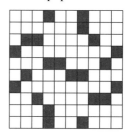

COMMUNICATING
The Ideas

In your journal, explain how these figures are related: square, rectangle, parallelogram. Draw some diagrams to illustrate the similarities and the differences among these three figures.

BOGGLE YOUR MIND

In 1992, a Canadian company lost $20 000 000 000. Newspaper articles at the time reported that if this amount of money were converted into loonies, it would fill a room about 120 m long, 120 m wide, and 2.4 m high. Measure your classroom. Estimate how many classrooms like yours the loonies would fill.

Review

1. Multiply.
   a) 37×0.0001
   b) 37×0.001
   c) 37×0.01
   d) 37×0.1
   e) 37×1
   f) 37×10

2. Divide.
   a) $1320 \div 0.0001$
   b) $1320 \div 0.001$
   c) $1320 \div 0.01$
   d) $1320 \div 0.1$
   e) $1320 \div 1$
   f) $1320 \div 10$

3. Determine each product. Predict what the next line should be. Check your prediction with your calculator.

   a)
   $9 \times 6 = \blacksquare$
   $99 \times 66 = \blacksquare$
   $999 \times 666 = \blacksquare$

   b)
   $4 \times 4 = \blacksquare$
   $34 \times 34 = \blacksquare$
   $334 \times 334 = \blacksquare$

   c)
   $1 \times 8 + 1 = \blacksquare$
   $12 \times 8 + 2 = \blacksquare$
   $123 \times 8 + 3 = \blacksquare$

   d)
   $7 \times 7 = \blacksquare$
   $67 \times 67 = \blacksquare$
   $667 \times 667 = \blacksquare$

4. a) Multiply.
   i) 495×1001
   ii) 650×1001
   iii) 286×1001
   iv) 193×1001
   What do you notice about the products?
   b) Write any 3 three-digit numbers. Predict the product when you multiply each number by 1001. Check your predictions with a calculator.
   c) Write any four-digit number. Suppose you multiply this number by 10 001. What do you think the product would be? Check your prediction with a calculator.

5. Refer to the multiplication table on page 27.
   a) The numbers in the second row of the table are multiples of 2. What are their final digits?
   b) Look at the row with multiples of 4. What are their final digits?
   c) Look at the row with multiples of 6. What are their final digits?
   d) Compare the patterns of final digits for parts a, b, and c. What do you notice?

   e) In what other row would you expect the final digits to have a similar pattern? Explain. Check your prediction.

6. Draw a division table like the one below. The numbers in the top line are the dividends. The numbers in the side column are the divisors. Use your calculator to complete the table. Find as many patterns in the table as you can.

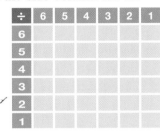

7. Write each number as a power of 10.
   a) 100
   b) 1000
   c) 1 000 000
   d) 100 000 000
   e) There are more than 100 000 lakes in Saskatchewan.
   f) The temperatures of some stars are greater than 10 000°C.

8. Write the power of 10 that is closest to each number.
   a) 85
   b) 37 800
   c) 4100
   d) 9200
   e) There are about 1 234 400 different species of animals.
   f) Starlight takes about 90 000 years to cross our galaxy.
   g) There are about 390 000 different species of plants.

9. In each pair, which is the smaller unit?
   a) centimetre, metre
   b) millimetre, metre
   c) decimetre, metre
   d) metre, kilometre

10. In each pair: Would you multiply or divide to convert? By what would you multiply or divide?
    a) metres to millimetres
    b) centimetres to millimetres
    c) metres to centimetres
    d) millimetres to decimetres

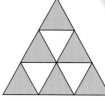

11. Change each measurement to centimetres.
    a) 1.5 m
    b) 50 mm
    c) 360 mm
    d) 0.5 m
    e) The calculator is 140 mm long.
    f) Canada's tallest tree is 73.4 m high.

12. Change each measurement to metres.
    a) 3 km
    b) 400 cm
    c) 350 mm
    d) 0.1 km
    e) The speed-skating oval for the Olympic Winter Games is 0.4 km long.
    f) The batter's box in baseball is 210 cm long and 90 cm wide.

13. Convert each measurement to kilometres.
    a) 826 m
    b) 82 570 cm
    c) 6793 cm
    d) 96 m
    e) The tallest office building in the world is the Sears Tower in Chicago. It is 520 m tall.
    f) The longest floating bridge in the world is Second Lake Bridge in Seattle, Washington. It is 3839 m long.
    g) The world record for the highest free fall parachute jump is about 23 160 m for men and about 14 020 m for women.

14. Many people collect sports cards. These cards have a photograph of an athlete on one side and information about the athlete's career on the other.
    a) Measure the length of a sports card.
    b) Susan has 243 sports cards. Suppose the cards were lined up end to end on the floor. Use your answer to part a to determine the length of the line. Express your answer in the unit of measure you think most appropriate.

15. a) Measure the thickness of this book.
    b) How many books would be in a stack that measures about 1 m?
    c) How many books would be in a stack that measures about 1 km?

16. Ann planted trees 3 m apart in 6 equal rows. The rows were 5 m apart and 24 m long.
    a) How many trees were planted?

b) What are the dimensions of the rectangle containing the trees?

17. These figures were made using a Draw program on a computer.

1 and 1   3 and 4   6 and 9

a) Look at the pattern of triangles. Sketch the next figure in this pattern. What pair of numbers would you write beneath it?
b) Suppose we used the number pairs 1 and 0, 3 and 1, 6 and 3 to describe the three figures. What number pair would we use to describe the fourth figure?
c) Draw your own pattern of three figures that could be described by these number pairs: 4 and 6, 6 and 10, 8 and 14. Is there another pattern of numbers that could describe your figures?

18. This square has a hole in the shape of a cross in the centre. Trace this square. Cut out the pieces.

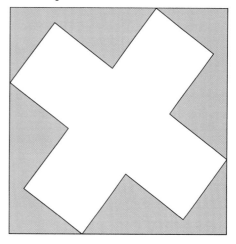

Rearrange the pieces to form each figure.
a) a square without a hole in the centre
b) a cross with a hole in the shape of a square in the centre

Patterns with Numbers and Quadrilaterals

Throughout this chapter you may have noticed examples of patterns in arithmetic and geometry that occur together. In this project you will investigate other examples of patterns in arithmetic and geometry that occur together.

ACTIVITY 1

You will need several copies of the number array below. You can make them yourself on graph paper, or your teacher will provide them.

1	2	3	4
5	6	7	8
9	10	11	12
13	14	15	16

The centres of the squares in the number array form vertices of quadrilaterals. Here are four examples.

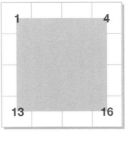
square

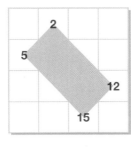
rectangle

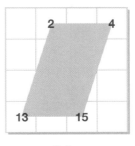
parallelogram

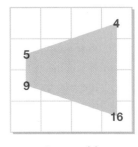
trapezoid

Add the four numbers at the vertices of each quadrilateral. What do you notice about the sums?

Draw several more examples of quadrilaterals like these. Add the four numbers at the vertices of each quadrilateral, and compare the results.

Draw some examples of quadrilaterals for which the sum of the four numbers is different from that above. How do these quadrilaterals differ from those above?

Why do you think the sums of the four numbers are the same in so many of these examples?

ACTIVITY 2

Repeat *Activity 1* using number arrays in which the numbers from 1 to 16 are arranged differently. Here are some examples to get you started.

1	2	3	4
8	7	6	5
9	10	11	12
16	15	14	13

1	3	6	10
2	5	9	13
4	8	12	15
7	11	14	16

1	2	3	4
12	13	14	5
11	16	15	6
10	9	8	7

ACTIVITY 3

Repeat *Activity 1* using larger number arrays such as these.

1	2	3	4	5
6	7	8	9	10
11	12	13	14	15
16	17	18	19	20
21	22	23	24	25

1	2	3	4	5	6
7	8	9	10	11	12
13	14	15	16	17	18
19	20	21	22	26	24
25	26	27	28	29	30
31	32	33	34	35	36

ACTIVITY 4

Repeat *Activity 1* using arrays of sixteen numbers that you would find on a calendar.

1	2	3	4
8	9	10	11
15	16	17	18
22	23	24	25

6	7	8	9
13	14	15	16
20	21	22	23
27	28	29	30

How many different arrays of sixteen numbers are possible on a calendar? What pattern is formed by the sums of the four numbers at the vertices of quadrilaterals on these arrays?

COMMUNICATING

The Ideas

Write a report that summarizes the results of your investigations. Include diagrams to illustrate your results.

TWO-DIMENSIONAL GEOMETRY

WHAT'S COMING UP?

DEPARTMENTS

Linking Ideas

Quest

Minds on Math Project

Start With What You Know

Since humans first constructed buildings, they have used geometric ideas in their designs. These concepts are evident in buildings from all cultures and ages. Four famous buildings are shown on these pages.

One of the great architectural wonders of the world is the Parthenon, built by the ancient Greeks between 448 B.C. and 432 B.C.

1. In each photograph:
   a) Identify objects that are almost geometric figures. Describe differences between the objects and geometric figures that they suggest. Explain how you identified these figures.
   b) Find straight lines and curved lines.

2. a) Look for pairs of equal angles. Explain how you know they are equal.
   b) Look for angles that are square corners, angles that are smaller than square corners, and angles that are greater than square corners.

3. Each building contains parts that have the same size and shape. Describe as many of these parts as you can.

4. Does any building contain parts that have the same shapes with different sizes? Describe these parts.

The spectacular palace at Versailles, France, was constructed between 1669 and 1685. The photograph shows the Royal Chapel of the palace.

This is the dome of a mosque in Cordoba, Spain. The mosque was designed over 1000 years ago by Muslim architects.

Another wonder of the architectural world is the Taj Mahal in India. This building was constructed between 1632 and 1654.

1.1 CONSTRUCTING TRIANGLES USING COMPASSES AND RULER

Developing the Ideas

Archimedes was probably the greatest mathematician of ancient times. He lived in Syracuse, which is in present-day Sicily. Archimedes was also a great inventor. Over 2200 years ago, he designed catapults with adjustable ranges. Huge rocks, with masses of several tonnes, were tossed at invading Roman ships. Archimedes' catapults and other ingenious inventions helped the Greeks hold off invading Roman forces for almost three years.

Some of the tools for geometric construction used by Archimedes were the compasses and the straightedge. A straightedge is a piece of wood, metal, or plastic with a straight edge—similar to a ruler without markings. In this section, you will use these tools to draw figures and solve problems.

▶ ▶ *Through Activities*

ACTIVITY 1

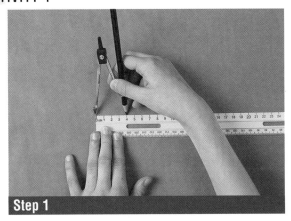

Step 1

Set your compasses to 4 cm.

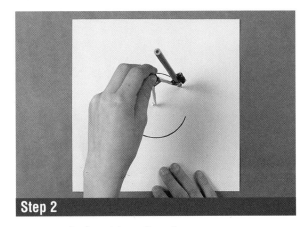

Step 2

Draw a circle with radius 4 cm.

1. Label the centre of the circle P. Label any point Q on the circle.
   a) How far is Q from P? How do you know?
   b) Is there any point 4 cm from P that is not on the circle? Explain.

2. Label any other point R on the circle.
   a) How far is R from Q through centre P? How do you know?
   b) What is the diameter of this circle? How can you know without measuring?

3. How could you use a string to determine the approximate circumference?

ACTIVITY 2

Follow the steps to construct a triangle with sides of lengths 10 cm, 8 cm, and 6 cm.

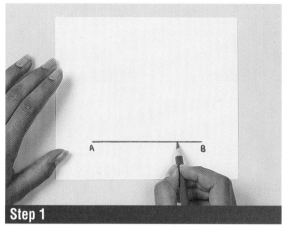

Step 1

Draw a line segment 10 cm long. Label it AB.

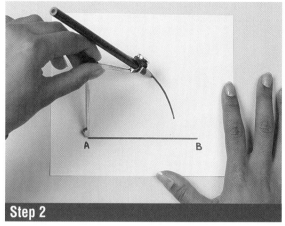

Step 2

Set your compasses to 8 cm. With compasses point on A, draw an arc.

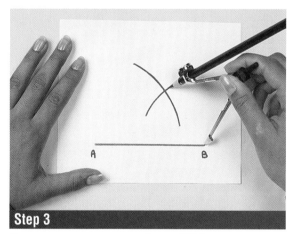

Step 3

Set your compasses to 6 cm. With compasses point on B, draw an arc to intersect the first arc you drew.

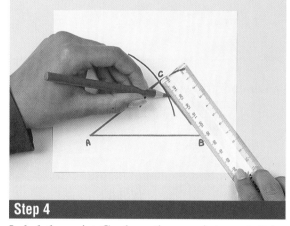

Step 4

Label the point C where the arcs intersect. Join AC and CB. You have drawn △ABC. Label each side of the triangle with its length.

1. Compare your triangle with those of other students. Do all the triangles look the same?

2. Use ruler and compasses to draw a triangle with each set of sides.
   a) 5 cm, 6 cm, 7 cm
   b) 10 cm, 10 cm, 10 cm
   c) 6 cm, 10 cm, 14 cm
   d) 8.5 cm, 8.5 cm, 6.0 cm
   e) 9.5 cm, 5.5 cm, 5.5 cm
   f) 6.5 cm, 6.5 cm, 6.5 cm

Keep these triangles. You will use them later on pages 60 and 61.

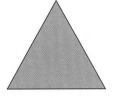 **Through Instruction**

We can classify triangles by the lengths of their sides.

A triangle with three equal sides is an *equilateral triangle*.	A triangle with at least two equal sides is an *isosceles triangle*.	A triangle with no equal sides is a *scalene triangle*.

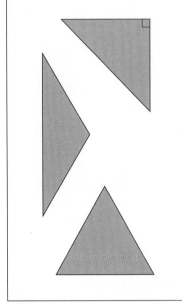

- For each triangle you drew in *Activity 2*, write whether it is equilateral, isosceles, or scalene.

BOGGLE YOUR MIND

Trace the isosceles triangle on the right. Glue your tracing onto a piece of cardboard. Cut out the tracing along the white lines. You now have five pieces. Use all five pieces to form each of the figures shown below. What other figures can you form using all five pieces?

1.

2.

3.

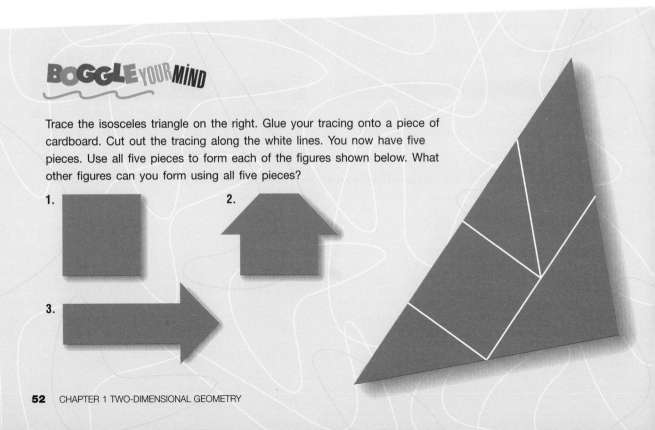

Working with Mathematics

Something to talk about

1. A circle with centre A and radius 4 cm is drawn. Are there any points inside this circle that are 4 cm from A? Explain how you know.

2. Is it possible to construct a triangle with sides of lengths 5 cm, 8 cm, and 21 cm? If your answer is yes, construct the triangle. If your answer is no, explain why it cannot be constructed.

3. Explain how you find out whether three certain lengths can be the lengths of the sides of a triangle.

Practice

4. Classify each triangle as scalene, isosceles, or equilateral. Use a ruler if necessary.

a)

b)

c)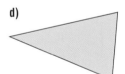

d)

e)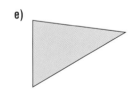

f)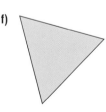

5. Use a ruler and compasses. Construct a triangle for each set of side lengths. Identify each type of triangle you constructed.
   a) 8 cm, 8 cm, 8 cm
   b) 12.5 cm, 9.0 cm, 12.5 cm
   c) 16 cm, 12 cm, 20 cm
   d) 10.0 cm, 5.5 cm, 13.5 cm
   e) 12 cm, 10 cm, 6 cm
   f) 5 cm, 12 cm, 13 cm

Work together

6. On a sheet of paper, construct the largest equilateral triangle you can. Measure the lengths of the sides of the triangle. Compare your triangle with those of your classmates. How can you tell who drew the largest triangle?

7. On a sheet of paper, construct the largest isosceles triangle you can. Measure the lengths of the sides of the triangle. Compare your triangle with those of your classmates. How can you tell who drew the largest triangle?

8. Construct a triangle with sides of lengths 10 cm, 8 cm, and 4 cm. Compare your triangle with those of your classmates. Are the triangles the same shape? Did anyone's triangle have a different shape?

On your own

9. Points P and Q are 9 cm apart. A third point R is 7 cm from P and 5 cm from Q. Using ruler and compasses, locate the two possible positions of R. Join P and Q to the two points R. Describe the diagram.

10. Is an equilateral triangle also an isosceles triangle? Explain your answer.

Extend your thinking

11. Obtain a paper strip with two parallel sides. Construct an isosceles triangle by folding the strip.

COMMUNICATING
The Ideas

In your journal, sketch each triangle below and explain how you identify it.
a) scalene triangle
b) isosceles triangle
c) equilateral triangle

Investigating the Medians of a Triangle

Sometimes we discover patterns in geometric figures that make us wonder *why*. Why is the circumference of a circle always π times the diameter, no matter how large or small the circle is? And why do the medians of a triangle … whoops … this is something you can discover using software like *The Geometer's Sketchpad*.

A *median* of a triangle is the line segment that joins a vertex to the midpoint of the opposite side.

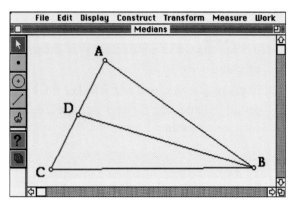

In the diagram, D is the midpoint of side AC. The line segment BD is a *median* of △ABC.

Start *The Geometer's Sketchpad*.

Construct a triangle using the Line Segment tool.

Choose the Selection tool. Select one side of the triangle by clicking on it. The two black squares on the line segment show that it has been selected.

From the Construct menu, select the Point At Midpoint command. This places a point at the midpoint of the line segment you selected. Hold down the shift key and select the point at the opposite vertex by clicking on it. From the Construct menu, select the Segment command.

This constructs the median from the vertex to the midpoint of the selected side.

Follow the procedure above to construct the other two medians of the triangle. Describe what you discover about the three medians of the triangle.

Do you think this property is true for all triangles?

To find out, click and drag one vertex of the triangle to create other triangles. Does this property of medians apply to all these triangles?

Write a statement that describes this interesting property of medians.

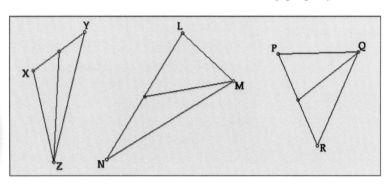

1.2 CONSTRUCTING TRIANGLES USING RULER AND PROTRACTOR

Developing the Ideas

In this section, you will use a ruler and a protractor to construct triangles. You have probably used a protractor to measure angles.

There are circular protractors where the scale is marked from 0° to 360°.

There are semicircular protractors where the scale is marked from 0° to 180°.

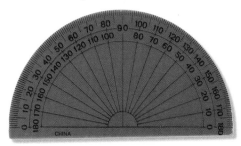

Most protractors have two scales. The scale we use depends on how we place the protractor on the angle.

In the following activities, you will learn how to use a semicircular protractor to construct a triangle.

ACTIVITY 1

Work with a partner.

Follow the steps to construct a triangle with two angles of 68° and 32°, so that the side between these angles has length 7 cm.

Step 1

Draw a line segment 7 cm long. Label it XY.

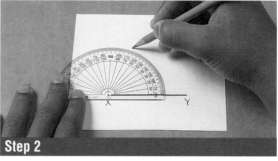

Step 2

Place the centre of the protractor at X. Use the inner scale. Mark a point on the paper at 68°.

Step 3

Use a ruler to draw the line through X and the point. Extend the line beyond the point.

Step 4

Place the centre of the protractor at Y. Use the outer scale. Mark a point on the paper at 32°.

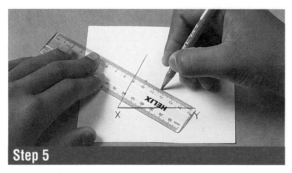

Step 5

Use a ruler to draw the line through Y and the point. Extend the line to intersect the line through X.

Step 6

Label Z as the intersection of the line through X and the line through Y.

You have drawn △XYZ. Label the triangle with the given angles and length.

1. Compare your triangle with those of other students. Do all the triangles look the same?

Work with a partner.

Follow the steps to construct a triangle with two sides of lengths 7 cm and 5 cm, and an angle of 44° between these sides.

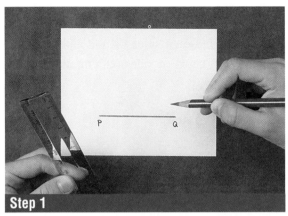

Step 1

Draw a line segment 7 cm long. Label it PQ.

Step 2

Place the centre of the protractor at P. Use the inner scale. Mark a point on the paper at 44°.

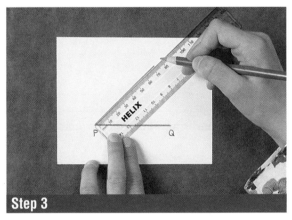

Step 3

Use a ruler to draw the line through P and the point. Extend the line beyond the point.

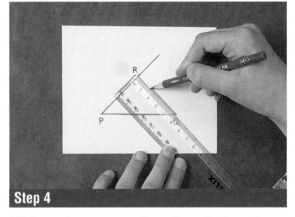

Step 4

With a ruler, measure 5 cm from P along the line you drew. Mark a point, and label it R. Join QR.

You have drawn △PQR. Label the triangle with the given lengths and angle.

1. Compare your triangle with those of other students. Do all the triangles look the same?

ACTIVITY 3

Work in a group.

1. Construct each triangle.

a) Side 6 cm between angles 36° and 46°	**b)** Angle 96° between sides 7.5 cm and 6.5 cm
c) Side 7.4 cm between angles 53° and 53°	**d)** Angle 114° between sides 5.7 cm and 4.6 cm
e) Side 8.3 cm between angles 124° and 14°	**f)** Angle 60° between sides 7.9 cm and 7.9 cm
g) Side 9.2 cm between angles 72° and 82°	**h)** Angle 75° between sides 5.4 cm and 5.4 cm
i) Side 10.4 cm between angles 60° and 60°	**j)** Angle 108° between sides 6.8 cm and 9.7 cm

2. Compare each triangle you constructed in exercise 1 with those of other students. For each set of measurements, are all the triangles the same? If they are not the same, explain how they are different.

▷ ▶ *Through Instruction*

We classify angles by their measures.

<table>
<tr>
<td>

An angle measuring less than 90° is an *acute angle*.

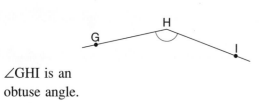

∠ABC is an acute angle.

</td>
<td>

An angle measuring 90° is a *right angle*.

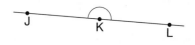

∠DEF is a right angle.

</td>
</tr>
<tr>
<td>

An angle measuring more than 90° and less than 180° is an *obtuse angle*.

∠GHI is an obtuse angle.

</td>
<td>

An angle measuring 180° is a *straight angle*.

∠JKL is a straight angle.

</td>
</tr>
</table>

We can use the types of angles in a triangle to classify triangles.

<table>
<tr>
<td>

A triangle with three acute angles is an *acute triangle*.

</td>
<td>

A triangle with a right angle is a *right triangle*.

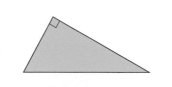

</td>
<td>

A triangle with an obtuse angle is an *obtuse triangle*.

</td>
</tr>
</table>

• For each triangle you drew in *Activity 3*, write whether it is acute, right, or obtuse.

Working with Mathematics

Something to talk about

1. Tell whether each angle is right, acute, obtuse, or straight. Explain how you know.

a)

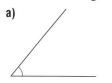

b)

c)

d)

e)

f)

Practice

2. Tell whether each triangle is acute, right, or obtuse. Explain how you know.

a)

b)

c)

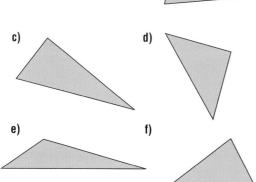

d)

e)

f)

3. Name as many acute angles as you can in this diagram.

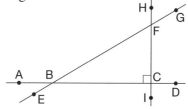

4. Use a ruler and a protractor. Construct a triangle for each set of measurements. Identify each type of triangle you constructed.

  a) angle 60° between sides 7 cm and 7 cm

  b) side 7.1 cm between angles 30° and 45°

  c) side 12.7 cm between angles 63° and 63°

  d) angle 74° between sides 5.3 cm and 9.6 cm

  e) angle 117° between sides 6.4 cm and 5.8 cm

  f) side 8.5 cm between angles 90° and 53°

5. Refer to the triangles in exercise 2. Find an example of each type.

  a) an obtuse scalene triangle

  b) an acute isosceles triangle

  c) a right scalene triangle

  d) an obtuse isosceles triangle

  e) an acute scalene triangle

  f) a right isosceles triangle

Work together

6. a) Trace this diagram. Draw a triangle whose vertices are on the dots.

b) How many kinds of triangles can you draw in this way? Identify each triangle.

c) Compare your triangles with those of your partner. Did you draw all possible triangles?

7. a) State whether it is possible for a triangle to be drawn:

    i) with 2 equal sides and 1 right angle

    ii) with 2 equal sides and 1 obtuse angle

    iii) with 3 equal sides and 1 right angle

    iv) with no equal sides and 3 equal angles

  b) Draw each triangle in part a that can be drawn. Compare your triangles with those of your partner.

8. A tunnel is to be constructed through a mountain. The surveyor drew line segment XY to represent the tunnel. She measured the distances to X and Y from a point Z. She found that ZX is 500 m and ZY is 700 m. Angle XZY is 125°.

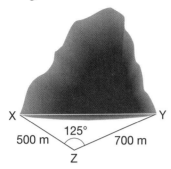

a) Is △XYZ acute, right, or obtuse?

b) Why must the length of the tunnel be greater than the length of XZ and greater than the length of YZ?

c) Why must the length of the tunnel be less than the sum of the lengths of XZ and YZ?

d) Visually estimate the length of the tunnel in metres. Explain your method. How can you use parts b and c to estimate?

e) Compare your estimate with estimates of other students.

On your own

9. a) Name one acute angle and one obtuse angle in each diagram.

i)

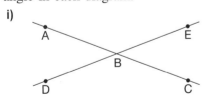

ii)

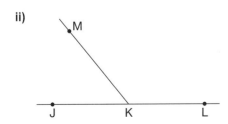

iii)

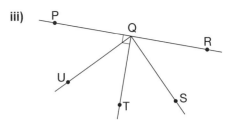

b) Compare your answers with those of another student. Did you select the same angles?

10. a) Construct a triangle with sides of lengths 3 cm, 4 cm, and 5 cm.

b) Classify the triangle in two ways.

11. Look at the equilateral triangles you constructed in *Activity 2*, page 51. How else can you classify each triangle?

12. Look at the isosceles triangles you constructed in *Activity 2*, page 51. How else can you classify each triangle?

13. a) Draw an example of each triangle, if possible.
   i) an acute isosceles triangle
   ii) an obtuse isosceles triangle
   iii) a right isosceles triangle

b) Compare each triangle with those drawn by other students. How are the triangles the same? How are the triangles different?

14. a) Draw an example of each triangle, if possible.
   i) a right scalene triangle
   ii) an obtuse scalene triangle
   iii) an acute scalene triangle

b) Compare each triangle with those drawn by other students. How are the triangles the same? How are the triangles different?

15. Draw an example of each triangle, if possible.
   a) an obtuse equilateral triangle
   b) a right equilateral triangle

16. A sailor wants to know her distance from a lighthouse. She measures the angle to the lighthouse when she is at point B. She then proceeds due west a distance of 1000 m. She measures the angle to the lighthouse from point A. She sketches the diagram below.

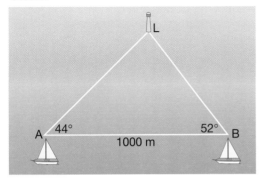

a) Classify △ABL in two ways.

b) Suppose the angles at A and B were equal. Would △ABL be scalene, isosceles, or equilateral? How do you know?

c) Draw △ABL with a 44° angle at A and at B. Classify this triangle in two ways.

d) Repeat part c for an angle of 52°.

17. Measure the angles of each equilateral triangle you drew in *Activity 2*, page 51. Measure the angles of any other equilateral triangles in the text or in your notebook. Compare your results with those of other students. What do you notice?

18. Measure the angles of each isosceles triangle you constructed in *Activity 2*, page 51. Measure the angles of any other isosceles triangles in the text or in your notebook. Compare your results with those of other students. What do you notice?

19. Find three triangular objects.

a) For each object, measure the angles. Tell whether the object represents an acute, a right, or an obtuse triangle. Explain how you know.

b) For each object, measure the lengths of the sides. Tell whether the object represents a scalene, an isosceles, or an equilateral triangle. Explain how you know.

Extend your thinking

20. A line segment joining a vertex of a triangle to the midpoint of the opposite side is called a *median*.

a) How many medians does every triangle have?

b) Are the medians of every triangle inside the triangle? Explain your answer.

c) Is it possible for a side of a triangle to be a median? Explain your answer.

COMMUNICATING

The Ideas

Look through magazines and newspapers. Cut out examples of angles and triangles. Label each angle with its type. Label each triangle with its type, in more than one way if possible. Post these pictures on a bulletin board display in your classroom.

Where Is the Treasure Buried?

Captain Crossbones buried treasure on a desert island. No one else knows where the chest containing gold and jewels is buried. A cryptic poem on a map was found in a bottle washed ashore. You are to decode this message and locate the hidden treasure. Describe the position of the treasure relative to the point of intersection of the two diagonals of the square.

X — 100 paces — Y

100 paces

100 paces

Ye Olde Treasure Map

On a remote desert island in old Pirate's Cove,
I have buried a fortune in jewels and gold.
Four coconut palms; during high tide,
Make corners of a square, hundred paces per side.

To find all this treasure, go there if you dare.
Start at the point that is inside the square
Forty paces from X and eighty from Y;
Use as your compass, the sun in the sky.

Travel south fifty paces — think "treasure chest"
Turn degrees forty-five and face the southwest
Then turn about face, 180 degrees
And march twenty paces toward the northeast.

Then move to the point that is nearest by
And equally distant from palms X and Y
It is here that a fortune lies buried until...
Found by a sleuth with geometry skill.

100 paces

Understand the problem

- What figure is formed by the four palm trees?
- What is the length of each side of this figure?
- Relative to what point are you asked to describe the position of the treasure?
- In what units will you express the distance of the treasure from that point?
- What are you asked to find?

Think of a strategy

- Trace the treasure map. Follow the instructions in the poem and use any geometry tools you need.

Carry out the strategy

- What is the length of one side of the map in paces? What is the length in centimetres? Use these measurements to find the length of one pace to the nearest tenth of a millimetre.
- How many paces is the starting point from X? From Y? How can you find these distances on your map to the nearest millimetre? What are the distances?
- What geometric figure represents all points 40 paces from X? All points 80 paces from Y?
- How many points lie 40 paces from X and 80 paces from Y?
- What direction is south on the map?
- How many paces south of this point do you travel? How can you find this distance in millimetres on your map?
- How can you find the distance on your map for 20 paces?
- What point on XY is the same distance from X and from Y? Suppose you draw a vertical line at right angles to XY through the midpoint of XY. Why is each point on it the same distance from X and from Y?
- Where is the treasure?

Look back

- What geometric constructions were needed to solve this problem?
- What property of the circle was needed to locate the starting point?
- What other geometric facts did you use?
- Draw your own treasure map. Invent instructions to find buried treasure. Exchange maps and instructions with a classmate. Find the position of your classmate's buried treasure.

Communicating the Ideas

In your journal, write a description of this problem and your solution. Include the answers to the questions in *Look back*.

1.3 CONGRUENT FIGURES

Developing the Ideas

▷▷ *Through Discussion*

Two figures are congruent if they are identical in size and shape. No two things are exactly alike. However, when we say that two figures are congruent, we mean that they are so close to being identical that we cannot tell the difference between them.

In a jigsaw puzzle, each piece is congruent to the space it fits. If a piece is not congruent to the space, it will not fit into the space. In most jigsaw puzzles, only one piece is congruent to each space.

A partly finished puzzle provides clues for completing the puzzle as you visualize which puzzle piece is congruent to the space it fits. People often use other clues, such as colour, shading, and items in the picture.

The picture on the box provides clues. Each part of the picture on the box is the same shape as the corresponding part of the puzzle, but usually the parts are not the same size.

Figures that have the same shape are *similar*.

Figures that have the same shape and the same size are *congruent*.

Work with a partner or in a group. You will need a geoboard, elastic bands, a ruler, compasses, and dot paper.

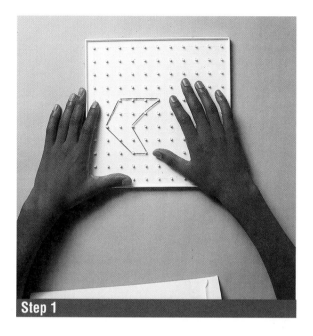

Step 1

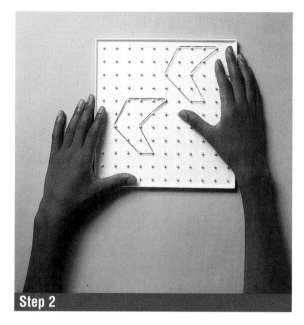

Step 2

Make a figure with at least four sides on the geoboard.

Make a congruent figure on the same geoboard.

1. What do you notice about the lengths of the sides of your figures?

2. What do you notice about the measures of the angles of your figures?

3. How do you know the figures are congruent?

4. Copy one of the figures from your geoboard to dot paper.

5. Is the figure on dot paper congruent to the figures on your geoboard? Explain.

Follow these steps to make congruent copies of a figure.

Step 1

Fold a piece of paper in half.

Step 2

Fold the paper in half again.

Step 3

Fold the paper in half a third time.

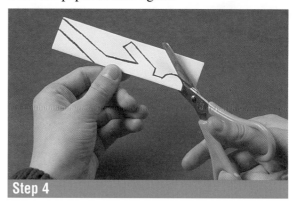

Step 4

Along the fold line, draw a figure or object on your paper. Cut out the figure.

1. Describe any symmetry in your figures.

To check that two of the figures are congruent, place one on top of another so they match exactly. You should find that they overlap so that one figure is completely covered by the other. Two figures match like this only if they have the same size and shape. Checking that two figures match exactly is one way to check that they are congruent.

2. How many congruent figures did you make?

Working with Mathematics

Something to talk about

1. a) In *Using Manipulatives*, you copied a figure on to dot paper. Suppose you made another copy of the figure on dot paper. Would the two copies be congruent? Explain.

b) Would these two copies be similar?

2. a) Are all photocopies of a figure congruent to the original figure? Explain.

b) Are all photocopies of a figure similar to the original figure? Explain.

3. Explain why congruence is important in the manufacture of these items.
- **a)** loonie dollars
- **b)** the tires on a car
- **c)** soft drink cans
- **d)** golf balls
- **e)** all the hiking boots of the same make, style, and size, for the left foot

Practice

4. In each diagram, are the figures congruent? If so, name the sides that are equal and the angles that are equal. If the figures are not congruent, explain why not.

a)

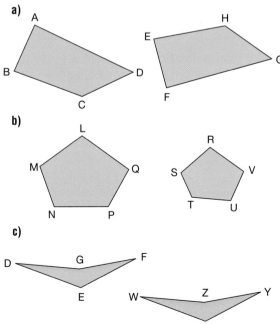

b)

c)

5. Which pictures of trilliums are congruent? Which pictures of trilliums are similar?

Work together

6. Explain whether each of these is congruent.
- **a)** statues are made with the same mould
- **b)** gear wheels on a bicycle

7. Use grid paper, dot paper, or tracing paper if you wish.
- **a)** Draw two figures that are congruent.
- **b)** Draw two figures that are not congruent.
- **c)** Draw two figures that are similar.
- **d)** Draw two figures that are not similar.

8. a) Explain how you could find out whether two circles are congruent without placing one over the other.

b) Are all circles similar? How do you know?

On your own

9. Mei Lin has three keys and a duplicate set. When her key chain broke, the keys were mixed. Use tracing paper to match each key with its duplicate.

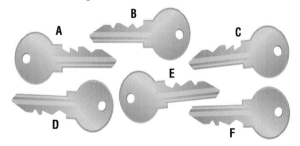

a) Write a pair of letters to match each key with its duplicate.

b) Which keys can be matched without flipping the tracing paper?

10. a) Do congruent keys open the same lock?

  b) If locks are congruent, can they be opened by the same key?

  c) If keys are not congruent, can they open the same lock?

11. Which quadrilaterals are congruent?

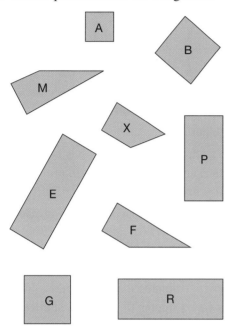

12. Make several copies of this 4 by 3 rectangle. The diagram shows one way to divide the rectangle into two congruent parts by joining the dots with lines parallel to the sides. How many other ways can you find?

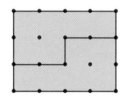

13. Determine if the figures in each pair are congruent. If they are, name the sides that are equal and the angles that are equal.

  a)

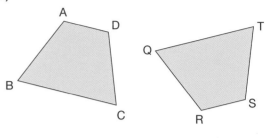

  b)

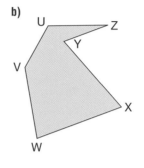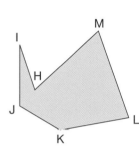

Extend your thinking

14. Which statements are true? Draw a diagram or write a statement to explain the reason.

  a) If figures are congruent, they are similar.

  b) All similar figures are congruent.

  c) No congruent figures are similar.

  d) If each figure in a set is congruent to the same figure, all the figures are congruent.

15. a) Find at least eight different ways to divide a square into four congruent parts.

  b) Find a way to divide a square into five congruent parts.

The Ideas

Look through newspapers and magazines for examples of congruent figures. Display these pictures on a bulletin board in your classroom.

1.4 CONGRUENT LINE SEGMENTS, ANGLES, AND TRIANGLES

Developing the Ideas

We can apply congruence to line segements, angles, and triangles.

▶▶ *Through Activities*

ACTIVITY 1

Work with a partner. You will need a ruler and a protractor.

1. Use tracing paper to determine which line segment is congruent to XY.

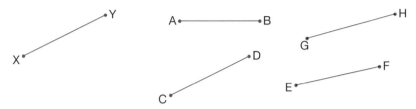

2. Use tracing paper to determine which angle is congruent to ∠XYZ.

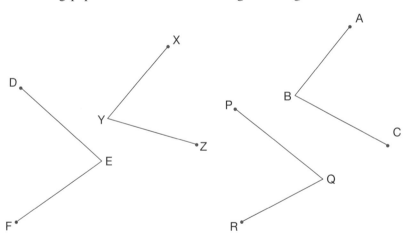

3. Check your answers to exercises 1 and 2 with other students. If you do not agree on the answers, try to find the mistakes.

4. a) In exercise 1, how could you find which line segment is congruent to XY without tracing?
   b) In what way are congruent line segments *equal*?
   c) Draw two line segments that are congruent to XY.

5. a) In exercise 2, how could you find which angle is congruent to ∠XYZ without tracing?
   b) In what way are congruent angles *equal*?
   c) Draw two angles that are congruent to ∠XYZ.

ACTIVITY 2

Work with a partner. You will need a ruler and a protractor.

1. Use tracing paper to determine which triangle is congruent to △PQR.

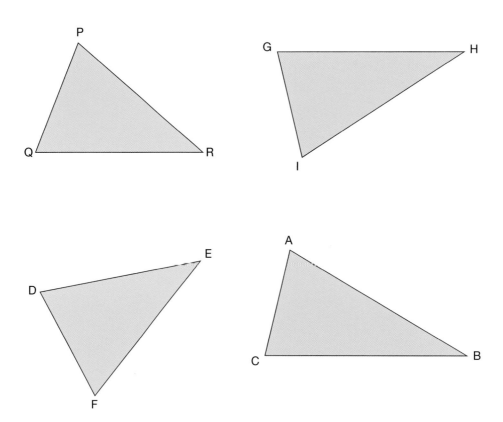

2. Check your answers to exercise 1 with other students. If you do not agree on the answer, try to find the mistakes.

3. a) In exercise 1, how could you find which triangle is congruent to △PQR without tracing?

 b) If you know that two triangles are congruent, what can you say about their sides and their angles?

▶▶ *Through Instruction*

Recall that two figures are congruent if they match exactly when one is placed on top of the other.
The matching sides are called *corresponding sides*.
The matching angles are called *corresponding angles*.

To determine if two triangles are congruent, measure their sides and their angles. If the measures for one triangle are equal to the measures for the other triangle, then the triangles are congruent.

Working with Mathematics

Something to talk about

1. Explain what is meant by each statement.
   a) AB is congruent to CD.
   b) ∠ABC is congruent to ∠DEF.
   c) △ABC is congruent to △XYZ.

2. Is every line segment of length 5 cm congruent to all other line segments of length 5 cm? Explain your answer.

3. **a)** Are these angles congruent?

   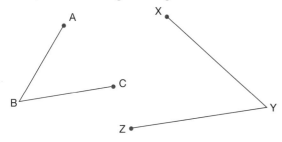

   b) Is every angle with a measure of 50° congruent to all other angles with measures of 50°? Explain your answer.

4. **a)** Do two congruent triangles have the same area? Explain.
   b) Are all triangles with the same area congruent? Explain.

5. **a)** Do two congruent triangles have the same perimeter? Explain.
   b) Are all triangles with the same perimeter congruent? Explain.

6. The diagram shows △ABC and △DEF. ∠ABC and ∠DEF both have a measure of 45°.
   a) Is ∠ABC congruent to ∠DEF? Explain.
   b) Is △ABC congruent to △DEF? Explain.

   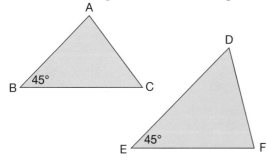

Practice

7. Measure each angle. Find two angles that are congruent.

   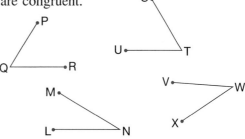

8. Each diagram shows congruent triangles. Name the equal angles and the equal sides.

   a)

   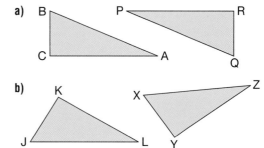

   b)

   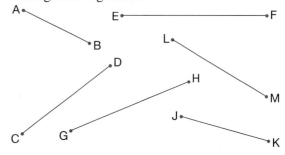

9. Measure each line segment. Find two congruent segments.

   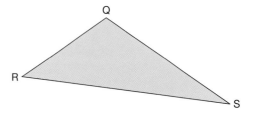

10. **a)** Draw a triangle that is congruent to △QRS. Label the vertices of the triangle that you draw.

    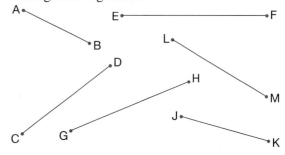

    b) Name the corresponding angles and sides for these congruent triangles.

Work together

11. In each diagram, are the triangles congruent? If they are, name the corresponding sides and corresponding angles.

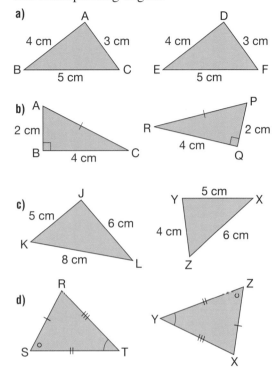

12. Only one pair of triangles in this set is congruent. By measuring with a ruler or protractor, find the matching pair.

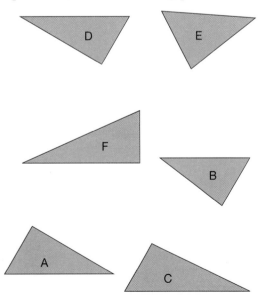

13. **a)** Construct a rectangle. Draw the diagonals.

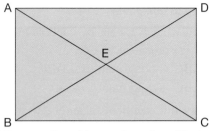

b) Measure the sides and angles. Find as many congruent triangles as possible. Name the congruent triangles.

c) Name corresponding sides in each pair of congruent triangles.

d) Name corresponding angles in each pair of congruent triangles.

On your own

14. In each diagram, name the congruent angles.

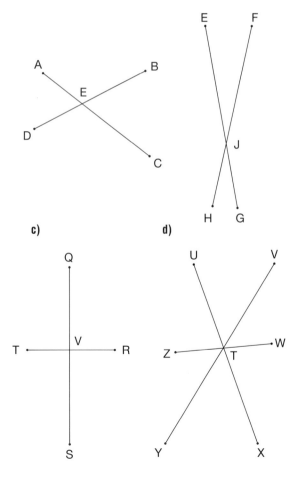

15. Recall that a triangle with three equal sides is an equilateral triangle.
    a) Draw an equilateral triangle. Cut out the triangle.
    b) Fold the triangle to divide it into congruent triangles.
    c) Repeat parts a and b several times. Each time, fold the triangle a different way.
    d) Describe the congruent triangles in parts b and c.

16. Use tracing paper to identify as many pairs of congruent triangles as you can. For each pair, name the corresponding angles and the corresponding sides.

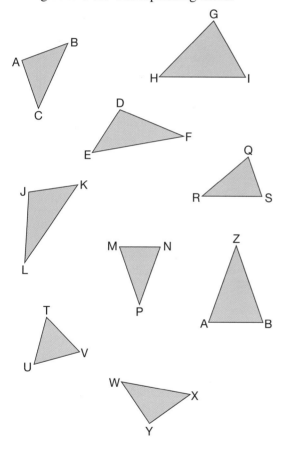

Extend your thinking

17. Recall that a triangle with at least two equal sides is an isosceles triangle. Construct three different isosceles triangles. Record the measures of the angles of each triangle.
    a) Describe any pattern you discover in the measures of the angles opposite the congruent sides.
    b) For each triangle, draw a line of symmetry. What can you say about the two figures formed by the line of symmetry?
    c) Fold your paper along the line of symmetry. Check that the line of symmetry divides the isosceles triangle into two congruent figures. Does the line of symmetry divide the angle into two equal parts? Explain how you know.

18. In each figure, find as many pairs of congruent triangles as you can.
    a)

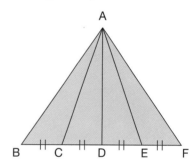

    b)

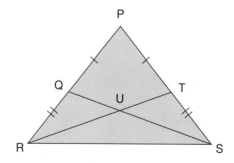

The Ideas

In your journal, explain what *congruence* is. Draw diagrams to show congruent segments, congruent angles, and congruent triangles.

Fingerprints

THE SKIN OF YOUR FINGERS HAS A UNIQUE PATTERN of ridges. No two sets of fingerprints are alike, even those of identical twins. Secretions are produced by glands under the surface of the skin and released through holes called pores. When you touch something, these secretions cause you to leave behind an invisible copy of your fingerprint pattern.

Fingerprints are one of the best ways to identify people. Fingerprint records are used to identify criminals, and dead or injured people. If the fingerprint of an unknown person is congruent to a fingerprint on record, then the unknown person can be identified. The system for classifying fingerprints is based on two things: class and ridges.

There are ten classes. These are shown below.

Ulnar loop (right hand)

Radial loop (right hand)

Double loop

Whorl

Arch

Tented arch

Lateral pocket loop

Central pocket loop

Composite

Accidental

There are five ridge characteristics.
These are shown below.

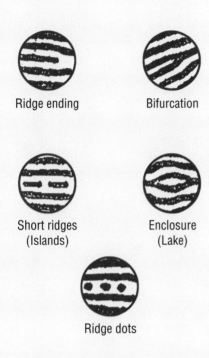

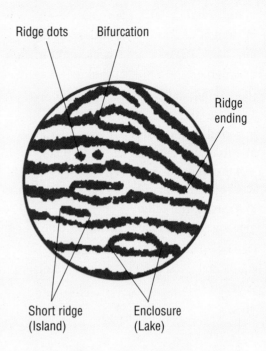

Matching prints have the same class, and the same number of ridges between shapes.

Complete the following exercises to classify your thumb print using these diagrams. You need an ink pad, blank paper, and a magnifying glass.

Work with a partner.

1. Lightly roll your right thumb face down over the ink pad. Slowly roll your thumb onto a blank piece of paper. Record your name underneath.

2. Make notes under the print to answer these questions.
   a) What is the class?
   b) Are there any identifying marks like cuts or scars?
   c) Are there any bifurcations, islands, or lakes?
   d) Count the ridges from the centre shape outwards to a new shape.
   e) Draw a sketch of the general shape.

3. Make a new thumb print on another piece of paper. Exchange prints with your partner. Repeat exercise 2 for your partner's print.

4. With your partner, compare your notes for both thumb prints.
   a) How well did you agree on your classification?
   b) What difficulties did you have in classifying the prints?

Mathematics & Science

Linking Ideas

Review

1. Explain each term.
   a) right angle
   b) equal
   c) straight angle
   d) scalene triangle
   e) acute triangle
   f) acute right triangle
   g) congruent
   h) similar

2. Use a ruler and compasses to draw each figure.
   a) a circle with radius 6.5 cm
   b) a triangle with side lengths 6.0 cm, 4.0 cm, and 7.5 cm
   c) a triangle with sides 5 cm, 8 cm, 5 cm
   d) a circle with radius 4 cm
   e) a triangle with sides 8 cm, 15 cm, 17 cm

3. Determine whether each triangle is equilateral, isosceles, or scalene. Explain your answers.

   a)
   b)

   c)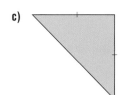
   d)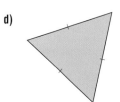

4. Is it possible to construct a triangle with side lengths 6.5 cm, 9.0 cm, and 11.5 cm? If your answer is yes, construct the triangle. If your answer is no, explain.

5. Draw each type of triangle.
   a) scalene
   b) right

6. Tell whether each angle is right, acute, obtuse, or straight. Explain how you know.

   a)
   b)

7. Use a ruler and a protractor to draw each triangle.
   a) angle 74° between sides 7.3 cm and 4.6 cm
   b) side 8.7 cm between angles 57° and 64°
   c) side 10.4 cm between angles 105° and 37°
   d) angle 124° between sides 5.1 cm and 8.5 cm

8. Determine whether each triangle is acute, right, or obtuse.

   a)
   b)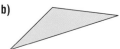

   c)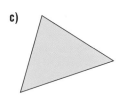
   d)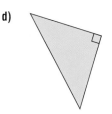

9. Draw each type of triangle.
   a) right isosceles
   b) acute equilateral
   c) obtuse scalene
   d) right scalene
   e) obtuse isosceles

10. In each part, are the figures congruent? If so, name the congruent sides and congruent angles. If not, explain why not.
    a)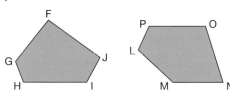

    b)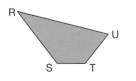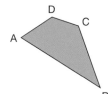

11. a) Which Canadian flags are congruent?
  b) Which Canadian flags are similar?

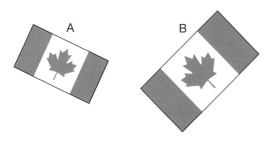

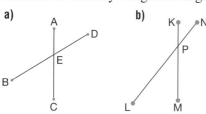

  c) Are all Canadian flags similar? Explain.

12. For each pattern block, sketch how this yellow block can be divided into congruent figures and tell how many congruent figures result.

  a) green block

  b) red block

  c) blue block

13. Measure to identify congruent angles.

  a)   **b)**

14. Measure each line segment. Determine which line segments are congruent to AB.

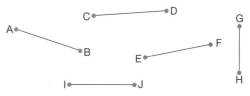

15. Which triangle is congruent to △ABC?

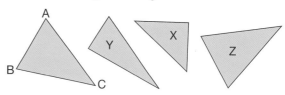

16. Name the equal angles and the equal sides in each pair of congruent triangles.

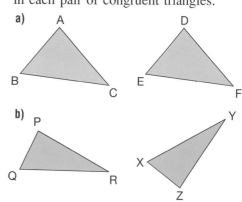
  a)

  b)

17. Each diagram shows congruent triangles. Name the corresponding angles and sides.

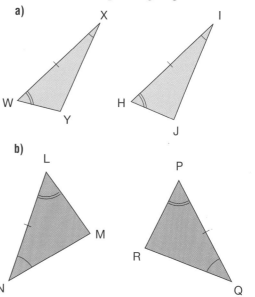
  a)

  b)

Writing a Solution Manual for a Geometric Puzzle

You create a geometric puzzle when you divide a geometric figure into smaller figures that can be put together in many ways. The tangram, which begins with a square, is one of the most famous geometric puzzles. It has been a popular toy for over 200 years. Tangram pieces can be combined to form hundreds of figures, some of which resemble people or animals.

Suppose you have been hired to develop a new geometric puzzle that starts with the parallelogram shown here. Your task is to prepare a manual to accompany the puzzle. The manual will use words or pictures to describe the figures people will create. It will also show the solutions to these puzzles. As well, you may add one additional challenge that you create.

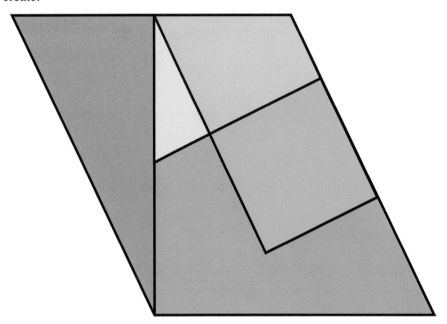

First, make your own copy of the puzzle. Trace the parallelogram on paper. Glue the paper onto a piece of cardboard. Cut out the five figures.

ACTIVITY 1

Arrange the pieces of the puzzle to form each figure below. Trace the outline of each figure so that someone using the puzzle can see what figure she or he should try to create. Record your solutions by tracing the outline of each piece.

    a) a square   **b)** a rectangle   **c)** a right triangle

ACTIVITY 2

A geometric figure that resembles an addition sign is called a *Greek cross*. An example is shown on the right. Arrange the pieces of the puzzle to form a Greek cross. Trace the outline of the figure. Record your solution by tracing each piece.

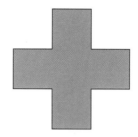

ACTIVITY 3

A quadrilateral that has no parallel sides is called a *trapezium*. Draw two examples of trapeziums to prove that such figures exist. Arrange the pieces of the puzzle to form a trapezium. Trace the outline of the figure. Record your solution by tracing each piece.

ACTIVITY 4

After rearranging the pieces to form the figures in *Activities 1* through *3*, it is easy to forget how the original parallelogram was pieced together. Without looking at the diagram on page 78, arrange the puzzle pieces to form a parallelogram. Trace the outline of the figure and record your solution by tracing each piece.

ACTIVITY 5

While you were working on the previous activities, you may have created an arrangement you thought was interesting and which was different from those described here. If not, try to create such a figure now. If you wish, name your figure. Make one sketch showing only the outline of your figure. Make another sketch showing the five pieces that make up your figure.

The Ideas

Prepare your solutions manual. Draw a title page and write an introduction. Include your drawings of the different figures people can make and the solutions you created in each activity. You may wish to order the problems according to difficulty—from easiest to most difficult.

Package your manual in a bag with a set of puzzle pieces. Make the package available to your family, friends, or classmates who have not completed this project.

Cumulative Review

1. Multiply.
   a) $2.8 \times 10\ 000$ b) 2.8×1000
   c) 2.8×100 d) 2.8×10
   e) 2.8×1 f) 2.8×0.1
   g) 2.8×0.01 h) 2.8×0.001

2. Divide.
   a) $149 \div 1000$ b) $149 \div 100$
   c) $149 \div 10$ d) $149 \div 1$
   e) $149 \div 0.1$ f) $149 \div 0.01$

3. Determine each product. Predict what the next line should be. Check your prediction with your calculator.
   a) $5 \times 9 = \blacksquare$ b) $3 \times 3 = \blacksquare$
      $55 \times 99 = \blacksquare$ $33 \times 33 = \blacksquare$
      $555 \times 999 = \blacksquare$ $333 \times 333 = \blacksquare$
   c) $1 \times 9 + 1 = \blacksquare$ d) $9 \times 8 = \blacksquare$
      $12 \times 9 + 2 = \blacksquare$ $99 \times 88 = \blacksquare$
      $123 \times 9 + 3 = \blacksquare$ $999 \times 888 = \blacksquare$

4. In each pair, which is the larger unit?
   a) metre, kilometre
   b) centimetre, millimetre
   c) metre, centimetre
   d) kilometre, millimetre
   e) centimetre, kilometre
   f) millimetre, metre

5. Which unit would you use to measure each item?
   a) the width of a floppy disk
   b) the length of a fence around a playground
   c) the width of a spaghetti noodle
   d) the height of a person
   e) the height of an office tower
   f) the length of a mosquito

6. Would you multiply or divide each unit below to convert to metres? By what would you multiply or divide?
   a) centimetres
   b) millimetres
   c) kilometres

7. Change each measurement to metres.
   a) 270 cm   b) 8 km   c) 0.95 km
   d) 693 mm   e) 0.043 km   f) 85 cm

8. Copy and complete.
   a) 15 cm = $\blacksquare$ mm   b) 2.1 km = $\blacksquare$ m
   c) 14.5 m = $\blacksquare$ cm   d) 90 mm = $\blacksquare$ cm
   e) 1.8 km = $\blacksquare$ m   f) 59 cm = $\blacksquare$ mm
   g) 101 m = $\blacksquare$ km   h) 73 mm = $\blacksquare$ m

9. a) Measure the width of this book and the length of your classroom.
   b) How many books would fit side-by-side across your classroom?
   c) How many books would fit side-by-side from the front door of your school to the door of your kitchen?

10. Look at the pattern of squares. Suppose the pattern was continued.

   1 and 2   2 and 4   3 and 6

   a) Sketch the fourth, fifth, and sixth figures.
   b) What pair of numbers would be beneath each of the fourth, fifth, and sixth figures?
   c) Suppose we use the number pairs 1 and 3, 2 and 6, 3 and 9, to describe the first three figures. What number pairs could we use to describe each of the fourth, fifth, and sixth figures?
   d) What 2 pairs of numbers could we use to describe the seventh figure?

11. Serena will plant tomato plants in a rectangular garden. She wants to plant 6 rows with 12 plants in each row. The plants must be 1 m apart.
   a) How long must the garden be for Serena to plant 12 plants in each row?
   b) How wide must the garden be for Serena to plant 6 rows of plants?

12. Write each power of 10 as a product and as a numeral.
   a) 10^6 b) 10^4 c) 10^8
   d) 10^1 e) 10^5 f) 10^7

13. Write the power of 10 closest to each number.
  a) An avalanche in British Columbia's interior mountain ranges can carry as much as 22 000 t of snow.
  b) Canada has about 1 300 000 km^2 of wetlands.
  c) Manitoulin Island, in Ontario, is the world's largest island in a lake. It has an area of 2766 km^2.
  d) Hudson Bay is one of the world's largest bays, with an area of over 1 000 000 km^2.

14. Use a ruler and compasses. Construct a triangle for each set of side lengths.
  a) 9.2 cm, 9.2 cm, 9.2 cm
  b) 6 cm, 8 cm, 10 cm
  c) 7.5 cm, 7.5 cm, 5.8 cm

15. Tell whether each angle is right, acute, obtuse, or straight. Explain how you know.
  a)   **b)**

16. Use a ruler and protractor. Construct a triangle for each set of side lengths. Identify each type of triangle you constructed.
  a) side 8 cm between angles 30° and 60°
  b) angle 60° between sides 6.5 cm and 6.5 cm
  c) side 4 cm between angles 110° and 45°

17. Is it possible to construct a triangle with an obtuse angle and a right angle? Explain.

18. a) If a photograph is copied to make a poster, are the pictures congruent? Are they similar?
  b) If a photograph is copied on a postcard, are the pictures congruent? Are they similar?

19. a) Use grid paper or dot paper to draw a pair of similar triangles.
  b) Use a transparent mirror to draw three congruent figures.

20. The figures in each pair are congruent. Identify the corresponding sides and angles.
  a)

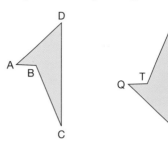

  b)

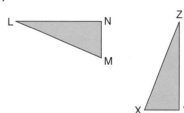

21. This circle is divided into 4 sectors. Explain how you can determine whether the sectors are congruent:
  a) by tracing
  b) by measuring radii and angles

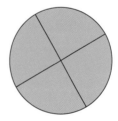

22. a) What is the measure of each angle at the centre of the circle in exercise 21?
  b) What is the sum of the angles in part a?
  c) What would the sum be if the circle was divided into 8 equal sectors? Into 12 equal sectors? Draw a diagram to explain your answer.

FRACTIONS AND DECIMALS

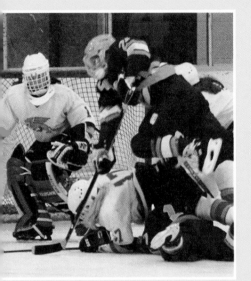

WHAT'S COMING UP?

DEPARTMENTS

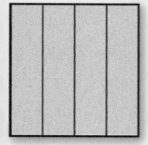

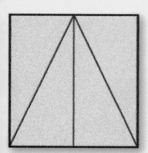

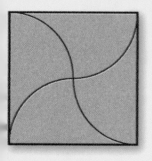

Linking Ideas

Quests

Minds on Math Project

Start With What You Know

The game of chess originated in India about 1500 years ago. It is played on a square board that has 8 rows of squares, with 8 squares in each row.

1. **a)** How many squares are there on a chessboard?
   b) How many of these squares are light?
   c) What fraction of the squares are light? Write this fraction in lowest terms.
   d) What fraction of the squares are dark? Write this fraction in lowest terms.

2. Each player begins the game with 16 pieces.

Pawn Pawn Pawn Pawn Pawn Pawn Pawn Pawn

Rook Knight Bishop Queen King Bishop Knight Rook

   a) What fraction of the white pieces are pawns? Write this fraction in lowest terms.
   b) What fraction of the white pieces are rooks? Write this fraction in lowest terms.

3. The photograph above shows the positions of the pieces at the beginning of the game.
   a) What fraction of the squares on the board are covered by pieces?
   b) What fraction of the squares on the board does each player's pieces cover?

4. Each diagram shows a chess piece on the board. The squares to which the chess piece can move are grey. For each chess piece, write the fraction of the squares on the chessboard to which it can move. Where possible, write the fraction in lowest terms.

a) King

b) Queen

c) Rook

d) Bishop

e) Knight

5. At the beginning of the game, a pawn may move forward one or two squares. To what fraction of the squares can this pawn move? Write this fraction in lowest terms.

Constructing Fraction Strips and Number Lines

You can use a Draw program on a computer to create the fraction strips and number lines on pages 88, 89, 90, and 91. Here is what you do in ClarisWorks.

Start a new drawing in ClarisWorks. Make sure the Autogrid is turned on. This ensures that whatever you draw goes to points on the grid.

Go under Format and choose Rulers. Set the ruler to measure in centimetres. Have 10 divisions per centimetre. This is what the screen should look like.

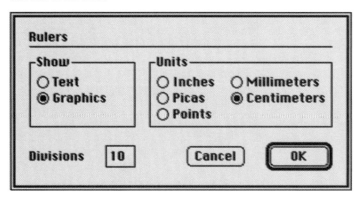

1. You should make your white 1-strip 16 cm long and 1.5 cm wide.

   What should the length of each of these strips be?

   a) yellow $\frac{1}{2}$-strip

   b) blue $\frac{1}{3}$-strip and blue $\frac{2}{3}$-strip

   c) red $\frac{1}{4}$-strip, red $\frac{3}{4}$-strip, and red $\frac{2}{4}$-strip

   d) green $\frac{1}{5}$-strip, green $\frac{4}{5}$-strip, green $\frac{2}{5}$-strip, and green $\frac{3}{5}$-strip

2. How many times as long as an orange $\frac{2}{8}$-strip is an orange $\frac{6}{8}$-strip?

3. How many times as long as a pink $\frac{2}{10}$-strip is a pink $\frac{8}{10}$-strip?

Carefully use the Rectangle tool in your Draw program to make each fraction strip on pages 88 and 89. Use the Line tool to make the divisions.

Use the Line tool to make the number lines on pages 90 and 91.

Each line for 0 to 1 should be 16 cm long.

Use small lines to mark the divisions on a line, in a similar way to marking the divisions on a strip.

Use the Text tool to label the strips and the number lines.

You could fill in the different fraction strips with different patterns.

Save your work and print it.

Mathematics & Technology

Linking Ideas

....2.1 *THE CONCEPT OF A FRACTION*

Developing the Ideas

The denominator of a fraction tells into how many parts one whole has been divided.

$$\frac{3}{4}$$

The numerator tells how many of those parts are being considered.

Fractions can be represented in different ways.

▶ ▶ *Through Activities*

ACTIVITY 1

1. A rectangle represents one whole. For each diagram, what fraction(s) are represented by the parts that are dark red?

   a)

   b)

   c)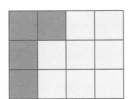

2. A circle represents one whole. For each diagram, name two fractions that are represented by the parts that are dark blue.

   a)

   b)

   c)

3. In each diagram, what fraction of the circles are dark green? What fraction are light green?

   a)

   b)

ACTIVITY 2

In many activities in this chapter, you will use paper strips to represent fractions.

Make your own set of fraction strips. You can copy pages 88 and 89, or use copies that your teacher gives you. Colour each rectangle as indicated, and cut out the rectangles. Keep your strips in an envelope.

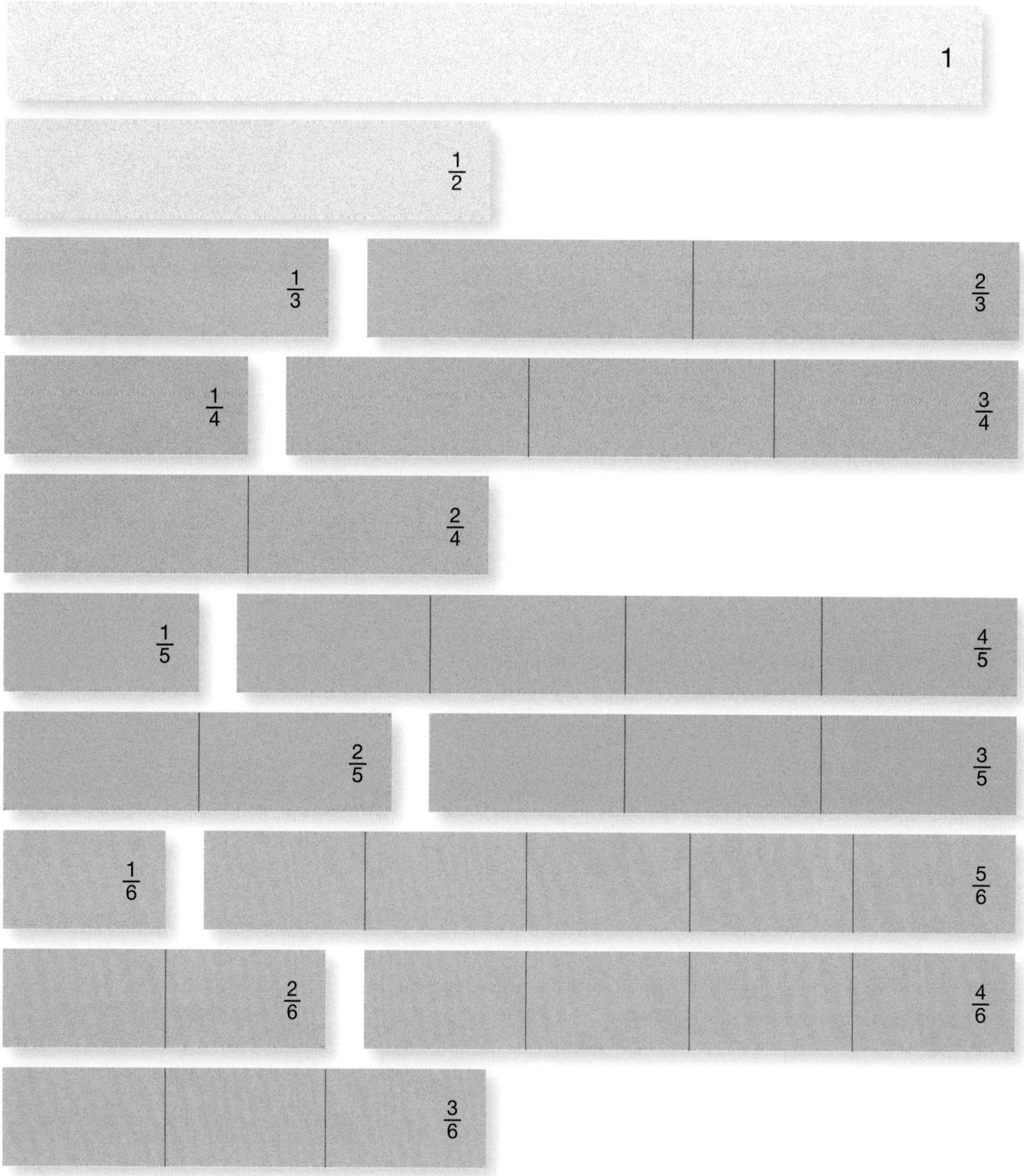

1

$\frac{1}{2}$

$\frac{1}{3}$ $\frac{2}{3}$

$\frac{1}{4}$ $\frac{3}{4}$

$\frac{2}{4}$

$\frac{1}{5}$ $\frac{4}{5}$

$\frac{2}{5}$ $\frac{3}{5}$

$\frac{1}{6}$ $\frac{5}{6}$

$\frac{2}{6}$ $\frac{4}{6}$

$\frac{3}{6}$

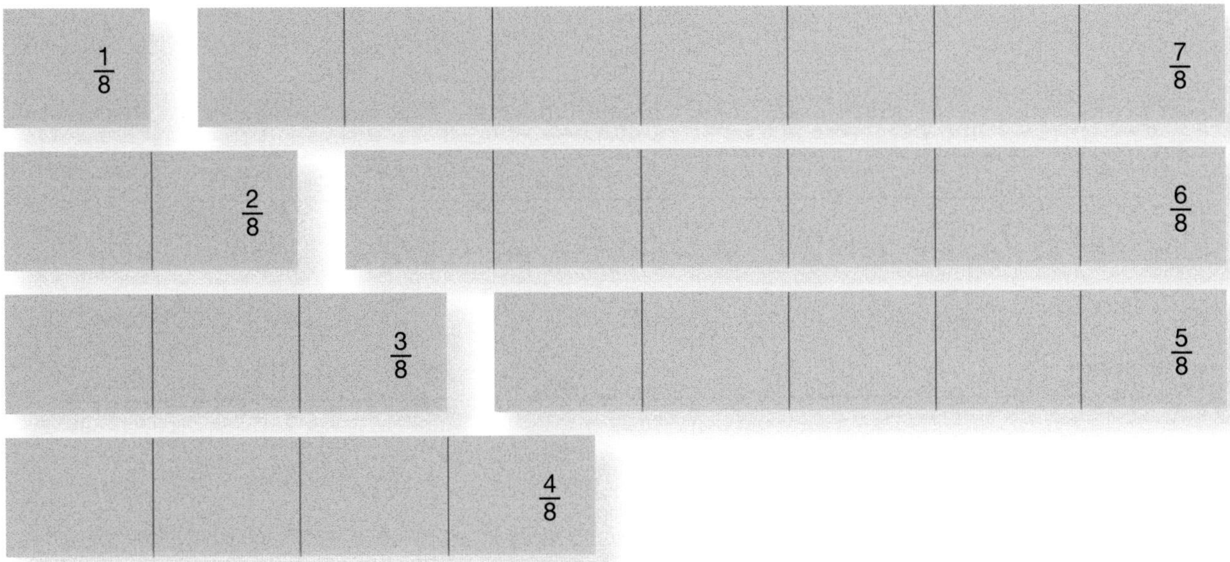

The strips shown represent the following fractions:

$\frac{1}{8}$ $\frac{7}{8}$

$\frac{2}{8}$ $\frac{6}{8}$

$\frac{3}{8}$ $\frac{5}{8}$

$\frac{4}{8}$

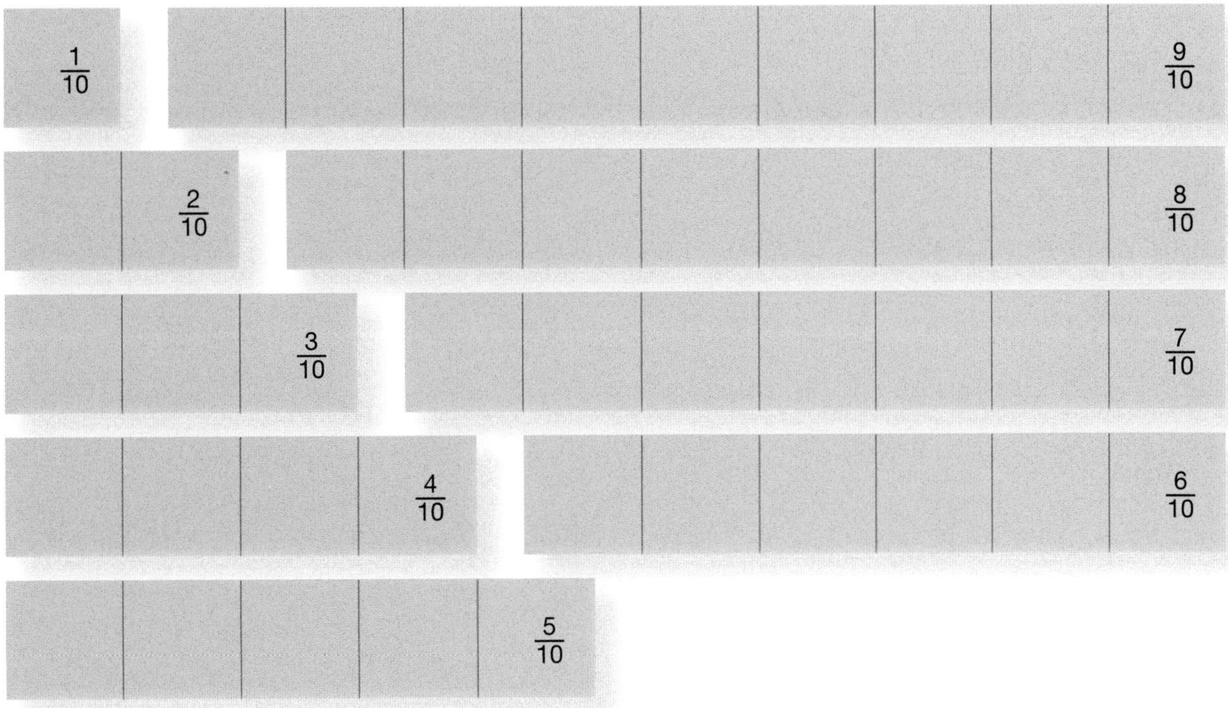

$\frac{1}{10}$ $\frac{9}{10}$

$\frac{2}{10}$ $\frac{8}{10}$

$\frac{3}{10}$ $\frac{7}{10}$

$\frac{4}{10}$ $\frac{6}{10}$

$\frac{5}{10}$

1. a) Find four strips that have the same length. List the fractions represented by these strips. These are examples of *equivalent fractions*. List some other fractions that are equivalent to these.

b) Find other strips that have the same length. List the fractions they represent. List some other fractions that are equivalent to them.

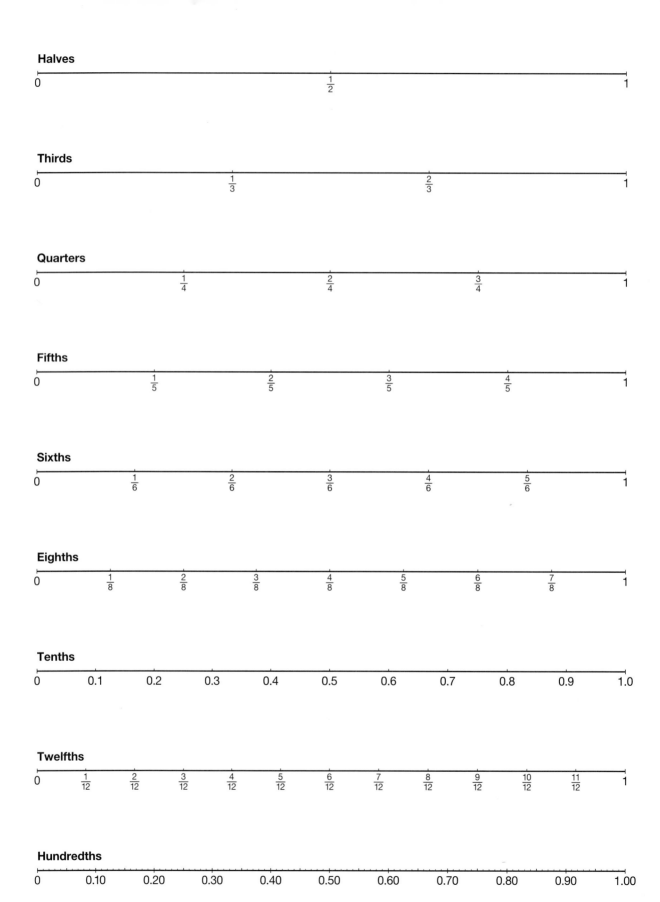

Halves

0          $\frac{1}{2}$ 1

Thirds

0      $\frac{1}{3}$ $\frac{2}{3}$ 1

Quarters

0     $\frac{1}{4}$ $\frac{2}{4}$ $\frac{3}{4}$ 1

Fifths

0    $\frac{1}{5}$ $\frac{2}{5}$ $\frac{3}{5}$ $\frac{4}{5}$ 1

Sixths

0   $\frac{1}{6}$ $\frac{2}{6}$ $\frac{3}{6}$ $\frac{4}{6}$ $\frac{5}{6}$ 1

Eighths

0   $\frac{1}{8}$ $\frac{2}{8}$ $\frac{3}{8}$ $\frac{4}{8}$ $\frac{5}{8}$ $\frac{6}{8}$ $\frac{7}{8}$ 1

Tenths

0   0.1   0.2   0.3   0.4   0.5   0.6   0.7   0.8   0.9   1.0

Twelfths

0   $\frac{1}{12}$ $\frac{2}{12}$ $\frac{3}{12}$ $\frac{4}{12}$ $\frac{5}{12}$ $\frac{6}{12}$ $\frac{7}{12}$ $\frac{8}{12}$ $\frac{9}{12}$ $\frac{10}{12}$ $\frac{11}{12}$ 1

Hundredths

0   0.10   0.20   0.30   0.40   0.50   0.60   0.70   0.80   0.90   1.00

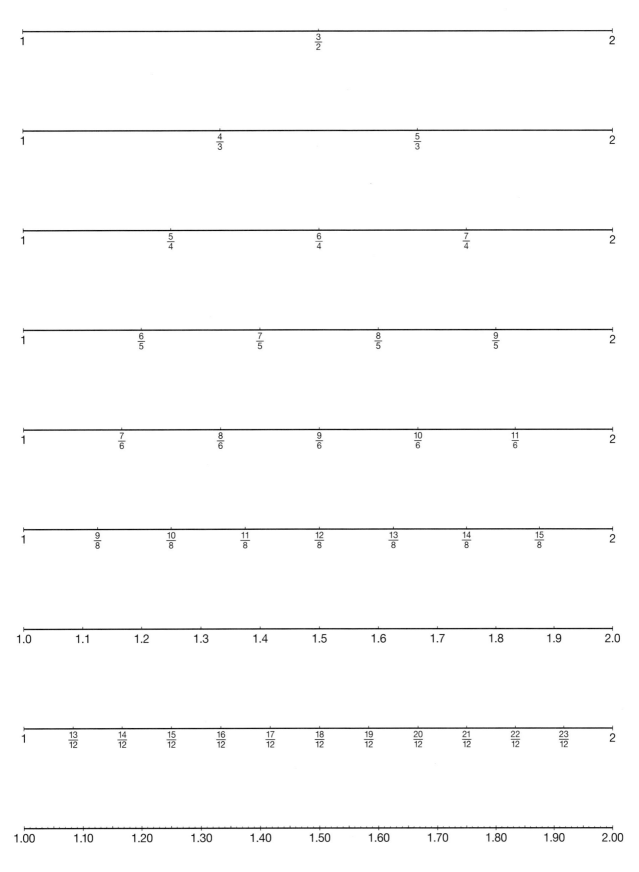

ACTIVITY 3

For many activities in this chapter, you will use the number lines on the previous two pages. Make your own set of number lines. You can copy pages 90 and 91, or use copies that your teacher gives you. Overlap, then tape adjacent lines together so you have each number line from 0 to 2, as shown below.

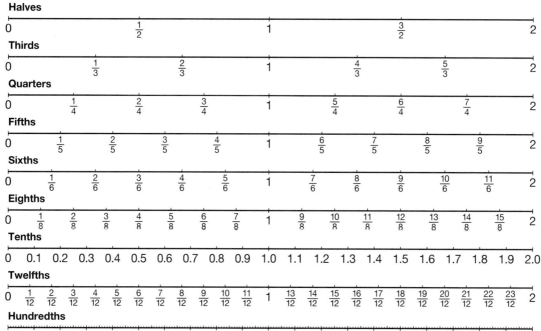

1. Check that your fraction strips fit on the number lines.

   a) For example, take the yellow $\frac{1}{2}$-strip and place it on the top number line so that one end is at 0. Notice the point on the number line at the other end of the strip.

   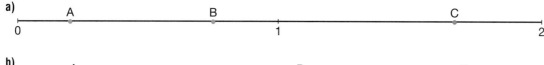

   b) Place the $\frac{1}{2}$-strip on the other number lines in the same way. What do you notice?

   c) What other strips will cover the same space as the $\frac{1}{2}$-strip?

   d) Repeat parts a, b, and c using some of the other strips.

2. Estimate a fraction that each labelled point represents.

   a)

   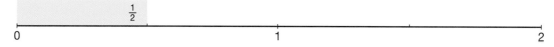

   b)

For the birthday cake, 3 of 12 equal parts, or 1 of 4 equal parts has been served.
$\frac{3}{12}$, or $\frac{1}{4}$ of the cake has been served.

$\frac{3}{12}$ and $\frac{1}{4}$ are equivalent fractions.
They describe the same amount of cake.

In *Activity 2* you found that some fraction strips have the same length. The fractions they represent are equivalent fractions.

For example, $\frac{2}{3} = \frac{4}{6}$

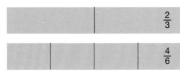

In *Activity 3* you found that some fractions name the same point on the number line. They are equivalent fractions.

For example, $\frac{1}{2} = \frac{4}{8}$

Halves

0                    $\frac{1}{2}$ 1

Eighths

0    $\frac{1}{8}$ $\frac{2}{8}$ $\frac{3}{8}$ $\frac{4}{8}$ $\frac{5}{8}$ $\frac{6}{8}$ $\frac{7}{8}$ 1

Observe the pattern in the two examples above.

$$\overset{\times 2}{\frac{2}{3}} = \underset{\times 2}{\frac{4}{6}} \qquad \overset{\times 4}{\frac{1}{2}} = \underset{\times 4}{\frac{4}{8}}$$

Suppose a fraction is given. To form an equivalent fraction, multiply or divide both the numerator and the denominator by the same number (not zero).

In *Activities 1* and *3* you found that some fractions are greater than 1.

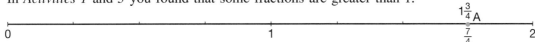

Point A is 7 units to the right of 0 on the number line above. So, point A can be represented by the fraction $\frac{7}{4}$. Point A is also 3 units to the right of 1. So, point A can also be represented by the mixed number, $1\frac{3}{4}$.

▶▶ *Through Guided Examples*

Example 1

Write two equivalent fractions for $\frac{6}{10}$.

Solution

$$\frac{6}{10} = \frac{6 \times 3}{10 \times 3} \qquad\qquad \frac{6}{10} = \frac{6 \div 2}{10 \div 2}$$
$$= \frac{18}{30} \qquad\qquad\qquad = \frac{3}{5}$$

In *Example 1*, the only common factor of the numerator and denominator of $\frac{3}{5}$ is 1. The fraction $\frac{3}{5}$ is in *simplest form*.

To express a fraction in simplest form, determine the greatest common factor of the numerator and the denominator. Then divide the numerator and the denominator by the greatest common factor.

Example 2

Express $\frac{12}{16}$ in simplest form.

Solution

$$\frac{12}{16} = \frac{12 \div 4}{16 \div 4} \qquad \text{◁ 4 is the greatest whole number that divides 12 and 16.}$$
$$= \frac{3}{4} \qquad\qquad \text{We say that 4 is the } \textit{greatest common factor} \text{ of 12 and 16.}$$

Example 3

a) Write $\frac{9}{4}$ as a mixed number.

b) Write $2\frac{2}{3}$ as an improper fraction.

Solution

a) $\frac{9}{4}$ means 9 quarters.

Separate the quarters into groups of 4 quarters each.
There are 2 groups of 4 quarters, or 2 wholes.
There is 1 quarter left.
So, $\frac{9}{4} = 2\frac{1}{4}$

b) Replace each whole number with 3 thirds.
There are 2 groups of 3 thirds, or 6 thirds.
Add the 2 thirds. This makes a total of 8 thirds.
So, $2\frac{2}{3} = \frac{8}{3}$

Working with Mathematics

Something to talk about

1. Does the numerator of a fraction have to be less than the denominator? Illustrate your answer with one or more examples.

2. Create an example in which you can form an equivalent fraction by dividing the numerator and denominator by the same number.

3. Match each diagram with the equivalent fractions that name the dark red part.

$$\frac{1}{2}, \frac{4}{8} \qquad \frac{1}{5}, \frac{2}{10} \qquad \frac{2}{3}, \frac{6}{9} \qquad \frac{3}{4}, \frac{9}{12}$$

a)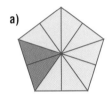

b)

c)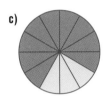

d)

4. Which fractions are in simplest form?
   a) $\frac{2}{3}$ b) $\frac{9}{12}$ c) $\frac{5}{5}$ d) $\frac{5}{4}$
   e) $\frac{8}{10}$ f) $\frac{7}{16}$ g) $\frac{15}{10}$ h) $\frac{11}{8}$
   i) $\frac{14}{21}$ j) $\frac{8}{6}$ k) $\frac{13}{5}$ l) $\frac{4}{9}$

Work together

5. Which fractions in the box are equivalent to each fraction?
   a) $\frac{2}{3}$ b) $\frac{3}{4}$ c) $\frac{4}{5}$

$\frac{6}{8}$	$\frac{4}{6}$	$\frac{12}{16}$	$\frac{8}{12}$
$\frac{8}{10}$	$\frac{9}{12}$	$\frac{12}{15}$	$\frac{6}{9}$

6. Write two fractions equivalent to $\frac{12}{18}$:
   a) by multiplying   b) by dividing

7. Write an equivalent fraction for each fraction.
   a) $\frac{2}{3}$ b) $\frac{3}{4}$ c) $\frac{6}{5}$ d) $\frac{7}{2}$
   e) $\frac{3}{10}$ f) $\frac{2}{8}$ g) $\frac{15}{6}$ h) $\frac{3}{11}$

Get a set of pattern blocks. Use the blocks shown here to complete exercises 8 to 11.

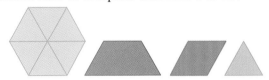

8. a) Suppose the yellow block represents one whole. What does each of the other 3 blocks represent?
   b) Suppose the green block represents one whole. What does each of the other 3 blocks represent?
   c) Suppose the blue block represents one whole. What does each of the other 3 blocks represent?
   d) Suppose the red block represents one whole. What does each of the other 3 blocks represent?

9. a) Suppose the yellow block represents one whole. State what each set of blocks below represents.
   b) Suppose the green block represents one whole. State what each set of blocks below represents.

i)

ii)

iii)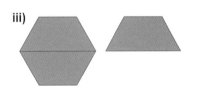

iv)

c) Suppose the parallelogram made from 4 blocks in part iv represents one whole. What does each of the 4 pattern blocks represent?

10. Hexagonal work tables can be separated into 2 half-tables that are trapezoids. Suppose you have 9 half-tables.
   a) Use pattern blocks to show how many work-tables you can make with the half-tables.
   b) Use your model to explain how to write $\frac{9}{2}$ as a mixed number.

11. A chocolate bar can be broken into 6 equal pieces. Suppose you have $2\frac{2}{6}$ of these bars to share with 4 friends.
   a) Use pattern blocks to determine whether you have enough so that you can each have two $\frac{1}{6}$ pieces.
   b) Use pattern blocks to determine whether you have enough so that you can each have three $\frac{1}{6}$ pieces.
   c) Use your model to explain how to write $2\frac{2}{6}$ as an improper fraction.

On your own

12. From a sheet of paper, cut two strips about 2 or 3 cm wide. Each strip represents one whole.
   a) Fold your strips as shown below. Then unfold them. What fractions do the fold lines represent?
   i)   ii)

b) Fold the strips one more time. What fractions do the fold lines represent now?
   i) 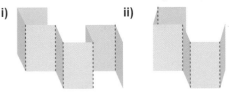   ii)

c) Suppose you folded the strips one more time. What fractions would the fold lines represent?

Save your strips from exercise 12. You will need them to do exercise 18.

13. Draw a diagram to represent each pair of equivalent fractions.
   a) $\frac{1}{3}, \frac{2}{6}$ b) $\frac{1}{4}, \frac{2}{8}$ c) $\frac{1}{2}, \frac{3}{6}$ d) $\frac{2}{5}, \frac{4}{10}$

14. Copy and complete.
   a) $\frac{2}{3} = \frac{\blacksquare}{15}$ b) $\frac{4}{5} = \frac{\blacksquare}{20}$
   c) $\frac{7}{4} = \frac{21}{\blacksquare}$ d) $\frac{9}{15} = \frac{3}{\blacksquare}$

15. Write in simplest form.
   a) $\frac{6}{8}$ b) $\frac{18}{6}$ c) $\frac{8}{12}$ d) $\frac{6}{4}$
   e) $\frac{4}{6}$ f) $\frac{9}{27}$ g) $\frac{24}{15}$ h) $\frac{14}{24}$

16. Write each improper fraction as a mixed number.
   a) $\frac{3}{2}$ b) $\frac{16}{5}$ c) $\frac{14}{3}$ d) $\frac{11}{6}$ e) $\frac{14}{9}$

17. Write each mixed number as an improper fraction.
   a) $4\frac{3}{4}$ b) $2\frac{5}{8}$ c) $1\frac{7}{9}$ d) $3\frac{2}{5}$ e) $6\frac{1}{3}$

Extend your thinking

18. Get the paper strips from exercise 12. Lay them out flat. Some of the folds point up towards you. These are called *mountain folds*. The folds that point down are called *valley folds*. For each paper strip, write the fraction of the folds that are mountain folds and the fraction that are valley folds. Is there any pattern in the results?

The Ideas

In your journal, write an explanation of what happens when you multiply or divide the numerator and denominator of a fraction by the same number. Illustrate your explanation with some examples.

Dividing a Square into Quarters

In how many different ways can you divide a square into quarters?
Try to find at least ten ways. Here are three to get you started.

 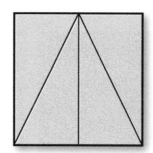 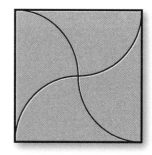

Understand the problem

- What does *quarters* mean?
- Do the four parts have to be identical?
- Suppose you find one way. If the four parts are rearranged inside the square, would that count as a different way?
- What are you asked to do?

Think of a strategy

- You may be able to think of one or two other "obvious" ways to divide the square into quarters.
- It might help to draw a square on grid paper.

Carry out the strategy

- Draw some squares on grid paper like the one below. Use the grid lines to help you find other ways to divide a square into quarters.
- Try larger squares if necessary.

Look back

- Share your results with other students. How many different ways did your class find?
- How many ways do you think there are to divide a square into quarters? Explain your answer.
- Try to find at least ten different ways to divide a square into halves.

Communicating the Ideas

In your journal, write a description of this problem and your solution.

Working with Mathematics

Something to talk about

1. What is the value of each underlined digit?

   a) 0.4<u>6</u>   **b)** 14.<u>7</u>82   **c)** 8.10<u>45</u>

   d) 482.0<u>90</u>   **e)** <u>5</u>26.05   **f)** 19.59<u>1</u>

   g) 308.1<u>10</u>   **h)** 27.401<u>6</u>   **i)** 24.0<u>89</u>

2. At his garage sale, Bryan priced comic books at 20 for $1.00. He wrote the price on each comic book as 0.05¢. Is this correct? Explain.

Practice

3. What number does each group of blocks represent?

   a)

   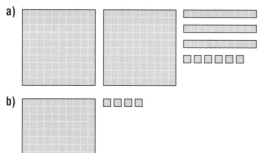

   b)

4. Use blocks to represent each number.

   a) 0.83   **b)** 3.24   **c)** 2.01   **d)** 5.20

5. Use blocks to determine the greater number in each pair.

   a) 3.2, 2.3   **b)** 1.06, 1.6

   c) 4.2, 4.25   **d)** 2.6, 2.53

6. Use the number lines from page 92 to explain how to determine the greater number in each part of exercise 5.

Work together

7. Make four cards as shown.

   [0] [.] [1] [4]

   a) Use some or all of the cards. Which of these numbers can you make?

   i) four and one tenth

   ii) fourteen and one tenth

   iii) four and one hundredth

   iv) one and four thousandths

   b) Name four other numbers you can make with the cards.

8. **a)** Draw a line segment 10 cm long. Mark the left end 4.1 and the right end 4.2.

   4.1   4.2
   •————————————————————————————•

   b) Which numbers in the box can be located between 4.1 and 4.2 on the segment? Use estimation to mark the location of each number.

4.15	4.11	4.01
4.19	4.151	4.09
4.105	4.21	4.175

9. Use only the [1], [0], [+], [−], [=], [.] keys on your calculator. Find a way to display each of the following numbers. Suppose each keystroke costs 1¢. What is the cheapest way to display each number?

   a) 13.49   **b)** 45.097   **c)** 354.35

   d) 1.7045   **e)** 0.2362   **f)** 0.0087

10. Sue bought a portable radio for $39.95. She paid for it with this cheque.

    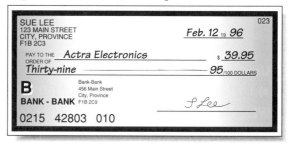

    Show how the cost of each item would be written on a cheque. Assume all taxes are included in the price.

    a) a skateboard for $27.49

    b) a pair of ski boots for $149.99

    c) a hockey stick for $12.89

    d) a tennis racket for $79.50 and a can of tennis balls for $8.95

On your own

11. Write each number in words and in expanded form.
    a) Cars travelling in opposite directions pass each other in about 0.07 s.
    b) In Olympic competition, each lane of a running track is 1.22 m wide.
    c) Every year, Hawaii is getting 0.069 m closer to Australia.
    d) One knot, one nautical mile per hour, is equal to 1.852 km/h.
    e) Some bacteria are 0.0003 mm long.

12. The table gives the areas and 1991 populations of the world's four largest countries. Arrange the countries in order of:
    a) decreasing population
    b) increasing area

Country	Population (millions)	Area (millions of square kilometres)
Canada	27.41	9.97
China	1158.23	9.57
Russia	148.54	17.08
U.S.A.	255.08	9.38

13. Use your calculator to display each number.
    a) two tenths less than 23.695
    b) eight hundredths more than 43.268
    c) six thousandths less than 12.482
    d) fifty-three hundredths more than 43.137
    e) fifty-three thousandths more than 43.137

14. Enter the first number in your calculator. Use only one operation. Have the calculator display the number in the box.
    a) 3.287   [3.087]   b) 69.542   [69.502]
    c) 49.755   [49.75]   d) 138.624   [138.612]
    e) 629.441 [629.331] f) 180.279   [180.178]

15. a) Enter the two numbers below on your calculator. After you enter each number, press [+].

    twenty and eight tenths
    three and five thousandths

    b) What number does your calculator display?

16. Replace each ▇ with >, <, or =.
    a) 0.96 ▇ 0.94   b) 0.61 ▇ 0.6
    c) 0.3 ▇ 0.30   d) 51.887 ▇ 51.878
    e) 0.0009 ▇ 0.0010   f) 304.11 ▇ 304.4

17. a) Enter the three numbers below on your calculator. After you enter each number, press [+].

    two and one hundred four thousandths
    seven hundred five and seven hundred five thousandths
    fourteen and one hundred fourteen ten thousandths

    b) What number does your calculator display?

Extend your thinking

18. Each planet in our solar system travels in an orbit around the sun. The table shows the average speed at which each planet moves around the sun. Scientists have found that the farther a planet is from the sun, the slower its speed.

Planet	Average speed (km/s)
Earth	29.76
Jupiter	13.03
Mars	24.13
Mercury	47.94
Neptune	5.47
Pluto	4.66
Saturn	9.65
Uranus	6.75
Venus	35.07

    a) List from least to greatest, the average speeds of the 4 planets farthest from the sun.
    b) List from greatest to least, the average speeds of the 4 planets closest to the sun.

The Ideas

Suppose two decimal numbers are given. In your journal, explain how you can tell which number is greater. Use examples to illustrate your explanation.

2.3 *FRACTIONS AND DECIMALS*

Developing the Ideas

▷ ▶ *Using Manipulatives*

You will need your fraction strips and number lines.

1. a) Place the green $\frac{2}{5}$-strip on the fifths line, starting at 0. Check the fraction on the number line at the right end of the strip.

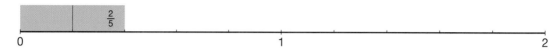

b) Place the $\frac{2}{5}$-strip on the tenths line. Express $\frac{2}{5}$ in decimal form.

c) Place the $\frac{2}{5}$-strip on the hundredths line. Express $\frac{2}{5}$ in decimal form.

d) Express these numbers in decimal form:

$$\frac{1}{5} \quad \frac{2}{5} \quad \frac{3}{5} \quad \frac{4}{5} \quad \frac{5}{5} \quad \frac{6}{5} \quad \frac{7}{5} \quad \frac{8}{5} \quad \frac{9}{5} \quad \frac{10}{5}$$

2. a) Place the red $\frac{3}{4}$-strip on each line in turn, so that the left end of the strip is at 0. If the right end coincides with a fraction, use the results to express $\frac{3}{4}$ in different ways.

b) Express these numbers in decimal form:

$$\frac{1}{4} \quad \frac{2}{4} \quad \frac{3}{4} \quad \frac{4}{4} \quad 1\frac{1}{4} \quad 1\frac{2}{4} \quad 1\frac{3}{4} \quad 1\frac{4}{4}$$

3. a) Place the blue $\frac{1}{3}$-strip on each line in turn, so that the left end of the strip is at 0. If the right end coincides with a fraction, use the results to express $\frac{1}{3}$ in different ways.

b) Repeat part a, using the blue $\frac{2}{3}$-strip.

c) You do not have a blue $\frac{3}{3}$-strip. What other strip could you use in its place? Repeat part a with this strip.

d) Use your strips to express $\frac{1}{3}$, $\frac{2}{3}$, and $\frac{3}{3}$ in decimal form as hundredths. Compare the results. Do you think your answers are exact, or are they only approximate?

e) Express these numbers in decimal form to the nearest hundredth:

$$\frac{1}{3} \quad \frac{2}{3} \quad \frac{3}{3} \quad 1\frac{1}{3} \quad 1\frac{2}{3} \quad 1\frac{3}{3} \quad 2\frac{1}{3} \quad 2\frac{2}{3}$$

▷ ▶ *Through Discussion*

Any number can be written in many ways in both fraction form and in decimal form. For example, here are many ways of writing the number "one and one-half."

In fraction form

$$1\frac{1}{2} \quad 1\frac{2}{4} \quad 1\frac{3}{6} \quad \dots \qquad 1\frac{5}{10} \quad 1\frac{50}{100} \quad 1\frac{500}{1000} \quad \dots$$

$$\frac{3}{2} \quad \frac{6}{4} \quad \frac{9}{6} \quad \dots \qquad \frac{15}{10} \quad \frac{150}{100} \quad \frac{1500}{1000} \quad \dots$$

In decimal form

1.5   1.50   1.500   ...

Decimal form is just another way of writing fractions with denominators 10, 100, 1000, ... Writing $1.50 = 1.5$ corresponds to writing $1\frac{50}{100} = 1\frac{5}{10}$

Any number that is expressed in fraction form can also be expressed in decimal form. You can use fraction strips and the hundredths line, or division, to do this. When you use fraction strips, the results may be approximate.

Using fraction strips and the hundredths line

$\frac{1}{4} = 0.25$

Since the result is not exact, we write
$\frac{1}{3} \doteq 0.33$

Using division

$$\begin{array}{r} 0.25 \\ 4\overline{)1.00} \\ \underline{8} \\ 20 \\ \underline{20} \\ 0 \end{array}$$

$$\begin{array}{r} 0.33 \\ 3\overline{)1.00} \\ \underline{9} \\ 10 \\ \underline{9} \\ 1 \end{array}$$

$\frac{1}{4} = 0.25$

$\frac{1}{3} \doteq 0.33$

Using a calculator

Press: **1 ÷ 4 =**

Display: **0.25**

$\frac{1}{4} = 0.25$

Press: **1 ÷ 3 =**

Display: **0.3333333**

$\frac{1}{3} \doteq 0.33$

The division does not terminate. The number in decimal form is rounded to a few decimal places.

Using a computer

Start a new document in a spreadsheet program.

In Microsoft Works:

In cell A1, type =1/4, and press Return.

In cell A2, type =1/3, and press Return.

	A	B
1	0.25	
2	0.3333333333	

In ClarisWorks:

Click on A to select that column.

Go into Format and choose Number.

In Number, choose Fixed and Precision 6.

Repeat the typing sequence for Microsoft Works.

	A	B
1	0.250000	
2	0.333333	

Working with Mathematics

Something to talk about

1. How could we write 1 as a fraction on each number line?
   - **a)** the halves line
   - **b)** the thirds line
   - **c)** the quarters line
   - **d)** the fifths line
   - **e)** the sixths line
   - **f)** the eighths line
   - **g)** the tenths line
   - **h)** the twelfths line

2. Several ways of writing the number "one and one-half" are shown on page 102. Locate as many as possible on the number lines on pages 90 and 91. What additional number line would be needed to show the remaining way of writing "one and one-half"? How would this number line differ from those on pages 90 and 91?

3. Compare the numbers on page 90 with the numbers on page 91.
   - **a)** When the numbers are written in decimal form, how are they the same? How are they different?
   - **b)** When the numbers are written in fraction form, how are they the same? How are they different?

4. **a)** If you made fraction strips for 0.40 and 0.4, how would they be the same? How would they be different?
   - **b)** Explain why 0.40 and 0.4 represent the same number.

Practice

5. Write each fraction as a decimal.
   - **a)** $\frac{3}{10}$
   - **b)** $\frac{81}{100}$
   - **c)** $\frac{7}{10}$
   - **d)** $\frac{27}{10}$
   - **e)** $\frac{9}{100}$
   - **f)** $\frac{479}{1000}$
   - **g)** $\frac{93}{1000}$
   - **h)** $\frac{127}{100}$

6. Write each decimal as a fraction with denominator 100. Where possible, write each fraction in simplest form as well.
   - **a)** 0.26
   - **b)** 0.51
   - **c)** 0.41
   - **d)** 0.65
   - **e)** 0.37
   - **f)** 0.74
   - **g)** 0.96
   - **h)** 1.18

7. On pages 90 and 91, find some fractions on the number lines that are one above another. What kind of fractions are they?

8. Use your fraction strips and number lines to write each number in decimal form.
   - **a)** $\frac{5}{8}$
   - **b)** $\frac{13}{8}$
   - **c)** $1\frac{1}{4}$
   - **d)** $1\frac{5}{6}$
   - **e)** $3\frac{1}{2}$
   - **f)** $\frac{5}{6}$
   - **g)** $\frac{11}{6}$
   - **h)** $1\frac{2}{5}$
   - **i)** $1\frac{2}{3}$
   - **j)** $2\frac{3}{4}$

9. Use division to write each number in decimal form.
   - **a)** $\frac{21}{8}$
   - **b)** $\frac{2}{9}$
   - **c)** $\frac{20}{9}$
   - **d)** $\frac{3}{7}$
   - **e)** $1\frac{3}{7}$
   - **f)** $\frac{17}{6}$
   - **g)** $\frac{5}{9}$
   - **h)** $\frac{5}{11}$
   - **i)** $\frac{10}{11}$
   - **j)** $\frac{15}{7}$

10. Write each number in fraction form.
    - **a)** 0.8
    - **b)** 0.25
    - **c)** 1.5
    - **d)** 2.1
    - **e)** 2.67
    - **f)** 0.75
    - **g)** 0.6
    - **h)** 0.9
    - **i)** 1.33
    - **j)** 2.5

Work together

11. One way to convert a fraction to a decimal is to use mental math to find an equivalent fraction with a denominator of 10 or 100. For each fraction, decide whether you can use this method. If you can, do so. If you cannot, explain why not.
    - **a)** $\frac{3}{5}$
    - **b)** $\frac{5}{8}$
    - **c)** $\frac{3}{2}$
    - **d)** $\frac{13}{25}$
    - **e)** $\frac{9}{20}$
    - **f)** $\frac{1}{6}$
    - **g)** $\frac{27}{30}$
    - **h)** $\frac{99}{300}$

12. **a)** Use your calculator to find the decimal equivalent for $\frac{1}{3}$.
    - **b)** Use blocks to explain why the decimal in part a repeats. Here is how to start. Let the thousand cube represent 1. You want to divide it by 3. Since you cannot divide the cube, trade it for 10 flats. Make 3 sets of 3 flats, or 300. Take one set. So far, you have 3 flats, or 0.3 of the thousand cube, and 1 flat left over.

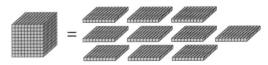

Trade the remaining flat for 10 rods and continue. Why does the decimal repeat?

13. When fractions are expressed in decimal form, patterns often occur.

   a) Use your calculator to convert each fraction to a decimal. Record what you see on the display.

   i) $\frac{1}{9}$ ii) $\frac{2}{9}$ iii) $\frac{3}{9}$

   b) Describe the pattern in your answers to part a. Use the pattern to predict the decimal form of each of these fractions. Use your calculator to check your predictions.

   i) $\frac{4}{9}$ ii) $\frac{6}{9}$ iii) $\frac{8}{9}$

   c) Based on the pattern you described in part b, predict the fraction form of each decimal. Use your calculator to check your predictions.

   i) 0.555 555...   ii) 0.777 777...

14. Explain how you could order these numbers from least to greatest using your halves number line. Order the fractions.

   $1\frac{1}{3}, \frac{3}{5}, \frac{7}{8}, 1\frac{4}{9}, \frac{1}{6}$

15. Explain how you could order these numbers from least to greatest using your thirds number line. Order the fractions.

   $\frac{3}{4}, \frac{2}{9}, 1\frac{5}{12}, 1\frac{2}{7}, \frac{3}{8}$

16. Is $1\frac{3}{8}$ between 1.2 and 1.3 or between 1.3 and 1.4?

17. Is $\frac{5}{6}$ between 0.8 and 0.9 or between 0.7 and 0.8?

DATA DISK

18. Use the *Baseball* database on the data disk. Choose one of the baseball players.

   a) What is this player's batting average?

   b) How was the batting average determined?

   c) Check your answer to part b, using your calculator. Is your answer the same as that for part a?

19. Replace each ▇ with > or <.

   a) $\frac{3}{8}$ ▇ $\frac{2}{5}$ b) $\frac{2}{3}$ ▇ $\frac{3}{4}$ c) $\frac{3}{8}$ ▇ $\frac{4}{12}$

   d) 0.7 ▇ $\frac{9}{12}$ e) $\frac{7}{8}$ ▇ 0.9   f) $\frac{5}{6}$ ▇ $\frac{4}{5}$

20. Estimate the numerator of each fraction. Explain how you can use a calculator to check your estimate.

   a) $0.75 < \frac{▇}{6} < 0.90$ b) $0.3 < \frac{▇}{8} < 0.5$

   c) $0.25 > \frac{▇}{11} > 0.10$ d) $0.75 < \frac{▇}{7} < 0.90$

   e) $1.3 < \frac{▇}{6} < 1.5$ f) $1.3 > \frac{▇}{7} > 1.2$

21. Estimate the numerator or denominator of each fraction. Explain how you can use a calculator to check your estimate.

   a) $0.70 < \frac{4}{▇} < 0.85$ b) $0.6 < \frac{5}{▇} < 0.7$

   c) $0.25 > \frac{▇}{13} > 0.15$ d) $0.80 > \frac{▇}{9} > 0.75$

   e) $1.6 > \frac{3}{▇} > 1.0$ f) $1.3 > \frac{6}{▇} > 1.1$

22. a) Use your fraction strips and number lines to write each number in decimal form.

   $\frac{1}{6}$ $\frac{2}{6}$ $\frac{3}{6}$ $\frac{4}{6}$ $\frac{5}{6}$ $\frac{6}{6}$

   b) Record your results from part a in a table.

Fraction form	Decimal form
$\frac{1}{6}$	

   c) Use the data in the table to draw a graph.

   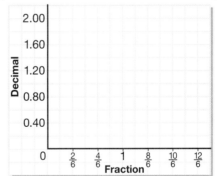

   d) Use your table and graph to write each number in decimal form.

   $\frac{7}{6}$ $\frac{8}{6}$ $\frac{9}{6}$ $\frac{10}{6}$ $\frac{11}{6}$ $\frac{12}{6}$

23. Use your results from exercise 22 to write the numbers below in decimal form. Check your results using the fraction strips and number lines.

   $\frac{1}{12}$ $\frac{2}{12}$ $\frac{3}{12}$ $\frac{4}{12}$ $\frac{5}{12}$ $\frac{6}{12}$ $\frac{7}{12}$ $\frac{8}{12}$

   $\frac{9}{12}$ $\frac{10}{12}$ $\frac{11}{12}$ $\frac{12}{12}$

24. Suppose 2 pizzas are to be divided equally among three people. How much pizza will each person get? Draw a diagram to explain your answer.

On your own

25. Is $1\frac{3}{4}$ between 1.7 and 1.8 or between 1.8 and 1.9?

26. Is $\frac{5}{8}$ between 0.6 and 0.7 or between 0.7 and 0.8?

27. In the activity on page 102, you found that $\frac{2}{5} = 0.4$. Use this result to write each number in decimal form.

   a) $\frac{1}{5}$ b) $\frac{4}{5}$ c) $7\frac{2}{5}$ d) $\frac{20}{5}$ e) $\frac{2}{50}$

28. In the activity on page 102, you found that $\frac{2}{3} \doteq 0.67$. Use this result to write an approximation to each number in decimal form.

   a) $\frac{20}{3}$ b) $\frac{200}{3}$ c) $\frac{2000}{3}$ d) $\frac{2}{30}$ e) $\frac{2}{300}$

29. Create two other exercises similar to exercises 27 and 28, and complete them.

30. Replace each ▮ with > or <.

   a) $\frac{5}{3}$ ▮ $\frac{3}{2}$ b) $\frac{7}{4}$ ▮ $\frac{9}{5}$ c) 1.1 ▮ $\frac{9}{8}$

   d) 1.7 ▮ $\frac{13}{8}$ e) $\frac{21}{12}$ ▮ 1.8   f) $\frac{21}{12}$ ▮ 1.7

31. a) Write each number in decimal form.

   i) $\frac{3}{6}$ $\frac{4}{6}$ $\frac{5}{6}$ ii) $\frac{3}{6}$ $\frac{2}{6}$ $\frac{1}{6}$

   iii) $\frac{3}{6}$ $\frac{3}{8}$ $\frac{3}{10}$ iv) $\frac{3}{6}$ $\frac{3}{5}$ $\frac{3}{4}$

   b) Does a fraction increase or decrease if:
      i) the numerator is increased? Decreased?
      ii) the denominator is increased? Decreased?

32. We can use a computer to write numbers in decimal form. We shall use the numbers
$\frac{1}{8}$ $\frac{2}{8}$ $\frac{3}{8}$ $\frac{4}{8}$ $\frac{5}{8}$ $\frac{6}{8}$ $\frac{7}{8}$ $\frac{8}{8}$
Start a new document in a spreadsheet program. Type the information shown below. In Microsoft Works, precede each fraction in column A with a double quotation mark.

TEMPLATE DISK

	A	B	C
1	The Eighths		
2	1/8	=1/8	
3	2/8	=2/8	
4	3/8	=3/8	
5	4/8	=4/8	
6	5/8	=5/8	
7	6/8	=6/8	
8	7/8	=7/8	
9	8/8	=8/8	

What do you see in cells B2 to B9?

Extend your thinking

33. a) Place the yellow $\frac{1}{2}$-strip on the thirds line with its left end at 0. To how many thirds does the right end of the strip correspond? How could you write $\frac{1}{2}$ in terms of thirds?

   b) Write $\frac{1}{2}$ in terms of fifths, and $\frac{1}{4}$ in terms of fifths and thirds.

COMMUNICATING

The Ideas

In your journal, explain how decimals and fractions are the same and how they are different. Use examples to illustrate your explanation.

BOGGLEYOUR**MIND**

Try to write 30 using any three identical digits and any mathematical symbols you wish. How many different ways can you do this?

Investigating Repeating Decimals

The world around us is full of patterns. You can find patterns in natural objects and objects created by humans. Numbers can also involve patterns of repeating digits. You may notice that such patterns sometimes occur when you express fractions in decimal form. You can use a spreadsheet to explore these patterns.

1. Start a new spreadsheet file. Enter the numbers and formulas shown below. Format column C to show numbers as fixed decimals with 10 places. You may need to make column C wider so there is room to display all the digits. Copy the formulas in row 3 to row 4.

TEMPLATE DISK

	A	B	C
1	Numerator	Denominator	Decimal
2		1	99	=A2/B2
3	=A2+1	=B2	=A3/B3

a) What does the formula in cell C2 tell the computer to do?

b) What does the formula in cell A3 tell the computer to do?

c) What fractions are being expressed as decimals? Write the decimal form for each of these fractions.

2. a) Based on your results of exercise 1, predict the decimal form for each fraction.
$$\frac{4}{99}, \frac{5}{99}, \frac{12}{99}, \frac{28}{99}, \frac{53}{99}, \frac{66}{99}$$

b) Use your spreadsheet to check your predictions to part a. What are some different ways to do this?

3. a) Revise your spreadsheet. Use it to express $\frac{1}{999}$, $\frac{2}{999}$, and $\frac{3}{999}$ as repeating decimals.

b) Based on the results of part a, predict the decimal form for each following fraction. Check your predictions using your spreadsheet.
$$\frac{4}{999}, \frac{5}{999}, \frac{14}{999}, \frac{37}{999}, \frac{685}{999}$$

4. Use your spreadsheet to investigate the decimals for these fractions.

a) $\frac{1}{6}, \frac{2}{6}, \frac{3}{6} \cdots$

b) $\frac{1}{11}, \frac{2}{11}, \frac{3}{11} \cdots$

c) $\frac{1}{16}, \frac{2}{16}, \frac{3}{16} \cdots$

d) $\frac{1}{33}, \frac{2}{33}, \frac{3}{33} \cdots$

e) $\frac{1}{37}, \frac{2}{37}, \frac{3}{37} \cdots$

f) $\frac{1}{64}, \frac{2}{64}, \frac{3}{64} \cdots$

g) $\frac{1}{101}, \frac{2}{101}, \frac{3}{101} \cdots$

h) $\frac{1}{271}, \frac{2}{271}, \frac{3}{271} \cdots$

5. Express each fraction in decimal form.

a) $\frac{55}{101}$

b) $\frac{10}{32}$

c) $\frac{25}{74}$

d) $\frac{30}{91}$

Mathematics & Technology

Linking Ideas

Fractions and Decimals in Baseball and Hockey

1. A batting average in baseball is a fraction.

$$\frac{\text{number of hits}}{\text{number of times at bat}}$$

A batting average is reported as a decimal rounded to the nearest thousandth.

From 1943 to 1954, there was an All-American Girls Professional Baseball League. Many Canadian women played for the league. Here are the statistics for five of these women for 1944. Use your calculator to determine each batting average.

	Player	Hits	Times at bat
a)	Helen Callaghan	114	397
b)	Lucella MacLean	13	66
c)	Vickie Panos	106	403
d)	Lena Surkowski	71	335
e)	Mildred Warwick	71	342

2. The goals-against average for a hockey goalie is also a fraction.

$$\frac{\text{number of goals allowed}}{\text{number of games played}}$$

A goals-against average is reported as a decimal rounded to the nearest hundredth. Four goalies from university hockey teams are listed below. The statistics are for the 1994/95 season up to November 1994. Use your calculator to determine each goals-against average.

	Goalie	Goals allowed	Games played
a)	Michelle Clayton	46	12
b)	Jennifer Dewar	22	12
c)	Christine Goodyear	40	12
d)	Joan Westman	9	12

3. **a)** List the batting averages in order from greatest to least.
   b) Who has the best batting average?

4. **a)** List the goals-against averages in order from greatest to least.
   b) Who has the best goals-against average?

5. **a)** Why do you think these averages are always reported as decimals?
   b) Why do you think batting averages are rounded to the nearest thousandth, but goals-against averages are only rounded to the nearest hundredth?

6. Why do you think people say a batting average is 427 when it appears in the newspaper as .427?

7. Give an example of another average in sports that is reported as a decimal. If you need ideas, use the sports pages of a newspaper.

Mathematics & Sports

Linking Ideas

2.4 ADDING FRACTIONS

Developing the Ideas

▶▶ *Using Manipulatives*

You will need your fraction strips and number lines.

1. Consider the addition $\frac{3}{5} + \frac{1}{5}$.

a) Use your green $\frac{3}{5}$-strip. Place it on the fifths line, starting at 0.
Place the green $\frac{1}{5}$-strip beside it. What is the answer to $\frac{3}{5} + \frac{1}{5}$?

b) Determine these sums in the same way.

   i) $\frac{1}{5} + \frac{1}{5}$ **ii)** $\frac{2}{5} + \frac{3}{5}$ **iii)** $\frac{3}{5} + \frac{4}{5}$

2. Consider the addition $\frac{1}{2} + \frac{3}{4}$.

a) Use your yellow $\frac{1}{2}$-strip. Place it on the halves line, starting at 0.
Place the red $\frac{3}{4}$-strip beside it. The right end of the $\frac{3}{4}$-strip does not coincide with a fraction on the halves line.

b) Use another line to determine the answer to $\frac{1}{2} + \frac{3}{4}$. Which line did you use? Why?

c) Determine these sums in the same way.

   i) $\frac{1}{2} + \frac{1}{4}$ **ii)** $\frac{3}{2} + \frac{1}{4}$ **iii)** $\frac{3}{2} + \frac{3}{4}$

3. Consider the addition $\frac{1}{3} + \frac{1}{2}$.

a) Use your blue $\frac{1}{3}$-strip. Place it on the thirds line, starting at 0.
Place the yellow $\frac{1}{2}$-strip beside it. The right end of the $\frac{1}{2}$-strip does not coincide with a fraction on this line.

b) Use another line to determine the answer to $\frac{1}{3} + \frac{1}{2}$. Which line did you use? Why?

c) Use the hundredths line to express the answer in decimal form.

d) Determine these sums in the same way.

   i) $\frac{2}{3} + \frac{1}{2}$ **ii)** $\frac{1}{3} + \frac{3}{2}$ **iii)** $\frac{4}{3} + \frac{1}{2}$

4. Use your fraction strips and number lines to add.

   a) $\frac{1}{5} + \frac{5}{6}$ **b)** $\frac{1}{4} + \frac{3}{8}$ **c)** $\frac{2}{5} + \frac{1}{2}$

   d) $\frac{1}{4} + \frac{1}{6}$ **e)** $\frac{3}{4} + \frac{2}{3}$ **f)** $\frac{4}{3} + \frac{1}{4}$

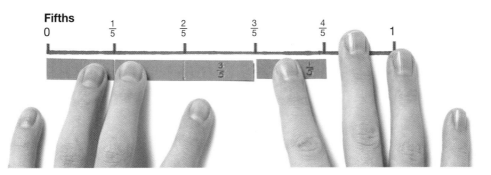

▶ ▶ *Through Guided Examples*

To add fractions, place the corresponding fraction strips end-to-end on the number lines. You can use the hundredths line to express the answers in decimal form, but they will sometimes be approximate answers.

Example 1 ....

Add: $\frac{1}{8} + \frac{5}{8}$

Express your answer in fraction form and in decimal form.

Solution

Place the orange $\frac{1}{8}$-strip on the eighths line with its left end at 0.

Place the $\frac{5}{8}$-strip beside it.

The right end coincides with $\frac{6}{8}$.

We write: $\frac{1}{8} + \frac{5}{8} = \frac{6}{8}$, or $\frac{3}{4}$, or 0.75

Example 2 ....

Add: $\frac{3}{4} + \frac{5}{8}$

Express your answer in fraction form and in decimal form.

Solution

Place the red $\frac{3}{4}$-strip on the quarters line, with its left end at 0.

Place the orange $\frac{5}{8}$-strip beside it. The right end of this strip does not coincide with a fraction on this line.

Place the strips on the eighths line.

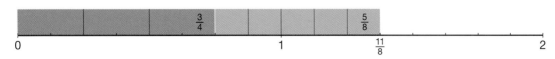

The right end of the $\frac{5}{8}$-strip coincides with $\frac{11}{8}$.

We write: $\frac{3}{4} + \frac{5}{8} = \frac{6}{8} + \frac{5}{8}$

$= \frac{11}{8}$, or $1\frac{3}{8}$, or 1.375

Example 3

Add: $\frac{1}{4} + \frac{1}{3}$

Express your answer in fraction form and decimal form.

Solution

Place the red $\frac{1}{4}$-strip on the quarters line with its left end at 0. Place the blue $\frac{1}{3}$-strip beside it. The right end of this strip does not coincide with a fraction on this line.

Use a number line that has equivalent fractions for $\frac{1}{4}$ and $\frac{1}{3}$.

Place the strips on the twelfths line.

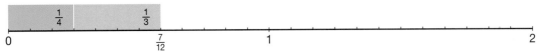

The right end of the $\frac{1}{3}$-strip coincides with $\frac{7}{12}$.

We write: $\frac{1}{4} + \frac{1}{3} = \frac{3}{12} + \frac{4}{12}$

$= \frac{7}{12}$

Place the strips on the hundredths line.

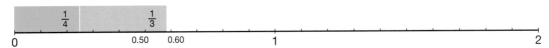

We write: $\frac{1}{4} + \frac{1}{3} \doteq 0.58$

You can always add fractions by expressing them in decimal form and adding the decimals. The answer will be in decimal form.

Example 4

Add: $\frac{2}{3} + \frac{4}{5}$

Solution

Use division to express each fraction in decimal form.

$\frac{2}{3} \doteq 0.67 \qquad \frac{4}{5} = 0.80$

We write: $\frac{2}{3} + \frac{4}{5} \doteq 0.67 + 0.80$

$= 1.47$

Some calculators have a special fraction key for doing calculations with fractions. The answer will be in fraction form.

We will use the *TEXAS INSTRUMENTS Math Explorer* calculator. If your calculator is different, look in your manual to find out how to work with fractions.

Example 5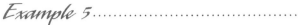

Use a calculator with a fraction key to add: $\frac{2}{3} + \frac{4}{5}$

Solution

Press: **2** / **3** + **4** / **5** =

Display: **22/15**

Press: Ab/c to display **1 u 7/15**

We write: $\frac{2}{3} + \frac{4}{5} = \frac{22}{15}$, or $1\frac{7}{15}$

BOGGLE YOUR MIND

Raymond had a box of candy bars.
He gave Monique half of what he had, plus half a bar.
He then gave Claude half of what he had left, plus half a bar.
He then gave Mei-Lin half of what he had left, plus half a bar.
Finally, he gave Laura half of what he had left, plus half a bar.
Raymond then had no bars left.
He didn't break any bars in half.
How many candy bars did Raymond have to start?

Working with Mathematics

Something to talk about

1. a) Which of these sums is greater than 1?

    i) $\frac{1}{2} + \frac{1}{3}$ ii) $\frac{1}{3} + \frac{3}{4}$ iii) $\frac{3}{4} + \frac{1}{6}$

   b) Which of these sums is less than 1?

    i) $\frac{1}{4} + \frac{2}{3}$ ii) $\frac{1}{4} + \frac{5}{6}$ iii) $\frac{1}{4} + \frac{7}{8}$

2. The sum of two fractions is between 0 and 1. One fraction is between 0 and $\frac{1}{2}$. What can you say about the other fraction?

3. a) Use your fraction strips and number lines to check the answer to *Example 4*.

   b) Use your calculator to check that the answer to *Example 5* is the same as the answer to *Example 4*.

Practice

4. Use your fraction strips and number lines to add.

    a) $\frac{1}{3} + \frac{1}{3}$ b) $\frac{1}{3} + \frac{2}{3}$ c) $\frac{1}{3} + \frac{1}{2}$

    d) $\frac{1}{3} + \frac{1}{4}$ e) $\frac{1}{3} + \frac{1}{6}$ f) $\frac{1}{3} + \frac{3}{4}$

    g) $\frac{1}{3} + \frac{4}{3}$ h) $\frac{1}{3} + 1\frac{2}{3}$ i) $\frac{1}{2} + \frac{3}{4}$

5. Use your fraction strips and number lines to add.

    a) $\frac{1}{2} + \frac{2}{3}$ b) $\frac{2}{5} + \frac{3}{10}$ c) $\frac{1}{8} + \frac{1}{4}$

    d) $\frac{5}{8} + \frac{1}{2}$ e) $\frac{3}{4} + \frac{3}{2}$ f) $\frac{1}{2} + \frac{2}{5}$

    g) $\frac{1}{6} + \frac{2}{3}$ h) $\frac{3}{4} + \frac{5}{6}$ i) $\frac{3}{10} + \frac{6}{5}$

6. Use your fraction strips and number lines to add.

    a) $\frac{5}{6} + \frac{1}{3}$ b) $1\frac{1}{3} + \frac{1}{3}$ c) $\frac{7}{8} + \frac{5}{4}$

    d) $1\frac{1}{2} + \frac{3}{4}$ e) $1\frac{3}{5} + \frac{2}{5}$ f) $\frac{1}{6} + 1\frac{5}{6}$

    g) $2\frac{3}{10} + \frac{7}{10}$ h) $1\frac{1}{2} + 1\frac{1}{2}$ i) $\frac{7}{8} + 1\frac{1}{8}$

Work together

7. Use your fraction strips and number lines to determine each sum. Then write the addition statement.

    a) $\frac{1}{6} + \frac{1}{6}$ b) $\frac{1}{6} + \frac{5}{6}$ c) $\frac{1}{6} + \frac{1}{4}$

    d) $\frac{1}{6} + \frac{1}{3}$ e) $\frac{1}{6} + \frac{1}{2}$ f) $\frac{1}{6} + \frac{1}{4} + \frac{1}{3}$

    g) $\frac{1}{2} + \frac{1}{4}$ h) $\frac{1}{2} + \frac{1}{3}$ i) $\frac{3}{4} + \frac{5}{6}$

    j) $\frac{3}{5} + \frac{1}{2}$ k) $\frac{5}{4} + \frac{4}{3}$ l) $\frac{2}{3} + \frac{3}{4} + \frac{1}{2}$

8. In *Example 1* we found that $\frac{1}{8} + \frac{5}{8} = \frac{6}{8}$. Use this result, and your knowledge of fraction strips, to complete these additions.

    a) $\frac{1}{8} + \frac{1}{8}$ b) $\frac{1}{8} + \frac{3}{8}$ c) $\frac{1}{8} + \frac{7}{8}$

    d) $\frac{1}{4} + \frac{5}{4}$ e) $\frac{1}{2} + \frac{5}{2}$ f) $\frac{1}{7} + \frac{5}{7}$

9. In *Example 2* we found that $\frac{3}{4} + \frac{5}{8} = 1\frac{3}{8}$. Use this result to complete these additions.

    a) $1\frac{3}{4} + \frac{5}{8}$ b) $2\frac{3}{4} + \frac{5}{8}$

    c) $3\frac{3}{4} + \frac{5}{8}$ d) $2\frac{3}{4} + 1\frac{5}{8}$

    e) $3\frac{5}{8} + 2\frac{3}{4}$ f) $4\frac{5}{8} + 6\frac{3}{4}$

10. Add by expressing the fractions in decimal form.

    a) $\frac{1}{4} + \frac{2}{5}$ b) $\frac{2}{3} + \frac{5}{8}$ c) $\frac{3}{4} + \frac{1}{6} + \frac{3}{5}$

11. Use a calculator to add.

    a) $\frac{1}{5} + \frac{3}{7}$ b) $\frac{4}{9} + \frac{5}{6}$ c) $\frac{4}{3} + \frac{5}{6} + \frac{6}{11}$

12. Is $\frac{3}{5} + \frac{1}{4}$ between 0.8 and 0.9 or between 0.9 and 1.0?

13. Is $\frac{5}{8} + \frac{1}{3}$ between 0.8 and 0.9 or between 0.9 and 1.0?

14. Copy and complete an addition table like this. Find as many patterns as you can.

+	$\frac{1}{4}$	$\frac{1}{2}$	$\frac{3}{4}$	1	$\frac{5}{4}$	$\frac{3}{2}$
$\frac{1}{4}$						
$\frac{1}{2}$						
$\frac{3}{4}$						
1						
$\frac{5}{4}$						
$\frac{3}{2}$						

On your own

15. Use your fraction strips and number lines to determine each sum. Then write the addition statement.

    a) $\frac{1}{4} + \frac{1}{2}$ b) $\frac{1}{4} + \frac{1}{3}$ c) $\frac{1}{4} + \frac{1}{4}$

    d) $\frac{1}{4} + \frac{1}{5}$ e) $\frac{1}{4} + \frac{1}{6}$ f) $\frac{1}{4} + \frac{1}{8}$

    g) $\frac{5}{8} + \frac{1}{4}$ h) $\frac{3}{2} + \frac{1}{6}$ i) $\frac{4}{3} + \frac{1}{2}$

    j) $\frac{2}{5} + \frac{1}{10}$ k) $\frac{5}{6} + \frac{3}{4}$ l) $\frac{1}{2} + \frac{1}{3} + \frac{1}{4}$

16. In *Example 3* we found that $\frac{1}{4} + \frac{1}{3} = \frac{7}{12}$. Use this result to determine each sum.

    a) $1\frac{1}{4} + \frac{1}{3}$ b) $\frac{1}{4} + 2\frac{1}{3}$ c) $3\frac{1}{4} + 4\frac{1}{3}$

    d) $\frac{2}{4} + \frac{2}{3}$ e) $\frac{1}{4} + \frac{1}{3} + \frac{1}{2}$ f) $\frac{1}{8} + \frac{1}{6}$

17. In *Example 5* we found that $\frac{2}{3} + \frac{4}{5} = 1\frac{7}{15}$. Use this result to determine each sum.

    a) $1\frac{2}{3} + \frac{4}{5}$ b) $4\frac{2}{3} + \frac{4}{5}$ c) $3\frac{2}{3} + 4\frac{4}{5}$

18. Add by expressing the fractions in decimal form.

    a) $\frac{1}{2} + \frac{4}{5}$ b) $\frac{6}{5} + \frac{3}{4}$ c) $\frac{7}{3} + \frac{5}{8}$

19. Use a calculator to add.

    a) $\frac{3}{5} + \frac{5}{6}$ b) $\frac{1}{8} + \frac{2}{3}$ c) $\frac{1}{2} + \frac{2}{5} + \frac{3}{7}$

20. Is $\frac{1}{5} + \frac{7}{8}$ between 0.9 and 1.0 or between 1.0 and 1.1?

21. Is $\frac{2}{3} + \frac{1}{6}$ between 0.7 and 0.8 or between 0.8 and 0.9?

MPLATE DISK

22. Find two fractions that add to a number that is close to 1, but not equal to 1.
    Start a new document in a spreadsheet program.

	A	B	C
1			=A1+B1
2			

Type a fraction in cell A1. Precede it with =
Type a fraction in cell B1. Precede it with =
Type the formula in cell C1 as shown.

a) What does the formula in cell C1 do?

b) How close to 1 is the sum of your fractions?

c) How can you get closer to 1?

   i) Choose two more fractions and type them in cells A2 and B2. What formula should you type in cell C2?

   ii) How close to 1 is the sum of your fractions?

d) Find three fractions that add to a number that is close to 4, but not equal to 4.

   i) Type these fractions in cells A3, B3, and C3. What formula should you type in cell D3?

   ii) Choose three different fractions to get closer to 4.

23. On Monday, Mike ran for $\frac{1}{4}$ of an hour in the morning and $\frac{1}{2}$ an hour in the afternoon. What fraction of an hour did Mike run on Monday?

24. Ken ate $\frac{3}{8}$ of a pizza and Nola ate $\frac{1}{4}$ of it. What total fraction of the pizza was eaten?

Extend your thinking

25. Fractions of the form $\frac{1}{n}$, where n is a natural number, are called *unit fractions*.

    a) Is it possible for two different unit fractions to have a sum of 1? Explain your answer using fraction strips.

    b) Use your fraction strips to find three different unit fractions whose sum is 1.

    c) Use your fraction strips to find four different unit fractions whose sum is 1.

COMMUNICATING

The Ideas

In your journal, explain how to add two fractions. Use some examples to illustrate your explanation.

2.5 SUBTRACTING FRACTIONS

Developing the Ideas

▶▶ Using Manipulatives

You will need your fraction strips and number lines.

1. Use your fraction strips to subtract.

    a) $\dfrac{3}{4} - \dfrac{1}{4}$ **b)** $\dfrac{5}{8} - \dfrac{1}{2}$ **c)** $\dfrac{5}{6} - \dfrac{1}{3}$

2. Use your fraction strips and number lines to subtract.

    a) $\dfrac{2}{3} - \dfrac{1}{3}$ **b)** $\dfrac{3}{4} - \dfrac{1}{2}$ **c)** $\dfrac{3}{2} - \dfrac{3}{4}$

    d) $\dfrac{5}{12} - \dfrac{1}{6}$ **e)** $\dfrac{3}{4} - \dfrac{1}{6}$ **f)** $\dfrac{5}{3} - \dfrac{5}{6}$

▶▶ Through Guided Examples

To subtract fractions, you may only need the two fraction strips for some examples. In other examples, you will need the number lines and one fraction strip. You can use the hundredths line to express the answers in decimal form, but they will sometimes be approximate answers.

Example 1 ···

Subtract: $\dfrac{7}{8} - \dfrac{3}{8}$

Solution

We don't need a number line.

Place the orange $\dfrac{3}{8}$-strip on top of the $\dfrac{7}{8}$-strip, with the right ends together. The answer to $\dfrac{7}{8} - \dfrac{3}{8}$ is the section of the $\dfrac{7}{8}$-strip that is not covered by the $\dfrac{3}{8}$-strip.

The section that is not covered is $\dfrac{4}{8}$.

We write: $\dfrac{7}{8} - \dfrac{3}{8} = \dfrac{4}{8}$

Example 2

Subtract: $\frac{2}{3} - \frac{1}{2}$

Solution

We don't need a number line.

Place the yellow $\frac{1}{2}$-strip on top of the blue $\frac{2}{3}$-strip, with the right ends together. The answer to $\frac{2}{3} - \frac{1}{2}$ is the section of the $\frac{2}{3}$-strip that is not covered by the $\frac{1}{2}$-strip. We cannot tell how much this is.

Replace the strips with equivalent ones of the same colour.
Replace the $\frac{2}{3}$-strip with the purple $\frac{4}{6}$-strip. Replace the $\frac{1}{2}$-strip with the purple $\frac{3}{6}$-strip.

The section that is not covered is $\frac{1}{6}$.

We write: $\frac{2}{3} - \frac{1}{2} = \frac{4}{6} - \frac{3}{6}$

$$= \frac{1}{6}$$

next please

BOGGLE YOUR MIND

Donna deposited $10 in her bank account.
She then withdrew half the balance.
The next day, Donna deposited $10 and then withdrew half the balance.
On the third day, she deposited $10 again and withdrew half the balance.
The balance was then $100.
How much did Donna have in her account at the beginning?

17. Use your fraction strips and number lines to subtract.

a) $\frac{1}{2} - \frac{1}{3}$ b) $\frac{1}{3} - \frac{1}{4}$ c) $\frac{1}{4} - \frac{1}{6}$

d) $2 - \frac{2}{3}$ e) $\frac{11}{6} - \frac{4}{3}$ f) $\frac{7}{4} - \frac{2}{3} - \frac{1}{2}$

18. In *Example 3* we found that $\frac{11}{12} - \frac{2}{3} = \frac{1}{4}$.

Use this result to determine each difference.

a) $1\frac{11}{12} - \frac{2}{3}$ b) $2\frac{11}{12} - \frac{2}{3}$ c) $5\frac{11}{12} - 2\frac{2}{3}$

19. In *Example 4* we found that $\frac{4}{3} - \frac{3}{4} = \frac{7}{12}$.

Use this result to determine each difference.

a) $\frac{7}{3} - \frac{3}{4}$ b) $\frac{10}{3} - \frac{3}{4}$ c) $\frac{7}{3} - \frac{7}{4}$

20. Simplify.

a) $\frac{3}{4} - \frac{1}{2} + \frac{1}{8}$ b) $\frac{3}{2} + \frac{2}{3} - \frac{5}{6}$

c) $\frac{1}{2} + \frac{1}{3} - \frac{1}{4}$ d) $\frac{5}{3} - \frac{3}{4} + \frac{1}{6}$

21. Subtract by expressing the fractions in decimal form.

a) $\frac{3}{2} - \frac{4}{5}$ b) $\frac{9}{5} - \frac{5}{4}$ c) $\frac{3}{8} - \frac{1}{6}$

22. Is $\frac{8}{5} - \frac{5}{6}$ between 0.6 and 0.7 or between 0.7 and 0.8?

23. Is $\frac{7}{3} - \frac{3}{8}$ between 2.0 and 2.1 or between 1.9 and 2.0?

24. Use a calculator to subtract.

a) $\frac{7}{5} - \frac{2}{3}$ b) $\frac{3}{7} - \frac{1}{4}$ c) $\frac{1}{9} - \frac{1}{11}$

25. Find two fractions whose difference is close to 1, but less than 1.
Start a new document in a spreadsheet program.

	A	B	C
1			
2			

Type a fraction in cell A1. Precede it with =. Type a smaller fraction in cell B1. Precede it with =.

a) What formula should you type in cell C1?
b) How close to 1 is the difference of your fractions?
c) How can you get closer to 1?
d) How can you find two fractions whose difference is close to 1, but greater than 1?

Compare your answers with those of other students. Did anyone get closer than you?

26. Karen usually saves $\frac{1}{4}$ of her allowance each week and uses the rest for spending money. One week she spent $\frac{1}{2}$ of her allowance. What fraction of her allowance did Karen have left that week?

27. Jackie had $\frac{3}{4}$ of a tank of gas on Monday. She did not fill up the tank that week. On Friday, Jackie had $\frac{1}{8}$ of a tank left. What fraction of the tank had she used since Monday?

Extend your thinking

28. Develop a rule that you could use to add or subtract any two fractions without using fraction strips or number lines. Test your rule using some examples.

COMMUNICATING

The Ideas

In your journal, explain how to subtract two fractions. Use some examples to illustrate your explanation.

2.6 USING PLACE-VALUE BLOCKS TO MULTIPLY WITH DECIMALS

Developing the Ideas

▷▶ *Using Manipulatives*

You will need place-value blocks, with values as assigned on page 99.

The flat represents 1.   The rod represents 0.1   The small cube represents 0.01.

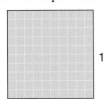

1. Use blocks to make this figure. You can use the blocks to determine
   the product 4.2×2.3.

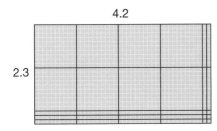

   a) How many flats are there in the product? What number do they
   represent?

   b) How many rods are there in the product? What number do they
   represent?

   c) How many small cubes are there in the product? What number do
   they represent?

   d) Use the blocks and the diagram to determine the product 4.2×2.3.

   e) How do the blocks and the diagram show that your answer is
   reasonable?

   f) Use estimation to check whether your answer is reasonable. You
   multiplied a number a little greater than 4 by a number a little
   greater than 2. Should your answer be greater or less than 8?

2. Here are two ways to determine the product 4.2×2.3 using paper
   and pencil. Choose one of these ways. Explain the procedure. Use the
   blocks or the above diagram to help you.

   a)
   $$
   \begin{array}{r}
   4.2 \\
   \times\,2.3 \\
   \hline
   .06 \\
   1.20 \\
   .40 \\
   8.00 \\
   \hline
   9.66
   \end{array}
   $$

   b)
   $$
   \begin{array}{r}
   4.2 \\
   \times\,2.3 \\
   \hline
   1.26 \\
   8.40 \\
   \hline
   9.66
   \end{array}
   $$

Working with Mathematics

Something to talk about

1. What product does each diagram represent?

a)

b)

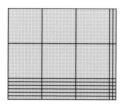

c)

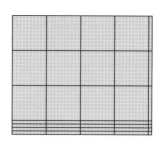

Work together

2. Use blocks to determine each product. Explain your method. Use estimation to check whether your answer is reasonable.

a) 3.2×2.4 **b)** 1.5×3.1

c) 2.7×2.2 **d)** 5.1×2.4

3. Determine each product in exercise 1. Explain your method.

4. What product does each diagram represent? Use the diagram to determine the product.

a)

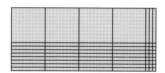

b)

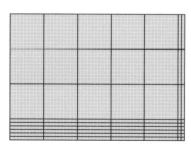

5. Multiply.

a) 1.2×1.3 **b)** 1.4×2.1

c) 2.4×1.8 **d)** 3.2×0.7

e) 6.4×1.8 **f)** 7.5×2.7

g) 3.6×2.9 **h)** 8.2×4.2

6. A floppy disk sells for $1.45. A box of 10 sells for $12.50. How much is saved by buying the box?

On your own

7. Use blocks to determine each product. Explain your method. Use estimation to check whether your answer is reasonable.

a) 3.1×2.5 **b)** 1.6×3.2

c) 2.8×2.3 **d)** 5.2×2.3

8. Multiply.

a) 4.3×2.1 **b)** 1.3×1.5

c) 3.4×1.3 **d)** 0.8×3.1

e) 1.7×4.5 **f)** 2.9×5.2

g) 6.2×1.7 **h)** 8.1×2.3

9. A single bus fare costs $1.30. A book of 8 tickets costs $10.00. How much is saved by buying the book?

Extend your thinking

10. *Without* using the ☒ key, use your calculator to determine each product.

a) 35×12 **b)** 4.7×24

c) 6.5×29 **d)** 8.3×1.5

The Ideas

In your journal, explain how multiplication and addition are related. Make up an example to illustrate your explanation.

2.7 USING PLACE-VALUE BLOCKS TO DIVIDE WITH DECIMALS

Developing the Ideas

▶ ▶ *Using Manipulatives*

Gita has 10.5 m of electrical wire for fixing lamps. She needs 2.4 m of wire for each lamp.
How many lamps can she fix?

We think:
The number of lamps she can fix is 10.5 ÷ 2.4.
How many 2.4s are there in 10.5?

You will need place-value blocks, with values as assigned on page 99.

2.4

1. a) Get 10 flats and 5 rods to represent 10.5.
   Try to form a rectangle with the blocks, with one side 2.4. Arrange 2 flats and 4 rods as shown. This represents the wire needed to fix one lamp. How many flats and how many rods do you have left?

   2.4

   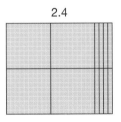

   b) Exchange one flat for 10 rods, then place 2 flats and 4 rods below the first group you made, as shown. This represents the wire needed to fix two lamps. How many flats and how many rods do you have left?

   c) Continue placing 2 flats and 4 rods in this way. How many times can you do this? How many flats and rods do you have left over?

   d) What is the quotient of 10.5 ÷ 2.4?

   e) How many lamps can Gita fix? How much electrical wire is left?

   f) Use estimation to check whether your answer is reasonable. The amount of wire Gita has is close to 10 m. The amount required for each lamp is between 2 m and 3 m. So, the number of lamps she can repair should be between $\frac{10}{2}$ and $\frac{10}{3}$. Is your answer between these numbers?

Working with Mathematics

Something to talk about

1. Use your calculator to divide 10.5 by 2.4. How is the answer you got with the blocks related to the answer on the calculator?

2. What quotient does each diagram represent?

   a)

   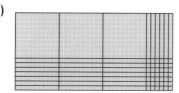

   b)

   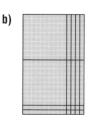

Work together

3. Determine each quotient in exercise 2. Explain your method.

4. Use blocks to divide. Explain your method.

   a) $2.1 \div 1.4$ **b)** $6.5 \div 1.3$
   c) $6.72 \div 3.2$ **d)** $5.52 \div 2.3$
   e) $3.23 \div 1.9$ **f)** $0.42 \div 0.14$

5. Use blocks to divide. Write the result as a whole number, with an amount left over. Explain your method. Use estimation to check whether your answer is reasonable.

   a) $6.5 \div 1.4$ **b)** $9.6 \div 2.3$
   c) $6.8 \div 1.5$ **d)** $4.3 \div 1.2$
   e) $4.4 \div 1.4$ **f)** $3.9 \div 2.1$
   g) $9.5 \div 2.7$ **h)** $6.28 \div 2.4$

6. **a)** Jason bought 13.2 m of fabric to make Halloween costumes. Each costume takes 2.4 m of fabric. How many costumes can he make? Solve this problem in two ways:

   i) using blocks
   ii) using your calculator

   b) Explain how the answers you get using each method are related.

On your own

7. Use blocks to divide. Explain your method.

   a) $4.8 \div 1.6$ **b)** $7.4 \div 2.0$
   c) $6.65 \div 1.9$ **d)** $2.38 \div 1.7$
   e) $7.44 \div 3.1$ **f)** $5.06 \div 2.2$

8. Use blocks to divide. Write the result as a whole number, with an amount left over. Explain your method. Use estimation to check whether your answer is reasonable.

   a) $4.6 \div 1.2$ **b)** $7.2 \div 2.6$
   c) $5.5 \div 1.5$ **d)** $4.9 \div 1.3$
   e) $2.9 \div 1.3$ **f)** $7.7 \div 3.1$
   g) $2.3 \div 0.42$ **h)** $5.84 \div 1.7$

9. **a)** Mayumi bought 10.0 m of framing material to make frames for pictures. Each picture requires 1.5 m of framing material. How many frames can she make? Solve this problem in two ways:

   I) using blocks   II) using your calculator

   b) Explain how the answers you get using each method are related.

10. **a)** Jorge has $3.72 to buy tiger fish. Each tiger fish costs 65¢. How many tigerfish can he buy? Solve this problem in two ways:

    i) using blocks   ii) using your calculator

    b) Explain how the answers you get using each method are related.

Extend your thinking

11. *Without* using the ÷ key, use your calculator to determine each quotient.

    a) $168 \div 14$ **b)** $52.7 \div 1.7$
    c) $80.5 \div 3.5$ **d)** $17.28 \div 2.7$

The Ideas

In your journal, explain how division and subtraction are related. Make up an example to illustrate your explanation.

Designing a Bookcase

Anita wants to convert a cabinet into a bookcase with two fixed shelves. If you count the bottom, there will be three spaces for books. Help Anita figure out where to put the supports so that the spaces for books all have the same height.

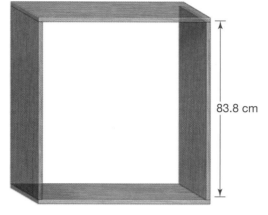

83.8 cm

1.9 cm

Understand the problem

- What is a support?
- What are you asked to do?
- Why can't Anita just divide 83.8 cm by 3?

Think of a strategy

- Anita has to allow for the thickness of two shelves.

Carry out the strategy

- Calculate the total thickness of the two shelves and subtract from the inside height of the cabinet.
- Divide by 3.
- How far from the bottom should Anita put the top edge of the support for the lower shelf?
- How far from the top should she put the top edge of the support for the upper shelf?

Look back

- How would the results change if Anita has another cabinet with inside height 1.0 cm greater? 1.0 cm less?
- How would the results change if Anita wants to put in an additional shelf?

Communicating the Ideas

In your journal, write a description of this problem and your solution. Include some diagrams to illustrate your explanation.

2.8 ORDER OF OPERATIONS

Developing the Ideas

▶▶ *Through Discussion*

Companies often give away prizes in promotional contests. If you have filled in an entry form for one of these contests, you may have noticed that it included a mathematical question. If your entry is drawn, you must have answered the mathematical question correctly to be declared the winner.

Lisa and Karen answered the skill-testing question on the entry form shown here. They each had different answers.

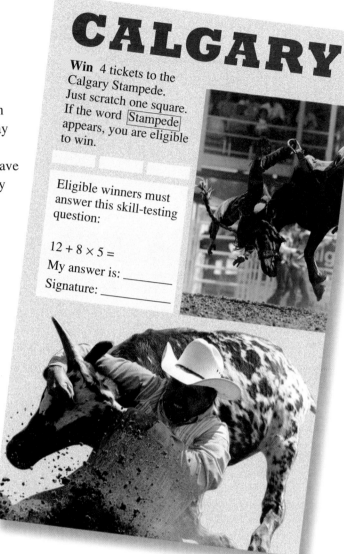

CALGARY

Win 4 tickets to the Calgary Stampede. Just scratch one square. If the word $\boxed{\text{Stampede}}$ appears, you are eligible to win.

Eligible winners must answer this skill-testing question:

$12 + 8 \times 5 =$

My answer is: _____
Signature: _____

Lisa

$$12 + 8 \times 5$$
Multiply: $\quad = 12 + 40$
Add: $\qquad = 52$

Karen

$$12 + 8 \times 5$$
Add: $\qquad = 20 \times 5$
Multiply: $\quad = 100$

Discuss these questions in a group or with a partner.

1. Why did Lisa and Karen get different answers?

2. Which answer do you think is correct? Why?

▶▶ *Through Guided Examples*

To avoid confusion, mathematicians have agreed on the order in which operations are to be performed. When this order is followed, everyone should get the same answer.

• • • • • • • • • •

Order of Operations

- Do all operations in brackets first.
- Do multiplication and division next, in the order they occur.
- Do addition and subtraction last, in the order they occur.

Example 1 ....

Simplify.

a) $5 + 9 \times 3$

b) $(5 + 9) \times 3$

Solution

a) $5 + 9 \times 3$ ← Multiply.

     $= 5 + 27$ ← Add.

     $= 32$

b) $(5 + 9) \times 3$ ← Do the operation in brackets.

     $= 14 \times 3$ ← Multiply.

     $= 42$

Example 2 ....

Simplify.

a) $7.5 - 1.5 \times 3.2$

b) $(7.5 - 1.5) \times 3.2$

Solution

a) $7.5 - 1.5 \times 3.2$ ← Multiply.

     $= 7.5 - 4.8$ ← Subtract.

     $= 2.7$

b) $(7.5 - 1.5) \times 3.2$ ← Do the operation in brackets.

     $= 6.0 \times 3.2$ ← Multiply.

     $= 19.2$

When you follow the order of operations, always do one operation at a time.

Example 3 ....

Simplify.

a) $20 - 18 \div 6 - 2$

c) $20 - 18 \div (6 - 2)$

b) $(20 - 18) \div (6 - 2)$

d) $20 - (18 \div 6 - 2)$

Solution

a) $20 - 18 \div 6 - 2$ ← Divide.

     $= 20 - 3 - 2$ ← Subtract.

     $= 17 - 2$ ← Subtract.

     $= 15$

b) $(20 - 18) \div (6 - 2)$ ← Do the operation in the first pair of brackets.

     $= 2 \div (6 - 2)$ ← Do the operation in brackets.

     $= 2 \div 4$ ← Divide.

     $= 0.5$

c) $20 - 18 \div (6 - 2)$ ← Do the operation in brackets.

     $= 20 - 18 \div 4$ ← Divide.

     $= 20 - 4.5$ ← Subtract.

     $= 15.5$

d) $20 - (18 \div 6 - 2)$ ← Divide.

     $= 20 - (3 - 2)$ ← Do the operation in brackets.

     $= 20 - 1$ ← Subtract.

     $= 19$

Working with Mathematics

Something to talk about

1. Why is it necessary to have rules for the order of operations?

2. a) Which operation must be done first?
   - i) $2 \times 3 + 4 \times 5$
   - ii) $2 \times 3 + (4 \times 5)$
   - iii) $2 \times (3 + 4) \times 5$
   - iv) $2 \times (3 + 4 \times 5)$

   b) How is the order changed when brackets are used?

3. a) Answer each skill-testing question.

   i)
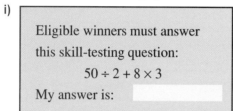

   Eligible winners must answer this skill-testing question:

   $50 \div 2 + 8 \times 3$

   My answer is: ____

   ii)

   SKILL-TESTING QUESTION

   Fifty divided by two _____

   Add eight _____

   Multiply by 3 _____

   My answer is: ____

   b) How is the order changed when the instructions are given in words?

Practice

4. Simplify.
   - a) $6 \times 5 + 2$
   - b) $(6 \times 5) + 2$
   - c) $6 \times (5 + 2)$
   - d) $6 + 5 \times 2$
   - e) $6 + (5 \times 2)$
   - f) $(6 + 5) \times 2$

5. Simplify.
   - a) $5 + 3 \times 4 + 2$
   - b) $(5 + 3) \times 4 + 2$
   - c) $5 + 3 \times (4 + 2)$
   - d) $5 \times 3 + 4 \times 2$
   - e) $5 \times (3 + 4) \times 2$
   - f) $(5 \times 3 + 4) \times 2$

6. How many different answers can you get by replacing each ▦ with an operation sign?
   - a) $8 \ ▦ \ 4 \ ▦ \ 2$
   - b) $8 \ ▦ \ (4 \ ▦ \ 2)$

7. Simplify.
   - a) $6 \times 8 + 7$
   - b) $29 - 4 \times 7$
   - c) $13 + 24 \div 2$
   - d) $16 - 4 \times 3$
   - e) $(16 - 4) \times 3$
   - f) $14 + (44 - 20)$
   - g) $(4 + 9) \times 3$
   - h) $5 \times (12 - 6)$
   - i) $38 - 16 \div 4$
   - j) $6 \times (8 + 7)$
   - k) $14 + 3 + 5 \times 2$
   - l) $(15 - 5) - (25 - 19)$

Work together

8. Simplify.
   - a) $2.3 + 3.7 \times 4.1$
   - b) $(6.4 + 4.1) \times 1.5$
   - c) $18.9 - 7.9 + 22.6$
   - d) $4.3 \times (8.8 - 5.5)$
   - e) $6.4 \div 3.2 \div 2$
   - f) $6.4 \div (3.2 \div 2)$

9. Use brackets. Write each expression so that it equals the number in blue.
   - a) $8 + 2 \times 5$ 50
   - b) $6 \times 3 + 1$ 24
   - c) $1 + 6 \times 3 + 1$ 25
   - d) $2 + 8 \times 5 - 1$ 49
   - e) $7 + 14 \div 7 - 5$ 14
   - f) $12 \div 2 \times 5 - 4$ 2

10. Use each of the numbers 2, 4, 6, 8, and any operations or brackets. Write an expression that equals each number.
    - a) 10
    - b) 20
    - c) 40
    - d) 60

In exercises 11 and 12, which expression gives the correct answer?

11. Mr. Polischuk bought 6 cases of mini-juice packets for his 3 children. Each case has 24 packets. How many packets should each child get?
    - a) $6 \times 3 \div 24$
    - b) $6 \times 24 \times 3$
    - c) $6 \times 24 \div 3$
    - d) $24 \div 6 \times 3$

12. Joyce bought 2 CDs at $7.95 each and 3 posters at $4.50 each. What was the total cost?
    - a) $2 \times \$7.95 + 3$
    - b) $2 \times \$7.95 + 3 \times \$4.50$
    - c) $(2 + 3) \times (\$7.95 + \$4.50)$

13. Replace each ▓ with +, −, ×, or ÷ so each equation is true.
   a) $(9 ▓ 3) ▓ 2 = 12$ **b)** $(9 ▓ 3) ▓ 2 = 24$
   c) $(9 ▓ 3) ▓ 2 = 54$ **d)** $(9 ▓ 3) ▓ 2 = 6$
   e) $(9 ▓ 3) ▓ 2 = 29$ **f)** $(9 ▓ 3) ▓ 2 = 4$

On your own

14. Simplify.
   a) $(3.2 + 4.8) \times 6.7$
   b) $5.7 + 2.5 \times 1.2$
   c) $16.3 - 4.5 \times 0.2$
   d) $8.8 - (7.9 - 4.3)$
   e) $(6.1 - 2.4) \times 1.5$
   f) $8.4 \div (2.8 \times 1.5)$

In exercises 15 and 16, which expression gives the correct answer?

15. Mrs. Azarshahi ordered 5 sweaters at $47.95 each. She returned 3 of them. How much did she spend?
   a) $5 \times \$47.95 - 3$
   b) $(5 - 3) \times \$47.95$
   c) $5 - (3 \times \$47.95)$

16. To train for a marathon run, Katie runs 20 km 4 days a week and 30 km 2 days a week. How many kilometres does she run each week?
   a) $20 \times 4 \times 30 \times 2$
   b) $4 + 20 \times 30$
   c) $4 \times 20 + 2 \times 30$

17. Use brackets. Write each expression so that it equals the number in red.
   a) $43 + 7 \times 2$ 100
   b) $4 \times 9 - 2$ 28
   c) $8 + 9 - 2 \times 4$ 36
   d) $15 - 13 - 8 \times 3$ 0
   e) $6 + 2 \times 5 - 1$ 14
   f) $8 \times 3 + 2 \times 2$ 80

18. Place brackets in each equation to make it true.
   a) $8 - 3 - 2 + 5 = 12$
   b) $3 + 1 + 2 \times 5 = 18$
   c) $3 + 4 \times 6 + 1 = 49$
   d) $2 \times 5 + 3 \times 4 = 64$
   e) $24 - 4 \div 2 \times 10 = 1$
   f) $16 + 2 \times 50 \div 10 = 26$

19. How many different answers can you get by using brackets with the expression $1 + 2 \times 3 + 4$?

20. Use each of the numbers 1, 2, 3, 4 and any operations or brackets. Write an expression for each whole number from 1 to 10. For example, $1 + 24 \div 3 = 9$.

21. Replace each ▓ with +, −, ×, or ÷ so each equation is true.
   a) $(7.4 ▓ 2.1) ▓ 14 = 25.5$
   b) $(7.4 ▓ 2.1) ▓ 14 = 19.3$
   c) $(7.4 ▓ 2.1) ▓ 14 = 1.54$
   d) $(7.4 ▓ 2.1) ▓ 14 = 1.11$
   e) $(7.4 ▓ 2.1) ▓ 14 = 74.2$
   f) $(7.4 ▓ 2.1) ▓ 14 = 133$

Extend your thinking

22. Replace each ▓ with +, −, ×, or ÷ so each equation is true.
   a) $9 ▓ 3 ▓ 4 ▓ 2 = 1$
   b) $9 ▓ 3 ▓ 4 ▓ 2 = 0$
   c) $9 ▓ 3 ▓ 4 ▓ 2 = 18$
   d) $9 ▓ 3 ▓ 4 ▓ 2 = 25$
   e) $9 ▓ 3 ▓ 4 ▓ 2 = 24$
   f) $9 ▓ 3 ▓ 4 ▓ 2 = 20$

23. Use three 4s and any operations or brackets. Write an expression that equals each number below.
   a) 12   **b)** 4   **c)** 32   **d)** 2   **e)** 20

The Ideas

In your journal, explain why we need rules for the order of operations. Include a list showing the order in which operations in a mathematical expression should be completed.

Measurement Tools in the Community

In this project, you will explore the many
different ways people use measurement tools.
You will learn about a variety of tools that
measure quantities involving length, area,
volume, capacity, mass, time, and angles.

ACTIVITY 1

Find as many measurement tools as you can in your home. Measure something with each tool. Make a list identifying each tool, the item you measured, and the measurement.

ACTIVITY 2

Interview some friends or relatives about the kinds of measurement tools they use. Make a list identifying each tool and its purpose.

ACTIVITY 3

Make arrangements to visit some businesses and services in your community. Prepare questions on how these people use measurement. Try to find examples of all types of measurement. Look for common and unique methods of measuring. Here are some suggestions of businesses and services to visit:

- lumberyard
- drugstore
- fabric store
- garden centre
- bakery

- post office
- airport
- food packaging firm
- paving firm
- hardware store

- carpet store
- paint and wallpaper store
- gas station
- surveying firm

COMMUNICATING The Ideas

Choose at least 3 of the most interesting measurement tools you learned about in the Activities. Prepare a poster about these tools and how they are used in the community. Your poster should explain what each tool is used for and describe the types of occupations that would use each tool. Illustrate your poster with photos or diagrams.

PERCENT AND PROBABILITY

3

Start With What You Know

On October 30, 1995, Quebec held a referendum. Quebecers were asked whether they thought the province should leave Canada after it offered the country a new partnership.

In the weeks before the vote, many surveys or polls were conducted in Quebec. As well as asking people how they would vote, many polling companies asked questions to help them predict how undecided people would vote.

On September 30, the Toronto Star reported that 55% of Quebecers had decided to vote No, or were likely to vote No. This meant that out of every 100 Quebecers surveyed, 55 supported No. We can show this on a 100-square. The squares shaded red represent the people surveyed who supported No.

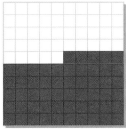

1. **a)** What fraction of the 100-square is red? Express this fraction in lowest terms.
   b) Did more than half the people surveyed support No?
   c) What fraction of the 100-square is not shaded? Express this fraction as a percent. What does this percent represent?

On October 26, 1995, this article appeared on the front page of the Toronto Star. Read the article.

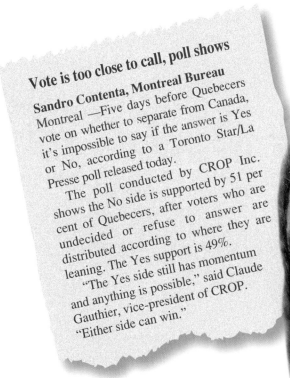

Vote is too close to call, poll shows

Sandro Contenta, Montreal Bureau

Montreal —Five days before Quebecers vote on whether to separate from Canada, it's impossible to say if the answer is Yes or No, according to a Toronto Star/La Presse poll released today.

The poll conducted by CROP Inc. shows the No side is supported by 51 per cent of Quebecers, after voters who are undecided or refuse to answer are distributed according to where they are leaning. The Yes support is 49%.

"The Yes side still has momentum and anything is possible," said Claude Gauthier, vice-president of CROP. "Either side can win."

2. **a)** Of every 100 people surveyed, how many supported No?
   b) Of every 100 people surveyed, how many supported Yes?
   c) Some people would not say how they would vote or had not decided. How did the survey take these people into account? Do you think this was a good idea, or should they have been left out of the survey? Explain.

3. **a)** Use a 100-square. Colour squares red to represent those people who said they supported No.
   b) Compare your 100-square to the one on page 136. Which has more red squares? How many more?
   c) How did the percent of people who said they supported No change between the two surveys?

The chart below shows the results of the referendum.

	Votes	Percent
Yes	2 308 028	49.4%
No	2 361 526	50.6%

4. Which answer received more votes? How many more votes did it receive?

5. **a)** What percent of those who voted marked No on their ballot?
   b) Compare the percent of No support in each survey to the actual result. Did the September or October survey provide a more accurate prediction of the result? Give reasons.

6. Why might the results of a survey differ from the results of a vote?

7. Each of these facts about Quebec is expressed as a percent. Shade squares on a 100-square to show each percent. Answer each question.
   a) Quebec makes up about 15% of Canada's land area. For every 100 km^2 of land in the country, how many square kilometres are in Quebec?
   b) In 1991, about 25% of Canada's population lived in Quebec. For every 100 Canadians, how many lived in Quebec? How many lived outside Quebec?
   c) In 1991, French was the first language of about 82% of Quebecers. For every 100 Quebecers, how many spoke French as their first language? For how many was French not a first language?
   d) In 1991, Quebec farmers produced about 39% of the milk sold in Canada. For every 100 L of milk sold, how many litres were produced in Quebec? How many were produced outside Quebec?

3.1 PERCENT

Developing the Ideas

▶▶▶ *Through Discussion*

Percents are everywhere around us, in newspapers, store windows, and on food packaging. They are used to describe discounts, sales tax, and the quantities of various ingredients in our foods.

1. One of the signs above is "Save 25%."
   a) Suppose an article originally cost $100. How much do you save if you buy the article in the sale? What does it cost in the sale?
   b) Suppose an article originally cost $200. How much do you save if you buy the article in the sale? What does it cost in the sale?

2. The sign on the shop window is "Up to 50% off."
   a) Suppose an article originally cost $100. How much might you save if you buy the article in the sale? What might it cost in the sale?
   b) Suppose an article originally cost $200. How much might you save if you buy the article in the sale? What might it cost in the sale?

3. A sign in a bank says "$5\frac{3}{4}\%$ per annum on Savings Accounts."
   a) Suppose you put $100 in your savings account. What interest will you have after one year?
   b) How much will be in your account after one year?
   c) Suppose you put $200 in your savings account. How much will be in your account after one year?

▶ ▶ Through Instruction

Here is a square that is divided into 100 equal parts. We call it a *100-square*. Each small square is *one-hundredth* of the 100-square. We can use percent to describe fractions of a 100-square.

In the 100-square on the right,

We see: 73 of the 100 squares are shaded.

We think: $\frac{73}{100}$ of the 100-square is shaded.

We say: 73 percent of the 100-square is shaded.

We write: 73% of the 100-square is shaded.

73% means *73 parts out of 100 equal parts*.

Recall that $\frac{73}{100}$ is written in decimal form as 0.73.

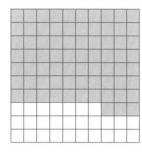

▶ ▶ Through Guided Examples

Example 1 ....

Convert each fraction to a percent.

a) $\frac{9}{50}$ b) $\frac{1}{4}$ c) $\frac{7}{10}$

Solution

The denominator of each fraction is a factor of 100. To convert each fraction to a percent, find the equivalent fraction with denominator 100.

a) $\frac{9}{50} = \frac{9 \times 2}{50 \times 2}$ b) $\frac{1}{4} = \frac{1 \times 25}{4 \times 25}$ c) $\frac{7}{10} = \frac{7 \times 10}{10 \times 10}$

$= \frac{18}{100}$ $= \frac{25}{100}$ $= \frac{70}{100}$

$= 18\%$ $= 25\%$ $= 70\%$

Example 2 ....

Convert each fraction to a percent.

a) $\frac{5}{12}$ b) $\frac{3}{8}$

Solution

Neither denominator is a factor of 100. To convert each fraction to a percent, express each fraction as a decimal then multiply by 100%.

a) $\frac{5}{12} \times 100\% \doteq 0.42 \times 100\%$ b) $\frac{3}{8} \times 100\% = 0.375 \times 100\%$

$\doteq 42\%$ $= 37.5\%$

In *Example 2a*, the decimal is 0.416 666.... It was rounded to 2 decimal places before multiplying by 100%.

▶ ▶ *Through an Activity*

A recent study found that our garbage is composed of paper, plastic, metal, glass, organic material (food, garden waste, and so on), and other materials. The amount of each material is given in the table below.

Material	Percent
Paper	50%
Plastic	10%
Metal	6%
Glass	1%
Organic	13%
Other	20%

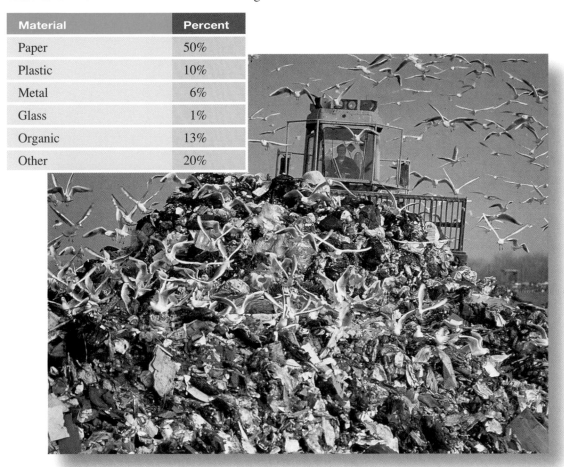

We will use a 100-square to graph these data. On squared paper, outline a 100-square.

1. How many squares will represent *paper*? Colour these squares red.

2. How many squares will represent *plastic*? Colour these squares blue.

3. How many squares will represent *metal*? Colour these squares black.

4. How many squares will represent *glass*? Colour these squares yellow.

5. How many squares will represent *organic*? Colour these squares orange.

6. How many squares represent *other*? Leave these squares white.

7. Name some materials that might be described as "other."

You have drawn a *box graph* to represent the makeup of garbage.

In a box graph, each item is represented by the area of part of the square.

8. In what way is a box graph better than other graphs to represent these data?

Working with Mathematics

Something to talk about

1. What is the meaning of the word *percent*?

2. Restate each sentence using a fraction.
   a) Jasmine scored 82% on her mathematics test.
   b) The milk in this carton is 1% butter fat by volume.
   c) The sales tax on an item is 11%.
   d) At the end of winter, skis sell for 30% off.

3. Restate each sentence using percent.
   a) About 14 out of every 100 Canadians are under 5 years of age.
   b) A furniture salesperson receives about $5 commission on every $100 worth of furniture she sells.
   c) Ian scored 78 out of 100 on his English examination.
   d) Every 100 mL of air contains about 21 mL of oxygen.
   e) The area of Africa is about one-fifth the total land area in the world.

4. What percent of each set is shaded?
   a)
   b)
   c)
   d)

5. State what percent of each 100-square is shaded.
   a) 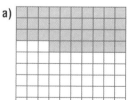   b)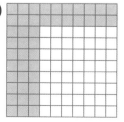

c) 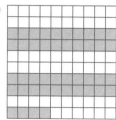   d)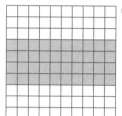

6. Estimate what percent of each square is shaded. How did you arrive at your estimate?
   a)    b)
   c)    d)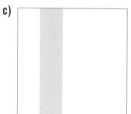

7. The shaded part of the 100-square shows the fraction of Canadians who are 14 years of age or younger.

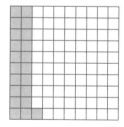

   a) How many small squares are shaded?
   b) How many small squares are there altogether?
   c) For every 100 Canadians, how many are 14 years of age or younger?
   d) What fraction of Canadians are 14 years of age or younger?
   e) What percent of Canadians are 14 years of age or younger?

Practice

8. Shade a 100-square to show each percent. Write each percent as a decimal and as a fraction in lowest terms.

   a) 35%   b) 46%   c) 15%   d) 69%

   e) 75%   f) 87%   g) 7%   h) 96%

9. Write each fraction as a percent, then as a decimal.

   a) $\frac{37}{100}$ b) $\frac{4}{100}$ c) $\frac{7}{50}$ d) $\frac{3}{25}$

   e) $\frac{3}{10}$ f) $\frac{1}{5}$ g) $\frac{3}{4}$ h) $\frac{7}{7}$

10. A survey shows that 9 out of 20 people dine out at least once a week. Suppose you have a group of 100 people. How many would you expect to dine out at least once a week? Express your answer as a percent.

11. A survey shows that 6 out of 10 people prefer coffee over tea. How many people out of 100 would you expect to prefer coffee over tea? Express your answer as a percent.

12. Express each fraction as a decimal, then as a percent.

   a) $\frac{11}{15}$ b) $\frac{33}{40}$ c) $\frac{57}{75}$ d) $\frac{43}{60}$

   e) $\frac{66}{80}$ f) $\frac{5}{8}$ g) $\frac{5}{6}$ h) $\frac{11}{12}$

13. a) Use the box graph to write the percent of Canadians in each age group.

   i) under 15 years old

   ii) between 15 and 34 years old

   iii) 35 years and older

   iv) under 35 years old

   Ages of Canadian population

   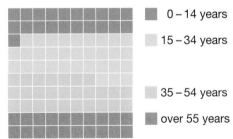

   b) What percent of Canadians do you think are under 125 years old?

14. The circle represents the world's total ocean area. Estimate the area of each ocean as a percent of the total area.

   Areas of oceans

   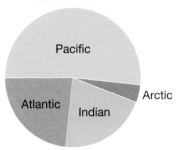

Work together

15. The Great Lakes form the largest body of fresh water in the world. The area of each lake as a percent of the total area is shown in the box graph.

   a) What percent of the area of the Great Lakes is each lake?

   i) Lake Superior   ii) Lake Erie

   iii) Lake Ontario

   Areas of the Great Lakes

   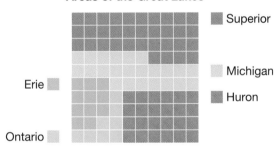

   b) What percent of the area of the Great Lakes is the combined area of the two largest lakes?

   c) Make up a question about this graph. Ask a classmate to answer your question.

16. A group of 100 students was asked, "What is your favourite season?" The results are shown in the tally chart below.

Spring	Summer	Fall	Winter
＋＋＋＋ ＋＋＋＋ ＋＋＋＋ III	＋＋＋＋ ＋＋＋＋ ＋＋＋＋ ＋＋＋＋	＋＋＋＋ ＋＋＋＋ ＋＋＋＋ ＋＋＋＋ III	＋＋＋＋ ＋＋＋＋ ＋＋＋＋ ＋＋＋＋ ＋＋＋＋ I

Colour a 100-square to show these data in a box graph.

a) What season is the most popular?

b) What season is the least popular?

c) What percent of students chose winter as their favourite season?

d) Is it correct to say that about one-quarter of the students chose winter as their favourite season?

e) What percent of students did not choose summer as their favourite season?

17. Start a new document in a Draw program. Create a small circle. Duplicate the circle and place it next to the first circle. Continue to duplicate until you have a row of 10 circles. Select the whole row and duplicate the row. Place this below the first row. Continue to duplicate until you have 10 rows of 10 circles.

a) Suppose each pattern below is continued. What percent of the circles will be shaded?

i)

ii)

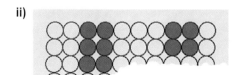

b) Create a pattern in which 80% of the circles are shaded.

c) Create a pattern in which 75% of the circles are unshaded.

18. You know that you breathe in oxygen; and you use carbon, as charcoal, in a barbecue, but did you know that your body is made up of these elements, along with others listed below?

Element	Percent by mass
Oxygen	65%
Carbon	18%
Hydrogen	10%
Nitrogen	3%
Calcium	2%
Other elements	2%

a) Colour a 100-square to show these elements in a box graph.

b) What percent of your body's mass is contributed by the three elements, carbon, hydrogen, and oxygen?

c) Make up a question about the box graph. Ask a classmate to answer your question.

Extend your thinking

19. The mass of an animal's lungs is about 1% of the mass of its body. The mass of an animal's heart is about 50% of the mass of its lungs. What is the mass of the heart of each animal?

a) a 6000-kg elephant **b)** a 6-kg cat

c) a 600-g hamster **d)** a 60-kg sheep

COMMUNICATING
The Ideas

The word *percent* derives from the Latin words *per centum*, meaning "out of 100." How many pennies are there in a dollar? What fraction of a dollar is a penny? What percent of a dollar is a penny? In your journal, use the answers to these questions to explain why we refer to a penny as a cent.

3.2 VISUALIZING AND ESTIMATING PERCENTS

Developing the Ideas

▶▶ *Through an Activity*

You will need a centimetre ruler, a large flat rubber band, and a pen or marker.

- Cut the rubber band and mark a percent scale on it. The scale should be 10 cm long, with markings 1 cm apart.

- Place the rubber band along the edge of the ruler, with the 0% mark at 0 on the ruler. Keeping the 0% mark at 0, stretch the rubber band so that the 100% mark moves from 10 cm to 30 cm on the ruler. What happens to the other percent marks as you do this?

Use your rubber band and the ruler to help you estimate the answer to each problem.

1. Last weekend, 14 cm of snow fell. Sixty-five percent of this fell on Saturday night. How much snow fell on Saturday night?

2. Julie had 11 hits in 19 at-bats. For what percent of her at-bats did she get a hit?

3. The Westview Marauders won 8 games last year. This was 40% of the games they played. How many games did they play?

▶ ▶ *Through Instruction*

It is not practical to use the rubber band for all percent problems, but thinking about it can help you to visualize percents. To do this, think of two scales. One scale is like the ruler—it contains the numbers in the situation with which you are dealing. The other scale is like the rubber band—it contains a percent scale. Imagine that this scale can be stretched or shrunk to match the first scale according to the numbers in the problem.

Consider this example.
A lacrosse team won 27 out of 45 games. What percent of its games did it win?

Visualize a scale of games from 0 to 45, with a percent scale from 0 to 100 below it. The 100% mark is at 45.

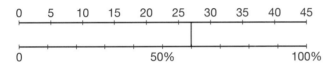

What mark on the percent scale will be at 27 on the games scale?

27 out of 45 is more than halfway along the scale.

The team won about 60% of its games.

Here is another example.
VCRs are on sale for $299. This is 70% of the regular price. What was the regular price?

Visualize a scale of prices from $0 to $300 and beyond, with a percent scale from 0 to 100 below it. The 70% mark is at $300.

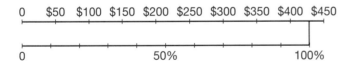

What number on the scale of prices is at the 100% mark?

If $300 is 70%, then 100% is just over one-third more.

The regular price was approximately $430.

Working with Mathematics

Something to talk about

1. Refer to the lacrosse team on page 145. What percent of the games did the team win if it won:
   a) 15 games?   b) 20 games?   c) 35 games?

2. Refer to the VCRs on sale on page 145. How would the regular price change if the sale price of $299 were:
   a) greater than 70% of the regular price?
   b) less than 70% of the regular price?

Work together

In exercises 3 and 4, sketch two scales. Use your visualization skills to estimate the answers.

3. There are 34 students in Ms. Smith's grade 8 class. Twenty of these students play a musical instrument. What percent of the students play a musical instrument?

4. Karol's best high jump is 1.62 m. This is 80% of the world record. What is the world record?

5. Estimate the percent of earnings each student saved.

	Earned ($)	Saved ($)
Adrian	41	10
Siobhan	49	20
Linda	23	18
Atul	33	25

6. Which percent in the box is closest to:
   a) $\frac{1}{2}$?   b) $\frac{1}{5}$?   c) $\frac{3}{10}$?   d) $\frac{3}{4}$?

58%	32%	69%
39%	47%	78%
12%	24%	92%

On your own

7. Central Junior High has 575 students. Sixty-four percent of them have pets. How many students have pets?

8. In Glen Acres School, 295 of the 410 students take music. About what percent of the students take music?

9. Resolute Bay, N.W.T., is so far north there is no daylight for about 93 days each year. What percent of the days of the year have no daylight?

10. About 289 000 km of Canada's 825 700 km of roads are paved. About what percent of the roads are paved?

11. Which fraction in the box is closest to:
    a) 100%?   b) 50%?   c) 25%?   d) 10%?

	$\frac{2}{3}$		$\frac{5}{6}$	$\frac{1}{5}$
$\frac{5}{8}$		$\frac{4}{9}$	$\frac{3}{5}$	
	$\frac{4}{5}$		$\frac{7}{8}$	$\frac{1}{10}$

12. An iceberg is 138 m tall. Only 15 m are visible above the water. About what percent is below the water?

Extend your thinking

13. Estimate the percent of each Great Lake that is in Canada.

Lake	Area (km²)	
	Canada	U.S.A.
Superior	28 700	53 400
Huron	36 000	23 600
Michigan	0	57 800
Erie	12 800	12 900
Ontario	10 300	9 300

COMMUNICATING The Ideas

Make a poster or a display that explains how your rubber band can be used to estimate the answer to a problem involving percent.

3.3 SALES TAX

Developing the Ideas

▶ ▶ *Through an Activity*

Sales tax is money paid to the government on certain things that we buy. The sales tax rates in 1997 are shown in the table.

New Brunswick, Nova Scotia, and Newfoundland and Labrador have a harmonized sales tax of 15%, which is usually included in the selling price and not added separately at the cash register. In Prince Edward Island and Quebec, PST is calculated on the price of an item after the GST has been added.

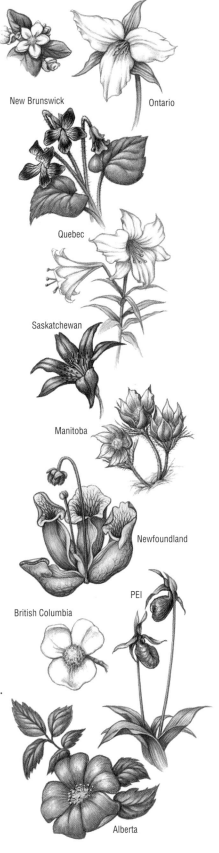

Nova Scotia

New Brunswick   Ontario

Quebec

Saskatchewan

Manitoba

Newfoundland

PEI

British Columbia

Alberta

Province	Provincial sales tax	Federal goods & services tax (GST)
Alberta	No tax	7%
British Columbia	7%	7%
Manitoba	7%	7%
Northwest Territories	No tax	7%
Ontario	8%	7%
Prince Edward Island	10%	7%
Quebec	7.5%	7%
Saskatchewan	7%	7%
Yukon	No tax	7%

Work in a group or with a partner.

1. What does each percent mean? Illustrate your answer by expressing each percent as a fraction.

   a) 6%   **b)** 7%   **c)** 8%   **d)** 9%   **e)** 10%   **f)** 11%   **g)** 12%

2. Pens are sometimes on sale for $1. Suppose you bought one pen for $1. Use the table to determine, for your province:
   a) the provincial sales tax (PST) you must pay
   b) the federal goods and services tax (GST) you must pay.

3. What would the PST and GST be in your province if you bought each number of pens?

   a) 2 pens   **b)** 3 pens   **c)** 4 pens   **d)** 5 pens

4. Copy and complete this table, using the sales tax rate for your province.

Number of pens	Cost of pens	PST	GST
1			
2			
3			
4			
5			

▶ ▶ Through Instruction

Here is one pattern in the table (using the sales tax rate for Saskatchewan).

Number of pens	Cost of pens	PST at 7%	GST at 7%	Think...
1	$1.00	$0.07	$0.07	→ $0.07 \times 1 = 0.07$
2	$2.00	$0.14	$0.14	→ $0.07 \times 2 = 0.14$
3	$3.00	$0.21	$0.21	→ $0.07 \times 3 = 0.21$
4	$4.00	$0.28	$0.28	→ $0.07 \times 4 = 0.28$
5	$5.00	$0.35	$0.35	→ $0.07 \times 5 = 0.35$

We see: The provincial tax rate is 7%, or 0.07. In any row of the table, if you multiply the cost by 0.07, the result is the provincial sales tax a person in Saskatchewan must pay.
The GST rate is 7%, or 0.07. If you multiply the cost of the pens by 0.07, the result is the GST a person must pay.

We say: A person in Saskatchewan pays 7¢ PST and 7¢ GST on every dollar spent.

▶ ▶ Through a Guided Example

To calculate the sales tax on an item, multiply the cost of the item by the sales tax rate, expressed in decimal form.

Example ....

Russ lives in Manitoba. He wants to buy his favourite rock group's CD, which sells for $15.95. Calculate the total cost of the CD, including sales tax.

Solution

The provincial sales tax in Manitoba is 7%, and the GST is 7%. This means that for every $1.00 Russ spends, he must pay 7¢ provincial tax and 7¢ GST.

Price of CD : $ 15.95
Provincial sales tax: $15.95 $\times$ 0.07 = $ 1.12
GST: $15.95 $\times$ 0.07 = $ 1.12
Total cost: $ 18.19

Working with Mathematics

Unless stated otherwise, use the current rate of sales tax in your province when you do these exercises. If you live in a region with no sales tax, choose a province that does have sales tax, and complete the exercises.

Something to talk about

1. Why do governments charge sales tax? Why are the rates of sales tax not the same in every province?

Practice

2. On each item, what is the provincial sales tax? What is the GST?

a)

b)

c)

d)

e)

f)

3. In British Columbia, the PST and GST add to almost 15%. Emma estimates the final cost of an item by estimating 10%, or $\frac{1}{10}$, plus 5%, or half of $\frac{1}{10}$ of the price. Then she adds the estimate to the price. Use Emma's method to estimate the final cost in British Columbia of each item in exercise 2. Use a calculator to determine the costs. How close are the estimates?

4. Sales clerks sometimes use a chart like this to determine the sales tax to charge customers.

Cost of item	Sales tax at 7%	Cost of item	Sales tax at 7%
8¢ – 21¢	1¢	$5.08 – $5.21	36¢
22¢ – 35¢	2¢	$5.22 – $5.35	37¢
36¢ – 49¢	3¢	$5.36 – $5.49	38¢
50¢ – 64¢	4¢	$5.50 – $5.64	39¢
65¢ – 79¢	5¢	$5.65 – $5.78	40¢
80¢ – 93¢	6¢	$5.79 – $5.92	41¢
94¢ – $1.07	7¢	$5.93 – $6.07	42¢
$1.08 – $1.21	8¢	$6.08 – $6.21	43¢
$1.22 – $1.35	9¢	$6.22 – $6.35	44¢
$1.36 – $1.49	10¢	$6.36 – $6.49	45¢
$1.50 – $1.64	11¢	$6.50 – $6.64	46¢
$1.65 – $1.78	12¢	$6.65 – $6.78	47¢
$1.79 – $1.92	13¢	$6.79 – $6.92	48¢
$1.93 – $2.07	14¢	$6.93 – $7.07	49¢
$2.08 – $2.21	15¢	$7.08 – $7.21	50¢
$2.22 – $2.35	16¢	$7.22 – $7.35	51¢
$2.36 – $2.49	17¢	$7.36 – $7.49	52¢
$2.50 – $2.64	18¢	$7.50 – $7.64	53¢
$2.65 – $2.78	19¢	$7.65 – $7.78	54¢
$2.79 – $2.93	20¢	$7.79 – $7.92	55¢
$2.94 – $3.07	21¢	$7.93 – $8.07	56¢
$3.08 – $3.21	22¢	$8.08 – $8.21	57¢
$3.22 – $3.35	23¢	$8.22 – $8.35	58¢
$3.36 – $3.50	24¢	$8.36 – $8.49	59¢
$3.51 – $3.64	25¢	$8.50 – $8.64	60¢
$3.65 – $3.78	26¢	$8.65 – $8.78	61¢
$3.79 – $3.92	27¢	$8.79 – $8.92	62¢
$3.93 – $4.07	28¢	$8.93 – $9.07	63¢
$4.08 – $4.21	29¢	$9.08 – $9.21	64¢
$4.22 – $4.35	30¢	$9.22 – $9.35	65¢
$4.36 – $4.49	31¢	$9.36 – $9.49	66¢
$4.50 – $4.64	32¢	$9.50 – $9.64	67¢
$4.65 – $4.78	33¢	$9.65 – $9.78	68¢
$4.79 – $4.92	34¢	$9.79 – $9.92	69¢
$4.93 – $5.07	35¢	$9.93 – $10.07	70¢
		$20.00	$1.40
		$30.00	$2.10
		$40.00	$2.80
		$50.00	$3.50

a) In which provinces would this sales tax chart be used? Explain how you know.

b) Use the sales tax chart to determine the provincial sales tax in these provinces for the items in exercise 2.

3.4 *WORKING WITH PERCENT*

Developing the Ideas

▶ ▶ *Through an Activity*

A region in the St. Lawrence River is known
as the Thousand Islands. Some of the islands
in this region belong to Canada and the others
belong to the United States. A table like
this one appeared in an article in *Canadian
Geographic* magazine.

The Thousand Islands		
	Islands in Canada	Islands in the U.S.A
Islands with names	241	126
Islands without names	424	358

Group 1

1. How many of the Thousand Islands are in Canada?

2. Estimate the percent of the Thousand Islands in Canada that have
   names.

3. **a)** Calculate the percent of the Thousand Islands in Canada that have
   names.
   b) Calculate the percent of the Thousand Islands in Canada that do not
   have names.

Group 2

1. How many of the Thousand Islands are in the U.S.A.?

2. Estimate the percent of the Thousand Islands in the U.S.A. that
   have names.

3. **a)** Calculate the percent of the Thousand Islands in the U.S.A. that
   have names.
   b) Calculate the percent of the Thousand Islands in the U.S.A. that do
   not have names.

Group 3

1. **a)** What is the total number of islands in the Thousand Islands region?
   b) How many of these islands have names?
   c) How many do not have names?

2. Estimate the percent of the islands in the Thousand Islands region
   that have names.

3. **a)** Calculate the percent of these islands that have names.
   b) Calculate the percent of these islands that do not have names.

▶▶ *Through Guided Examples*

Some percent problems can be solved in more than one way. It does not matter which method you use. One method may seem easier or more obvious to you than another method.

Example 1

Cassette tapes are on sale for $3.60. This is 80% of the regular price. What is the regular price?

Solution

You want to know: 100% of the regular price is ▨.
You do know: 80% of the regular price is $3.60.

1% of the regular price is $\frac{\$3.60}{80}$.

100% of the regular price is $\frac{\$3.60}{80} \times 100\% = \$4.50$

The regular price is $4.50.

Check: 80% of $4.50 = 0.8 × $4.50
$= \$3.60$

Example 2

An open-air concert is held each year. This year the attendance was 2400. This is 75% of the attendance last year. What was the attendance last year?

Solution

To change from last year's attendance to this year's attendance, you multiply by 0.75.
So, to change from this year's attendance to last year's attendance, you divide by 0.75.

Last year's attendance $= \frac{2400}{0.75}$
$= 3200$

Check by visualizing:

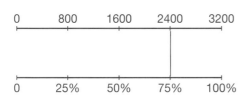

The relative frequency of an outcome can also be called the *experimental probability*.

In *Activity 1*, we would expect that after many tosses we would get about the same number of heads as tails. We would also have predicted that the relative frequency of heads would be $\frac{1}{2}$.

For the toss of a coin:

We think: There are 2 equally-likely outcomes. The relative frequency of each outcome should be about $\frac{1}{2}$, or 50%.

We say: The *probability* of heads is 50%, and the probability of tails is 50%.

▶ ▶ *Through a Guided Example*

Example ....

Suppose a die is rolled.

a) What are the possible outcomes?

b) Are the outcomes equally likely?

c) What is the probability of obtaining ?

Solution

a) There are 6 outcomes.

b) If we roll a die many times, we would expect each outcome to occur about the same number of times. The outcomes are equally likely.

c) The relative frequency for each outcome should be approximately $\frac{1}{6}$.

Hence, the probability of obtaining is $\frac{1}{6}$, or almost 17%.

This item appeared in a newspaper the day before the 1994 World Cup Soccer final. The world's population is between 5 billion and 6 billion. What fraction of the world's population was expected to watch the game?

Viva Italia! Olê, Olá, Brasil!

Any way you say it, tomorrow's World Cup final in Pasadena between Italy and Brazil is a mega-event for soccer lovers.

With about 2 billion TV viewers expected to tune in for the 4 p.m. start, the only thing that might surpass the match's intensity is the spontaneous partying by fans before the action, and after.

Working with Mathematics

Something to talk about

1. In *Activity 1*, some students decided to save time by tossing 5 coins 10 times. Do you think this will affect the results?

2. In *Activity 2*:
   a) Are the outcomes *point up* and *point down* equally likely?
   b) How would the results change if you use a thumbtack with:
      i) a longer point?   ii) a shorter point?

3. Only two of these statements are true. Which ones do you think they are? Explain your thinking.
   a) If you toss a coin 10 times, you will never get 10 heads.
   b) If you toss a coin 10 times, you could get 10 heads, but this is very unlikely.
   c) If you toss a coin 10 times, you will always get exactly 5 heads.
   d) If you toss a coin many times, the number of heads should be approximately $\frac{1}{2}$ of the number of tosses.

Practice

4. Express each fraction as a decimal, rounded to two decimal places, and as a percent.
   a) $\frac{13}{80}$ b) $\frac{37}{50}$ c) $\frac{38}{60}$ d) $\frac{11}{30}$
   e) $\frac{17}{20}$ f) $\frac{9}{15}$ g) $\frac{9}{25}$ h) $\frac{46}{75}$
   i) $\frac{153}{200}$ j) $\frac{86}{150}$ k) $\frac{85}{140}$ l) $\frac{462}{500}$

5. For each experiment, state the possible outcomes. Are the outcomes equally likely? Explain.
   a) The pointer on a spinner is spun. The spinner is divided into 3 equal sectors labelled Win, Lose, and Tie.
   b) One marble is chosen from a bag with 15 blue, 20 green, and 10 striped marbles.
   c) One candy is chosen from a bag containing 8 toffees, 8 mints, 8 chocolates, and 8 pieces of licorice.

d) A store distributes scratch-and-save discount coupons. They distribute one hundred twenty 30% coupons, two hundred fifty 20% coupons, and five hundred 10% coupons. You scratch the spot on your coupon to determine the discount you will receive.

Work together

In each activity, express the relative frequencies in decimal form, rounded to two decimal places, and as percents.

6. For this activity you will need a deck of 52 playing cards.
   a) Suppose a card is picked from the deck and its value is recorded. What are the possible outcomes, if the card's suit does not matter?
   b) Do you think the outcomes in part a are equally likely, or are some more likely than others? Explain.
   c) Draw a table like this. Pick a card from the deck and record its value in the table. Return the card to the deck. Repeat this 25 times.

Outcome	Tally	Frequency	Relative frequency
Ace			
King			
Queen			
.			
.			
3			
2			

   d) Calculate the relative frequency for each outcome in the table.
   e) Do the results confirm your prediction in part b?
   f) Combine your results with those of other students. What is the probability of drawing a queen from a deck?

7. For this activity you will need a die.
   a) When a die is rolled, what are the possible outcomes?

b) Do you think these outcomes are equally likely, or are some more likely than others?

c) Design and conduct an experiment to determine relative frequencies for these outcomes. Copy and complete this table.

Outcome	Tally	Frequency	Relative frequency

d) Did the results confirm your prediction in part b?

8. When you roll a die, what is the probability of obtaining  ?

9. For this activity you will need a paper cup. When a paper cup is tossed, there are three possible outcomes: it can land top up, top down, or on its side.

a) Which outcome do you think is most likely? Which outcome do you think is least likely?

b) Design and conduct an experiment to determine relative frequencies for these outcomes. Record the results in a table like this.

Outcome	Tally	Frequency	Relative frequency
Top up			
Top down			
Side			

c) Did the results confirm your prediction?

10. For this activity you will need two coins. When two coins are tossed, there are three possible outcomes: they can land both heads, both tails, or one head and one tail.

a) Do you think these outcomes are equally likely, or is one more likely than another?

b) Design and conduct an experiment to determine relative frequencies for these outcomes. Copy and complete this table.

Outcome	Tally	Frequency	Relative frequency
2 heads			
2 tails			
1 head, 1 tail			

c) Did the results confirm your prediction?

d) Combine your results with those of other students. What do you think the probabilities are for the three outcomes?

Save your results from the experiments in exercises 9 and 10. You will need them later.

Extend your thinking

11. An experiment was once conducted in which coins were tossed thousands of times. The results showed that a coin may be slightly more likely to land tails than heads. Look at a coin very closely. Compare the heads side with the tails side. Can you think of a reason why a coin might be slightly more likely to land with the head side down?

12. You intend to toss a coin 100 times to determine the relative frequency of heads. Investigate whether it makes a significant difference if you toss:

a) 1 coin, 100 times

b) 2 coins, 50 times

c) 4 coins, 25 times

d) 10 coins, 10 times

The Ideas

In your journal, write a few sentences to explain what *frequency* and *relative frequency* mean. Use an example to illustrate your explanation.

. . . 3.6 *MAKING PREDICTIONS*

Developing the Ideas

▷ ▶ *Through an Activity*

Work with a partner or in a group. You will need 10 coins and a cup.

1. Place the 10 coins in the cup and shake them to mix them thoroughly. Then drop them on a flat surface. Count the number of heads that appear. Repeat this experiment many times. Copy and complete this table.

Number of heads	Tally	Frequency
0		
1		
2		
3		
4		
5		
6		
7		
8		
9		
10		

2. Copy the grid below. Use your data to construct a bar graph showing the frequencies for the different numbers of heads.

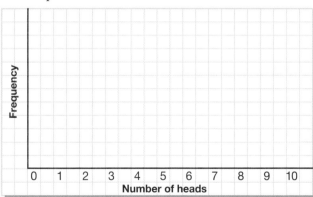

3. Compare your graph with other students or groups. Did everyone's graph look the same? Do you think the graphs should look the same?

4. Combine your results with those of other students to get results for as many experiments as you can.

  a) For the combined experiments, construct a table like the one in exercise 1.

  b) Use the table to construct a graph like the one in exercise 2.

  c) Compare the graph with the graphs for the individual experiments.

5. What was the most frequent number of heads? How could you have predicted this without doing the experiment?

▶ ▶ *Through a Guided Example*

If the outcomes of an experiment are equally likely, the probability of an event is the number of outcomes favourable to the event divided by the total number of outcomes.

Probability = $\dfrac{\text{Number of favourable outcomes}}{\text{Total number of outcomes}}$

Suppose you repeat an experiment many times. You can predict the number of times an event will occur by multiplying the probability by the number of repetitions.

When you toss a coin, the probability of obtaining heads is $\frac{1}{2}$. When you toss a coin many times, you should expect that it will turn up heads and tails about the same number of times.

Example ···

Suppose you roll a die 60 times. Predict how many times  or will appear. Explain your answer.

Solution

There are 6 equally likely outcomes:

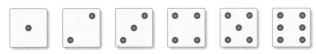

The probability of obtaining or is $\frac{2}{6}$, or $\frac{1}{3}$.

In 60 rolls, the number of times or will appear should be approximately $\frac{1}{3} \times 60 = 20$

This does not mean that or will appear 20 times. It means only that the number of times or appears will probably be close to 20.

Working with Mathematics

Something to talk about

1. Suppose another class does the activity on page 163.
   a) How would the individual graphs obtained by that class in exercise 2 compare with yours?
   b) How would the combined graph obtained by that class in exercise 4 compare with the combined graph for your class?

2. Suppose you toss a coin 10 times and record the number of heads. You repeat this experiment many times. Only one of the statements below is true, no matter how many times you repeat the experiment. Which one do you think it is? Explain your thinking.
   a) You will get 5 heads each time you repeat the experiment.
   b) The number of heads will probably be around 5 each time.
   c) You will get 5 heads in half of the experiments.

3. In the cartoon below, suppose the cartoonist had used 75% instead of 50% in the first picture.
   a) What percent would appear in the second picture?
   b) Would the cartoon be as effective if this change were made?

Practice

4. Simplify. Round each answer to the nearest whole number.
   a) $\frac{1}{3} \times 60$ b) $\frac{1}{2} \times 45$ c) $\frac{1}{4} \times 75$
   d) $\frac{1}{6} \times 20$ e) $\frac{1}{7} \times 80$ f) $\frac{1}{5} \times 24$
   g) $\frac{1}{10} \times 50$ h) $\frac{1}{3} \times 100$ i) $\frac{1}{20} \times 50$

5. Calculate the probability of each outcome in exercise 5 on page 161.

6. What is the probability of each event?
   a) rolling a 4 on a die
   b) rolling an odd number on a die
   c) rolling a number less than 4 on a die
   d) rolling a 1 or a 6 on a die
   e) drawing the 7 of hearts from a deck of cards
   f) drawing a red card from a deck of cards
   g) drawing a spade from a deck of cards
   h) drawing a jack, queen, or king from a deck of cards
   i) drawing an even number from a deck of cards
   j) drawing a red 3 from a deck of cards
   k) drawing a number less than 6 from a deck of cards

7. Compare your answers to parts a to d of exercise 6 with the relative frequencies of these events in the experiment you conducted in exercise 7 on page 161. How close are the relative frequencies and the probabilities?

8. Compare your answers to parts e to k of exercise 6 with the relative frequencies of these events in the experiment in exercise 6 on page 161. How close are the relative frequencies and the probabilities?

Work together

9. Suppose a die is rolled 60 times. How many times would you expect each event in parts a to d of exercise 6 to occur?

10. Suppose a card is drawn from a deck of 52 cards. Its value is recorded, and it is returned to the deck. This is done 50 times. About how many times would you expect each event in parts e to k of exercise 6 to occur? Why do we use the word *about* in this exercise?

11. Suppose you roll a die 60 times. Predict how many times each event will occur.
    a) [die showing 1]   b) an even number
    c) a number greater than 4

12. Get the results of your paper cup experiment (see page 162, exercise 9). Suppose you toss the paper cup 1000 times. Predict how many times each outcome will occur.
    a) top up   b) top down   c) on its side

13. Get the results of your two-coin experiment (see page 162, exercise 10). Suppose you toss two coins 1000 times. Predict how many times each event will occur.
    a) two heads   b) two tails
    c) one head and one tail

14. Suppose you roll a die 60 times, and record the number of times [die showing 5] appears. Only one statement below is true, no matter how many times you repeat the experiment. Which one do you think it is? Why?
    a) [die showing 5] will appear 10 times each time you repeat the experiment.
    b) The number of times you get [die showing 5] will probably be around 10 each time.
    c) If you repeat the experiment 600 times, you will get [die showing 5] 100 times.

On your own

15. Suppose you toss a coin 40 times. Predict how many times heads will appear.

16. Get the results of your thumbtack experiment (see page 159). Suppose you toss the thumbtack 1000 times. Predict how many times each outcome will occur.
    a) with the point up
    b) with the point down

17. This clipping appeared in a newspaper.

One in 10,000 chance you'll live to be 100

What are your chances of living to be 100?

About one in 10,000. According to actuarial statistics, one person in 10,000 living in developed countries can expect to make it to the century mark and only one in 2.1 billion people can expect to live beyond the age of 115.

Although there have been great gains in average life-span, so more and more people are living into their 80s, the maximum length of human life has not been extended during recorded history.

Use a database or reference book and the information in the clipping to predict:
a) the number of people in Canada who will reach age 100
b) the number of people in the world who will reach age 100

Extend your thinking

18. Use the data in the *Activity* on page 163. Determine the mean number of times heads appeared:
    a) in your experiment
    b) for the combined experiments

COMMUNICATING

The Ideas

In your journal, explain why you cannot be sure how many heads you will get if you toss a coin 10 times

Sharing a Birthday

In a group of 30 people, what is the probability that two people have the same birthday?

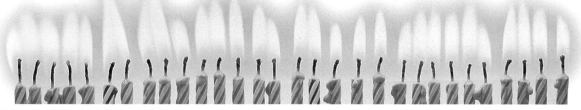

Understand the problem

- In a group of 30 people, is it possible that no two people have the same birthday?
- Is it possible that every person in the group has the same birthday? How probable is it?
- If you were in a group of 30 people, would you be surprised if there were two people who had the same birthday?

Think of a strategy

- How could you conduct a study to answer the question above?
- Is it sufficient to consider two or three groups of 30 people?
- How could you get your classmates to help with the study?

Carry out the strategy

- Find a group of 30 different people. Ask each student in the class to do the same. You could use family members and friends, books from the "Who's Who" series, or choose groups of 30 people at random from an encyclopedia. If you have access to a computer bulletin board, leave a message asking people to respond with their first names and birthdays.
- For each group of 30 people, record whether two people have the same birthday. Pool your results with those of your classmates. Calculate the probability that in a group of 30 people, two people have the same birthday.

Look back

- The probability that, in a group of 30 people, two people have the same birthday is about 71%. How does this value compare with your value? If your value is different, give reasons why.
- Use your results for groups of 30 people to find the probability that, in a group of 60 people, two people have the same birthday.

Communicating the Ideas

Write a description of this problem in your journal. Include reasons why your answer might have been different from the value given above.

3.7 *INDEPENDENT EVENTS*

Developing the Ideas

▶ ▶ *Through Discussion*

Some probability experiments involve two experiments that occur separately. When the outcome of one experiment does not affect the outcome of the other experiment, the two experiments are said to be *independent*. The outcomes of these independent experiments are called *independent events*.

Suppose we toss two coins. We can think of the toss of each coin as a separate experiment. The outcomes of successive tosses of two coins are independent events because the outcome of the first toss does not affect the outcome of the second toss. The possible outcomes of the *combined* experiment are summarized in the table below.

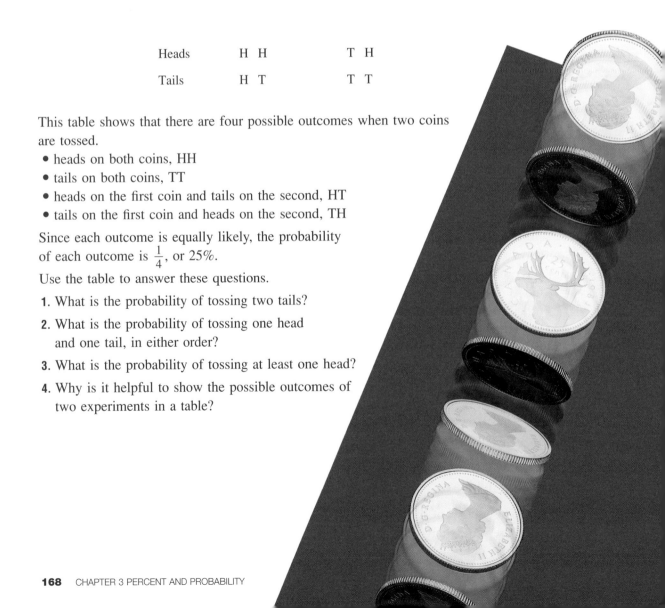

Heads	H H		T H
Tails	H T		T T

This table shows that there are four possible outcomes when two coins are tossed.
- heads on both coins, HH
- tails on both coins, TT
- heads on the first coin and tails on the second, HT
- tails on the first coin and heads on the second, TH

Since each outcome is equally likely, the probability of each outcome is $\frac{1}{4}$, or 25%.

Use the table to answer these questions.

1. What is the probability of tossing two tails?

2. What is the probability of tossing one head and one tail, in either order?

3. What is the probability of tossing at least one head?

4. Why is it helpful to show the possible outcomes of two experiments in a table?

▶ ▶ *Through a Guided Example*

Example ···

Janet and Harish are playing a game of paper, scissors, or rock. The 2 players count aloud together. On the count of 3 each makes one of these hand signs: a flat palm to represent paper, 2 outstretched fingers to represent scissors, or a closed fist to represent rock. If they make the same sign, there is a tie and they play again. If they make different signs, the winner is declared according to these rules:
- Rock blunts scissors, so rock wins over scissors.
- Scissors cut paper, so scissors win over paper.
- Paper covers rock, so paper wins over rock.

a) What is the probability that Janet and Harish tie?

b) What is the probability that Janet wins?

Solution

Create a table. Assume that each player chooses randomly which hand sign to make. So, consider each person's choice to be a probability experiment with 3 equally likely outcomes: paper, scissors, or rock. This means that all the outcomes in the table are equally likely. Also, since both players make their choices at the same time, their choices are independent.

		Janet's call		
		Scissors	**Paper**	**Rock**
Harish's call	Scissors	Tie	Harish wins.	Janet wins.
	Paper	Janet wins.	Tie	Harish wins.
	Rock	Harish wins.	Janet wins.	Tie

a) There are 9 possible outcomes.
Three of these outcomes result in a tie.
The probability of a tie is:

$$\frac{\text{Number of outcomes that result in a tie}}{\text{Total number of outcomes}} = \frac{3}{9}, \text{ or } \frac{1}{3}$$

The probability of a tie is $\frac{1}{3}$, or $33\frac{1}{3}\%$.

b) There are 9 possible outcomes.
In 3 of these outcomes, Janet wins.
The probability that Janet wins is:

$$\frac{\text{Number of outcomes in which Janet wins}}{\text{Total number of outcomes}} = \frac{3}{9}, \text{ or } \frac{1}{3}$$

The probability that Janet wins is $\frac{1}{3}$, or $33\frac{1}{3}\%$.

c) Use your table to determine the probability of each event.
  i) a circle and a 4
  ii) a square and an even number
  iii) a circle or triangle and an odd number
  iv) neither a circle nor an even number

14. Use your table from exercise 13 to write the probability of each event.
  a) i) spinning a circle
  ii) spinning a 4
  iii) spinning a circle and a 4
  b) i) not spinning a circle
  ii) not spinning a 3
  iii) spinning neither a circle nor a 3
  c) i) spinning an even number
  ii) spinning a triangle
  iii) spinning an even number and a triangle
  d) Do your answers to parts a to c support the conclusion you made in exercise 12d?

15. A jar contains 5 balls: 1 blue, 1 red, 1 green, 1 purple, and 1 yellow. Players are blindfolded and asked to select a ball from the jar. The ball selected is returned to the jar and the same player selects a ball again. Make a table to show all the possible outcomes of the selection of the two balls from the jar. What is the probability of each event?
  a) A blue ball is selected on both draws.
  b) A red ball is selected on the first draw and a purple ball on the second.
  c) A green ball and a yellow ball are selected, in either order.
  d) Neither ball is green.
  e) At least one ball is purple.

Extend your thinking

16. A card is drawn from a deck of 52 cards. The value of the card is recorded. The suit does not matter. The card is returned to the deck and another card is drawn.
  a) How many possible outcomes are there?

b) What is the probability of each outcome?
  i) Both cards are aces.
  ii) Neither card is an ace.
  iii) At least one of the cards is an ace.

17. A cereal company inserts a plastic figurine in each box of cereal. There are three types of figurines: Batman, Superman, and Wonder Woman. Half the boxes contain a Wonder Woman figurine, one-quarter contain a Superman figurine, and one-quarter contain a Batman figurine.
  a) Suppose you buy 2 boxes of the cereal. Make a table to show the possible figurines you could receive. How can you design your table to show that there are twice as many Wonder Woman figurines as Superman or Batman?
  b) The boxes of cereal are distributed randomly throughout the country. If you buy 2 boxes, what is the approximate probability of each event?
    i) You receive two Wonder Woman figurines.
    ii) You receive two Batman figurines.
    iii) You receive a Batman and a Wonder Woman figurine.
    iv) You receive at least one Wonder Woman figurine.
  c) Is the type of figurine in the second box affected by the type of figurine in the first box? Explain your answer. Does this make much difference in calculating the probability?

The Ideas

In your journal, explain the meaning of the term *independent events*. Give an example of an experiment that involves two independent events. Explain how you know they are independent.

3.8 MONTE CARLO METHODS

Developing the Ideas

To estimate some probabilities, we simulate an experiment by doing a different experiment which has the same probability. This technique is known as a *Monte Carlo* method. For example, to simulate guessing the answer on a true/false question, we toss a coin. Heads on the coin corresponds to a correct answer. Tails on the coin corresponds to a false answer.

▶ ▶ *Through Activities*

ACTIVITY 1

Suppose you have to complete a true/false test with 10 questions. If you guess each answer, what is the probability that you will get at least 5 questions right?

We can design an experiment to simulate this situation.

The probability of guessing the correct answer to each question is $\frac{1}{2}$.

The probability of getting heads when a coin is tossed is $\frac{1}{2}$.

We simulate the problem by tossing 10 coins many times.

- With a partner, toss 10 coins.
- Record the number of heads that occurred.
- Conduct the experiment 20 times.
- Write the number of times 5 or more heads appeared as a fraction of 20. This corresponds to the probability of guessing 5 or more questions correctly on the test.
- Combine your results with those of four other groups. Calculate the probability again.
- Do you think it is wise to complete a true/false test by guessing?

ACTIVITY 2

For a group of 5 students in your class, what do you think the probability is that at least 2 will have birthdays in the same month?

We assume that the probability of being born in a particular month is $\frac{1}{12}$.

We simulate this situation with a coin and a die. We assign each month with heads or tails, and a number from 1 to 6.

January H1   February H2   March H3   April H4   May H5
June H6   July T1   August T2   September T3   October T4
November T5   December T6

Conduct this experiment with a partner.

- Toss a coin and roll a die 5 times. Record whether any month occurred more than once.
- Conduct the experiment 20 times.
- What is your estimate of the probability that in a group of 5 students at least 2 were born in the same month?
- Combine your results with those of 4 other groups. Estimate the probability again.
- Do the combined results change your estimate of the probability?

When designing an experiment, we must be careful to match the method used with the conditions of the problem.

In *Activity 1*, a coin was used because there are two equally likely outcomes, just as there are two possible answers to a true/false question.

In *Activity 2*, a coin and a die were used because there are 12 equally likely outcomes, one for each month.

Both activities could be conducted by using other experiments.

TEMPLATE DISK

▶ *Using a Computer*

We will simulate the rolling of two dice in two ways. Start a new document on your spreadsheet. Enter the information shown below.

In ClarisWorks

	A	B	C	D	E
1	Die 1	Die 2	Die 1 + Die 2		Die 1 and Die 2 together
2	=RAND(6)	=RAND(6)	=A2+B2		=RAND(11)+1

In Microsoft Works

	A	B	C	D	E
1	Die 1	Die 2	Die 1 + Die 2		Die 1 and Die 2 together
2	=Int(Rand()*6)+1	=Int(Rand()*6)+1	=A2+B2		=Int(Rand()*11)+2

- Copy the formulas in row 2 to 20 or more rows below.
- Choose Calculate Now. Record the number of times each number from 2 to 12 appears in column C and in column E.
- Repeat this several times. Tally your results.
- Which method, column C or column E, is the better simulation for rolling two dice?
- Combine your results with those of your classmates. Use the spreadsheet to record, tally, and graph the results of your experiment. Use the graphs to explain your conclusions.
- Why is 7 such an important number in dice games?

Working with Mathematics

Something to talk about

1. A multiple-choice test has 10 questions. Each question has 4 answers. Explain how this spinner could be used to estimate the probability of guessing at least 3 correct answers.

2. **a)** Explain what is meant by *simulation*.
   b) Why do we use a simulation to calculate a probability?
   c) Why do we expect the results of a simulation to provide a good estimate of the probability?

3. To simulate each event, would you use one or more of: a coin, a die, a spinner, or some other object?
   a) the birth of a girl
   b) the selection of a month of the year
   c) the correct answer to a multiple-choice question which has four choices
   d) the selection of an even number

4. Describe a simulation you could conduct to estimate each probability.
   a) the probability that in a family of 4 children there are exactly 3 boys
   b) the probability that you will guess correctly more than 5 answers on an 8-question true/false test

On your own

5. A student guesses each answer for an 8-question true/false quiz. Design an experiment to estimate the probability that the student will get exactly 5 answers correct.

6. A student guesses each answer for a 10-question multiple-choice test. For each question there are 3 possible answers. Design an experiment to estimate the probability that a student will guess at least 7 answers correctly.

Work together

7. According to a news report, one in every six railroad cars is defective. Design an experiment to estimate the probability that a 7-car train contains 2 or more defective cars. What is the probability that the train has no defective cars?

8. A batter is hitting 0.500; that is, she gets a hit 50% of the times she comes to bat. Design an experiment to estimate the probability that she will get at least 3 hits in her next 5 times at bat.

9. The first traffic light the school bus reaches each morning is green for 25 s, yellow for 10 s and red for 25 s out of every minute. Design a simulation to estimate the probability that the light, when first seen by the driver, will be green at least 3 times in a week.

Extend your thinking

10. A survey indicates that 75% of all consumers prefer Brand A cola to Brand B cola. A sample of 10 consumers is chosen. What is the probability that 8 or more of them prefer Brand A?

The Ideas

Only 4 of the 6 students who volunteered to organize the spring dance are needed to put up the decorations. In your journal, explain how Monte Carlo methods could be used to select the students.

Review

1. Shade a 100-square to show each percent. What percent does the unshaded portion of each 100-square represent?
   a) 36%   b) 47%   c) 83%   d) 28%
   e) 78%   f) 94%   g) 7%   h) 66%

2. Convert each fraction to a percent. If the percent is not a whole number, round it to 1 decimal place.
   a) $\frac{2}{5}$ b) $\frac{17}{20}$ c) $\frac{34}{50}$ d) $\frac{1}{10}$
   e) $\frac{16}{25}$ f) $\frac{77}{100}$ g) $\frac{3}{4}$ h) $\frac{15}{20}$
   i) $\frac{25}{30}$ j) $\frac{8}{15}$ k) $\frac{48}{65}$ l) $\frac{145}{200}$

3. Convert each percent to a decimal.
   a) 24%   b) 72.6%   c) 28%   d) 18%
   e) 5.7%   f) 84.3%   g) 68.1%   h) 0.4%

4. Convert each decimal to a percent.
   a) 0.56   b) 0.37   c) 0.47   d) 0.827
   e) 0.471   f) 0.057   g) 0.265   h) 0.001

5. Estimate the percent of electricity in Nova Scotia that is produced by each source.
   a) water
   b) coal
   c) oil

   Sources of Nova Scotia's electricity

   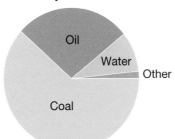

6. For each item, calculate the provincial sales tax (PST), the goods and services tax (GST), and the total cost.
   a) a raincoat that sells for $42.69 in P.E.I.
   b) an exercise treadmill that sells for $1254.59 in Ontario
   c) a gold necklace that sells for $134.99 in Newfoundland
   d) a pair of gloves that sells for $16.89 in Quebec
   e) a pair of snowshoes that sells for $36.59 in the Northwest Territories

7. At a restaurant, Craig orders the items shown below. There is a sales tax of 11%, and he leaves a 15% tip.

Salad	$2.50
Entree	$7.55
Dessert	$3.65
Beverage	$1.75

   a) Find the total cost of the meal if Craig calculates the tip:
      i) before sales tax is added
      ii) after sales tax is added
   b) Which method of calculating the tip in part a is more reasonable? Why?

8. Heather, who lives in Saskatchewan, would like to buy a canister set for her mother. She finds a set that is on sale for 30% off. The canister set is regularly priced at $54.95.
   a) Find the discount price.
   b) Find the PST, GST, and total cost.
   c) Heather has only $50.00. Can she afford to buy the canister set?

9. Calculate the sale price for each item.
   a) A toaster, regularly priced at $26.98, is on sale for 15% off.
   b) A sofa, regularly priced at $476.69, is on sale for 20% off.
   c) A T-shirt is on sale for 10% off. It is regularly priced at $12.35.
   d) A car battery is on sale for 25% off. It is regularly priced at $87.65.

10. Use mental math to estimate each percent. Explain your estimation strategies.
    a) Canada covers an area of about 9 980 000 km². British Columbia covers an area of about 950 000 km². What percent of the area of Canada is the area of British Columbia?
    b) In 1991, 69 557 000 m³ of crude oil were produced in Canada. That year, 52 246 000 m³ were produced in Alberta. What percent of Canada's crude oil production was this?

c) In 1991, there were 12 369 000 head of cattle in Canada. That year, there were 4 403 000 head of cattle in Alberta. What percent of Canada's cattle were in Alberta?

d) In 1991, the population of Saskatchewan was 988 920. There were 138 090 people in Saskatchewan whose first language was neither French nor English. What percent of the population was this?

11. Last season a hockey team won 47 of the 65 games it played. There were no ties.
a) What percent of its games did it win?
b) What percent of its games did it lose?

12. Oakridges Junior High has 675 students. Forty-eight percent of them take the bus to school. How many students take the bus?

13. The attendance at a Blue Jays' home opener was 45 800. This was about 85% of the previous year's attendance at the home opener. What was the attendance that year?

14. For each experiment, state the possible outcomes. Are the outcomes equally likely? Explain.
a) A die is rolled.
b) A spinner is spun. The spinner is divided into 4 equal sectors labelled Yes, No, Probably Yes, and Probably No.
c) A name is drawn from a bag containing papers: 2 papers for Martha, 1 for Bryan, 3 for Connor, 4 for Edna.

15. What is the probability of each event?
a) rolling an even number on a die
b) drawing a black 10 from a deck of cards
c) drawing an ace from a deck of cards
d) drawing a face card from a deck of cards
e) drawing a queen or king from a deck of cards

16. A coin is tossed and a die is rolled.
a) Are the outcomes independent? Explain.
b) Refer to exercise 6b on page 170. Are the outcomes of this experiment equally likely? Explain.
c) What is the probability of the coin showing heads and the die showing 6?
d) What is the probability of the coin showing heads and the die showing an odd number?
e) Toss the coin and roll the die 20 times. Record your results in a table like this.

Outcome	Tally	Frequency	Relative frequency

f) What were the relative frequencies of the outcomes in parts c and d? How similar were they to the probabilities you calculated?

17. A potato chip manufacturer has randomly placed one of 4 prizes in each bag of chips it manufactures. Design an experiment to determine how many bags of chips need to be purchased to collect at least one of each prize. Use cards or pieces of paper numbered from 1 to 4 to simulate the prizes. Repeat your experiment at least 10 times. Record the results of each trial in a table like the one below.

Trial	Prize 1	Prize 2	Prize 3	Prize 4	Total number of draws
1					
2					
⋮					

Newspaper Advertising

The advertisements in many newspapers are simple fractions of a page, such as $\frac{1}{2}$-page, $\frac{2}{5}$-page, and $\frac{3}{4}$-page. In this project you will investigate which fractions are used for the advertisements in a newspaper. You will also investigate the percent of a newspaper that is devoted to advertising. You will need a newspaper that has different sizes of advertisements.

ACTIVITY 1

Find as many different sizes and shapes of advertisements as you can in your newspaper. For each size and shape of advertisement:

a) Record the page number and the company.

b) Estimate the fraction of the page it occupies. Express the fraction as a percent.

Record your estimates in a table.

Page	Company	Estimated fraction	Estimated percent

ACTIVITY 2

Measure the width and the height of each advertisement. Record your data in a new table. Try to include a full-page advertisement in your table. If there are no full-page advertisements in your newspaper, measure the width and the height of a full page of print, not including the margins.

Calculate the area of each advertisement. Calculate the area of a full page. Record these areas in your table.

Page	Company	Width (cm)	Height (cm)	Area (cm²)	Area Full page	Estimated fraction	Estimated percent

ACTIVITY 3

For each advertisement, calculate the fraction $\dfrac{\text{Area of the advertisement}}{\text{Area of a full page}}$ as a decimal. Record the decimal in the table. Express the decimal as a percent and record it in the table

Use this result to estimate a simple fraction of the page each advertisement occupies. Record your estimated fractions in the table.

ACTIVITY 4

Compare your estimated fractions and percents with your estimates in *Activity 1*. Were your estimates in *Activity 1* reasonable?

ACTIVITY 5

Many newspapers have a *rate card*, which contains a table of advertisement sizes and costs. Most newspapers describe the dimensions of an advertisement by the number of columns and lines it fills. Create a table of advertisement sizes for the rate card for your newspaper. You may use fractions, percents, or columns and lines to describe advertisement sizes.

T.V. SCENE GENERAL

Unit Size	1x
Full page	$2,249
2/3 page	1,574
1/2 page	1,237
1/3 page	865
1/6 page	460

ACTIVITY 6

Calculate the total area of all the advertisements in the newspaper, including the want advertisements. Then carry out calculations to determine the percent of the newspaper that is devoted to advertising.

COMMUNICATING
The Ideas

Prepare a report of the results of your investigations. Include tables and newspaper pages showing the different sizes of advertisements.

Cumulative Review

1. Multiply. Describe the pattern formed by the products.

a) 9.3×0.001 **b)** 9.3×0.01

c) 9.3×0.1 **d)** 9.3×1

e) 9.3×10 **f)** 9.3×100

2. Divide. Describe the pattern formed by the quotients.

a) $2790 \div 0.001$ **b)** $2790 \div 0.01$

c) $2790 \div 0.1$ **d)** $2790 \div 1$

e) $2790 \div 10$ **f)** $2790 \div 100$

3. Copy and complete.

a) $340 \text{ mm} = \blacksquare \text{ cm}$ **b)** $860 \text{ cm} = \blacksquare \text{ m}$

c) $13.5 \text{ m} = \blacksquare \text{ cm}$ **d)** $1122 \text{ m} = \blacksquare \text{ km}$

e) $2.7 \text{ km} = \blacksquare \text{ m}$ **f)** $56.6 \text{ cm} = \blacksquare \text{ mm}$

4. Use a ruler and compasses. Construct a triangle for each set of side lengths.

a) 5 cm, 5 cm, 5 cm

b) 6 cm, 6 cm, 3 cm

c) 6 cm, 7 cm, 8 cm

5. Identify the corresponding sides and angles in these congruent figures.

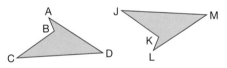

6. Write two equivalent fractions for the dark purple part of each figure.

a)   **b)**

c)   **d)**

7. For each fraction, write an equivalent fraction with denominator 12.

a) $\frac{2}{3}$ **b)** $\frac{5}{6}$ **c)** $\frac{3}{4}$ **d)** $\frac{3}{2}$ **e)** $\frac{18}{24}$

8. Here are some facts about birds from *The Guinness Book of Records*. Write each number in words and in expanded form.

a) The largest living bird is the North African ostrich. Some males are 2.74 m tall and have a mass of 156.5 kg.

b) The world's smallest bird is the bee hummingbird. The male is 5.7 cm long, including the beak and tail. It has a mass of 1.6 g.

c) In 1973, a Ruppell's vulture collided with a plane at an altitude of 11 277 m. This is the highest altitude ever recorded for a bird.

d) The red-billed quelea of Africa has one of the world's largest bird populations. There are about 1.5 billion adult quelea.

9. Replace each $\blacksquare$ with >, <, or =.

a) $\frac{1}{2} \blacksquare \frac{1}{3}$ **b)** $\frac{5}{7} \blacksquare \frac{5}{6}$ **c)** $\frac{3}{5} \blacksquare \frac{2}{3}$

d) $\frac{3}{8} \blacksquare \frac{2}{5}$ **e)** $0.75 \blacksquare \frac{7}{9}$ **f)** $\frac{5}{4} \blacksquare 1.25$

g) $\frac{4}{7} \blacksquare 0.6$ **h)** $1.2 \blacksquare 0.8$ **i)** $1.4 \blacksquare 1.37$

10. Use your fraction strips and number lines to add.

a) $\frac{1}{3} + \frac{1}{3}$ **b)** $\frac{1}{6} + \frac{1}{3}$ **c)** $\frac{3}{5} + \frac{1}{2}$

d) $\frac{1}{3} + \frac{1}{4}$ **e)** $\frac{2}{5} + \frac{3}{10}$ **f)** $\frac{5}{8} + \frac{1}{2}$

11. In a survey about spicy chicken wings, $\frac{2}{5}$ of the people preferred mild, $\frac{1}{4}$ preferred medium, and $\frac{3}{10}$ preferred hot. The remaining people did not like any type of spicy chicken wings.

a) What fraction of the people surveyed liked spicy chicken wings?

b) What fraction of the people surveyed preferred medium or hot wings?

c) What fraction of the people surveyed did not like any type of spicy chicken wings?

12. Use your fraction strips and number lines to subtract.

a) $\frac{1}{4} - \frac{1}{6}$ **b)** $\frac{11}{12} - \frac{1}{2}$ **c)** $\frac{3}{2} - \frac{1}{3}$

d) $1 - \frac{7}{8}$ **e)** $\frac{7}{10} - \frac{3}{5}$ **f)** $2 - \frac{5}{6}$

13. Multiply.
    a) 4.3×1.8 b) 2.5×6.9
    c) 2.4×7.6 d) 0.05×46.1

14. Canada's record for the greatest rainfall in 6 h is 26.5 cm. This record was set in 1984 in British Columbia.
    a) Suppose rain continued to fall at this rate for 1 day. What would be the total rainfall?
    b) Suppose rain continued to fall at this rate for 1 week. What would be the total rainfall? Express your answer in centimetres and in metres.

15. Use blocks to divide.
    a) $9.6 \div 3.2$ b) $4.5 \div 0.9$
    c) $6.51 \div 2.1$ d) $1.4 \div 2.0$

16. Simplify.
    a) $8.4 \times 3.1 + 10.7$
    b) $(13.08 + 5.4) \div 2.2$

17. Write each fraction as a percent, then as a decimal.
    a) $\frac{83}{100}$ b) $\frac{7}{100}$ c) $\frac{8}{50}$ d) $\frac{6}{25}$
    e) $\frac{4}{10}$ f) $\frac{3}{5}$ g) $\frac{2}{4}$ h) $\frac{6}{6}$

18. For each item, calculate the provincial sales tax (PST), the Goods and Services Tax (GST), and the total cost. Use the PST rate for your province.
    a) a blouse that costs $34.95
    b) a pair of pants that cost $59.95
    c) a winter coat that costs $174.99
    d) a baseball bat that costs $42.99
    e) a soccer ball that costs $19.95
    f) a croquet set that costs $28.99

19. The store that sells the items in exercise 18 offers a 15% discount on all clothing, and a 20% discount on all sporting goods. Calculate the sale price of each item.

20. The average Canadian uses about 350 L of water every day. Of this, 40% is flushed down the toilet, 35% is used for showers and baths, 20% is used for washing laundry and dishes, and 5% is used for drinking and cooking. Calculate the amount of water the average Canadian uses each day and each year for each activity.

21. For this exercise, you will need a die numbered 1 to 6. Suppose the die is rolled.
    a) What is the probability of rolling a 5?
    b) What is the probability of rolling an odd number?
    c) Suppose you roll the die 30 times. How many times would you expect each event in parts a and b to occur?
    d) Roll the die 30 times. Each time, record in a table the number on the die.
    e) Compare the relative frequency of each event in parts a and b with its probability. How close are they?
    f) Compare the frequency of each event in parts a and b with your answer to part c. How close are they?

22. Suppose a coin is tossed and the pointer on the spinner below is spun.

    a) Does this experiment involve independent events? Explain.
    b) Make a table to show the possible outcomes of the experiment. Use your table to determine the probability of each event.
       i) The coin shows heads and the pointer lands on blue.
       ii) The pointer lands on green.
       iii) The coin shows tails and the pointer lands on yellow or purple.
       iv) The pointer does not land on purple.
       v) The coin shows heads and the pointer does not land on green.

DATA MANAGEMENT

Mathematics File

Quests

Minds on Math Project

Start With What You Know

The elephant is the world's largest land animal. It is on the brink of extinction. People have been invading the animals' living space. Many elephants have been killed for the ivory from their tusks. The peril of the African elephant is so serious that it has become the symbol of human concern for the environment.

1. In this pictograph, each 🐘 stands for 40 000 elephants. For numbers less than 40 000, the graph shows a fraction of the symbol.

Number of elephants in Africa in 1989

| West Africa | Southern Africa | East Africa | Central Africa |

a) What does 🐘 stand for?
b) Make a table to show the approximate number of elephants in each region of Africa in 1989.
c) Name the region with the fewest elephants. Name the region with the most elephants.
d) About how many elephants were there in Africa in 1989?

Elephant tusks were sold to make ivory artifacts. To prevent the killing of elephants for ivory, the elephant was placed on the endangered species list. A ban on the ivory trade was instituted in 1990.

2. a) What does this bar graph show?

Mass of ivory exported by each country in 1986

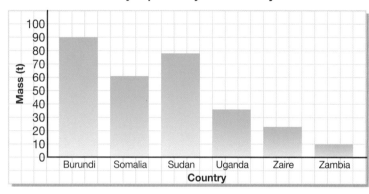

b) Which country exported the most ivory in 1986? How many tonnes did it export?

c) Which country exported the least ivory in 1986? How many tonnes did it export?

d) How much ivory was exported by Uganda, Zaire, and Zambia combined? Was this as much as Sudan exported?

3. a) What does this broken-line graph show?

Total mass of ivory exported in 1981–89

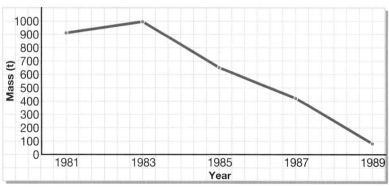

b) Describe how the exports of ivory changed during the 1980s.

4.1 *INTERPRETING AND CONSTRUCTING GRAPHS*

Developing the Ideas

▶▶ *Through Discussion*

We find graphs everywhere we find information; in newspapers, magazines, books, and on computers. The ability to read, interpret, and construct graphs is an important skill.

Study each graph, then answer the questions below it.

Double-Bar Graph

A double-bar graph combines two bar graphs. We use a double-bar graph to make comparisons.

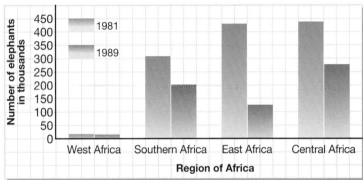

African elephant populations — 1981 and 1989

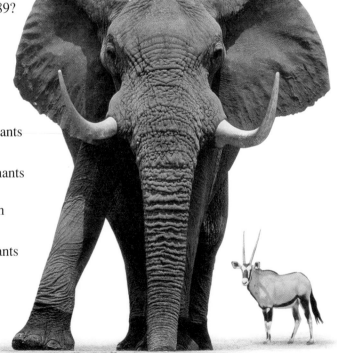

1. **a)** Which of each pair of bars represents 1981?
   b) Which of each pair of bars represents 1989?

2. **a)** What region of Africa had the most elephants in 1989?
   b) How many did it have?

3. What region of Africa had the fewest elephants in 1989?

4. What was the total number of African elephants in 1981 and in 1989?

5. **a)** What region of Africa lost the most elephants between 1981 and 1989?
   b) Estimate how many elephants were lost in that region.

6. What region of Africa lost the fewest elephants between 1981 and 1989?

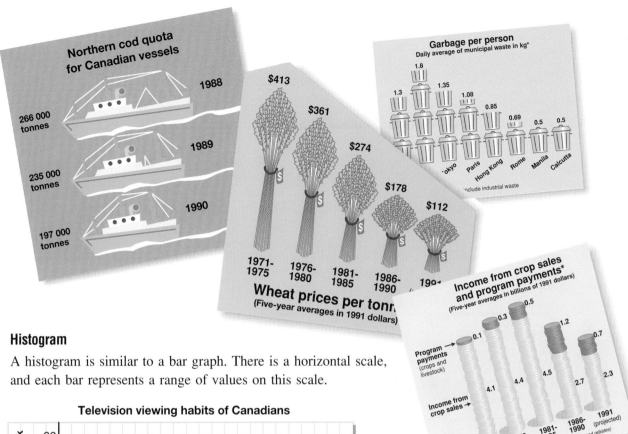

Northern cod quota for Canadian vessels

1988 — 266 000 tonnes
1989 — 235 000 tonnes
1990 — 197 000 tonnes

Wheat prices per tonne
(Five-year averages in 1991 dollars)

$413 — 1971-1975
$361 — 1976-1980
$274 — 1981-1985
$178 — 1986-1990
$112 — 199-

Garbage per person
Daily average of municipal waste in kg*

1.8 Tokyo
1.3
1.35 Paris
1.08 Hong Kong
0.85
0.69 Rome
0.5 Manila
0.5 Calcutta

*include industrial waste

Income from crop sales and program payments*
(Five-year averages in billions of 1991 dollars)

Program payments (crops and livestock):
0.1 — 1971-1975
0.3 — 1976-1980
0.5 — 1981-1985
1.2 — 1986-1990
0.7 — 1991 (projected)

Income from crop sales:
4.1 — 1971-1975
4.4 — 1976-1980
4.5 — 1981-1985
2.7 — 1986-1990
2.3 — 1991 (projected)

*(includes insurance, stabilization payments, and rebates)

Histogram

A histogram is similar to a bar graph. There is a horizontal scale, and each bar represents a range of values on this scale.

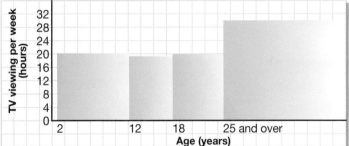

Television viewing habits of Canadians

TV viewing per week (hours) vs. Age (years)

7. What does this graph show?

8. a) What age group watches the most television?
   b) About how many hours per week do these people watch?

9. a) What age group watches the least television?
   b) Estimate how many hours per week these people watch.
   c) Why do you think this group watches the least television?

10. a) Use the graph to estimate how many hours of television Canadians age 18 to 24 years watch per week.
    b) Statistics Canada tells us that on average, a Canadian male between 18 and 24 years old watches about 17.7 h of television per week. Do you think it is possible to use this information and the information in part a to estimate how many hours a Canadian female between 18 and 24 years old spends per week watching television? Explain.

Double Broken-Line Graph

A broken-line graph shows how data change. Only the endpoints of the line segments represent data. This double broken-line graph combines two broken-line graphs.

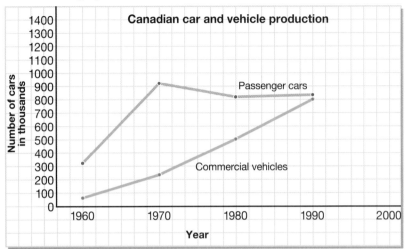

Canadian car and vehicle production

11. This information was taken from the *E-STAT* database.
    a) What does the upper broken line represent?
    b) What does the lower broken line represent?

12. How many passenger cars were manufactured in Canada in 1960 and in 1990?

13. How many commercial vehicles were manufactured in Canada in 1960 and in 1990?

14. Describe how the number of passenger cars manufactured in Canada changed between 1960 and 1990. Compare this with the change in the number of commercial vehicles made in Canada during that same period.

15. Use the graph to estimate the numbers of passenger cars and commercial vehicles that will be manufactured in Canada in the year 2000. How did you get your answers?

In the preceding pages, you reviewed and learned about these graphs:

- pictograph
- bar graph
- double-bar graph
- broken-line graph
- double broken-line graph
- histogram

A set of data may often be illustrated with more than one type of graph. You have to decide which type of graph is best to display the data.

Working with Mathematics

Something to talk about

1. a) Describe how a bar graph and a double-bar graph are alike.

b) How are they different?

2. Compare a broken-line graph and a double broken-line graph. Give an example of data that might be presented using a double broken-line graph.

3. a) How is a histogram like a bar graph?

b) How are they different?

4. Which type of graph would you use to display the data in each table? Give a reason for your choice.

a) To show how your $20 was spent

Item	movies	snack	cassette	bus fare
Cost	$7.00	$3.35	$8.00	$1.65

b) To compare the sales of domestic cars and foreign cars in Canada for three years

Year	1970	1980	1990
Domestic cars	497 000	741 000	670 000
Foreign cars	143 000	191 000	320 000

c) To show the number of Canadians in each age group

Age group	Number of Canadians
under 10	3 605 000
10 to 19	3 712 000
20 to 44	10 421 000
45 and over	7 570 000

d) To show the number of passenger cars in Canada and Brazil for four years

Year	Brazil	Canada
1977	6 900 000	9 600 000
1980	8 300 000	10 300 000
1985	9 500 000	11 100 000
1987	10 000 000	11 500 000

On your own

5. Populations of Alberta and British Columbia, 1930–90

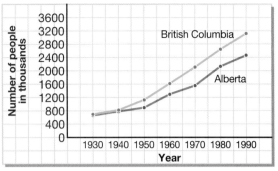

a) What were the approximate populations of Alberta and British Columbia in 1930?

b) i) In which year did the population of British Columbia reach 1 600 000?

ii) How many years later did Alberta reach this population?

c) What was the approximate difference in the populations of Alberta and British Columbia in 1990?

d) During the period from 1960 to 1990, which province was growing faster? How do you know?

6. This double-bar graph was produced from the *Occupations* database on the data disk.

DATA DISK

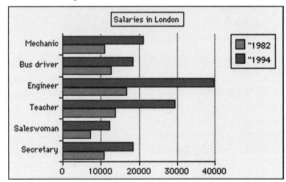

a) For which years are the salaries graphed?

b) For which occupation was there the greatest salary increase?

c) For which occupation was there the least salary increase?

d) For these occupations and years, use the *Occupations* database to calculate:

i) the greatest salary increase

ii) the least salary increase

DATA DISK

7. Choose a city from the *Occupations* database. Use a spreadsheet program to create a table of the salaries of six occupations for 2 years. Have the computer draw a double-bar graph. Answer the questions in exercise 6 for your city.

8. a) What type of graph is this? How do you know?

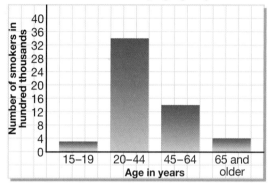

Canadian smokers by age group in 1991

b) What age group has the most smokers?

c) What age group has the fewest smokers?

d) About how many Canadians between 20 and 44 years are smokers?

e) Compare the number of smokers in the age group 20 to 44 with the number in the age group 45 to 64. Why do you think there were more smokers in the age group 20 to 44?

f) Why were there so few smokers over age 64?

g) About how many Canadians were smokers in 1991?

h) Why do so many younger adults smoke when they know it can kill them?

9. Many species of whales are now endangered because of excess hunting. The table shows some of these species and their estimated numbers in 1950 and in 1990.

Species	1950	1990
Blue	80 000	7 000
Bowhead	35 000	8 000
Humpback	85 000	12 000
Right	25 000	3 000

a) For each species, calculate the difference between the numbers in the two years.

b) Which species suffered the greatest loss between 1950 and 1990?

Work together

10. The table shows the places where Canadians say their friendship with their closest friend started. The numbers are in thousands.

Place	Number
School	5700
Work	4100
Club or organization	1400
Religious organization	700
Home or neighbourhood	4300
Through family	1200
Through friend	1100
Other	600

a) How many people were included in this survey?

b) Draw a bar graph to represent these data.

c) Where did most people meet their best friend?

d) What might the *Other* category represent?

11. The table shows the populations of Nova Scotia and Newfoundland.

	Nova Scotia	Newfoundland
1950	638 000	351 000
1960	727 000	448 000
1970	782 000	517 000
1980	845 000	565 000
1990	895 000	572 000

a) Draw a double broken-line graph.

b) Use your graph to determine which province grew faster in the period from 1960 to 1970.

c) Which province grew faster in population between 1950 and 1990? How do you know?

12. Draw each graph you suggested in exercise 4. Compare your graphs with those of other students. Did you all draw the same type of graph for each part of exercise 4?

13. Use the *Baseball* database on the data disk. Select the Sort option to order the players from those who stole the most bases to those who stole the fewest bases. Look at the top 20 players, and the positions they played. Is this statement true or false? "The best base stealers are usually outfielders." We'll use a tally chart and bar graph to find out.

  a) Make a tally chart with headings that are the seven playing positions.

  b) For each of the top 20 players, put a tally mark for each position played.

  c) Draw a bar graph to display the results.

  d) Give reasons to explain why you think the statement is true or false.

14. Forty women and 60 men were asked who does certain household tasks when both partners are working outside the home. The numbers are written as percents.

What the women say:

Task	Women	Men	Shared equally	Other
Meal preparation	76	9	12	3
Cleaning/laundry	74	6	13	6
Maintenance/outside work	7	71	6	16

What the men say:

Task	Women	Men	Shared equally	Other
Meal preparation	74	11	12	3
Cleaning/laundry	74	7	13	6
Maintenance/outside work	5	78	3	14

  a) i) According to the women, how many of them prepare the meals?

  ii) According to the men, how many women prepare the meals?

  iii) Why are the answers to parts i and ii different?

  b) For each task, what might the column headed *Other* represent?

  c) Draw graphs to represent these data. Compare your graphs with those of other students. Did you draw the same types of graph?

Extend your thinking

15. The world's population is growing at an alarming rate. This threatens the survival of animals as we cut down rain forests to provide living space for humans. It also threatens our food supply.

Year	1950	1960	1970	1980	1990
Population (in millions)	2565	3050	3721	4477	5333

  a) Construct a broken-line graph to show the growth in the world population between 1950 and 1990.

  b) Use your graph to estimate the years when the world population reached 3 billion, 4 billion, and 5 billion.

  c) Estimate the year when the world population will reach 6 billion.

  d) The world population reached 2 billion in 1925. How many years did it take the world population to increase from 2 billion to 3 billion?

  e) How many years did it take the world population to increase from:
  i) 3 billion to 4 billion?
  ii) 4 billion to 5 billion?

  f) Predict the year in which the world population will reach 7 billion. What assumptions are you making?

COMMUNICATING

The Ideas

When given a set of data, how do you decide which type of graph is appropriate to represent the data? Write a few sentences in your journal to explain.

Drawing Circle Graphs

The following information was obtained from the *Baseball* database on the data disk.

Baseball

Name	Andre Dawson
Team(s)	Montreal (N.L.), Chicago (N.L.), Boston (A.L.)
Position(s)	Outfield
Games played	2431
At bats	9351
Runs	1303
Hits	2630
Second base hits	473
Third base hits	95
Home runs	412
Runs batted in	1492
Stolen bases	312
Batting average	0.281

1. How many times was Andre at bat?

2. How many hits did Andre have?

3. What is Andre's batting average?

4. How many second base hits (doubles) did Andre have?

5. How many third base hits (triples) did Andre have?

6. How many home runs did Andre have?

We shall construct a circle graph that shows how Andre's at bats are divided into hits and no hits.

Start a new document in your spreadsheet. Input the following data.

TEMPLATE DISK

	A	B
1	Batting statistics	Andre Dawson
2	Hits	2630
3	Did not hit	=B5-B2
4		
5	At bats	9351

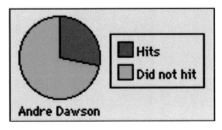

Andre Dawson

- Hits
- Did not hit

Use the mouse to select the cells from A1 to B3. Do not select row 5. In ClarisWorks, use the Options menu. Choose the Make Chart option, and click on the Pie icon. Click OK.

In Microsoft Works, use the Chart menu. Select the New Chart option. The graph will be drawn as a bar graph. Double-click on the graph and change the graph type to Pie. Click OK.

In most spreadsheet programs, circle graphs are called *pie* graphs.

You should see a circle graph of batting statistics.

PLATE DISK

We shall now construct a circle graph that shows how Andre's hits are divided into singles, doubles, triples, and home runs. Use the same spreadsheet document but extend it as follows:

7			
8	Batting statistics	Andre Dawson	
9	Singles	=B2-(B10+B11+B12)	
10	Doubles	473	
11	Triples	95	
12	Home runs	412	
13			
14			

7. How does the formula in cell B9 calculate Andre's singles?

ATA DISK

Select the cells from A8 to B12. Have the computer draw a circle graph. We will compare this circle graph with one for another player. Copy the information in cells A1 to A12. Paste this information in column C. In column D, enter the statistics for Marquis Grissom. You can get these from the *Baseball* database. Use column B entries as a guide.

In cell D3, type =D5–D2

In cell D9, type =D2–(D10+D11+D12)

Have the computer draw a circle graph for Marquis' batting statistics.

8. What do the two batting statistics graphs tell you about how the players compare?

Mathematics & Technology
Linking Ideas

4.2 *CIRCLE GRAPHS*

Developing the Ideas

▶ ▶ *Through Discussion*

In May 1991, *National Geographic* magazine published a three-dimensional box graph similar to this, to show the composition of our garbage.

The volume of each ingredient in the garbage is shown as a percent of the volume of a box.

Recall that you drew a box graph of these data in the *Activity* on page 140.

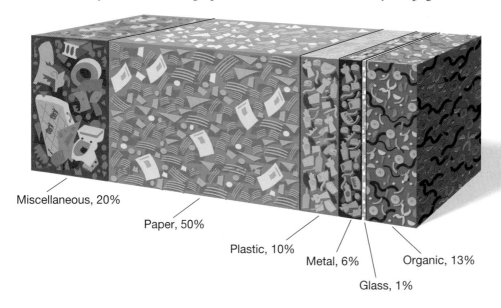

Miscellaneous, 20%

Paper, 50%

Plastic, 10%

Metal, 6%

Glass, 1%

Organic, 13%

It is more common to display these data using a circle graph. A circle graph shows one whole divided into parts.

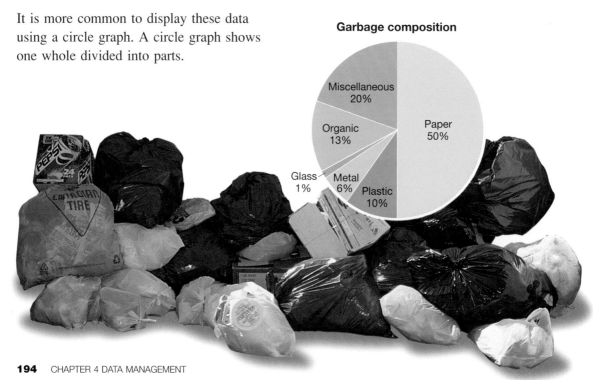

Garbage composition

Miscellaneous 20%

Organic 13%

Paper 50%

Glass 1%

Metal 6%

Plastic 10%

1. **a)** What percent of the garbage is paper?
   b) Write this percent as a fraction.
   c) Use the fraction to calculate how much paper would be in 10 m³
   of garbage.

2. **a)** What percent of the garbage is metal?
   b) Write this percent as a decimal.
   c) Use the decimal to calculate how much metal would be in 20 m³
   of garbage.

3. What volume of each material would you expect to find in 100 m³
   of garbage?
   a) organic   **b)** glass   **c)** plastic

4. The composition of the garbage shown in the graphs is based on
   samples taken from various garbage dumps. Would you expect the
   composition of garbage in all dumps to be the same? Explain why
   or why not.

▶▶ *Through a Guided Example*

Example ···

Use this circle graph to answer the questions below.

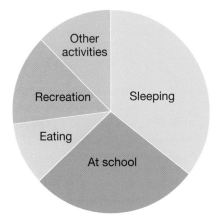

**Hours spent in a typical
student's day**

a) What is the total number of hours for all the activities?

b) i) What activity in a typical student's day uses the most time?
   ii) Estimate what fraction of the day is spent on this activity.

c) i) Estimate what fraction of a student's day is spent at school.
   ii) About how many hours is this?

d) On which activity does a typical student spend more time,
   eating or recreation?

e) i) Name three activities that together use about half a student's day.
   ii) About how many hours is this?

Solution

a) The total number of hours for all the activities is the number of hours in a day: 24 h.

b) i) The activity that uses the most time is the one with the largest sector. This is sleeping.

ii) This sector is about $\frac{1}{3}$ of the circle, so $\frac{1}{3}$ of a student's day is spent sleeping.

c) i) The sector for *At school* is about $\frac{1}{4}$ of the circle. A student spends about $\frac{1}{4}$ of the day at school.

ii) There are 24 h in a day. One quarter of 24 h is $\frac{24 \text{ h}}{4} = 6$ h

d) The sector for *Recreation* is larger than the sector for *Eating*. A student spends more time for recreation than eating.

e) i) The three sectors: *Recreation*, *Eating*, and *At school* make up about half the circle. These are the three activities that use about half of a student's day.

ii) One half of 24 h is $\frac{24 \text{ h}}{2} = 12$ h

For data to be illustrated on a circle graph, they must be listed as parts of one whole. That is, they must be listed as percents, so that their total is 100%; or as fractions, so their total is 1.

Working with Mathematics

Something to talk about

1. **a)** Can data displayed in a box graph always be displayed in a circle graph?
   b) Can data displayed in a circle graph always be displayed in a box graph?
   Explain your answers.

2. **a)** Which tables below contain data that could be displayed on circle graphs? Give reasons for your answers.

   i)

Canadian population by mother tongue	
English	60%
French	24%
Italian	2%
Chinese	2%
Other	12%

   ii)

Percent of Canadian families with these appliances in 1991	
Air conditioners	27%
Cars	83%
Camcorders	10%
Home computers	20%
Colour TV	98%

   iii)

Karat rating corresponding to the percent of gold	
24 karat	100%
18 karat	75%
12 karat	50%
10 karat	42%

   iv)

Production of the world's gold	
South Africa	32%
Russia	15%
U.S.A.	11%
Canada	7%
Other	35%

   b) For each table that could not be displayed on a circle graph, state what graph you would use to display it.

Practice

3. Write as a percent.
   a) $\frac{1}{2}$ **b)** $\frac{3}{4}$ **c)** $\frac{2}{5}$ **d)** $\frac{7}{10}$
   e) $\frac{3}{20}$ **f)** $\frac{2}{3}$ **g)** $\frac{1}{9}$ **h)** $\frac{5}{6}$

4. Write as a fraction.
   a) 25% **b)** 50% **c)** 20% **d)** 5%
   e) 15% **f)** 7% **g)** $33\frac{1}{3}\%$ **h)** 1%

5. Estimate each product. Explain your estimation strategy. Calculate to check your estimate.
   a) $\frac{1}{4} \times 120$ **b)** $\frac{3}{5} \times \$800$
   c) $\frac{3}{5} \times 2400$ kg **d)** $\frac{5}{12} \times 45\,000$
   e) $\frac{1}{6} \times \$6000$ **f)** $\frac{1}{16} \times 4000$ L

6. Estimate. Explain your estimation strategy. Calculate to check your estimate.
   a) 18% of \$45 000 **b)** 11% of \$38 000
   c) 5% of 40 000 t **d)** 60% of 32 000 kg
   e) 12% of 1800 L **f)** 15% of 560 000

7. In a spreadsheet, enter each data set in exercise 2 you would display in a circle graph. Use the spreadsheet's charting capabilities to draw a circle graph for each data set.

Work together

8. **a)** What does this circle graph show?

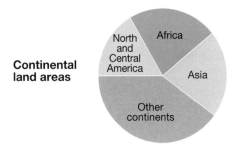

Continental land areas

   b) About what percent of the total land area is Asia?
   c) Express the area of Asia as a fraction of the world's total land area.
   d) About what fraction of the total land area is Africa?

e) What fraction of the total land area is North and Central America?

f) In the graph, *Other continents* refers to South America, Europe, Oceania, and the former USSR. What fraction of the world's land area is contained in these continents?

g) Suppose you added the fractions in parts c, d, e, and f. What should the result be?

9. Recall the box graph in exercise 15, page 142. The circle graph below represents the same data.

Areas of the Great Lakes

a) Which lake is about one quarter of the total area of all the lakes?

b) Which lake is about one third of the total area of all the lakes?

c) List the Great Lakes in order from greatest to least area.

d) Look at the box graph in exercise 15, page 142. Could you answer parts a, b, and c above more easily from the box graph or the circle graph? Give reasons for your answer.

10. There are 24 students in Megan's class, including Megan.

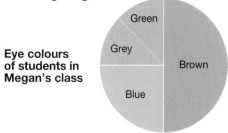

Eye colours of students in Megan's class

a) What does this circle graph show?

b) About how many students have:

   i) brown eyes?   **ii)** blue eyes?

   iii) grey eyes?   **iv)** green eyes?

11. The world's population in 1993 was about 5 570 000 000. Use the information in the circle graph to estimate the number of people in the world who speak each language.

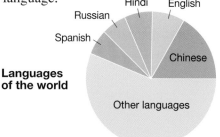

Languages of the world

a) Chinese   **b)** English

c) Hindi   **d)** Russian

e) Spanish   **f)** other languages

On your own

12. The Goreski family has a budget. This graph shows how the family spends its money.

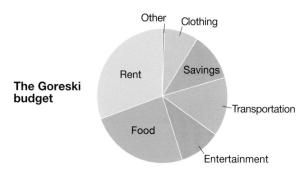

The Goreski budget

a) List the expenditures from least to greatest.

b) About what percent of the Goreski budget is assigned to rent?

c) What expenditure accounts for about one quarter of the budget?

d) Name 2 expenditures that together account for about one quarter of the budget.

e) About what fraction of the budget is assigned to food and rent combined?

f) Suppose the Goreski's income is $40 000. About how much will be spent on food and rent combined?

13.

**Sources of
New Brunswick's electricity**

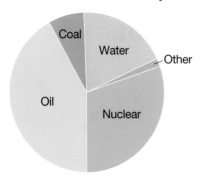

**Sources of
Alberta's electricity**

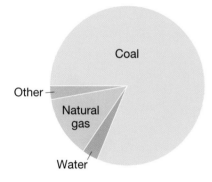

a) What do these circle graphs show?
b) i) How are the graphs the same?
 ii) How are the graphs different?
c) From where does Alberta get most of its electricity?
d) What source of electricity does New Brunswick have that Alberta does not have?
e) Suggest what the label *Other* on the graphs might represent.

Extend your thinking

14. a) What do these circle graphs show?

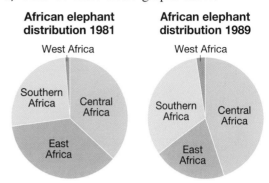

b) Estimate what percent of the elephants were in East Africa in 1981 and in 1989.
c) What happened in East Africa during the 1980s?
d) Estimate the percent of the elephants in Central Africa in 1981 and in 1989. Did the percent of elephants in Central Africa increase during the 1980s? Explain your answer.
e) Did the number of elephants increase in Central Africa during the 1980s? Explain.
f) Compare the second circle graph with the pictograph on page 184. What information can you get from the pictograph that you cannot get from the circle graph?

15. About 18% of landfill by volume is newspaper.
 a) Approximately what volume of newspaper would be found in a landfill site containing 200 000 m^3 of garbage?
 b) Do you think the mass of the newspaper in the landfill is more or less than 18% of the total mass? Give reasons for your answer.

CATING

The Ideas

In your journal, explain how a circle graph is used to display data as parts of one whole. Give an example of data that cannot be displayed using a circle graph. You may use data from some of the earlier sections of this chapter.

Can You Construct a Circle Graph from a Bale of Garbage?

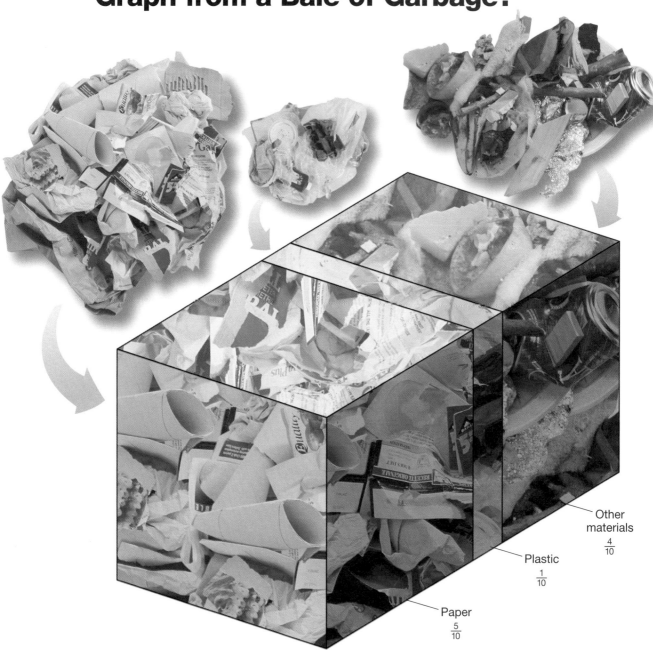

Other materials $\frac{4}{10}$

Plastic $\frac{1}{10}$

Paper $\frac{5}{10}$

Five tenths of the bale of garbage is paper, $\frac{1}{10}$ is plastic, and $\frac{4}{10}$ are other materials. How can we construct a circle graph showing these fractions?

You will need a circular object, a piece of string, a ruler, and scissors.

Understand the problem

- What are the three parts that make up the bale?
- What fraction of the bale is paper? What fraction is plastic? What fraction is other materials?
- Into what fractions must we divide the circle?

Think of a strategy

- The fraction of each type of garbage is related to the circumference of the circle.
- If we can divide the circumference in the same fractions as the garbage, we can draw each sector.

Carry out the strategy

- Draw around a circular object.
- Fold the circle in half and crease along the diameter. Open the circle, and fold it in half a different way. Crease along the diameter. Mark the centre of the circle with a dot.
- Colour red the part of the circle that represents *paper*.
- Cut a piece of string equal to the circumference.
- Measure the string. What fraction of the string represents plastic? What length of the string represents plastic? Cut off this length.
- Place this string along the circumference so one end coincides with the edge of the red sector. Mark a point on the circumference at the other end of the string.
- Draw and colour the sector that represents *plastic*.
- Colour the sector that represents *other materials*.
- Label each sector.

Look back

- Use your string to measure the part of the circumference for *other materials*. Divide this length by the circumference. Write your answer as a decimal. Is this decimal equivalent to $\frac{4}{10}$? Explain your answer.
- How could you construct this circle graph if you had a protractor?

Communicating the Ideas

In your journal, write a description of this problem and your solution. Include an explanation of how to construct a circle graph.

4.3 MEDIAN

Developing the Ideas

▶▶ *Through Discussion*

The table shows the seating capacities of Canada's major stadiums in order from largest to smallest seating capacity.

Stadium and City	Seating capacity
Commonwealth Stadium, Edmonton	60 081
B.C. Place, Vancouver	59 478
SkyDome, Toronto	53 595
Olympic Stadium, Montreal	43 739
McMahon Stadium, Calgary	38 408
Winnipeg Stadium, Winnipeg	32 648
Landsdowne Park, Ottawa	30 927
Ivor Wynne Stadium, Hamilton	29 183
Taylor Field, Regina	27 637

1. What is meant by the term *seating capacity*?

2. a) Which stadium has the largest seating capacity?
   b) How many people can it seat?

We can use the table to find the average seating capacity of the Canadian stadiums.

3. What do we mean by *average* seating capacity?

4. Could we consider Commonwealth Stadium to be average in seating capacity? Why or why not?

5. Could we consider Taylor Field to be average in seating capacity? Why or why not?

6. Look at the capacities of the stadiums. Which stadium would you select as average in seating capacity? Why?

▶▶ *Through Instruction*

For the average seating capacity, we choose a stadium that is in the middle in seating capacity. Of the nine stadiums listed, the capacity of McMahon Stadium in Calgary is the middle value. That is, there are four stadiums with greater capacities and four stadiums with smaller capacities. We say, of the nine seating capacities listed, McMahon Stadium has the *median* value, 38 408. The median is a measure of the average capacity.

When a set of numbers is arranged in order, the middle number is called the *median*.

For example, the median of the set of numbers 1, 3, 4, 9, 28 is 4 because the numbers are in order and the middle number is 4.

When there is an even number of numbers, there are two in the middle. To obtain the median, add the two middle numbers and divide by 2.

For example, the median of the set of numbers 3, 4, 19, 28, 56, 79 is $\frac{19 + 28}{2}$ or 23.5.

▶ ▶ *Through a Guided Example*

Half the numbers in a set are greater than or equal to the median, and the other half are less than or equal to the median.

Example

Canada won the Women's World Ice Hockey Championships in 1994. The table shows the number of goals scored by each team in the tournament.

Team	Goals scored
Canada	37
China	17
Finland	40
Germany	6
Norway	12
Sweden	22
Switzerland	10
U.S.A.	41

What was the median number of goals scored by a team during the tournament?

Solution

We arrange the number of goals scored in order from greatest to least.
41, 40, 37, 22, 17, 12, 10, 6

Since there is an even number of teams, there are two middle numbers, 22 and 17.

The median number of goals scored is $\frac{22 + 17}{2} = \frac{39}{2}$
$$= 19.5$$

It does not make sense to talk about half a goal. However, if we say that the median is 19.5, we know that there were the same number of teams with more than 19.5 goals as there were with fewer than 19.5 goals.

Working with Mathematics

Something to talk about

1. Explain what is meant by the *median* in a set of data.

2. Give an example where we may need to know the median in a set of data.

3. Explain how to find each number in a set of data.
   a) the smallest number
   b) the largest number
   c) the median

Practice

4. Name the median in each set of data.
   a) 6, 8, 8, 9, 11, 17, 21
   b) 5, 7, 10, 10, 16
   c) 14, 14, 21, 27, 44, 51
   d) 45, 47, 56, 56, 73, 94

5. Name the median in each set of data.
   a) 120, 142, 113, 140, 118, 163, 157
   b) 62, 46, 214, 147, 531, 27
   c) 56, 37, 112, 37, 37, 85, 61, 32, 28, 37
   d) 42, 34, 51, 29, 38, 34, 110, 67, 20, 50
   e) 38.5, 32.4, 19.6, 18.3, 14.7, 46.2, 38.9
   f) 1040, 977, 1228, 1310, 778, 1205, 990, 1150, 1302, 1033

6. All the students in Melissa's health class were weighed. The students' masses in kilograms are given below.

28	32	40	36	31	40
48	35	38	34	43	35
41	36	52	37	47	29
43	35	33	39	32	48
37	38	30	35	44	54

   a) Find the masses of the lightest and heaviest students in the class.
   b) What is the median mass of the students in Melissa's class?

Work together

7. a) Write a set of 5 numbers with a median of 12.
   b) Write a set of 8 numbers with a median of 20.
   c) Suppose you add 2 to each number in a set. If you think the median would change, describe how; if you think it would not change, explain why not. Check your answer using your set from part a.

8. When you buy a small box of raisins, do you wonder whether there are more raisins in your box than in the other boxes on the shelf? That is, how many raisins are there on average in a small box of raisins? You will need two partners and 15 small boxes of raisins.
   a) Count and record the number of raisins in each of 5 boxes of raisins.
   b) Record the numbers of raisins in the 15 boxes.
   c) What is the least number of raisins in a box? What is the greatest number of raisins in a box? What is the median number of raisins in a box?
   d) Compare and discuss your results with other groups of students.

9. Use the *Canadian Agriculture* database on the data disk. Sort the records so that all those for 1991 are together. Sort these records so the *Number of dairy cattle* are in order from greatest to least. What was the median number of dairy cattle in 1991?

DATA DISK

10. For one week, count the number of hours you spend watching TV. Collect the data for everyone in the class.
   a) Graph the data. Explain the reasons for your choice of graph.
   b) What is the median time spent watching TV?
   c) What does this median time represent?

On your own

11. Select 50 different books. Record the number of pages in each book.
    a) Graph the data. Explain the reasons for your choice of graph.
    b) Find the median number of pages in the 50 books.

12. The table shows the goals scored against each team in the Women's World Ice Hockey Championships in 1994.

Team	Goals scored against
Canada	7
China	34
Finland	8
Germany	46
Norway	33
Sweden	17
Switzerland	30
U.S.A.	10

What was the median number of goals scored against each team during the tournament?

13. Ask your teacher for the class list of marks for your last mathematics test.
    a) Graph the data. Explain the reasons for your choice of graph.
    b) What is the median mark?
    c) What does the median mark represent?

14. The table shows the life spans of 24 composers of classical music.

Bach	65	Debussy	56	Paderewski	81
Barber	71	Dukas	70	Prokofiev	62
Bartok	64	Dvorak	63	Rossini	76
Beethoven	57	Elgar	77	Saint-Saens	86
Berlioz	66	Haydn	77	Schubert	31
Bizet	37	Liszt	75	Schumann	46
Chopin	39	Mendelssohn	38	Sibelius	92
Copeland	90	Mozart	35	Strauss, R.	85

a) What are the longest and shortest life spans among these composers?
b) What is the median life span of these composers?

c) Consider only those composers with life spans less than 70 years. What is the median life span?

15. In 1989, ecologists estimated the number of elephants killed for ivory. They divided the mass of ivory exported by twice the average mass of an elephant's tusk. To find the average mass, the ecologists measured a sample of tusks and found the median.
    a) Find the median mass of these 28 masses of elephant tusks in kilograms.

4.3	4.9	5.2	3.9	5.1	4.0	4.7
5.1	3.6	4.5	4.9	5.8	4.3	5.4
5.0	4.5	4.2	5.6	4.2	4.6	4.8
5.1	4.3	4.5	5.0	4.9	4.8	4.1

b) About 6828 t of ivory were exported from Africa between 1979 and 1987. Use your answer from part a to estimate the number of elephants slaughtered for ivory.

Extend your thinking

16. a) Suppose you have 25 numbers arranged in order. Which one is the median?
    b) Which number would be the median if you had 35 numbers? 53 numbers?
    c) Suppose you have an odd number of numbers, arranged in order. Describe a rule you could use to determine which number is the median.
    d) Suppose you have an even number of numbers, arranged in order. Develop a rule you could use to determine the median.

COMMUNICATING The Ideas

Find a newspaper or magazine article that refers to average. In your journal, write a few sentences to explain the meaning of the average in the article. Is the average a median?

Exploring Mode

In the previous section, you used the median to describe a set of data. The *mode* is another measure you can use to describe a set of data. The mode is the number or response that occurs most often in the set.

The mode can be useful for determining the most common or most popular item in a set. For example, suppose you survey your classmates to determine the size of their bicycle helmets. Your results show that 3 students have size S helmets, 9 have size M, 8 have size L, and 5 have size XL. The mode of this set of data is size M because size M occurs most often. In this case, knowing the mode helps a store decide the quantities to order for the different sizes.

It is possible for a set of data to have more than one mode. Consider this list of numbers: 3, 5, 7, 6, 9, 6, 8, 9, 6, 2, 3, 9, 2. Both 6 and 9 occur three times, which is more than any of the other numbers. Thus, this set of data has two modes, 6 and 9.

It is also possible for a set of data to have no mode. Consider this list of numbers: 3, 5, 7, 6, 9, 6, 8, 9, 7, 3, 8, 5. Each number in this list occurs two times. No number occurs more often than the others. Thus, this set of data has no mode.

To explore modes using databases, open the *Occupations* database on the data disk. Browse through the information. Look at the field that shows the number of vacation days each person received in a year. Go to the List or Table view to see the records for many cities at the same time.

DATA DISK

1. Use the database's Find feature (ClarisWorks) or a Filter or Query (Microsoft Works) to select all the 1994 records for saleswomen. Use the data in the vacation days field to sort these 51 records from least to greatest. Look through the sorted data. Find the number of vacation days that occurs most often. In this database, what is the mode number of vacation days received by saleswomen?

2. Find the median record. Since the data are already sorted, the median record is the middle one. In this database, what is the median number of vacations days received by saleswomen?

3. Compare your answers to exercises 1 and 2 with the rest of the data. Does the mode or the median better describe a saleswoman's "typical" vacation? Explain.

4. Choose another occupation from the database.
   a) Repeat exercises 1, 2, and 3 for this occupation.
   b) How do the modes for saleswomen and the new occupation compare?
   c) How do the medians for saleswomen and the new occupation compare?

....4.4 MEAN

Developing the Ideas
▶ ▶ *Through Activities*

The greatest distance that your hand can stretch, from the tip of your thumb to the tip of your little finger, is called your *hand span*. Some great concert pianists have hands that are large enough to span several octaves on the keyboard.

ACTIVITY 1

To find an average hand span by measuring

Work in a group of 4. You will need scissors and string.
- Place your outstretched hands together like this:

- Place a string from the thumb end of the first span to the finger end of the last span. Cut the string so its length is equal to the combined hand span.
- Fold the string in half, and then in half again. Cut off one-quarter of the string. Measure and record the length of this piece to the nearest centimetre. This is your average hand span.

ACTIVITY 2

To find an average hand span by calculating

Work in the same group.
- Measure and record the hand span of each member of the group.

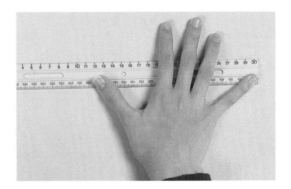

- Add the four hand spans.
- Divide the sum by 4. Round the result to the nearest centimetre. This is your average hand span.

Compare the results of *Activities 1* and *2*. Are they the same? Explain why or why not.

The average you obtained in *Activities 1* and *2* is called the *mean*.

• • • • • • • • •

> To find the mean of a set of numbers, add the numbers, and then divide by the number of numbers.

Through a Guided Example

You have now learned three different ways to describe an average in a set of data: the median, the mode, and the mean. These three numbers are called *measures of central tendency*.

Example ···

Here are the heights of the students in a grade 7 choir.

162 cm	157 cm	170 cm	158 cm	175 cm	182 cm
164 cm	162 cm	158 cm	176 cm	165 cm	168 cm
166 cm	162 cm	172 cm			

a) What is the mean height of the students?

b) How does the mean height compare with the median height?

c) What is the mode height?

d) Which measure of central tendency best represents the average height of the students?

Solution

a) Use a calculator to add the heights.
Total height is 2497 cm.
There are 15 students.
Divide the total height by 15.
$\frac{2497}{15} \doteq 166.466\ 67$
Round the answer to the nearest centimetre.
The mean height is about 166 cm.

b) Arrange the heights in order to find the median.
157, 158, 158, 162, 162, 162, 164, 165, 166, 168, 170, 172, 175, 176, 182
The median height is the middle height: 165 cm.

c) The mode height is 162 cm, which occurs 3 times.

d) The mean height is very close to the median height. Since the mean and median are nearly equal, either could be used to represent the average height of the students. The mode height is shorter than most of the other heights in the set. It does not represent a typical height.

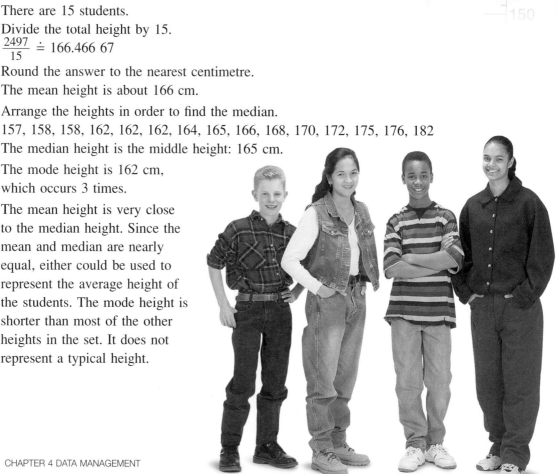

Working with Mathematics

Something to talk about

1. Compare the methods in *Activities 1* and *2* for calculating the mean.

   a) Why is the length of the string the same as the sum of the hand spans?

   b) Why did we fold the string into four parts?

   c) Why is folding the string in half twice the same as dividing by 4?

2. Can the method in *Activity 1* always be used to calculate the mean of several numbers? Explain.

3. Three books have a total mass of 3.9 kg. Calculate the mean mass of the books.

Practice

4. State the mean length of the sides of each polygon.

   a)

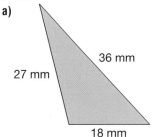

36 mm
27 mm
18 mm

   b)

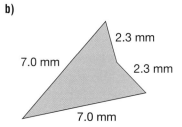

2.3 mm
7.0 mm
2.3 mm
7.0 mm

   c)

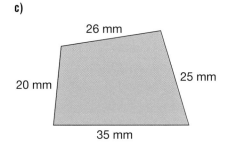

26 mm
20 mm
25 mm
35 mm

5. Find the mean, median, and mode for each set of data.

   a) 5, 5, 6, 7, 7

   b) 60, 65, 75, 80, 80, 60

   c) 5, 63, 71, 68, 73

   d) 52.5, 54.8, 61.3, 44.7, 22.1, 34.6

   e) 83, 188, 191, 177, 182, 186, 199

   f) 6.2, 66.1, 57.5, 49.4, 47.9, 63.3

6. A student was asked to record the time she spent on the bus to school each day for one month. The times, in minutes, are shown below. The day she spent 90 min getting to school was the day the bus had a flat tire.

14	20	14	14	19
20	14	19	90	17
22	20	14	14	20
15	14	21	14	20

   a) Why do you think the trip does not take the same time each day?

   b) Find the mean, median, and mode times.

   c) Which measurement best represents a typical bus trip? Explain your reasoning.

7. The manager of a local courier company wishes to find the average mass of packages the company delivers. She can then select the most appropriate type of delivery vehicle. A random survey of 24 packages yields the following masses, in kilograms.

200.0	0.1	3.0	20.0,	0.3	0.5
0.4	2.0	0.1	200.0	0.1	5.0
3.0	4.0	250.0	3.0	0.1	300.0
50.0	2.0	70.0	70.0	0.1	0.1

   a) Find the mean, median, and mode masses.

   b) Which measurement best represents a typical package? Explain your reasoning.

Work together

8. One measure of central tendency for a set of data is 100. There are 7 numbers in the set. What might the numbers in the set be? Write an example for each measure of central tendency. Describe how you choose the numbers in each set.

9. A typical piano keyboard has a length of about 120 cm. Use the mean hand span in your group. Calculate the approximate number of hand spans required to span such a keyboard.

10. Draw a large polygon on a piece of paper. Ask 10 students to estimate the perimeter of the polygon in centimetres without measuring it. Calculate the mean of the 10 estimates. Then measure the perimeter. Was the mean of the estimates close to the true perimeter?

11. a) Work in a group of 5 students. Measure the length of each person's shoe. Calculate the mean shoe length.
    b) Suppose 1000 people with this shoe length stood heel-to-toe. How far would the line stretch?

12. Take a stride. Hold it while your partner measures the length of your stride from the heel of your back foot to the heel of your front foot. Combine your answers with one other pair of students. Find the mean stride length. Use this length to estimate how many strides your group would take in walking a 1-km race.

13. In each case, which average is more appropriate? Explain your answer.
    a) To determine whether you are taller than the average student your age, would you want to know the mean or the median height of students your age?
    b) To determine whether you earn more or less for babysitting than the average student your age, would you calculate the mean or median wage per hour for a group of your classmates?
    c) To estimate the total value of tickets sold to the 38 000 fans at the baseball game, would you want to know the mean ticket price or the median ticket price?

14. A small advertising agency has 5 employees. The manager earns $120 000 per year, the sales representative earns $60 000 per year, the graphic artist earns $40 000 per year, and the receptionist and administrative assistant each earn $18 000 per year.
    a) Suppose you want to make the average salary look as attractive as possible to a new employee. Which measure of central tendency would you quote?
    b) Suppose you want to make the company look as though it does not pay its employees well. Which measure of central tendency would you quote?

15. A quality control inspector randomly selects boxes of cereal from the shipping department. She measures their masses. On one day she selects 20 boxes and finds that 15 have a mass of 400 g each. The masses of the remaining boxes are 390 g, 380 g, 390 g, 390 g, and 380 g.
    a) Choose the correct expression from the list below. Use it to find the mean mass.
       i) $(400 + 390 + 380) \div 3$
       ii) $(400 \times 15 + 390 \times 3 + 380 \times 2) \div 20$
       iii) $(390 + 380 + 390 + 390 + 380) \div 5$
    b) For the shipment of cereal to be acceptable, the mean mass must be at least 395 g. Is this shipment acceptable?

16. Some people bought jeans at a department store and paid $49.95 per pair. After several weeks, the store had a sale and sold the remaining stock for $39.99 per pair. What extra information do we need before we can compute the mean selling price per pair?

17. a) Write a set of 5 numbers with a mean of 20.
    b) Write a set of 5 numbers with a mean of 10 and a median of 12.
    c) Write a set of 6 numbers with a mean of 10 and a median of 12.
    d) Write a set of 5 numbers with a mean of 30 and a mode of 25.

18. The six members of Amira's family share a laser printer. During a three-month period, they printed a total of 4236 pages.
   a) What was the mean number of pages printed per month?
   b) What was the mean number of pages printed per person?
   c) What was the mean number of pages printed per month per person?

On your own

19. The table shows the number of tins collected each day for the one-week food drive in Ms. Evird's class.

Day	Number of tins
Monday	28
Tuesday	35
Wednesday	22
Thursday	31
Friday	46

What was the mean number of tins collected per day during that week?

20. According to Statistics Canada, in 1990, the average annual income of Canadian families was $51 342.
   a) Is this average the mean or the median?
   b) What was the average monthly income?

LATE DISK

21. Which average is included in a spreadsheet program on a computer: median or mean? To find out, start a new document in a spreadsheet program. Input some numbers in cells A1 to A5. In cell A6:
   • in ClarisWorks, type =Average(A1..A5)
   • in Microsoft Works, type =AVG(A1:A5)
   Look at the result. Which average is it?

22. An Asian elephant eats for about 18 h per day. It consumes about 70 000 kg of vegetation per year. What is the mean mass of vegetation that an Asian elephant eats per hour?

23. a) What does the table show?

Activity	Energy burned per hour (kilojoules)
Baseball	880
Basketball	1280
Racquetball	1800
Soccer	1640

   b) What is the mean energy burned per hour by these activities?
   c) Suppose each activity were done for 15 minutes. How much energy would be burned in one hour?
   d) Compare the answers to parts b and c. Explain a different way to find the mean energy burned per hour.

Extend your thinking

24. Suppose tennis is added to the list of activities in exercise 23. The mean energy burned per hour is then 1376 kJ. How much energy is burned per hour by playing tennis?

25. a) i) What is the mean of the whole numbers from 1 to 10 inclusive?
      ii) What is the median of these numbers?
   b) i) What is the mean of the whole numbers from 1 to 100 inclusive?
      ii) What is the median?
   c) In each of parts a and b, are the mean and median the same? Explain your answer.
   d) How does the mean of a set of numbers change if all the numbers are:
      i) increased by 7?   ii) doubled?

The Ideas

In your journal, write an example of data for which the mean is an appropriate measure of average, and an example of data for which the median is an appropriate measure of average.

4.5 *MEASURES OF DATA DISTRIBUTION*

Developing the Ideas

▶ ▶ *Through Instruction*

What is a typical age at which an actress wins an Academy Award for Best Actress? This table lists the names and ages of the winners of the Best Actress award from 1973 to 1991.

Year	Actress	Age	Movie
1973	Glenda Jackson	37	A Touch of Class
1974	Ellen Burstyn	42	Alice Doesn't Live Here Anymore
1975	Louise Fletcher	41	One Flew Over the Cuckoo's Nest
1976	Faye Dunaway	35	Network
1977	Diane Keaton	31	Annie Hall
1978	Jane Fonda	41	Coming Home
1979	Sally Field	33	Norma Rae
1980	Sissy Spacek	30	Coal Miner's Daughter
1981	Katharine Hepburn	74	On Golden Pond
1982	Meryl Streep	33	Sophie's Choice
1983	Shirley MacLaine	49	Terms of Endearment
1984	Sally Field	38	Places in the Heart
1985	Geraldine Page	61	Trip to Bountiful
1986	Marlee Matlin	21	Children of a Lesser God
1987	Cher	41	Moonstruck
1988	Jodie Foster	26	The Accused
1989	Jessica Tandy	80	Driving Miss Daisy
1990	Kathy Bates	42	Misery
1991	Jodie Foster	29	The Silence of the Lambs

We could calculate the mean, median, or mode age. The median and mean tell us the "middle" age. The mode tells us the most common age or ages. But none of these measures of central tendency tell us how close most of the data are to these ages.

In this section, you will learn about some measures that help us determine where the mean, median, and mode are in a set of data.

To see how the ages are distributed, we follow these steps to construct a *line plot*.

Step 1

Scan the ages to find the smallest and greatest numbers. These are called the *extremes*. In this example, the youngest actress to win was Marlee Matlin, at the age of 21. The oldest actress to win was Jessica Tandy, at the age of 80.

Step 2

Draw a number line. Mark on it all the ages between the two extreme values. For each age shown in the table, mark an X above that number on the number line. If an age appears more than once, mark an X for each time it occurs. The completed line plot is shown below.

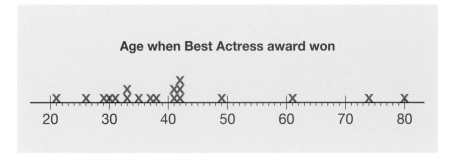

Age when Best Actress award won

We can see several things from the line plot.
* The difference between the greatest and smallest numbers in a set of data is called the *range*. The range tell us how spread out the data are. In this case, the range is 80 − 21 = 59 years.
* Most of the data are located between 29 and 42 on our plot. We say the data form a *cluster* between these ages. This means that, between 1973 and 1991, most winners of the Best Actress award were between the ages of 29 and 42.
* When we look beyond 42 on our line plot, we see there are large sections without any data points. For example, there are no Xs between 49 and 61. We say that there is a *gap* in the data between 49 and 61. This means that, between 1973 and 1991, none of the Best Actress winners were between 49 and 61 years old. There is another gap between 61 and 74.
* The age that occurs most often is 42, which has three Xs on our line plot. This is the mode age.

- There are 19 pieces of data. From previous work, we know the median is at the halfway point when the data are arranged in increasing order. In this case, the median is the tenth piece of data. Starting at the left, we count to the tenth X on the plot. The median age is 38 years.
- The number at the one-quarter point is called the *lower quartile*. Since there are 19 pieces of data, the one-quarter point is the fifth point. Starting at the left, count to the fifth X on the plot. The lower quartile is 31. This means that one quarter of the winners were 31 years of age or younger.
- The number at the three-quarters point is called the *upper quartile*. Since there are 19 pieces of data, the three-quarters point is the fifteenth point. Starting at the left, count to the fifteenth X on the plot. Alternatively, start at the right and count back 5 Xs. The upper quartile is 42. This means that one quarter of the winners were 42 years of age or older.

From previous work, we know that the mean age of the winners is the sum of all their ages divided by 19.

The sum of their ages is 784.

$$\frac{784}{19} \doteq 41.26$$

The mean age is about 41.3 years.

The line plot can help us decide whether the mean, median, or mode best represents the typical age.

The mean and the mode are 41.3 and 42. These ages are both near the end of the cluster. There are large gaps in the data after this cluster.

The median is 38. This is more toward the centre of the cluster.

So, the median best represents the typical age of a winner.

The range, extremes, gaps, clusters, and quartiles are all measures of data distribution.

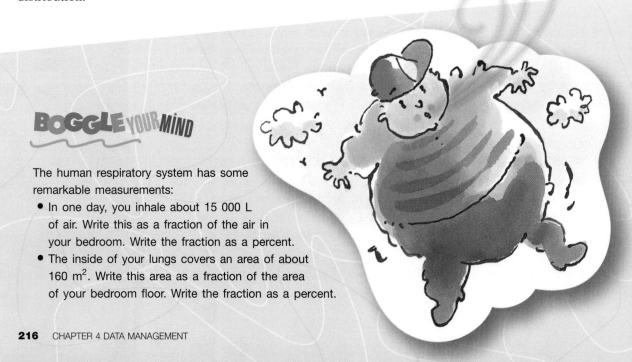

BOGGLE YOUR MIND

The human respiratory system has some remarkable measurements:
- In one day, you inhale about 15 000 L of air. Write this as a fraction of the air in your bedroom. Write the fraction as a percent.
- The inside of your lungs covers an area of about 160 m^2. Write this area as a fraction of the area of your bedroom floor. Write the fraction as a percent.

Working with Mathematics

Something to talk about

1. Explain each term.
   a) extremes   b) range
   c) lower quartile   d) upper quartile

2. How would the range and extremes of a set of data change if 3 is added to each number?

3. Suppose you make a line plot for a set of data. There is a large cluster of data in the centre of your plot, one very small number, and a few large numbers. What does this tell you about the data?

Practice

4. a) The lowest number in a data set is 9 and the highest is 20. Find the range.
   b) The lowest number in a data set is 12 and the range is 30. Find the highest number.
   c) The highest number in a data set is 52 and the range is 19. Find the lowest number.

5. Record the following set of numbers in order from least to greatest.
   25, 11, 18, 2, 30, 5, 7, 8, 10, 21, 25
   a) State the extremes and the range.
   b) If there is a mode, state it.
   c) Which number is the median? Circle that number.
   d) Look at the first five numbers. Draw a square around their median. This is the lower quartile.
   e) Look at the last five numbers. Draw a triangle around their median. This is the upper quartile.

6. Record the following set of numbers in order from least to greatest.
   55, 25, 21, 42, 30, 50, 48, 47, 36, 34, 23, 27
   a) State the extremes and the range.
   b) If there is a mode, state it.
   c) Calculate the median.
   d) Look at the first six numbers. Calculate their median. This is the lower quartile.
   e) Look at the last six numbers. Calculate their median. This is the upper quartile.

7. a) State the extremes and range for each set of data.
   b) If there is a mode, state it.
   c) Arrange each set in order from least to greatest. Determine the median, the lower quartile, and the upper quartile.
      i) 9, 12, 15, 21, 28, 30, 39, 40, 46
      ii) 63, 67, 70, 75, 81, 88, 89
      iii) 12, 14, 17, 23, 47, 65, 75, 87
      iv) 0.4, 1.9, 4.5, 5.6, 7.8, 9.6, 12.8, 15.7, 26.9, 30.8, 41.2, 50.0
      v) 106, 82, 46, 74, 61, 37, 93, 112
      vi) 88, 60, 100, 96, 66, 100, 80

Work together

8. Suppose you have 15 numbers arranged in order.
   a) Which will be the median?
   b) Which will be the lower quartile?
   c) Which will be the upper quartile?

9. Suppose you have 16 numbers arranged in order.
   a) How can you determine the median?
   b) How can you determine the lower quartile?
   c) How can you determine the upper quartile?

10. The table on page 206 shows the life spans of 32 notable western Canadian women.
    a) Find the extremes. Calculate the range.
    b) Make a line plot showing the life span distribution of these women.
    c) Use your line plot to find the lower quartile, the median, and the upper quartile.
    d) Describe any gaps or clusters you notice on your line plot. Are the data evenly distributed?
    e) What is the mode life span?

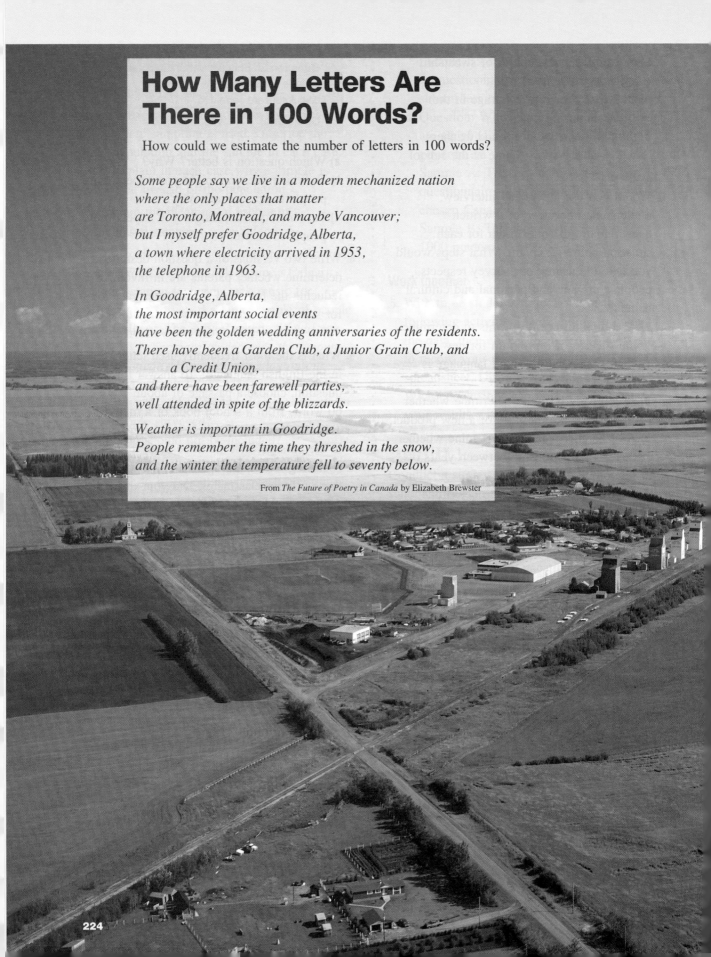

How Many Letters Are There in 100 Words?

How could we estimate the number of letters in 100 words?

Some people say we live in a modern mechanized nation
where the only places that matter
are Toronto, Montreal, and maybe Vancouver;
but I myself prefer Goodridge, Alberta,
a town where electricity arrived in 1953,
the telephone in 1963.

In Goodridge, Alberta,
the most important social events
have been the golden wedding anniversaries of the residents.
There have been a Garden Club, a Junior Grain Club, and
       a Credit Union,
and there have been farewell parties,
well attended in spite of the blizzards.

Weather is important in Goodridge.
People remember the time they threshed in the snow,
and the winter the temperature fell to seventy below.

From *The Future of Poetry in Canada* by Elizabeth Brewster

Understand the problem

- Where would we find 100 words?
- Would we use a mathematics text? A newspaper? A novel? A magazine?
- How do we know that the 100 words we choose are representative of the English language?
- What are we asked to find?

Think of a strategy

- Since we cannot count all the letters and words in everything that has ever been written, we must choose a sample passage.
- We need to find the mean numbers of letters in a word.

Carry out the strategy

- Choose a sample passage. For example, consider the excerpt from the poem *The Future of Poetry in Canada* by Elizabeth Brewster, on the facing page.
- Count the number of 1-letter words, 2-letter words, and so on, up to 13-letter words. Draw a tally chart to record your results.
- Use the tally chart to find the total number of words in this passage.
- Use the tally chart to find the total number of letters in this passage.
- Calculate the mean number of letters per word.
- Estimate how many letters there would be in a passage of 100 words.

Look back

- Do you think your estimate of the number of letters in a passage of 100 words will be close to the number for a passage taken from a newspaper? Select an article from a newspaper. Count 100 words. Count the number of letters in these words. How close was your estimate?
- Do you think that the sample passage on the facing page was a good one for estimating the number of letters per word in all passages? Explain why or why not.
- About how many letters would you expect there to be in a passage of 1000 words?
- Many word processing programs have a Word Count option. This calculates and reports the numbers of words, letters, characters (including spaces and punctuation), paragraphs, and pages. Input the poem and use the word processing program to find the total numbers of words and letters.

Communicating the Ideas

In your journal, write a description of this problem and your solution. Include a comparison of the results with the poem and with the newspaper article you chose.

Reporting on Canada's Waste

An article titled, *Canadians Leaders in Garbage*, was published in the Toronto Star on July 10, 1994. The article presented three graphs like those below to show how Canada compared in 1991 with other nations in three categories of waste.

In this project, you will write a report to accompany these graphs. The four Activities are designed to help you write your report.

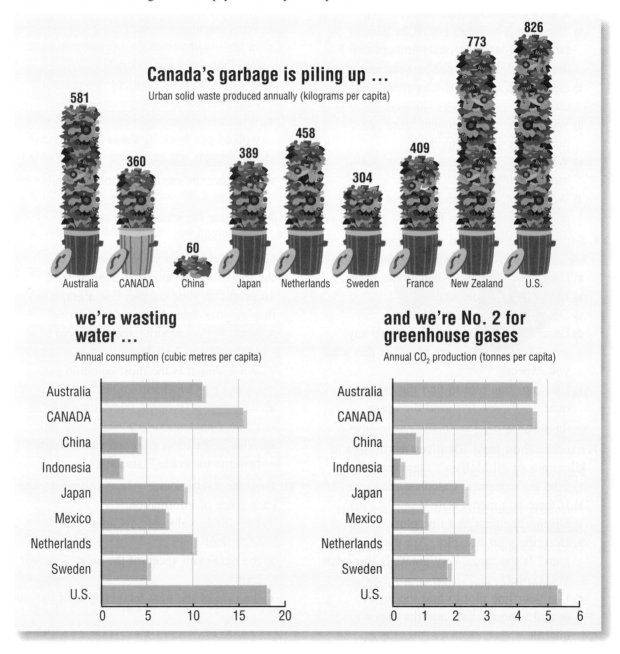

Canada's garbage is piling up ...
Urban solid waste produced annually (kilograms per capita)

581	360	60	389	458	304	409	773	826
Australia	CANADA	China	Japan	Netherlands	Sweden	France	New Zealand	U.S.

we're wasting water ...
Annual consumption (cubic metres per capita)

Australia, CANADA, China, Indonesia, Japan, Mexico, Netherlands, Sweden, U.S.

0   5   10   15   20

and we're No. 2 for greenhouse gases
Annual CO_2 production (tonnes per capita)

Australia, CANADA, China, Indonesia, Japan, Mexico, Netherlands, Sweden, U.S.

0   1   2   3   4   5   6

ACTIVITY 1

List the three categories of waste that are presented in the graphs.

Write several sentences to describe how each kind of waste threatens human survival.

ACTIVITY 2

Find the meaning of the expression *per capita*.

Find the population of Canada in 1991. Calculate the mass of solid waste produced by the Canadian population in that year.

Find the 1991 populations of Australia and the United States. Calculate the mass of solid waste produced by each country that year.

ACTIVITY 3

Use your populations from *Activity 2*. Calculate the total production of carbon dioxide (CO_2) in Canada, the United States, and Australia in 1991. What is the major cause of CO_2 production? Why do these countries produce so much carbon dioxide?

ACTIVITY 4

Suppose your family pays water bills. Use those water bills to determine how much water your family uses in a year. Suppose your family does not pay water bills. Use the information in the chart below to estimate the volume of water used in your home in a year. Divide the total by the number of people in your home. What is the annual water consumption per capita in your home? Express your answer in cubic metres. How does it compare to the data in the graph?

Activity	Typical water use (L)	Activity	Typical water use (L)
Toilet flush	15	Dish washing (for 3 meals)	40
Shower	20 L/min	Washing clothes	225
Bath	150	Washing car	400
Teeth brushing	10	Watering lawn	35 L/min

COMMUNICATING The Ideas

Prepare a report to accompany these graphs. Describe the ideas you investigated in *Activities 1* to *4*. Provide suggestions for reducing the amount of waste in each category.

INTEGERS

WHAT'S COMING UP?

DEPARTMENTS

5

239

Start With What You Know

ACTIVITY 1

Making Comparisons

Look at the photograph.

1. Write the difference between the number of basketball uniforms and the number of softball uniforms.

2. What other ways can the students be divided into two groups? For each way, write the difference between the numbers of the students in the two groups.

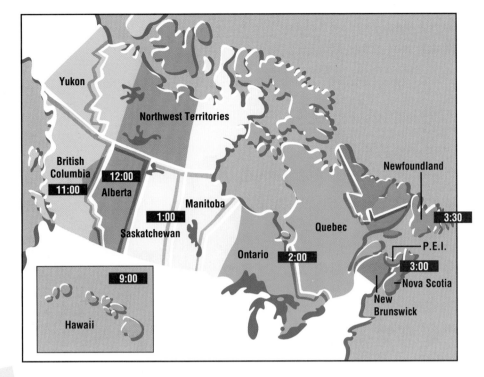

Nfld

Atlantic

Eastern

Central

Mountain

Pacific

ACTIVITY 2

Does Anyone Really Know What Time It Is?

1. On this map, locate the province or territory where you live. Suppose it is 12 noon in your province. What time is it in each of your neighbouring provinces or territory?

2. Jane lives in New Brunswick and Becky lives in Manitoba.
  a) When the time on Jane's watch is 10 o'clock, what time is it on Becky's watch?
  b) i) Is the time on Jane's watch ahead or behind the time on Becky's watch?
  ii) How many minutes ahead or behind is it?

3. Suppose you live in the Central Time Zone. Describe the time difference in minutes between the Central Time Zone and each zone listed.
  a) the Pacific Time Zone
  b) the Atlantic Time Zone
  c) the Newfoundland Time Zone

4. a) When it is 8:00 a.m. in the Mountain Time Zone, what time is it in Hawaii?
  b) What is this time difference in minutes?

5. Ask 10 of your classmates which city in Canada they would like to visit. For each city, calculate the time difference between it and where you currently live. Compared to where you live now:
  a) which city is furthest ahead in time?
  b) which city is furthest behind in time?

5.1 *WHAT IS AN INTEGER?*

Developing the Ideas

▶ ▶ *Through Instruction*

Until now, when you subtracted numbers, you were only able to subtract a small number from a larger number. Using integers, you will now be able to subtract a large number from a smaller number.

The following examples should help you understand what an integer is.

In this photograph,
there are 5 girls and 3 boys.

To describe the difference between the number of boys and the number of girls, we say, "There are 2 fewer boys than girls."
We represent the difference between the number of boys and the number of girls by using the integer −2.

We say, "Negative two."

The number −2 is a *negative integer*.

Similarly, to describe the difference between the number of girls and the number of boys, we say, "There are 2 more girls than boys."
We represent the difference between the number of girls and the number of boys by using the integer +2.

We say, "Positive two."

The number +2 is a *positive integer*.

The order in which we describe the difference is important. When we compare the number of boys to the number of girls, there are *fewer* boys. The integer describing this difference is *negative*.

When we compare the number of girls to the number of boys, there are *more* girls. The integer describing this difference is *positive*.

In this photograph, there are 4 boys and 4 girls.

To describe the difference between the number of girls and the number of boys, we say, "There is no difference between the number of girls and the number of boys."

We represent this difference by using the integer 0. Similarly, there is no difference between the number of boys and the number of girls.

• • • • • • • • •

An integer is any one of the numbers
... −3, −2, −1, 0, +1, +2, +3, ...

▶ ▶ *Through Discussion*

We have 2 yellow tiles and 1 red tile. As before, the order in which the tiles are compared is important. We shall consider the difference between the number of yellow tiles and the number of red tiles. There is 1 more yellow tile than red tile. Using an integer, we represent this difference as +1.

1. For each picture below, describe the difference between the number of yellow tiles and the number of red tiles: **i)** in words   **ii)** as an integer

a)   b)    c)

d)    e)

12. Each measurement below is recorded as an integer. With which number is it compared?
   a) The elevation of Mount Logan is +5951 m.
   b) The coldest permanently inhabited place is a village in Siberia. In 1933, the temperature reached −68°C.
   c) The elevation of Death Valley is −86 m.

13. Express each difference using an integer.
   a) After a night of baby-sitting, you have $24 more on Saturday than you had on Friday.
   b) After lending your brother $5 on Wednesday, you have $5 less than you had on Tuesday.
   c) If you deposit $110 into your bank account on Friday, you would have $110 more in the account than you had on Thursday.
   d) In the 1993 Classic golf tournament, Dawn Coe-Jones' score was 10 strokes under par.
   e) The stock market crash in 1929 resulted in losses of about $50 billion from one day to the next.

On your own

14. According to Statistics Canada, the populations of 10 cities in Canada in 1991 were as shown in the next column.
   a) Write an expression to describe the difference between the population of each city and the population of Halifax.
   b) Use an integer to represent the difference between the population of each city and the population of Halifax.

c) Use an integer to represent the difference between Edmonton's population and the population of each other city.

City	Population
Vancouver	1 602 502
Edmonton	839 924
Regina	191 692
Winnipeg	652 354
Whitehorse	17 925
Yellowknife	15 179
Toronto	3 893 046
Montreal	3 127 242
Saint John	124 981
Halifax	320 501
Charlottetown	15 396
St. John's	171 859

Extend your thinking

15. a) Suppose you have 10 yellow tiles. How many red tiles would you need to model a difference of +2 between the number of yellow tiles and the number of red tiles?
   b) Suppose you have 100 yellow tiles. How many red tiles would you need to model a difference of +2 between the number of yellow tiles and the number of red tiles?
   c) Suppose you have n yellow tiles. How many red tiles would you need to model a difference of +2 between the number of yellow tiles and the number of red tiles?
   d) Suppose you have n yellow tiles. How many red tiles would you need to model a difference of −5 between the number of yellow tiles and the number of red tiles?

COMMUNICATING

The Ideas

In your journal, write an integer that describes the difference between 4 yellow tiles and 2 red tiles. Describe how the integer would change if it were written to describe the difference between 2 yellow tiles and 4 red tiles.

Comparing Provincial Populations

The spreadsheet below contains data from the *Canadian Agriculture* database on the data disk. It shows the population of each province in 1971.

MPLATE DISK

	A	B	C
1		Population	Compare with
2		in 1971	Saskatchewan
3	Alberta	1627900	
4	British Columbia	2184600	
5	Manitoba	988200	
6	New Brunswick	634600	
7	Newfoundland	522100	
8	Nova Scotia	789000	
9	Ontario	7703100	
10	Prince Edward Island	111600	
11	Quebec	6027800	
12	Saskatchewan	926200	

1. Start a new document in a spreadsheet program. Input the data above.
   In cell C3, type the formula =B3–926200
   Copy this formula down to cell C12.
   a) Why are some of the integers in column C positive and others negative?
   b) What do the integers in column C represent?

2. Here is the population data from the data disk, for 1991.

Alberta	2 521 600	Nova Scotia	901 000
British Columbia	3 212 100	Ontario	9 917 300
Manitoba	1 094 400	Prince Edward Island	131 200
New Brunswick	727 600	Quebec	6 847 400
Newfoundland	575 700	Saskatchewan	994 200

Input these data in the correct rows in column E. In column F, input formulas to show the difference between each other province's 1991 population and the population of Saskatchewan.
   a) Which provinces' populations are closer to Saskatchewan in 1991 than in 1971?
   b) Which provinces are further away in population?
   c) Which provinces are growing faster than Saskatchewan?

Representing Integers

1. Suppose there are 5 chairs at a table and 3 people at the table. Write an integer that represents the difference between the number of people and the number of chairs.

2. Suppose there are 6 chairs and 4 people at the table. Write an integer that represents the difference between the number of people and the number of chairs.

3. Suppose there are 2 chairs and no people at the table. Write an integer that represents the difference between the number of people and the number of chairs.

In each case above, the same integer represents the difference between the number of people and the number of chairs.

4. Suppose 2 people are sitting at a table with 4 chairs.
   a) Write an integer that represents the difference between the number of people and the number of chairs.
   b) Four people join the group. A table with 4 chairs is added. There are now 6 people and 8 chairs. Write an integer that represents the difference between the number of people and the number of chairs.

Adding an equal number of chairs and people is the same as adding 0 because there is no difference between the number of chairs added and the number of people added.

5. Suppose 5 people left the group and 5 chairs were removed from the tables in exercise 4b. Write an integer that represents the difference between the number of people and the number of chairs remaining.

Subtracting an equal number of chairs and people is the same as subtracting 0 because there is no difference between the number of chairs removed and the number of people who left.

We can model the addition and subtraction of equal numbers of chairs and people by using red and yellow tiles.

7 yellow tiles and 4 red tiles model the integer +3.
Suppose we remove 3 yellow tiles and 3 red tiles.

4 yellow tiles and 1 red tile remain, which also model the integer +3.
Let's replace the tiles we removed, so we have 7 yellow tiles and 4 red tiles.
They again model +3.

Suppose we add 2 yellow tiles and 2 red tiles.

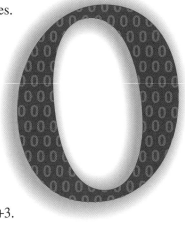

We now have 9 yellow tiles and 6 red tiles, which also model the integer +3.

- - - - - - - - -

Subtracting equal numbers of red and yellow tiles is the same as subtracting 0.
Adding equal numbers of red and yellow tiles is the same as adding 0.
That is, equal numbers of red and yellow tiles together model 0, because there is no difference between the numbers of red and yellow tiles.

6. Show why each statement is always true.
   a) Suppose the integer that represents the difference between the number of yellow tiles and the number of red tiles is +5. If we add equal numbers of red and yellow tiles, the difference is still +5.
   b) Suppose the integer that represents the difference between the number of yellow tiles and the number of red tiles is +2. If we subtract equal numbers of red and yellow tiles, the difference is still +2.

5.2 ORDERING INTEGERS

Developing the Ideas

▶▶ Through Discussion

1. Here is a thermometer that you would use in the science laboratory.

   a) Describe the numbers on this thermometer.

   b) i) How do we record a temperature below zero?

   ii) How do we record a temperature above zero?

When you use a thermometer you are measuring the difference between the temperature and 0.

A temperature of +10°C means the difference between the temperature and 0°C is 10.

A temperature of −10°C means the difference between the temperature and 0°C is −10.

2. In your notebook, draw a thermometer.

   The chart shows the highest temperature reached on one day in November in twelve Canadian cities.

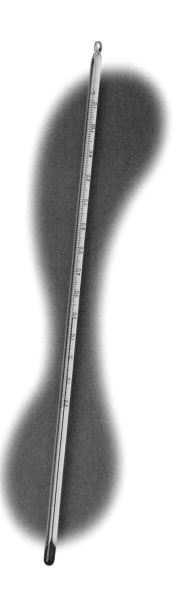

Vancouver	+7°C	Halifax	+1°C
Edmonton	−2°C	St. John's	−4°C
Saskatoon	−5°C	Charlottetown	0°C
Winnipeg	−10°C	Moncton	−1°C
Toronto	+2°C	Whitehorse	−15°C
Montreal	+5°C	Aklavik	−22°C

   a) Record these temperatures on the thermometer you drew.

   b) Write the temperatures in order from coldest to warmest.

   c) Write the cities in order, from the city with the coldest temperature to the city with the warmest temperature.

St. John's

Whitehorse

Winnipeg

ACTIVITY 1

Work with a partner. You will need grid paper.

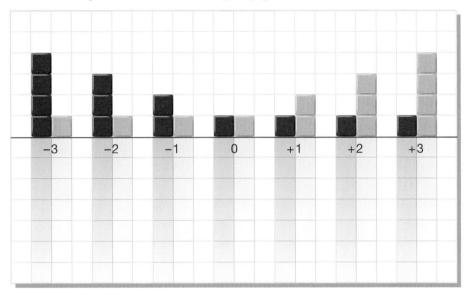

Look at the number line above. Copy the pattern on grid paper. Continue the pattern to the right until the difference between the number of yellow tiles and the number of red tiles is +10. Continue the pattern to the left until the difference between the number of yellow tiles and the number of red tiles is −10.

1. Record the integer that describes the difference between the number of yellow tiles and the number of red tiles in each pair of columns, from left to right.

2. As you look from left to right, what do you notice about the number of yellow tiles and the number of red tiles that each integer describes?

3. Using this number line, describe the numbers of yellow tiles and red tiles that are used to represent the integers +7 and −7.

4. Suppose the columns of yellow tiles and red tiles continued down the page forever.
   a) Could we tell how many red tiles there were in each red column?
   b) Could we tell how many yellow tiles there were in each yellow column?
   c) Do we need to know how many of each tile there are to be able to find their difference?

. . . .

The integers +7 and −7 are called *opposite* integers because +7 has seven more yellow tiles than red tiles and −7 has seven fewer yellow tiles than red tiles.

ACTIVITY 2

Work in a group of 4 students. You have a cup of
yellow chips and a cup of red chips.

1. Take turns. Close your eyes and remove some
   chips from each cup.

2. Write the difference between the number of
   yellow chips and the number of red chips as an
   integer. Record your group's four integers. Return
   the chips to the cups.

3. Repeat Steps 1 and 2. Your group should now
   have eight integers.

4. Look at the eight integers. How do you know
   which of two integers is greater or less than the
   other? Order your integers from least to greatest.
   Compare your group's ordering with another
   group's ordering.

▶▶ *Through Instruction*

To order integers, we can construct a number line.

```
 ┼──┼──┼──┼──┼──┼──┼──┼──┼──┼──┼──┼──┼──┼──┼──┼──┼──┼──┼──┼─
 −20 −18 −16 −14 −12 −10 −8  −6  −4  −2   0  +2  +4  +6  +8 +10 +12 +14 +16 +18 +20
```

Each positive integer on the line can be represented by that number of
yellow tiles and 0 red tiles. For example, +6 is 6 yellow tiles and 0 red
tiles because there are 6 more yellow tiles than red tiles.

Each negative integer on the line can be represented by that number of
red tiles and no yellow tiles. For example, −5 is 5 red tiles and 0 yellow
tiles because there are 5 fewer yellow tiles than red tiles.

Any integer that is to the right of another integer is greater than that integer.

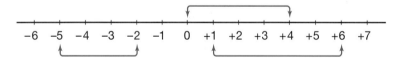

For example,
+6 is greater than +1; we write: +6 > +1
+4 is greater than 0; we write: +4 > 0
−2 is greater than −5: we write: −2 > −5

Any integer that is to the left of another integer is less than that integer.

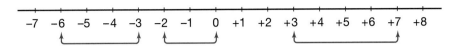

For example,
+3 is less than +7; we write: +3 < +7
−2 is less than 0; we write: −2 < 0
−6 is less than −3; we write: −6 < −3

When we read the numbers on the number line from left to right, they are in ascending order because they are increasing.

When we read the numbers on the number line from right to left, they are in descending order because they are decreasing.

▶ ▶ *Through a Guided Example*

Example ....

Arrange the following integers in ascending order.
+7, −6, +2, −3, +4, 0, +1, −2, +5

Solution

Draw a number line. Circle the integers listed above.

The integers are in ascending order when written from left to right.
−6, −3, −2, 0, +1, +2, +4, +5, +7

BOGGLE YOUR MIND

In 1994, a 70-year-old man, who had been collecting pennies for 65 years, decided it was time to cash them in. It took the man 4 days to cart the 40 garbage cans full of pennies to the bank. The pennies had a mass of 21 770 kg. The bank estimated that there were approximately 8 million pennies, worth $80 000!
Check this estimate. Find the mass of a 1¢ coin, then calculate the mass of 8 million coins.

Working with Mathematics

Something to talk about

1. Explain what opposite integers are. Suppose you mark an integer and its opposite on the number line. What can you say about the distances of these two integers from 0 on the number line?

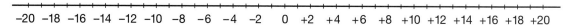

2. Why is zero important in the set of integers?

3. Explain what it means when integers are in ascending order.

4. Explain what it means when integers are in descending order.

5. Explain why +3 is greater than −2.

Practice

Use the number line in exercise 1 to complete exercises 6 to 10.

6. In each pair, which integer is greater than the other?
   a) −3 or +2   **b)** −2 or −5
   c) +3 or −1   **d)** 0 or −2

7. In each pair, which integer is less than the other?
   a) −4 or +1   **b)** −3 or −5
   c) +6 or −2   **d)** −5 or −9

8. −4 is less than +2. Is this statement true? Explain.

9. Write each set of integers in order from least to greatest.
   a) +4, −6, +1, +5, −7
   b) −13, −1, +10, 0, +3
   c) +4, +1, −15, +11, −5
   d) +7, 0, −12, +18, +4, −20
   e) +5, −17, +4, +17, −16

10. Write the integer that is:
   a) 3 units to the right of +6
   b) 7 units to the right of 0
   c) 10 units to the right of −3
   d) 6 units to the left of +1
   e) 7 units to the left of −4
   f) 9 units to the left of −1

Work together

11. Use red and yellow tiles to model four different integers. Have your partner record the integers in ascending order. Take turns using the tiles and ordering the integers.

12. The chart shows the mean January temperatures in a recent year.

City	January temperature (°C)
Calgary	−12
Halifax	−6
Regina	−18
Vancouver	+3
Winnipeg	−19

   a) Which cities had mean January temperatures lower than Halifax's mean temperature?
   b) Arrange the temperatures in order from highest to lowest.

13. Use the number line in exercise 1. Replace each ♦ with < or > to make a true statement.
   a) +5 ♦ +2   **b)** +7 ♦ 0
   c) −4 ♦ −1   **d)** −11 ♦ −14
   e) +8 ♦ −3   **f)** −15 ♦ +9
   g) +14 ♦ −14   **h)** −10 ♦ +10

14. Draw a number line to show the integers from −6 to +6. Write the integer that is:
   a) 4 greater than +1
   b) 5 less than 0
   c) 6 less than +3
   d) 7 greater than −5
   e) 8 greater than −4
   f) 2 less than −2

On your own

15. For each number line, name two integers that are greater than A, and two integers that are less than A.

a)
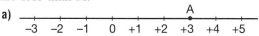
```
  ┼──┼──┼──┼──┼──┼──┼──┼──┼
 -3 -2 -1  0 +1 +2 +3 +4 +5
                     A
```

b)
```
  ┼──┼──┼──┼──┼──┼──┼──┼──┼
 -4 -3 -2 -1  0 +1 +2 +3 +4
        A
```

c)
```
  ┼──┼──┼──┼──┼──┼──┼──┼──┼
 -4 -3 -2 -1  0 +1 +2 +3 +4
  A
```

d)
```
  ┼──┼──┼──┼──┼──┼──┼──┼──┼
 -4 -3 -2 -1  0 +1 +2 +3 +4
                          A
```

16. The mean April temperatures of several cities are shown. Compared with Charlottetown, which city has a temperature:
a) 2° higher?
b) 6° higher?
c) 4° lower?
d) 9° lower?
e) 1° higher?
f) 13° lower?

```
°C
 8 ─ Toronto
 6
 4 ─ Edmonton
   ─ Winnipeg
 2 ─ Charlottetown
 0 ─ Whitehorse
 2 ─ Dawson
 4
 6
 8 ─ Yellowknife
10
12 ─ Churchill
```

17. For each set of numbers, describe the pattern that they appear to be forming. Write the next three integers.
a) +4, +2, 0, …
b) −5, −3, −1, …
c) +1, −2, +3, −4, …
d) +7, +4, +1, −2, …

18. Which integer is:
a) 3 less than −2?
b) 4 more than −1?
c) 6 more than −3?
d) 7 less than +2?
e) 5 less than +15?
f) 2 less than −8?

19. This diagram shows five pictures of "2 more stripes than dots." These pictures were drawn using a Draw program on a computer.

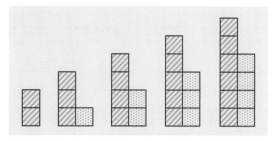

Start a new document in a Draw program.
a) Design your own "2 more stripes than dots" diagram with five pictures.
b) Draw a "5 more stripes than dots" diagram with five pictures in it.
c) By combining any picture from the "2 more" and any picture from the "5 more", show that together they make "7 more stripes than dots."
d) Repeat part c with another combination of a picture from each diagram.
e) i) Draw a "4 more stripes than dots" diagram with five pictures.
   ii) Draw a "1 fewer stripe than dots" diagram with five pictures.
   iii) Drag any two pictures together to show what "4 more" and "1 fewer" make.
   iv) Drag two different pictures to show the same result.

Extend your thinking

20. Which integer is:
a) 4 more than its opposite?
b) 6 less than its opposite?
c) equal to its opposite?

COMMUNICATING

The Ideas

Suppose you are given two different integers. In your journal, describe how you can tell which integer is greater.

The Coordinate Plane

You have worked with both horizontal and vertical number lines.

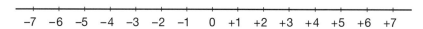

When a vertical number line and a horizontal number line intersect at right angles and at the point zero on each line, they form axes on a coordinate plane.

The number lines intersect at the *origin*, which we label zero. We label the horizontal axis with *x*, and the vertical axis with *y*.

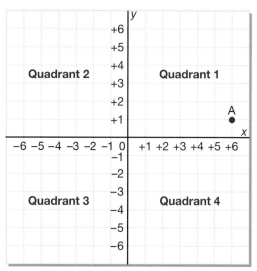

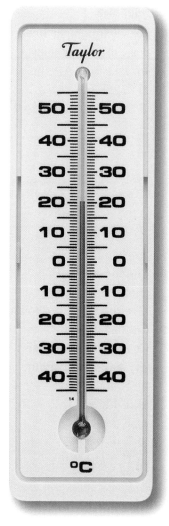

The axes divide the coordinate plane into four sections. These sections are known as *quadrants*. Any point in the plane can be described by its coordinates.

The coordinates of point A are (+6, +1). The first coordinate, or *x*-coordinate, is +6. It represents the distance and direction from zero along the horizontal number line. The second coordinate, or *y*-coordinate, is +1. It represents the distance and direction from zero along the vertical number line.

1. Suppose the first coordinate of a point is −3. What does this represent?

2. Suppose the second coordinate of a point is −5. What does this represent?

3. In which quadrant is each point located?
- **a)** P(+5, +1)
- **b)** Q(−2, +3)
- **c)** R(+4, −3)
- **d)** S(−1, −2)
- **e)** T(+3, −1)
- **f)** U(−5, +2)

4. a) In which quadrants do the coordinates of a point have the same sign?
   b) In which quadrants do the coordinates of a point have opposite signs?

5. Write the coordinates of any five points whose first coordinates are all −3. Then plot the points. What do these points have in common?

6. Write the coordinates of any five points whose second coordinates are all −5. Then plot the points. What do these points have in common?

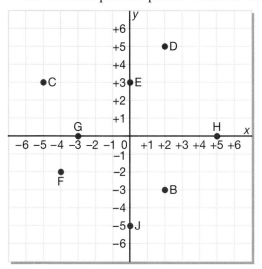

7. Name the coordinates for each point shown above.

8. Plot each set of points and join them in order to form a quadrilateral. Identify the quadrilateral.
   a) A(+1, +1), B(+1, +5), C(−3, +5), D(−3, +1)
   b) J(+1, −3), K(+5, +1), L(+8, +1), M(+4, −3)
   c) P(−3, 0), Q(−6, −2), R(+4, −4), S(+10, 0)

9. On grid paper, draw axes like those above. Connect the following points in order.
   (+2, +1), (+5, +5), (+1, +2), (0, +5), (−1, +2), (−5, +5), (−2, +1),
   (−5, 0), (−2, −1), (−5, −5), (−1, −2), (0, −5), (+1, −2), (+5, −5),
   (+2, −1), (+5, 0)
   What picture do you see?

10. Sit back-to-back with a partner. Take turns explaining how to plot (−3, +4) and (+5, 0). Take turns to choose the coordinates of a point and explain how to plot them.

11. Draw a design on coordinate axes. Ensure that each vertex is at the intersection of grid lines. List the coordinates of the vertices. Swap coordinates with a partner. Draw the design described by your partner's coordinates. Compare designs.

12. The points S(+2, +2) and T(−2, +2) are two vertices of a square. Plot these points on coordinate axes. What are the possible coordinates of the other two vertices?

5.3 *USING TILES TO ADD INTEGERS*

Developing the Ideas

▷ ▶ *Using Manipulatives*

In a previous section, you learned that an integer is used to represent the difference between the numbers of objects in two groups.

When one of the groups has 0 objects, the difference between the numbers is simply the number of objects in the other group.

For example, *3 yellow* tiles and 0 red tiles mean there are 3 more yellow tiles than red tiles. This is a model for the integer *+3*.

Also, 0 yellow tiles and *2 red* tiles mean there are 2 fewer yellow tiles than red tiles. This is a model for the integer *−2*.

We can use this idea to model an integer by using a number of tiles that represents the difference. For example, +3 can be modelled by 3 yellow tiles and 0 red tiles since the difference between the number of yellow tiles and the number of red tiles is +3.

Also, −2 is modelled by 0 yellow tiles and 2 red tiles since the difference between the number of yellow tiles and the number of red tiles is −2.

Each yellow tile models +1 because there is 1 more yellow tile than red tile.

Each red tile models −1 because there is 1 fewer yellow tile than red tile.

Using this model, we describe combining groups of tiles as *adding integers*.

Consider combining  and ■ ■ ■ ■ ■ ■ .

▨ ▨ ▨ ▨ models +4.

■ ■ ■ ■ ■ ■ models −6.

We can remove equal numbers of red and yellow tiles without changing the integer. That is, 1 yellow tile and 1 red tile together model 0; as do 4 yellow tiles and 4 red tiles together.

2 red tiles remain, which model −2.

We write: $(+4) + (−6) = −2$. This is the addition statement.

▶▶ Through an Activity

Combine each set of tiles. Write the result as an addition statement.

1. 3 yellow tiles and 5 red tiles

2. 2 red tiles and 6 yellow tiles

3. 4 yellow tiles and 7 yellow tiles

4. 2 red tiles and 8 red tiles

5. 4 red tiles and 4 yellow tiles

▶▶ Through a Guided Example

Example

Use yellow and red tiles to add each pair of integers.

a) $(+5) + (−4)$ **b)** $(+3) + (−7)$

c) $(−4) + (−3)$ **d)** $(+2) + (+1)$

Solution

a) $(+5) + (−4)$

represents
+1

$(+5) + (−4) = +1$

b) $(+3) + (−7)$

represents
−4

$(+3) + (−7) = −4$

c) $(−4) + (−3)$

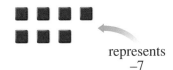

represents
−7

$(−4) + (−3) = −7$

d) $(+2) + (+1)$

represents
+3

$(+2) + (+1) = +3$

Working with Mathematics

Something to talk about

1. What is the result when the same numbers of yellow tiles and red tiles are added? Is this always true? Support your answer with examples.

Practice

2. Represent each set of tiles as an integer. Determine the sum of the integers and write the addition statement.
   a) 2 yellow tiles and 4 red tiles
   b) 4 yellow tiles and 1 red tile
   c) 1 red tile and 6 yellow tiles
   d) 2 yellow tiles and 7 red tiles
   e) 3 red tiles and 3 yellow tiles
   f) 5 red tiles and 3 yellow tiles
   g) 2 yellow tiles and 5 red tiles
   h) 1 red tile and 3 yellow tiles
   i) 1 yellow tile and 6 red tiles

3. Write the answers to exercise 2 in ascending order.

4. Use yellow and red tiles to represent each sum. Find the sum.
   a) $(-3) + (+3)$ b) $(+5) + (-5)$
   c) $(+6) + (-6)$ d) $(+2) + (-2)$
   e) $(-9) + (-4)$ f) $(+3) + (+9)$
   g) $(+5) + (-7)$ h) $(-1) + (+6)$
   i) $(-8) + (-3)$ j) $(-10) + (+6)$

Work together

5. Take turns. Create a group of red and yellow tiles. Have your partner write the addition statement that these tiles represent. Repeat this several times.

6. Write each addition expression and determine its sum.
   a) 12 yellow tiles and 10 red tiles
   b) 10 yellow tiles and 15 red tiles
   c) 8 yellow tiles and 13 red tiles
   d) 14 yellow tiles and 17 red tiles
   e) 20 yellow tiles and 11 red tiles
   f) 19 yellow tiles and 8 red tiles

7. Write each expression as an addition statement.
   a) Add −5 to +3.   b) Add +7 to +10.
   c) Add −2 to −9.   d) Add +4 to −11.
   e) Add −1 to +13.   f) Add +20 to −3.
   g) Add −3 to +2.   h) Add +8 to −3.
   i) Add +5 to −7.   j) Add −4 to −2.

8. Add.
   a) $(+5) + (-1)$ b) $(-3) + (-2)$
   c) $(-2) + (-4)$ d) $(-2) + (-7)$
   e) $(+4) + (-6)$ f) $(+2) + (-5)$
   g) $(+6) + (-1)$ h) $(-5) + (-6)$
   i) $(-1) + (+8)$ j) $(+3) + (+7)$
   k) $(-7) + (+3)$ l) $(-4) + (-5)$

9. Add.
   a) $(+1) + (-2) + (+4)$
   b) $(-3) + (+5) + (-7)$
   c) $(-2) + (-6) + (-1)$
   d) $(+5) + (+7) + (+2)$
   e) $(-1) + (+2) + (-4)$
   f) $(+3) + (-5) + (+7)$

On your own

10. Add.
   a) $(+3) + (+6)$ b) $(+5) + (+2)$
   c) $(+7) + (+3)$ d) $(+4) + (+6)$
   e) $(-5) + (-3)$ f) $(-3) + (-1)$
   g) $(-2) + (-7)$ h) $(-9) + (-9)$
   i) $(-9) + (+2)$ j) $(-21) + (+15)$

11. Add.
   a) $(+6) + (-4)$ b) $(+9) + (-2)$
   c) $(-2) + (+7)$ d) $(-1) + (+5)$
   e) $(+3) + (-8)$ f) $(+4) + (-7)$
   g) $(-6) + (+4)$ h) $(-2) + (+2)$
   i) $(-8) + (-2)$ j) $(-4) + (+13)$

12. Is each statement true or false? Justify your answer with examples.
   a) The result of adding two negative integers will always be a negative integer.
   b) The result of adding a negative integer and a positive integer will always be a negative integer.

c) The result of adding two positive integers will always be a positive integer.

d) The result of adding two opposite integers is always zero.

13. Add.

a) $(-3) + (-4) + (+5)$

b) $(+6) + (+8) + (+7)$

c) $(+6) + (-8) + (+7)$

d) $(+6) + (-8) + (-7)$

e) $(-6) + (-8) + (-7)$

f) $(-4) + (-10) + (+3)$

g) $(+5) + (-8) + (-5)$

h) $(+4) + (-6) + (+8)$

i) $(+3) + (-7) + (+5)$

14. Start a new document in a spreadsheet program.

In cell A1, type −8.
In cell A2, type =A1+1. Copy this formula down to cell A17.

TEMPLATE DISK

	A	B	C
1	-8		
2	=A1+1		
3			
4			

a) In cell B1, type =A1+4. Copy this formula down to cell B17. Look at the numbers in columns A and B. Explain what happens when a positive integer is added to an integer.

b) In cell C1, type =A1+(−4). Copy this formula down to cell C17. Look at the numbers in columns A and C. Explain what happens when a negative integer is added to an integer.

15. Add horizontally and vertically. Find the sum of the integers in each table in two different ways.

a)
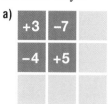

b)
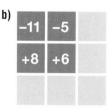

Extend your thinking

16. a) Does $(-32) + (+14) = (+14) + (-32)$? Justify your answer.

b) Does the result of part a hold when adding three or more integers?

c) In mathematics, this property is called the *commutative property*. Express the commutative property in your own words. Write another example of the commutative property.

17. Two integers have a sum of +5. One integer is +8. What is the other integer?

18. Two integers have a sum of −6. One integer is +3. What is the other integer?

The Ideas

When adding two integers, how can you predict when the result will be positive? How can you predict when the result will be negative? In your journal, write a rule for adding any two integers.

According to the estimates of Manitoba Agriculture, by the time a Canadian girl has reached age 18, she has cost her parents $151 649 in food, clothes, shelter, and all other expenses to raise her. A boy costs almost $2000 more. What is the mean annual cost for a girl and for a boy?

5.4 USING TILES TO SUBTRACT INTEGERS

Developing the Ideas

When we add integers, we combine groups of tiles. To subtract integers, we do the reverse; we remove tiles from a group of tiles.

▶ ▶ Using Manipulatives

We can use red and yellow tiles to model the subtraction of integers.

Model 1	Model 2
Consider 8 yellow tiles.	Consider 8 red tiles.

Model 1	Model 2
When we remove 3 tiles, we are subtracting +3.	When we remove 3 tiles, we are subtracting −3.

Model 1	Model 2
5 yellow tiles remain. We write: (+8) − (+3) = +5	5 red tiles remain. We write (−8) − (−3) = −5

Model 3

Suppose we reverse the process of Model 1, and attempt to take 8 yellow tiles from 3 yellow tiles.
We want to model this expression:
(+3) − (+8)

To be able to remove 8 yellow tiles, we need to put 5 more yellow tiles with the 3 yellow tiles.

Recall that we can add equal numbers of yellow and red tiles without changing the integer.

That is, 5 yellow tiles and 5 red tiles together represent 0. So, we put 5 yellow tiles and 5 red tiles with the 3 yellow tiles.

By adding 0, we haven't changed the integer that the yellow tiles represent. We can now remove the 8 yellow tiles.

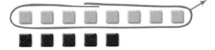

5 red tiles remain.

We write: (+3) − (+8) = −5

Model 4

What happens if we reverse the process of Model 2, and try to model this expression?
(−3) − (−8)

How can we take 8 red tiles from 3 red tiles?

To be able to remove 8 red tiles, we need to put 5 more red tiles with the 3 red tiles.

We know that 5 red tiles and 5 yellow tiles together represent 0. So, we put 5 red tiles and 5 yellow tiles with the 3 red tiles.

By adding 0, we haven't changed the integer that the red tiles represent.

We can now remove the 8 red tiles.

5 yellow tiles remain.

We write: (−3) − (−8) = +5

Model 5

How can we complete a sentence like this?
(+8) − (−3) =

How can we take 3 red tiles from 8 yellow tiles?

We know that 3 red tiles and 3 yellow tiles together represent 0. We add 3 red tiles and 3 yellow tiles to the 8 yellow tiles.

We can now remove the 3 red tiles.

11 yellow tiles remain.

We write: (+8) − (−3) = +11

▶ ▶ *Through an Activity*

Use red and yellow tiles to model each subtraction expression and its solution.

1. (+6) − (+2) =   **2.** (+2) − (+6) =   **3.** (−6) − (−2) =   **4.** (+6) − (−2) =

5. (+2) − (−6) =   **6.** (−2) − (−6) =   **7.** (−2) − (+6) =   **8.** (−6) − (+2) =

▶▶ Through Instruction

For each subtraction statement, let's consider a similar addition statement that gives the same answer.

Subtraction statement

$(+8) - (+3) = +5$

$(-8) - (-3) = -5$

$(+8) - (-3) = +11$

$(-8) - (+3) = -11$

Addition statement

$(+8) + (-3) = +5$

$(-8) + (+3) = -5$

$(+8) + (+3) = +11$

$(-8) + (-3) = -11$

In each case, the result of subtracting an integer is the same as adding its opposite. For example,

$(+8) - (\mathbf{+3}) = +5$

subtract +3

$(+8) + (\mathbf{-3}) = +5$

add −3

Think of our model of yellow and red tiles. These sentences illustrate that subtracting the tiles of one colour is the same as adding the tiles of the other colour. We can use this idea to subtract integers.

▶▶ Through a Guided Example

Example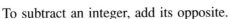

Subtract each pair of integers.

a) $(+5) - (-4)$

b) $(-3) - (+7)$

c) $(-4) - (-3)$

d) $(+2) - (+1)$

Solution

In each case, add the opposite.

a) $(+5) - (-4)$ becomes $(+5) + (+4) = +9$

b) $(-3) - (+7)$ becomes $(-3) + (-7) = -10$

c) $(-4) - (-3)$ becomes $(-4) + (+3) = -1$

d) $(+2) - (+1)$ becomes $(+2) + (-1) = +1$

· · · · · · · · · ·

To subtract an integer, add its opposite.

Working with Mathematics

Something to talk about

1. Describe the possible results in each case.
   a) Yellow tiles are subtracted from yellow tiles.
   b) Red tiles are subtracted from red tiles.
   c) Yellow tiles are subtracted from red tiles.
   d) Red tiles are subtracted from yellow tiles.

2. How is the subtraction of integers related to the addition of integers?

Practice

3. Use tiles to model the solution to each subtraction expression.
   a) 2 yellow tiles subtract 4 red tiles
   b) 2 red tiles subtract 5 yellow tiles
   c) 4 yellow tiles subtract 1 red tile
   d) 3 yellow tiles subtract 5 red tiles
   e) 6 yellow tiles subtract 1 red tile
   f) 7 red tiles subtract 4 red tiles
   g) 2 yellow tiles subtract 7 yellow tiles
   h) 3 yellow tiles subtract 1 yellow tile
   i) 3 red tiles subtract 3 red tiles
   j) 3 red tiles subtract 5 red tiles

4. Write the answers to exercise 3 in ascending order.

5. Use yellow and red tiles to represent each difference. Find the difference.
   a) $(-3) - (-1)$ b) $(-3) - (+1)$
   c) $(+4) - (+1)$ d) $(+4) - (-1)$
   e) $(-2) - (-3)$ f) $(-2) - (+3)$
   g) $(+3) - (+4)$ h) $(-3) - (+4)$
   i) $(+5) - (+2)$ j) $(-5) - (-2)$
   k) $(-4) - (-3)$ l) $(+4) - (-3)$

Work together

6. Use red and yellow tiles to model five different subtraction expressions. Have your partner do each subtraction and write the subtraction statement. Rewrite the subtraction statement as an addition statement.

7. Subtract. Check your answers with your partner.
   a) $(-5) - (+2)$ b) $(+7) - (+2)$
   c) $(+8) - (-6)$ d) $(+9) - (-3)$
   e) $(-9) - (-4)$ f) $(+3) - (-9)$
   g) $(+4) - (-4)$ h) $(-6) - (-7)$
   i) $(-4) - (-7)$ j) $(-1) - (+6)$
   k) $(+5) - (+3)$ l) $(-7) - (-5)$

8. Take turns with each statement. Give an example that makes it true. Give an example that makes it false.
   a) When a positive integer is subtracted from a positive integer, the result is a positive integer.
   b) When a negative integer is subtracted from a negative integer, the result is a negative integer.

9. Write each expression as a subtraction statement.
   a) Subtract +5 from −4.
   b) Subtract −8 from −7.
   c) Subtract +12 from +5.
   d) Subtract −6 from −8.
   e) Subtract +5 from 0.
   f) Subtract −3 from +3.
   g) Subtract +1 from +12.
   h) Subtract −4 from −4.

10. The graph shows the highest temperatures on a certain day in five cities.

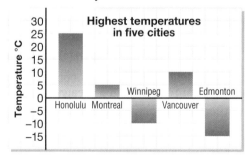

How much warmer was:
a) Winnipeg than Edmonton?
b) Honolulu than Winnipeg?
c) Montreal than Edmonton?

Cumulative Review

1. Use a ruler and a protractor. Construct a triangle for each set of measurements.
   a) angle 45° between sides 6 cm and 6 cm
   b) side 5.5 cm between angles 40° and 65°
   c) side 6 cm between angles 60° and 60°

2. Name the congruent triangles in each diagram. Explain how you know they are congruent. List pairs of corresponding equal sides and equal angles.

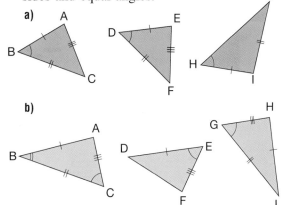

3. Express each fraction in simplest form.
   a) 8 eggs as a fraction of 1 dozen
   b) 75¢ as a fraction of $1
   c) 15 min as a fraction of 1 h
   d) 30 cm as a fraction of 1 m
   e) 6 h as a fraction of 1 day
   f) 6 slices of an 8-slice pizza
   g) 500 g as a fraction of 1 kg
   h) 3 months as a fraction of 1 year
   i) 200 m as a fraction of 1 km
   j) 4 pieces of a 12-piece cake

4. Express each fraction as a decimal. Round your answer to 2 decimal places, if necessary. Use your answers to write the fractions in order from least to greatest.
   a) $\frac{1}{10}$ b) $\frac{4}{5}$ c) $\frac{3}{20}$ d) $\frac{8}{25}$ e) $\frac{5}{6}$
   f) $\frac{7}{15}$ g) $\frac{29}{60}$ h) $\frac{21}{40}$ i) $\frac{11}{30}$ j) $\frac{4}{7}$

5. Write each fraction in exercise 4 as a percent.

6. Add or subtract.
   a) $\frac{3}{4} + \frac{1}{8}$ b) $\frac{2}{9} + \frac{2}{3}$ c) $\frac{3}{4} - \frac{1}{2}$
   d) $\frac{7}{12} - \frac{1}{3}$ e) $\frac{9}{10} + \frac{3}{5}$ f) $1 - \frac{2}{5}$

7. Write each fraction as a percent.
   a) $\frac{2}{5}$ b) $\frac{7}{10}$ c) $\frac{6}{6}$ d) $\frac{3}{4}$

8. Magda purchases 15 uniforms for her soccer team. Each uniform costs $32.95, not including taxes.
   a) How much would 15 uniforms cost, not including taxes?
   b) Use the PST rate for your province. Calculate the provincial sales tax (PST) and the goods and services tax (GST) on your answer to part a. What is the total cost?
   c) Show how the total cost would be written on a cheque.

9. A die numbered 1 to 6 is rolled.
   a) What is the probability of each event?
      i) a 6   ii) a 2 or a 5
      iii) an odd number
      iv) a number less than 4
      v) any number except 1
   b) Suppose the die is rolled 60 times. How many times would you expect each event in part a to occur?

10. The graph shows the mother tongues of residents of the Northwest Territories. The data were collected by Statistics Canada as part of the 1991 census. That year, the population of the Northwest Territories was 56 470. Calculate the number of people for whom each language, or group of languages, is the mother tongue.
    a) Aboriginal languages
    b) English
    c) French

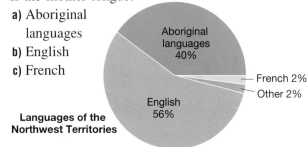

Languages of the Northwest Territories

11. The table lists the population of British Columbia each year from 1986 to 1994.
    a) Display the data on a graph. Explain how you decided which type of graph to draw.
    b) Describe any trends in the population. Can you think of reasons for these trends?
    c) Use your graph to predict the population of British Columbia in the year 2000.

Year	Population (thousands)
1986	3020
1987	3065
1988	3128
1989	3209
1990	3300
1991	3380
1992	3779
1993	3574
1994	3668

12. Find the mean, median, and mode for each set of data. Which measure of central tendency do you think best represents the data? Explain.
    a) The heights of 15 adults, in centimetres: 150, 170, 162, 180, 162, 198, 155, 173, 158, 166, 173, 166, 174, 186, 165
    b) The masses of 15 adults, in kilograms: 53, 88, 64, 75, 65, 48, 74, 64, 65, 99, 62, 92, 58, 65, 45
    c) The class marks on a science test, as percents: 84, 72, 65, 61, 58, 47, 67, 64, 93, 65, 81, 38, 73, 79, 54, 68, 73, 87, 63, 67, 77

13. One measure of central tendency for a set of data is 50. There are 7 numbers in the set. What might the numbers be? Write an example for each measure of central tendency. Describe how you chose the numbers in each set.

14. What integer does each set of red and yellow tiles represent?
    a) 2 yellow tiles and 4 red tiles
    b) 7 yellow tiles and 1 red tile
    c) 5 yellow tiles and 5 red tiles
    d) 3 yellow tiles and 4 red tiles
    e) 9 yellow tiles and 2 red tiles
    f) 1 yellow tile and 6 red tiles

15. State the opposite of each integer.
    a) −4   b) +5   c) +1   d) −100
    e) 0   f) +19   g) −26   h) +10

16. Add or subtract.
    a) $(-8) + (-10)$ b) $(+11) + (-5)$
    c) $(-16) + (-27)$ d) $(-12) + (+12)$
    e) $(+7) - (+12)$ f) $(-8) - (-9)$
    g) $(+17) - (-15)$ h) $(-25) - (+25)$

17. The table lists the daily maximum temperatures of 22 Canadian cities on November 9, 1995.

City	Temp. (C°)	City	Temp. (C°)
Calgary	−11	Saskatoon	−9
Charlottetown	15	St. John's	12
Edmonton	−11	Sudbury	−5
Fredericton	13	Thunder Bay	−5
Halifax	14	Timmins	−10
Moncton	14	Toronto	2
Montreal	2	Vancouver	14
Ottawa	3	Victoria	15
Quebec City	3	Whitehorse	−13
Regina	−9	Winnipeg	0
Saint John	13	Yellowknife	−13

    a) Find the extremes. Calculate the range.
    b) If there is a mode, state it.
    c) Display the data in a line plot.
    d) Describe your line plot. Are there any gaps or clusters? Is this what you expect?
    e) Use your line plot to find the median, the lower quartile, and the upper quartile.

18. Find the current daily maximum temperatures for some Canadian cities. Use the Internet or a daily newspaper. Find the extremes, the range, the median, the lower quartile, and the upper quartile for the data.

MEASUREMENT

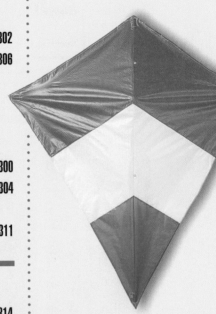

Mathematics Files

Quests

Minds on Math Project

Start With What You Know

1. Estimate, using an appropriate metric unit.

a) the height of the seat above the floor

b) the length of your thumb

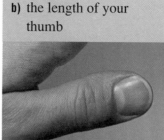

c) the height of the basket above the floor

d) the height of a parking meter

e) the height of a doorknob

f) your height

2. Find some things that are approximately 30 cm long.
   a) What is the longest object you can find that has a length less than 30 cm?
   b) What is the shortest object you can find that has a length greater than 30 cm?

3. Suppose the ball is rolled until it touches the wall. Will the other side of the ball be at A, B, or C?

A B C

4. Multiply mentally.

    a) 400×10 **b)** 30×2000 **c)** 600×5

    d) 700×300 **e)** 9×60 **f)** 5000×2

    g) $10 \times 10 \times 10$ **h)** $2 \times 2 \times 2$ **i)** $1 \times 1 \times 1$

5. Estimate each product.

    a) 403×11 **b)** 28×2012 **c)** 597×5.1

    d) 698×290 **e)** 8.8×62 **f)** 5007×1.9

    g) $11 \times 9 \times 9.8$ **h)** $1.9 \times 2.1 \times 1.8$ **i)** $0.9 \times 1.1 \times 0.8$

6. **a)** Would you suggest using a calculator for exercise 4? Explain.

    b) For exercise 5, which is faster, using a calculator or estimating?
       Why?

7. These are the side lengths of squares. Find the area of each square.

    a) 4 cm   **b)** 1.8 m   **c)** 90 cm   **d)** 700 mm

    e) 25 m   **f)** 60 cm   **g)** 1.2 m   **h)** 0.6 m

Work in a group or with a partner. You will need large sheets of paper, scissors, tape, and a metre stick.

8. Tape sheets of paper together to make a large square with sides 1 m. What is the area of this square?

9. Use your square metre to find something in your classroom that has an area of about one square metre.

    a) What is the largest thing you can find that has an area less than one square metre?

    b) What is the smallest thing you can find that has an area greater than one square metre?

Save your square metre for use later on page 308.

10. Choose the best estimate for each area.

    a) 40 cm² 400 cm² 4 m²   **b)** 1.5 cm² 150 cm² 1.5 m²   **c)** 18 cm² 180 cm² 1.8 m²

    d) 8 cm² 80 cm² 0.8 m²   **e)** 220 cm² 2.2 m² 22 m²   **f)** 1.8 m² 18 m² 180 m²

 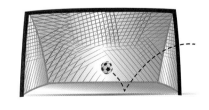

The Long and the Short of Canadian Mammals

The *Mammals of Canada* database on the data disk contains information on 160 Canadian mammals. Open the database and browse through a few records. Use the Find and Sort options in ClarisWorks or in Microsoft Works to complete these exercises.

DATA DISK

1. Name the fields in the database that contain measurements.
   a) What is being measured in each field?
   b) What is the unit of measurement?

All mammals, except the platypus, bear live young. The database gives the number of young a mammal has in 1 litter.

2. Find all the mammals in the seals and sea lions group.
   a) How many mammals are in this group?
   b) How many young do most of these mammals have in 1 litter?

3. a) How many mammals are in the insectivores group?
   b) How many young do most of these mammals have in 1 litter?
   c) How does this compare to the number of young by seals and sea lions?

4. Compare the longevity of the two groups of mammals in exercises 2 and 3. What do you notice?

For some mammals, the tail is critical to the animal's survival; for other mammals, a tail is less important. The database contains information on a mammal's average body length and average tail length. Average body length includes both the length of the body and length of the tail.

5. a) Choose 5 mammals from the cloven-hoofed group. Calculate the percent each mammal's tail length is of its body length.
   b) Choose 5 mammals from the rodent group. Calculate the percent each mammal's tail length is of its body length. How do your results compare with those in part a?
   c) For what purposes does a rodent use its tail? How does this explain why a rodent's tail forms a greater percent of its body length than does the tail of a cloven-hoofed mammal?

6. Which groups of mammals do not have a tail? Research to find out what these mammals have instead of a tail.

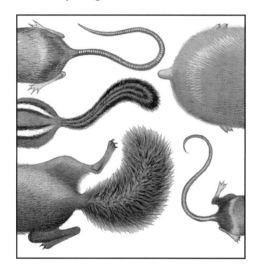

MEASUREMENT & DATA MANAGEMENT

Linking Ideas

6.1 *WORKING WITH PERIMETER AND AREA*

Developing the Ideas
▶ ▶ *Through Activities*

Work in a group to complete the two activities. Each group will need 36 square tiles.

Each tile has sides 1 unit long and an area of one square unit.

ACTIVITY 1

1. Make a rectangle using all 36 tiles.

   a) i) What is the length of the rectangle, in units?

      ii) What is the width of the rectangle?

   b) What is the area of the rectangle, in square units?

   c) Determine the perimeter of the rectangle.

   d) Record the length, width, area, and perimeter for use later.

2. a) i) Do you think you could make other shapes of rectangles using all 36 tiles?

      ii) Would they all have the same area as the rectangle you made?

     iii) Would they all have the same perimeter as the rectangle you made?

   b) Using all 36 tiles, make as many different rectangles as you can.
     Record the length, width, area, and perimeter of each rectangle in a table.

Rectangles with areas of 36 square units

Length (units)	Width (units)	Area (square units)	Perimeter (units)

   c) i) Do all the rectangles have the same area?

      ii) Do they all have the same perimeter?

   d) What kind of rectangle is the one that has the least perimeter?

3. Suppose you were planning a rectangular vegetable garden. You have enough topsoil to cover 36 m². Recall that m² is the symbol for square metres.

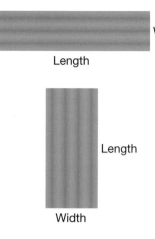

   a) What is the area of the vegetable garden you are planning?

   b) For each given length, determine the width and the perimeter of the garden.

     i) 6 m   **ii)** 9 m   **iii)** 12 m

     iv) 18 m   **v)** 24 m   **vi)** 36 m

   c) **i)** Do all the gardens have the same area?

     ii) Do they all have the same perimeter?

4. **a)** Record your results from exercise 3 in a table. Arrange the gardens so that their lengths are in order from least to greatest, as shown below.

Gardens with areas of 36 m²

Length (m)	Width (m)	Area (m²)	Perimeter (m)
6			
9			
12			
18			
24			
36			

   b) Find as many different patterns in the table as you can.

5. **a)** Use the data in the table to draw a graph of perimeter against length. Label the axes as shown.

   b) **i)** Is it possible for the lengths to be numbers between those in the table?

     ii) How could you show this on the graph?

     iii) How could you show this in the table?

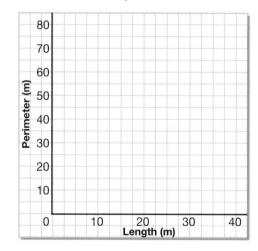

6. For rectangles with a fixed area:

   a) How does the width change as the length increases?

   b) How does the perimeter change as the length increases?

7. What are the dimensions of the vegetable garden that requires the least amount of fencing?

ACTIVITY 2

1. Using some of the tiles, make a rectangle that has a perimeter of 24 units.
   a) i) How many units are there in its length?
   ii) How many units are there in its width?
   b) Determine the area of the rectangle, in square units.
   c) Record the length, width, perimeter, and area for use later.

2. a) i) Do you think you could make other shapes of rectangles with perimeters of 24 units?
   ii) Would they all have the same area as the rectangle you made?
   b) Make as many different rectangles as you can that have a perimeter of 24 units. Record the length, width, area, and perimeter of each rectangle in a table.

Rectangles with perimeters of 24 units

Length (units)	Width (units)	Area (square units)	Perimeter (units)

   c) i) Do all the rectangles have the same perimeter?
   ii) Do they all have the same area?
   d) What kind of rectangle is the one that has the greatest area?

3. Suppose you were planning a rectangular flower garden. You have 24 m of fencing to go around the garden and you want to use it all.

Length

Width

Length

Width

   a) What is the perimeter of the flower garden you are planning?
   b) For each given length, determine the width and the area of the garden.
   i) 6 m   **ii)** 7 m   **iii)** 8 m   **iv)** 9 m   **v)** 10 m   **vi)** 11 m
   c) i) Do all the gardens have the same perimeter?
   ii) Do they all have the same area?

4. a) Record your results from exercise 3 in a table. Arrange the gardens so that their lengths are in order from least to greatest, as shown below.

Gardens with perimeters of 24 m

Length (m)	Width (m)	Area (m²)	Perimeter (m)
6			
7			
8			
9			
10			
11			

b) Find as many different patterns in the table as you can.

5. a) Use the data in the table to draw a graph of area against length. Label the axes as shown below.

b) **i)** Is it possible for the lengths to be numbers between those in the table?
ii) How could you show this on the graph?
iii) How could you show this in the table?

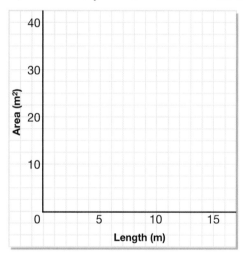

6. For rectangles with a fixed perimeter:
a) How does the width change as the length increases?
b) How does the area change as the length increases?

7. What are the dimensions of the garden with the greatest area?

Example ⋯⋯⋯⋯⋯⋯⋯⋯⋯⋯⋯⋯⋯⋯⋯⋯⋯⋯⋯⋯⋯⋯⋯⋯⋯⋯⋯⋯⋯

Sandeep is helping her mother decorate her bedroom. The room is rectangular, 4 m long and 3 m wide.

a) Carpeting for the floor costs $34.50 per square metre. About how much will it cost to carpet the floor?

b) Baseboard trim costs $4.79 per metre. It is installed along the edge of the floor. How much will the baseboard trim cost?

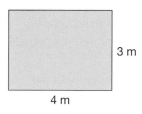

3 m

4 m

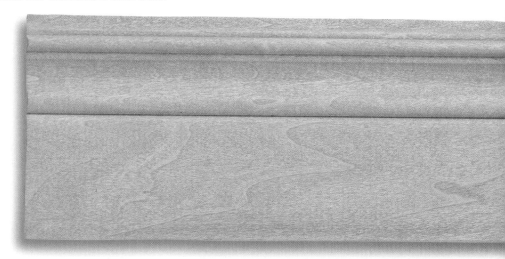

Solution

The room is rectangular.

a) Area = length × width
= 4 m × 3 m
= 12 m^2

The area of the floor is 12 m^2. Since carpet for one square metre costs $34.50, multiply by 12 to find the cost of the carpet.

Cost of carpet = 12 × $34.50
= $414

It will cost about $414 to carpet the floor.

Carpeting is usually cut from a large roll. Do you think there would be some waste that could not be used? How would this affect the answer to part a?

b) Perimeter = 2 × length + 2 × width
= 2 × 4 m + 2 × 3 m
= 8 m + 6 m
= 14 m

The perimeter of the floor is 14 m. Since one metre of baseboard trim costs $4.79, multiply by 14 to find the cost of the baseboard trim.

Cost of trim = 14 × $4.79
= $67.06

The baseboard trim will cost $67.06.

Working with Mathematics

Something to talk about

1. Use your table or your graph from *Activity 1* for this exercise.
   a) What is the perimeter of the vegetable garden that has an area of 36 m² and one side 3 m long?
   b) What are the dimensions of a vegetable garden that has an area of 36 m² and a perimeter of 26 m?
   c) Describe the vegetable garden that has the least perimeter.

2. Use your table or your graph from *Activity 2* for this exercise.
   a) What is the area of a flower garden with a perimeter 24 m and one side 4 m long?
   b) What are the dimensions of a flower garden that has a perimeter of 24 m and an area of 20 m²?
   c) Describe the flower garden that has the greatest area.

Practice

3. a) Find the length of a rectangle with area 15 cm² and width 3 cm.
   b) Find the length of a rectangle with width 8 cm and area 72 cm².
   c) Find the width of a rectangle with area 35 cm² and length 7 cm.
   d) Find the side length of a square with area 25 cm².
   e) Find the width of a square with area 64 cm².
   f) Find the length of a rectangle with width 7 cm and area 49 cm².

4. Determine the perimeter and area of each rectangle.
   a) length 5 m, width 7 m
   b) length 4.5 km, width 0.6 km
   c) length 3.8 cm, width 2.2 cm
   d) length 10.7 mm, width 3.1 mm

5. a) Find the length of a rectangle with width 3.8 cm and area 17.48 cm².
   b) Find the width of a rectangle with length 10.6 cm and area 25.44 cm².
   c) Find the length of a rectangle with width 100.8 km and area 20 301.12 km².
   d) Find the perimeter of a rectangle with length 18.9 cm and area 162.54 cm².

Work together

6. In *Activities 1* and *2*, you investigated rectangles made from tiles, and rectangular gardens.
   a) How are the investigations with the gardens the same as those with the tiles?
   b) How are the investigations different?

7. a) Determine the area and the perimeter of the green figure.

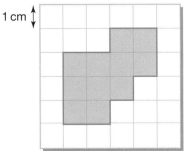

1 cm

   b) On a 4 by 4 grid, draw other figures on the grid lines that have the same perimeter as the green figure.
   c) What is the greatest area for a figure with this perimeter?
   d) What is the least area for a figure with this perimeter?

8. a) Determine the area and the perimeter of the yellow figure.

1 cm

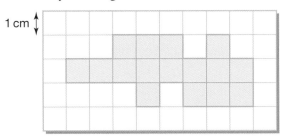

b) On 1-cm grid paper, draw other figures on the grid lines that have the same area as the yellow figure.

c) What is the greatest perimeter you can get for a figure with this area?

d) What is the least perimeter you can get for a figure with this area?

9. A rectangle and a square have one side in common. The area of the square is 64 cm². The perimeter of the rectangle is 40 cm.

a) Determine the perimeter of the square.

b) Determine the area of the rectangle.

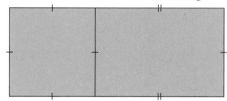

10. The world's first TV wristwatch was made by Seiko in Japan in 1982. It has a rectangular screen 3.0 cm long and 2.3 cm wide.

a) What is the perimeter of the screen?

b) What is the area of the screen, to the nearest square centimetre?

11. Kara is a landscape architect. She is designing a courtyard for a new building. The diagram below is a plan of the courtyard.

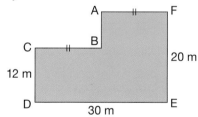

a) How does the diagram show that sides CB and AF have the same length?

b) All corners are 90°. What is the area of the courtyard?

c) Determine the area of the courtyard in a different way. How many ways can you find to determine the area of the courtyard?

12. The world's smallest TV set was made by Casio Computer Company in Japan in 1992. Its screen is 3.6 cm long and 2.7 cm wide.

a) What is the perimeter of the screen?

b) What is the area of the screen, to the nearest square centimetre?

13. Here is the floor plan of an apartment. Calculate the total cost of carpet and baseboard trim for each room listed.

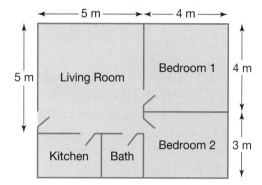

	Carpet cost per square metre	Baseboard cost per metre
Bedroom 1	$25.00	$3.25
Bedroom 2	$27.50	$3.65
Living room	$38.50	$4.35

14. Calculate the area and the perimeter of each figure.

a)

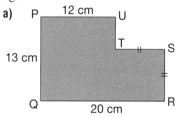

b)

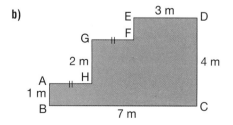

On your own

15. A tennis club has five tennis courts arranged as shown. What is the total area?

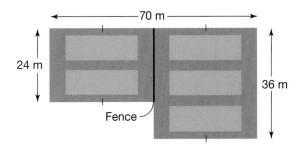

70 m

24 m

36 m

Fence

16. Suppose you were to paint your bedroom walls. You need to know their area to estimate how much paint to buy. You can use the spreadsheet below to calculate the area of the walls of your bedroom.

TEMPLATE DISK

Start a new document in a spreadsheet program and input the information in the table below.

If you use Microsoft Works, the formula in cell F5 is =SUM(B5:E5) and the formula in cell F10 is =SUM(B10:E10).

a) Measure the height and length of each wall. Enter the data in rows 3 and 4. What do the formulas in row 5 do?

b) Measure the height and length of every door and window. Enter the data in rows 8 and 9. What do the formulas in row 10 do?

c) What is the area of the walls in your bedroom?

d) One small can of paint covers 9 m². Each can costs $4.99. How much would it cost to paint the walls in your bedroom (excluding taxes)?

17. Calculate the area and the perimeter of each figure.

a)

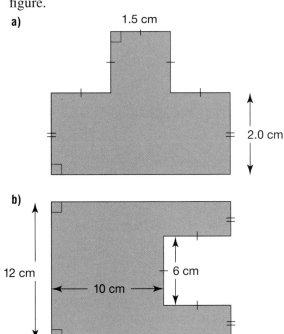

1.5 cm

2.0 cm

b)

12 cm

10 cm

6 cm

	A	B	C	D	E	F
1	Painting my bedroom walls					
2	Wall	North	West	South	East	Total
3	Height					
4	Length					
5	Area	=B3*B4	=C3*C4	=D3*D4	=E3*E4	=SUM(B5..E5)
6						
7	Door or window					
8	Height					
9	Length					
10	Area	=B8*B9	=C8*C9	=D8*D9	=E8*E9	=SUM(B10..E10)
11						
12	Paintable area	=B5-B10	=C5-C10	=D5-D10	=E5-E10	=F5-F10

18. The world's largest television screen was built for an exhibition near Tokyo, Japan, in 1985. It measured 45.6 m by 24.6 m.
   a) What is the perimeter of the screen?
   b) What is the area of the screen, to the nearest square metre?
   c) The screen was so large that it had to be assembled in sections. Each section was 7.6 m long and 4.1 m wide. How many sections were needed?

19. A large rectangular picture 1.5 m long and 1.2 m wide is framed with non-glare glass. One square metre of glass costs $36. One metre of frame costs $18.
   a) Calculate the cost of the glass.
   b) Calculate the cost of the frame.

20. A swimming pool and a wading pool are both surrounded by a walk 1 m wide.

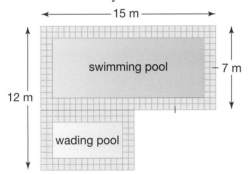

   a) Calculate the area of each pool.
   b) Calculate the area of the walk.

21. A rectangle is 16 cm long and 4 cm wide.
   a) A square has the same perimeter as this rectangle. What is the area of the square?
   b) Another square has the same area as this rectangle. What is the perimeter of the square?

Extend your thinking

22. From a sheet of 1-cm grid paper, cut out a 9 cm by 4 cm rectangle. Find a way to cut the rectangle into two pieces that can be rearranged to form a square.

23. Draw five different rectangles on grid paper.
   a) Divide the length of each rectangle by its width. Explain how you can use these quotients to order the five rectangles from the one most like a square to the one least like a square.
   b) Divide the width of each rectangle by its length. How can you use these quotients to order the five rectangles from the one most like a square to the one least like a square?

The Ideas

Suppose two rectangles both have a perimeter of 20 cm. Is it possible for them to have different areas? Write several sentences in your journal to convince someone that your answer is correct. Use examples to illustrate your explanation.

Suppose two rectangles both have an area of 16 cm². Is it possible for them to have different perimeters? Write several sentences in your journal to convince someone that your answer is correct. Use examples to illustrate your explanation.

6.2 AREA OF A PARALLELOGRAM

Developing the Ideas

▶ ▶ *Through an Activity*

Work with a partner or in a group. You will need 1-cm grid paper, a ruler, scissors, and some tape.

1. Use a ruler to draw these parallelograms on 1-cm grid paper.

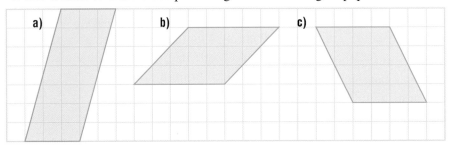

Any side of a parallelogram is the *base*. The perpendicular distance from the base to the opposite side is the *height*.

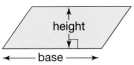
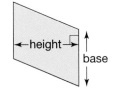

2. Carry out the following steps for each parallelogram.

Step 1	Step 2
Determine the area of the parallelogram by counting squares.	Identify the base and the height of the parallelogram.

Step 3	Step 4
Cut out the parallelogram. Then cut off a triangle along one of the grid lines.	Tape the two parts together to form a rectangle.

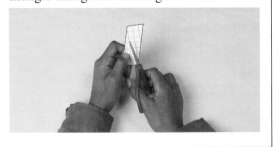

Step 5	Step 6
Compare the length and the width of the rectangle with the base and the height of the parallelogram you started with.	Determine the area of the rectangle. Compare it with the area of the parallelogram in Step 1.

3. If you know the base and the height of a parallelogram, how can you determine its area?

▶▶ *Through a Guided Example*

To determine the area of a parallelogram, multiply the base by the height.

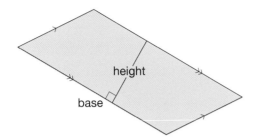

Area of parallelogram = base × height

Example ···············

Measure the base and the height of this parallelogram. Then calculate its area.

Solution ···············

One base is 3.6 cm and the height is 1.7 cm.

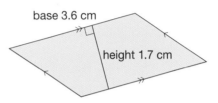

Area of parallelogram = base × height
= 3.6 cm × 1.7 cm
= 6.12 cm^2

The area of the parallelogram is about 6.1 cm^2.

 **BOGGLE** YOUR **MIND**

According to *The Guinness Book of Records*, the largest iceberg ever recorded was measured in the South Pacific Ocean in 1956. It was 335 km long and 97 km wide. What was the area of the iceberg as seen from the air?

Working with Mathematics

Something to talk about

1. **a)** Does the base of a parallelogram have to be at the bottom?
   b) Does the base of a parallelogram have to be horizontal?
   c) How are the base and the height of a parallelogram related?

2. In the solution of the *Example*, the longer side of the parallelogram was the base.
   a) Calculate the area of the parallelogram using the shorter side as the base.
   b) Is the area the same as in the solution of the *Example*? If it is not the same, can you explain why?

3. In the *Activity*, what other ways are there to cut each parallelogram into two parts to form a rectangle?

Practice

4. For each parallelogram, identify its base and its height. Then determine its area.

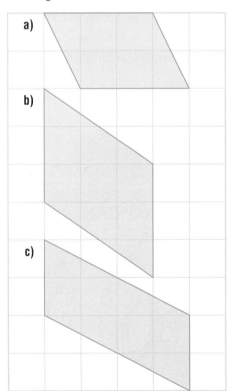

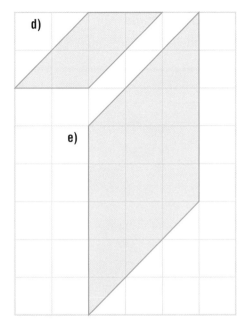

5. Determine the area of each parallelogram.
   a) One base is 3 m and the height is 2 m.
   b) The height is 4.2 cm and one base is 9 cm.
   c) One base is 20 cm and the height is 11 cm.
   d) The height is 1.6 m and one base is 2.5 m.

6. **a)** Find the area of a parallelogram with base 5 cm and height 7 cm.
   b) Find the base of a parallelogram with height 9 cm and area 63 cm^2.
   c) Find the height of a parallelogram with area 20 cm^2 and base 4 cm.
   d) Find the area of a parallelogram with base and height 8 cm.

Work together

7. On 1-cm grid paper, draw two different parallelograms with each area.
   a) 10 cm^2 **b)** 12 cm^2 **c)** 16 cm^2
   d) 18 cm^2 **e)** 24 cm^2 **f)** 28 cm^2

8. Two different parallelograms have areas of 36 cm^2.
   a) One parallelogram has a base of 9 cm. What is its height?
   b) The other parallelogram has a height of 6 cm. What is its base?

9. If you have access to a computer and *The Geometer's Sketchpad*® software, open the sketch entitled Parallelogram Area (Macintosh version) or paraarea.gsp (Windows version), which comes with the program. Follow the instructions on the screen. What do you see?

On your own

10. Calculate the area of one parking space.

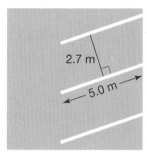

2.7 m

5.0 m

11. Measure the base and the height of each parallelogram. Then calculate its area to one decimal place.

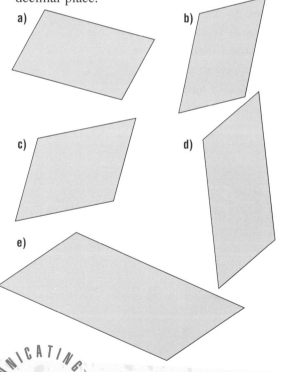

a)

b)

c)

d)

e)

12. Calculate the area of the coloured portion of each highway sign.

a)
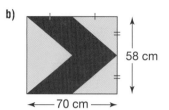
40 cm

80 cm

b)
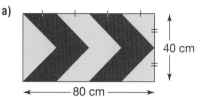
58 cm

70 cm

Extend your thinking

13. In the *Activity* on page 290, a triangle was cut from a parallelogram and the two parts were rearranged to form a rectangle. Do you think it is possible to do this for every parallelogram? If your answer is yes, explain why. If your answer is no, draw a parallelogram for which it is not possible to cut off a triangle and rearrange the two parts to form a rectangle.

14. By taking measurements from the diagram, calculate the area of the figure X.

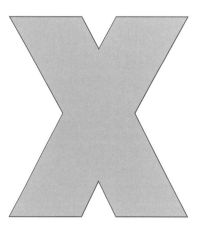

COMMUNICATING
The Ideas

In your journal, describe how to calculate the area of a parallelogram. Use an example to illustrate your explanation.

Triangle-Square Puzzle

Start a new document in a Draw program. In Microsoft Works, go to the Arrange menu and ensure that the Snap To Grid option is turned off. In ClarisWorks, go to the Options menu and choose Turn Autogrid off. Click on the Rectangle tool. Hold down the shift key. Make a large square. Use the Polygon tool. Make a triangle that has its vertices on three sides of the square. Fill the triangle with a pattern. Repeat the process until the square contains only filled triangles.

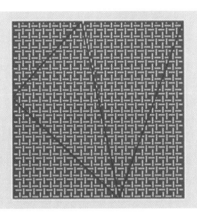  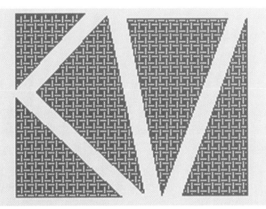

Carefully drag the triangles apart, ensuring that they do not change size or shape. Select each triangle in turn. In Microsoft Works, choose Rotate… from the Draw menu. In ClarisWorks, choose Rotate from the Arrange menu. Use a transformation to change the appearance of the triangle by rotating it and/or flipping it horizontally and/or vertically.

Print the document or give the computer file to another student. Ask her or him to make a square using your triangles. Tell the student if some or all of the triangles have been transformed.

What do you know about the area of the square?

6.3 AREA OF A TRIANGLE

Developing the Ideas

▷ ▷ *Through an Activity*

Work with a partner or in a group. You will need 1-cm grid paper,
a ruler, scissors, and some tape.

1. Use a ruler to draw these triangles on 1-cm grid paper.

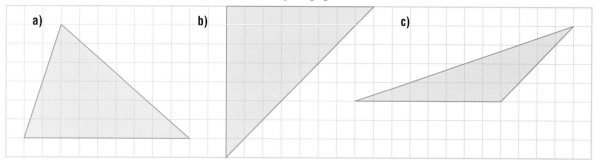

Any side of a triangle is the *base*. The perpendicular
distance from the base to the opposite vertex is the *height*.

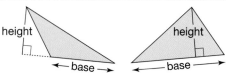

2. Carry out the following steps for each triangle.

Step 1
Determine the area of the triangle by counting squares.

Step 2
Identify the base and the height of the triangle.

Step 3
Use the ruler to draw another triangle that has the same size and shape as this triangle. Cut out the two triangles.

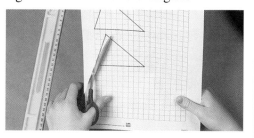

Step 4
Tape the two triangles together to form a parallelogram.

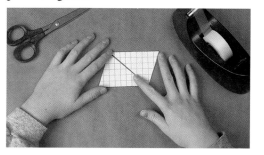

Step 5
How does the area of the triangle you started with compare with the area of the parallelogram?

Step 6
How could you use the area of the parallelogram to determine the area of the triangle?

3. If you know the base and the height of a triangle, how can you
determine its area?

To determine the area of a triangle, multiply the base by the height, and divide by 2.

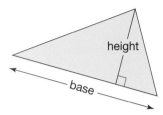

Area of triangle = $\dfrac{\text{base} \times \text{height}}{2}$

Example ....

What is the area of the triangular lot?

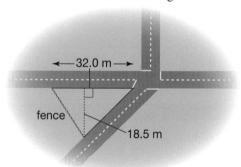

Solution ....

The base is 32.0 m and the height is 18.5 m.

$$\text{Area of triangle} = \frac{\text{base} \times \text{height}}{2}$$
$$= \frac{32.0 \text{ m} \times 18.5 \text{ m}}{2}$$
$$= \frac{592 \text{ m}^2}{2}$$
$$= 296 \text{ m}^2$$

The area of the triangular lot is 296 m².

This notice is printed on the back of a receipt for a parking fee. Assume that the notice is true. According to the Canadian Red Cross Society, how many people in Canada need blood in one year?

EVERY 20 SECONDS SOMEONE IN CANADA NEEDS BLOOD

20

The Canadian Red Cross Society

Please be a blood donor. For Mobile and Permanent Clinic Locations Call 974-9900

Working with Mathematics

Something to talk about

1. **a)** Does the base of a triangle have to be at the bottom? Give an example to support your answer.
   b) Does the base of a triangle have to be horizontal? Give an example to support your answer.
   c) How are the base and the height of a triangle related?

2. Does the height of a triangle always lie inside the triangle? Give an example to support your answer.

3. How could the *Activity* on page 295 be changed so that the area of the triangle is compared with the area of a rectangle?

4. Do the red and the white triangles in this photograph all have the same areas, or do they have different areas? Explain your answer.

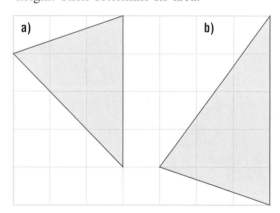

Practice

5. For each triangle, identify its base and its height. Then determine its area.

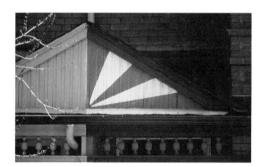

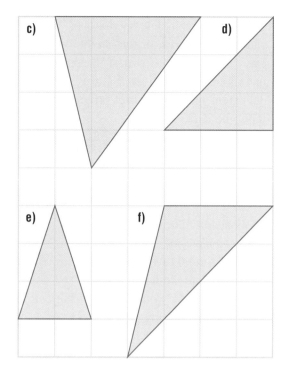

6. Determine the area of each triangle.
   a) Height is 4 m and base is 6 m.
   b) Base is 5 cm and height is 8 cm.
   c) Height is 12 cm and base is 10 cm.
   d) Base is 6.2 m and height is 3.5 m.
   e) Base is 10.2 cm and height is 8.3 cm.
   f) Base and height are 6.9 cm.

7. **a)** Find the base of a triangle with area 30.24 cm^2 and height 4.8 cm.
   b) Find the base of a triangle with height 7 cm and area 42 cm^2.
   c) Find the height of a triangle with area 90 cm^2 and base 9 cm.
   d) Find the height of a triangle with area 69.36 m^2 and base 6.8 m.
   e) Find the base of a triangle with height 14.6 cm and area 213.16 cm^2.
   f) Find the height of a triangle with base 15.9 m and area 354.57 m^2.

Work together

8. On 1-cm grid paper, draw two different triangles with each area.
   a) 5 cm^2 **b)** 8 cm^2 **c)** 10 cm^2
   d) 12 cm^2 **e)** 16 cm^2 **f)** 18 cm^2

TEMPLATE DISK

Here is an incomplete spreadsheet. It calculates the area, or the height, or the base of a triangle, if two of the three measurements are given. Start a new document in a spreadsheet program and input the data.

	A	B	C	D
1	Area of triangle is one-half base times height			
2				
3	Base		24	18
4	Height		17	16
5	Area		225	12

a) What formula would you input in cell B5 to calculate the area?

b) What formula would you input in cell C4 to calculate the height?

c) What formula would you input in cell D3 to calculate the base?

d) Input the formulas for parts a, b, and c. What number did you get in each cell?

   i) B5   ii) C4   iii) D3

10. Two different triangles have areas of 24 cm².
   a) One triangle has a base of 8 cm. What is its height?
   b) The other triangle has a height of 4 cm. What is its base?

11. If you have access to a computer and *The Geometer's Sketchpad* software, open the sketch entitled Triangle Area (Macintosh version) or triarea.gsp (Windows version), which comes with the program. Follow the instructions on the screen. What do you see?

12. Calculate the area of each figure PQRS.

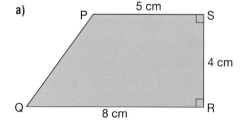
a)
P   5 cm   S
4 cm
Q   8 cm   R

b)
P   3.0 cm   Q
1.5 cm
S   1.0 cm   2.0 cm   R

On your own

13. Calculate the area of the larger sail on this sailboat. The sail approximates a right triangle.

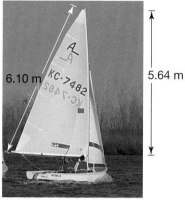
6.10 m   KC-7482   5.64 m

├— 2.97 m →┤

14. Calculate the area of the triangular wall (including the window).

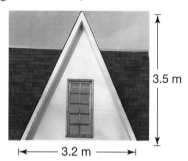
3.5 m

├—— 3.2 m ——→┤

15. Measure the base and the height of each triangle. Then calculate its area to one decimal place.

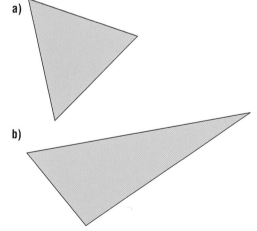
a)

b)

c) Check your answers with another student. In each case, did you use the same base and height?

16. Calculate the area of the kite.

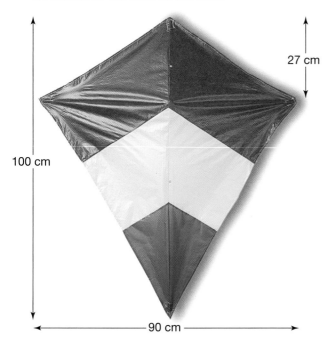

27 cm

100 cm

90 cm

17. Calculate the area of the red region of rectangle ABCD.

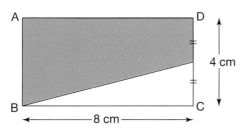

A   D

4 cm

B   C

8 cm

18. a) A square with perimeter 24 cm is cut into four pieces of equal area, which can be rearranged to form a triangle. The height of the triangle is 6 cm. How long is its base?

b) Draw the square in part a on cardboard and cut it out. Cut the square into the four pieces that form the triangle.

19. To find the area of a triangle, you multiply its base by its height and divide the result by 2. Which of the following products could you use instead to determine the area of a triangle? Explain your answers.

a) Multiply half the base by the height.

b) Multiply the height by half the base.

c) Multiply half the base by half the height.

d) Multiply 0.5 times the base times the height.

Extend your thinking

20. Determine the area of each pane of the leaded window.

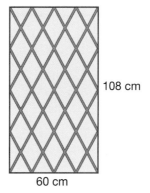

108 cm

60 cm

21. a) How many different pairs of bases and heights does a triangle have? Draw diagrams to illustrate your answer.

b) Is it possible for:

  i) only one of the heights to be outside the triangle?

  ii) all three of the heights to be outside the triangle?

c) Explain your answers to part b.

d) Will you always get the same area if you use any pair of base and height to calculate the area of a triangle? Explain your answer.

The Ideas

In your journal, describe how to calculate the area of a triangle.
Use an example to illustrate your explanation.

Do Triangles with Longer Sides Have Greater Areas than Triangles with Shorter Sides?

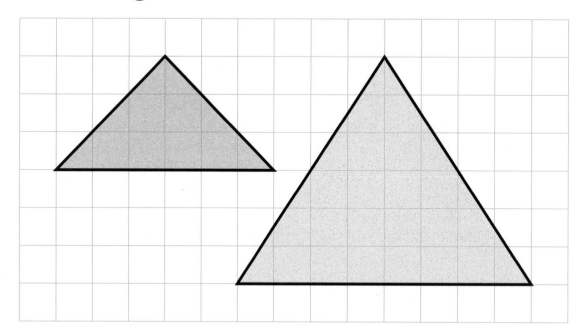

In this diagram, the sides of one triangle are all longer than the sides of the other triangle. Also, the area of the triangle with the longer sides is greater than the area of the triangle with the shorter sides.

Does this always happen? That is, suppose all three sides of one triangle are longer than all three sides of another triangle. Does this mean that the area of the triangle with the longer sides must be greater than the area of the triangle with the shorter sides?

Understand the problem

- How can you find the area of a triangle?
- What are you asked to do?

Think of strategies

- You could try changing the base and the height of the triangle with the longer sides.

- You could use a computer program that draws triangles and displays the lengths of their sides and their areas.

Carry out the strategies

- Try making the base of this triangle longer and the height smaller.
- Are the sides of this triangle longer than the sides of the other triangle?
- Is its area less than the area of the other triangle?

- Use *The Geometer's Sketchpad* to draw two triangles. One triangle should have shorter sides and a smaller area than the other triangle.
- Display the length of each side of the triangles.
- Display the area of each triangle. To do this, shift-click the three vertices and select Polygon Interior from the Construct menu. Click on the interior of the triangle, then choose Area from the Measure menu.
- Drag the vertices of the smaller triangle so that its sides become longer than those of the larger triangle. Can you do this so that the area of the smaller triangle remains less than the area of the larger triangle?

Look back

- Is it possible for the two triangles described above to have the same area?
- Suppose you make the base of a triangle longer and its height shorter. Could its area be larger, smaller, or the same as before?

Communicating the Ideas

In your journal, write a description of this problem and your solution. Include your answers to the questions in *Look back*.

Area of a Trapezoid

Work with a partner or in a group. You will need 1-cm grid paper, a ruler, scissors, and some tape.

All of these figures are trapezoids.

None of these figures is a trapezoid.

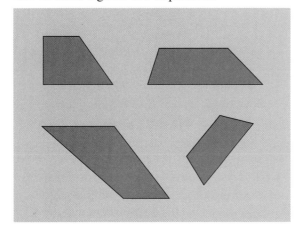
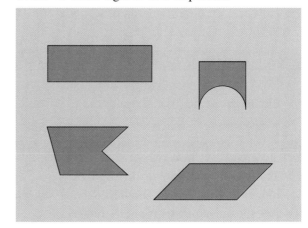

1. Which of these figures are trapezoids?

a)

b)

c)

d)

2. What is a trapezoid?

The distance between the two parallel sides of a trapezoid is called the *height*.

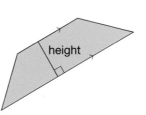

height

You already know how to determine the area of a triangle and the area of a parallelogram. You can use either of these figures to determine the area of a trapezoid. In the exercises that follow, you will use a trapezoid like this.

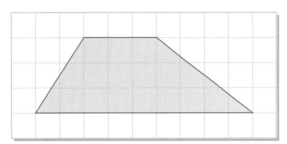

Using the area of a triangle

3. On 1-cm grid paper, use a ruler to draw a trapezoid like the one at the bottom of page 302. Then draw another trapezoid that is larger.

4. For each trapezoid:
a) Cut out the trapezoid.
b) Recall that you know how to calculate the area of a triangle. What could you do to the trapezoid so that you can calculate its area by calculating the areas of two triangles? Use your idea to calculate the area of the trapezoid.

5. Suppose you know the lengths of the two parallel sides of a trapezoid. Suppose you also know its height. How could you determine its area?

6. Calculate the area of each trapezoid.

a)
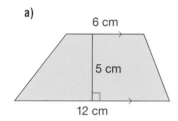
6 cm
5 cm
12 cm

b)
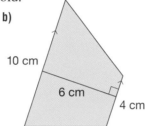
10 cm
6 cm
4 cm

c)
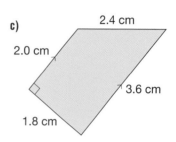
2.4 cm
2.0 cm
3.6 cm
1.8 cm

Using the area of a parallelogram

7. a) On 1-cm grid paper, use a ruler to draw two trapezoids like the one at the bottom of page 302.
b) Cut out the two trapezoids. Tape them together to form a parallelogram.
c) How does the area of one of the trapezoids compare with the area of the parallelogram?
d) Calculate the area of the parallelogram. What is the area of each trapezoid?

8. If you have access to a computer and *The Geometer's Sketchpad* software, open the sketch entitled Trapezoid Area (Macintosh version) or traparea.gsp (Windows version), which comes with the program. Follow the instructions on the screen. What do you see?

9. Repeat exercise 5. Can you find the area of a trapezoid a different way?

You should have discovered this formula.
Area of trapezoid = one-half the sum of the parallel sides × height
Use this formula to complete exercise 10.

10. Calculate the area of each trapezoid.

a)
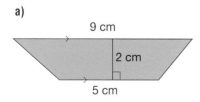
9 cm
2 cm
5 cm

b)
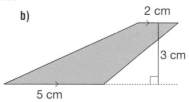
2 cm
3 cm
5 cm

c)
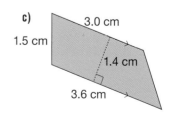
3.0 cm
1.5 cm
1.4 cm
3.6 cm

What Is the Area of a Newspaper?

If all the paper used to print today's 500 000 copies of The Star were stretched out, it would form a 1.65 m wide road that would reach from Toronto to Kamloops, 4120 km away. Instead of stretching it out, The Star keeps the paper in 900-kg rolls, ready for the presses.

The excerpt above appeared in *The Toronto Star*. Use your own newspaper. Calculate how far all the copies that were printed would reach if they were spread out on a road 1.65 m wide. Use the result to calculate the total area that could be covered by all the sheets of the newspaper printed on one day.

You will need a newspaper.

Understand the problem

- What are you asked to do?
- What information do you need about your newspaper? How will you get this information?

Think of a strategy

- Visualize arranging the sheets of your newspaper side by side in strips 1.65 m wide.
- You could calculate the number of strips from one newspaper and the total number of strips from all the newspapers printed.

Carry out the strategy

- Place some sheets side by side and measure the overall length.
  How many sheets do you need to form a strip 1.65 m long?
  How wide is this strip?
- Count the number of sheets in the newspaper. How many 1.65-m strips could you make with all the sheets?
- How many metres would these strips reach if they were placed side by side?
- Find out how many copies of the newspaper are printed each day. How many metres would they reach if all the sheets from all the copies were placed side by side in 1.65-m strips?
- How many kilometres is this?
- In this way, the sheets are arranged in a very long rectangle 1.65 m wide. Calculate the area of this rectangle.

Look back

- Check your result by calculating the total area of all the sheets in your newspaper in a different way.
- Is there enough information in the newspaper item above to check the claim that all the copies of *The Star* would reach from Toronto to Kamloops?
- Determine the mass of one newspaper. How many copies of this newspaper could be printed from a 900-kg roll of newsprint?

Communicating the Ideas

In your journal, write a description of this problem and your solution.

Regular Polygons

These road signs show polygons with all sides equal and all angles equal. Polygons like these are called *regular polygons*. Here are some examples of regular polygons.

| Equilateral triangle | Square | Regular pentagon | Regular hexagon | Regular octagon |

1. Identify at least two different polygons in each photograph. Are they regular polygons? Explain your answers.

a)

b)

c)

2. Two of Canada's coins have shapes that are almost regular polygons.
   a) Which coins are they?
   b) How many sides and angles does each coin appear to have?
   c) Why are the shapes "almost" regular polygons?

3. Sketch an example of each polygon.
   a) a hexagon with 6 equal angles that is not a regular hexagon
   b) a hexagon with 6 equal sides that is not a regular hexagon

4. Measure a side of each regular polygon preceding exercise 1. Then calculate its perimeter.

5. Suppose you know the number of sides in a regular polygon and the length of each side. How can you determine its perimeter?

6. Suppose a regular hexagon and a regular octagon have the same perimeter. Which one has the longer sides? Explain how you know.

7. Every regular polygon has a point called the *centre*. This point is the same distance from each side. For each regular polygon below, measure the length of a side and the distance from the centre to the side. Then calculate the area of the polygon.

a)   **b)**   **c)**   **d)**

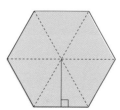
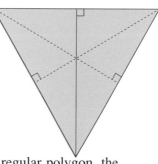
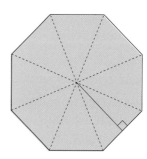

8. Suppose you know the number of sides in a regular polygon, the length of each side, and the distance from each side to the centre. How can you determine its area?

9. Calculate the perimeter of each regular polygon.
   a) a regular hexagon with side length 4.5 cm
   b) an equilateral triangle with side length 6.1 m
   c) a regular octagon with side length 7.9 km
   d) a regular hexagon with side length 0.6 cm
   e) a regular pentagon with side length 2 m
   f) a square with side length 8.9 km

6.4 WORKING WITH SQUARE UNITS

Developing the Ideas

▷ ▷ *Through an Activity*

Work in a group or with a partner. You will need many centimetre cubes and the square metre you made earlier.

1. **a)** Place some centimetre cubes along the edge of the square metre. How many would you need to go along the edge?
   b) Calculate how many centimetre cubes you would need to cover the square metre completely.

2. **a)** Express the length of each side of your square metre in centimetres.
   b) Calculate the area of your square metre in square centimetres.

▷ ▷ *Through Instruction*

You can express the area of your square in square metres or in square centimetres.

Area in square metres	*Area in square centimetres*

Area = 1 m × 1 m

    = 1 m^2

The area of the square is 1 m^2.

Area = 100 cm × 100 cm

    = 10 000 cm^2

The area of the square is 10 000 cm^2.

$$1 \text{ m}^2 = 10\ 000 \text{ cm}^2$$

Changing to a smaller unit

To change from metres to centimetres, multiply by 100.

To change from square metres to square centimetres, multiply by 100 × 100.

$$3.5 \text{ m}^2 = 3.5 \times 100 \times 100 \text{ cm}^2$$
$$= 3.5 \times 10\ 000 \text{ cm}^2$$
$$= 35\ 000 \text{ cm}^2$$

Changing to a larger unit

To change from centimetres to metres, divide by 100.

To change from square centimetres to square metres, divide by (100 × 100).

$$72\ 000 \text{ cm}^2 = \frac{72\ 000}{100 \times 100} \text{m}^2$$
$$= \frac{72\ 000}{10\ 000} \text{m}^2$$
$$= 7.2 \text{ m}^2$$

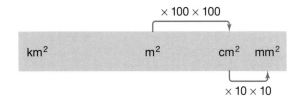

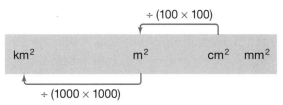

Working with Mathematics

Something to talk about

1. a) In the *Activity*, suppose you covered your square metre completely with centimetre cubes. How many would you need to do this?
b) Suppose you had one million centimetre cubes. What size square would they cover?

2. How many of your square metres would you need to cover one square kilometre?

3. Visualize what millimetre cubes would be like. Suppose you could cover your square metre completely with millimetre cubes. How many would you need to do this?

4. Visualize what a square centimetre looks like. Suppose you covered a square centimetre completely with millimetre cubes.
a) How many millimetre cubes would you need to go along each edge?
b) How many millimetre cubes would you need to cover the square centimetre completely?
c) How many square millimetres are there in one square centimetre?
d) How do you change from square centimetres to square millimetres?
e) How do you change from square millimetres to square centimetres?

5. How do you change from each unit to the other?
a) kilometres to metres
b) square kilometres to square metres
c) metres to kilometres
d) square metres to square kilometres

Practice

6. When you change from one unit to the other, will you have a larger or smaller number of units?
a) kilometres to metres
b) centimetres to metres
c) square metres to square centimetres

d) square centimetres to square millimetres
e) metres to kilometres
f) square kilometres to square metres
g) metres to centimetres
h) square centimetres to square metres
i) square metres to square kilometres
j) millimetres to centimetres

7. Change to centimetres.
a) 5 m   **b)** 800 m   **c)** 60 mm
d) 0.9 m   **e)** 45 m   **f)** 700 mm
g) 3 km   **h)** 6.5 mm   **i)** 48.2 m

8. Change to square centimetres.
a) 250 m^2 **b)** 25 m^2 **c)** 2.5 m^2
d) 0.25 m^2 **e)** 800 m^2 **f)** 60 mm^2
g) 0.9 m^2 **h)** 45 m^2 **i)** 700 mm^2

9. Change to metres.
a) 200 cm   **b)** 3 km   **c)** 8000 mm
d) 90 000 cm   **e)** 500 000 cm   **f)** 50 km
g) 80 mm   **h)** 25 km   **i)** 902 mm

10. Change to square metres.
a) $70\,000 \text{ cm}^2$ **b)** 7000 cm^2 **c)** 700 cm^2
d) 200 cm^2 **e)** 3 km^2 **f)** 8000 mm^2
g) $90\,000 \text{ cm}^2$ **h)** $500\,000 \text{ cm}^2$ **i)** 50 km^2

Work together

11. A square room has sides 10 m. Its floor is to be covered with tiles measuring 45 cm by 45 cm.
a) What is the area of the room?
b) What is the area of each tile?
c) Approximately how many tiles will be needed?

12. An area of land is measured in hectares. *One hectare* (1 ha) is the area covered by a square with sides 100 m. The diagram shows how 1 ha compares with the area of a baseball diamond and the infield.

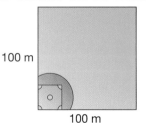

100 m

100 m

To see one hectare, you will need a piece of string 100 m long or a trundle wheel. Go outside and measure a square that has sides 100 m. Have four students stand at the vertices of the square. It has an area of 1 ha.

1 ha = 100 m × 100 m
     = 10 000 m^2

a) Change to square metres.

  i) 25 ha   **ii)** 250 ha

b) Change to hectares.

  i) 4600 m^2 **ii)** 460 m^2

13. a) Calculate the area, in square metres, of the part of a football field that is between the goal lines.

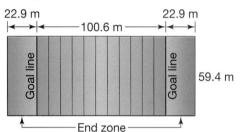

b) Express the answer to part a in hectares.

14. Draw each figure on 1-cm grid paper.

  a) a triangle with area 100 cm^2

  b) a trapezoid with area 50 cm^2

  c) a parallelogram with area 75 cm^2

On your own

15. Change 5 m^2 to each unit.

  a) square millimetres

  b) square centimetres

  c) square kilometres

16. Draw each figure on 0.5-cm grid paper.

  a) a triangle with area 50 cm^2

  b) a trapezoid with area 75 cm^2

  c) a parallelogram with area 100 cm^2

17. Change to square metres.

  a) 2.5 ha   **b)** 0.25 ha   **c)** 2500 ha

18. Change to hectares.

  a) 64 000 m^2 **b)** 640 000 m^2

19. Use the information in exercise 13.

  a) Calculate the area, in square metres, of the entire football field including the end zones.

  b) Express the answer to part a in hectares.

20. Read the article below. It was published in April, 1992.

IT'S ALIVE!
—and big as 23 football fields

A giant fungus found in a hardwood forest in northern Michigan may be the largest living organism on Earth, edging out the blue whale and the giant sequoia tree.

The fungus—a member of a species called *Armarillaria bulbosa* covers at least 15 hectares—about the size of 23 football fields—and has a mass of more than 10 tonnes and possibly as much as 100 tonnes, two University of Toronto biologists say.

It has been alive for 1500 years and has survived at least one major forest fire.

  a) Is the statement that 15 ha are about the size of 23 football fields correct?

  b) Does this refer to the entire football field or only the part between the goal lines?

Extend your thinking

21. The TransCanada highway is about 7820 km long. Its width varies. Assume a mean width of 7.2 m. Calculate the area of the pavement in each unit.

  a) square metres

  b) square kilometres

  c) hectares

The Ideas

In your journal, write several sentences to explain how square metres and square centimetres are related.

Review

1. a) Find the width of a rectangle with area 18 cm² and length 6 cm.

b) Find the length of a rectangle with area 20 cm² and width 4 cm.

c) Find the side length of a square with area 49 cm².

d) Find the length of a rectangle with area 81 cm² and width 9 cm.

2. Determine the perimeter and area of each rectangle.

a) length 15 cm, width 3 cm

b) length 1.5 km, width 0.4 km

c) length 26 m, width 23 m

d) length 10 mm, width 5 mm

e) length 8.5 cm, width 6.2 cm

f) length 2.4 m, width 1.5 m

3. Determine the area and the perimeter of this rectangle.

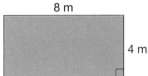

4. A square has the same perimeter as the rectangle in exercise 3.

a) Find the length of one side of the square.

b) Find the area of the square.

c) Compare the area of the square to the area of the rectangle.

d) Use the result of part c and the results of other exercises in this chapter. Make a general statement about the areas of rectangles and a square that have the same perimeter.

5. a) Find the area of this figure.

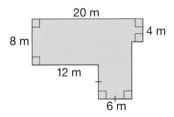

b) Find the perimeter of the figure.

6. a) Find the area of land for each crop.

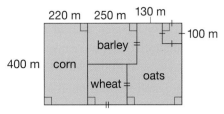

b) Find the length of the fence around the outside of the field.

c) Find the length of the fences that separate the crops.

d) Find the total length of all the fences.

7. A rectangle is 12 cm long and 3 cm wide.

a) A square has the same perimeter as the rectangle. Find the area of the square.

b) A square has the same area as the rectangle. Find the perimeter of the square.

8. The Giordano family are putting up a fence around their rectangular yard. It measures 25 m by 18 m.

a) What is the perimeter of the yard?

b) The charge for materials and labour is $22 per metre. How much will the fence cost?

9. Measure the sides of this figure.

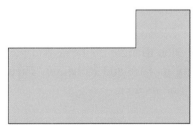

a) Calculate its perimeter.

b) Calculate its area.

10. A baseball diamond is a square with sides 27.4 m long. The bases are located at the vertices.

a) What is the area of the infield?

b) A home run occurs when a player runs a complete circuit of the bases without stopping. What distance must a player run to get a home run?

11. Decide whether each measurement involves perimeter or area.
    a) the length of a frame around a picture
    b) the amount of fertilizer needed for a field
    c) the distance run in one lap of a race track

12. Draw each parallelogram on 1-cm grid paper. Identify its base and its height. Then determine its area.

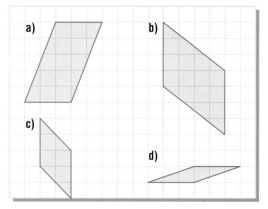

13. On 1-cm grid paper, draw four different parallelograms that each have an area of 36 cm².

14. Determine the area of each parallelogram.
    a) The base is 6 cm and the height is 9 cm.
    b) The height is 5.8 m and the base is 4.5 m.
    c) The base is 20.0 mm and the height is 16.2 mm.

15. Draw each triangle on 1-cm grid paper. Identify its base and its height. Then determine its area.

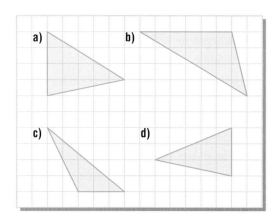

16. Calculate the area of each triangle.

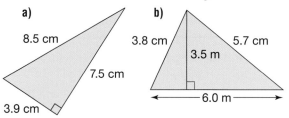

17. Determine the area of each triangle.
    a) The base is 6 cm and the height is 9 cm.
    b) The height is 5.8 m and the base is 4.5 m.
    c) The base is 20.0 mm and the height is 16.2 mm.

18. **a)** Find the base of a triangle with area 7.82 cm² and height 3.4 cm.
    b) Find the height of a triangle with area 20 m² and base 5 m.
    c) Find the base of a triangle with area 0.35 km² and height 1.4 km.
    d) Find the height of triangle with area 25.92 m² and base 8.1 m.
    e) Find the height of a triangle with area 9.6 cm² and base 4.8 cm.

19. On 1-cm grid paper, draw two different triangles with each area.
    a) 14 cm²   **b)** 20 cm²
    c) 6 cm²   **d)** 24 cm²

20. The area of each figure is given below. Create one set of dimensions so that each figure has the given area.
    a) A triangle has an area of 35 cm².
    b) A square has an area of 144 m².
    c) A rectangle has an area of 48 km².
    d) A parallelogram has an area of 56 m².
    e) A triangle has an area of 18 cm².
    f) A square has an area of 64 m².
    g) A rectangle has an area of 24 cm².
    h) A parallelogram has an area of 24 cm².

21. The dimensions of six flower beds are given.
   a) Which flower bed has the largest area?
   b) Which has the smallest?
   i) a rectangle with length 8.2 m and width 4.1 m
   ii) a square with side lengths 6.5 m
   iii) a triangle with base 9.4 m and height 7.8 m; the other two sides are 11.0 m and 8.4 m
   iv) a trapezoid with parallel sides 3.2 m, 6.6 m, and height 4.4 m; the other two sides are 4.8 m and 4.6 m long
   v) a parallelogram with height 5.9 m and base 6.4 m; the other two sides are 6.8 m long

22. a) What are the perimeters of the flower beds in exercise 21?
   b) Does the flower bed with the largest area have the longest perimeter?
   c) Does the flower bed with the smallest area have the shortest perimeter?

23. Find the area of each figure.

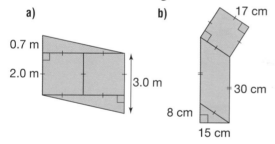

a)
b)

24. On 1-cm grid paper, draw three different triangles that each have an area of 36 cm².

25. Compare the triangles in exercise 24 to the parallelograms in exercise 13. Describe any patterns that you find.

26. When you change from one unit to the other, will you have more or fewer units?
   a) metres to centimetres
   b) square centimetres to square metres
   c) square metres to hectares
   d) hectares to square metres

27. Change to square centimetres.
   a) 12 m²   **b)** 250 mm²
   c) 0.6 m²   **d)** 10 mm²

28. Change to square metres.
   a) 15 000 cm²   **b)** 2 km²
   c) 14 ha   **d)** 300 000 mm²

29. Change to hectares.
   a) 2700 m²   **b)** 28 000 m²

30. Change 4 m² to each unit.
   a) square centimetres
   b) square kilometres
   c) square millimetres

31. The perimeter of this square is 80 cm.

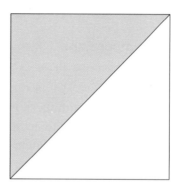

   a) Find the side length of the square.
   b) Find the area of the square.
   c) Find a height of the shaded triangle.
   d) Find a base of the shaded triangle.
   e) Find the area of the shaded triangle.
   f) Find the area of the unshaded triangle.
   g) Compare the area for part b with the areas for parts e and f.

32. Is each statement below true or false? Use diagrams to support your answer.
   a) To find the perimeter of a triangle, measure one side and multiply by 3.
   b) To find the perimeter of a parallelogram, all you need is the length of one side and the height.
   c) To find the perimeter of a square, measure one side and multiply by 4.

33. How many sides of each figure must you measure to find its perimeter?
   a) square   **b)** rectangle
   c) parallelogram   **d)** triangle
   e) trapezoid

Keeping Tabs on the Weather

Mark Twain once said, "Everyone talks about the weather but nobody ever does anything about it!" One thing you can do is make your own observations and compare them with predictions in newspapers and on television to see if the predictions were correct.

In the activities below, it is suggested that you collect the data for at least two weeks, and preferably longer. You will probably not be able to do all the activities at the same time.

ACTIVITY 1

Measuring Air Temperature

Use a thermometer to measure the air temperature at the same time each day.

Compare your temperatures with those predicted in newspapers or in TV weather forecasts. If your observed temperatures are different from the predicted temperatures, give reasons for the differences.

Summarize your observations and the predicted temperatures in a table. Draw a graph showing both your observations and the predicted temperatures.

ACTIVITY 2

Measuring Rainfall

Use a tin can to catch the rain that falls each day, and measure the depth of the water.

Compare your observations with those predicted in newspapers or in TV weather forecasts. Give reasons for any differences.

Summarize your observations and the predicted rainfall in a table.
Draw a graph showing both your observations and the predicted rainfall.

ACTIVITY 3

Measuring Snowfall

During the winter, use a tin can to catch the snow that falls each day, and measure its depth.

Compare your observations with those predicted in newspapers or in TV weather forecasts. Give reasons for any differences.

Summarize your observations and the predicted snowfall in a table. Draw a graph showing both your observations and the predicted snowfall.

Measuring snow more difficult than rain

The measurement of rainfall is fairly straightforward, but snowfall presents problems that make measurements "somewhat arbitrary", says a meteorologist at Pennsylvania State University.

For rain, the Penn State meteorology department uses a simple cylindrical tube to catch it. The amount that falls in a given period is poured into a smaller cylindrical tube that is carefully gradated and measured with something like a dipstick.

Many things can affect the depth of snow, especially wind and how frequently it is measured, both during and after a storm. Because the weight of the falling snow packs down what is underneath, it might compact from 10 inches to 8 inches as air holes fill in.

ACTIVITY 4

Measuring Relative Humidity

Find out what the term *relative humidity* means. Use a hygrometer to measure the relative humidity at the same time each day.

Ask your teacher for information to make a hygrometer like the one shown at the right.

Compare your observations with those predicted in newspapers or in TV weather forecasts. Summarize your observations and the predicted relative humidity in a table. Draw a graph showing both your observations and the predictions.

COMMUNICATING The Ideas

Prepare a report or a display to illustrate the results of your investigations. Include your tables and graphs in your report.

FROM ARITHMETIC TO ALGEBRA

WHAT'S COMING UP?

DEPARTMENTS

7

Linking Ideas

Quests

Minds on Math Project

Start With What You Know

Work with a partner or in a group.

ACTIVITY 1

In each list of numbers, the first four numbers and the tenth number of a pattern are given. Describe a pattern in each list of numbers. Determine the five missing numbers.

1. 3, 5, 7, 9, ■ , ■ , ■ , ■ , ■ , 21
2. 100, 110, 120, 130, ■ , ■ , ■ , ■ , ■ , 190
3. 33, 53, 73, 93, ■ , ■ , ■ , ■ , ■ , 213
4. 305, 310, 315, 320, ■ , ■ , ■ , ■ , ■ , 350
5. 56, 52, 48, 44, ■ , ■ , ■ , ■ , ■ , 20
6. 2, 4, 8, 16, ■ , ■ , ■ , ■ , ■ , 1024

ACTIVITY 2

1. On grid paper, draw a rectangle with area 72 cm^2.

2. Draw a different rectangle with area 72 cm^2.

3. How many different rectangles can you draw with area 72 cm^2? When the rectangles get too big to draw on the grid paper, draw them to scale.

4. Compare your rectangles with those of another group. Did you all draw the same rectangles?

5. On grid paper, draw a rectangle with perimeter 72 cm.

6. Draw a different rectangle with perimeter 72 cm.

7. How many different rectangles can you draw with perimeter 72 cm? When the rectangles get too big to draw on the grid paper, draw them to scale.

8. Compare your rectangles with those of another group. Did you all draw the same rectangles?

ACTIVITY 3

1. On grid paper, draw a 10 by 10 multiplication table. Label it as shown.

×	1	2	3	4	5	6	7	8	9	10
1										
2										
3										
4										
5										
6										
7										
8										
9										
10										

2. Complete the multiplication table.

3. Describe the pattern you see:
   a) as you read across each row from left to right
   b) as you read across each row from right to left
   c) as you read down each column
   d) as you read up each column

4. Add one row and one column to the table. Label them 11. Complete the row and column. Describe how you did this.

5. Look at the 7th row and the 7th column.
   a) What pattern do you see?
   b) How would you describe the numbers in the 7th row and the numbers in the 7th column?
   c) Is this description true for all other columns and rows of the same number?

6. **a)** Start at the upper left corner. Write the numbers along the diagonal to the bottom right corner.
   b) Describe the pattern in these numbers.
   c) Suppose the diagonal were to continue beyond the table. Write the next five numbers in the pattern.
   d) Explain how you decided which five numbers to write.

7. The diagonal in exercise 6 is called the *main diagonal* of the table. The table has many other diagonals. Where do you think these diagonals are? Write the numbers along some of these diagonals. Describe a pattern in the numbers in each diagonal.

7.1 EXTENDING GEOMETRIC PATTERNS

Developing the Ideas

In *Start With What You Know*, you worked with number patterns.

In the following activities and exercises, you will look at patterns of geometric figures. Try to find a rule that you can use to draw the next figure in each pattern.

▷▷ *Through Activities*

ACTIVITY 1

Work with a partner. You will need grid paper.

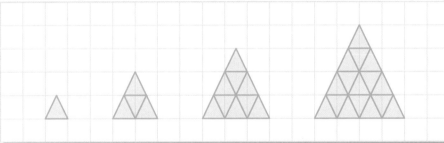

1. Look at the pattern of triangles above.
   a) How are the triangles in the pattern the same?
   b) How are the triangles in the pattern different?

2. On grid paper, draw the next three triangles in the pattern.

3. Copy and complete this table for the triangles you drew.

Length of base of large triangle (units)	1	2	3
Number of small triangles	1	4	9

4. **a)** What pattern do you see in the table?
   b) How is the number of small triangles needed to build the large triangle related to the length of the base of the large triangle?

5. Suppose this pattern continues. A large triangle has a base of 10 units. Use the pattern to determine how many small triangles there will be.

6. Suppose a large triangle has a base of 15 units. How many small triangles will there be?

In *Activity 1*, you should have found that the number of small triangles needed to build the large triangle is the length of the base of a triangle multiplied by itself.

For example, for the large triangle with base 3 units, the number of small triangles needed is $3 \times 3 = 9$.

There is a general way we can describe this relationship.

We represent the length of the base of a large triangle by n.

Then the number of small triangles needed is represented by $n \times n$.

We say that n is a variable, and $n \times n$ is an *algebraic expression*, or simply an *expression*.

• • • • • • • • •

A *variable* is a letter or symbol that is used to represent a quantity that can vary.

ACTIVITY 2

Work with a partner.

Each polygon has a side length of 3 cm.

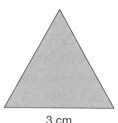

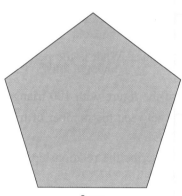

| 3 cm | 3 cm | 3 cm |

1. Look at the pattern of regular polygons. Name each polygon.
   a) How are the polygons in the pattern the same?
   b) How are the polygons in the pattern different?

2. The number of sides of a polygon is increasing by 1. Sketch the next three regular polygons in the pattern. Name each polygon you drew.

3. Count the number of sides of each polygon. Calculate the perimeter of each polygon. Copy and complete this table.

Number of sides	3	4	5	6	7	8
Perimeter (cm)						

4. a) Use the data in the table to draw a graph. On the horizontal axis, plot Number of sides; on the vertical axis, plot Perimeter.
   b) Describe the pattern in the table and graph.

5. Suppose this pattern continues. What is the perimeter of the polygon with 100 sides?

.....7.3 WHAT IS AN EQUATION?

Developing the Ideas

▶▶ *Through Activities*

ACTIVITY 1

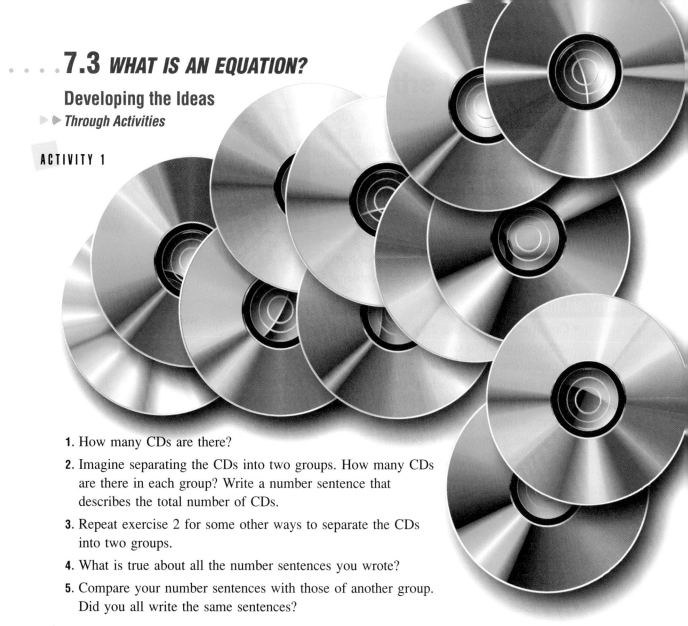

1. How many CDs are there?

2. Imagine separating the CDs into two groups. How many CDs are there in each group? Write a number sentence that describes the total number of CDs.

3. Repeat exercise 2 for some other ways to separate the CDs into two groups.

4. What is true about all the number sentences you wrote?

5. Compare your number sentences with those of another group. Did you all write the same sentences?

ACTIVITY 2

1. A number can be represented in many ways. The expression $18 + 8$ represents the number 26. It can also be represented by 2×13 and $30 - 4$.

   We say that $18 + 8$, 2×13, and $30 - 4$ are *equivalent expressions*, because they all represent the same number.

   a) Write each expression as a single number.

      i) $29 + 8$ **ii)** $47 - 5$ **iii)** 3×13 **iv)** $24 \div 2$

   b) For each expression in part a, write three equivalent expressions, using three different operations.

2. Compare your expressions with those of other students. For each expression given, did you all write the same equivalent expressions?

3. For any given expression, how many different equivalent expressions are there?

ACTIVITY 3

Here is a two-pan balance.

The pans balance because the total mass in the pan on the left is equal to the total mass in the pan on the right. We can write number sentences to describe the picture: $5 + 5 + 1 = 10 + 1$ or $2 \times 5 + 1 = 10 + 1$

1. Suppose you have many 1-g, 5-g, and 10-g masses. For each two-pan balance below:

   a) Determine some masses you could put in the empty pan so that it would balance.

   b) Write a number sentence to describe how the masses on the left side balance the masses on the right side.

   c) Write an equivalent expression, which is different from the masses in the picture, to describe the total mass in each pan.

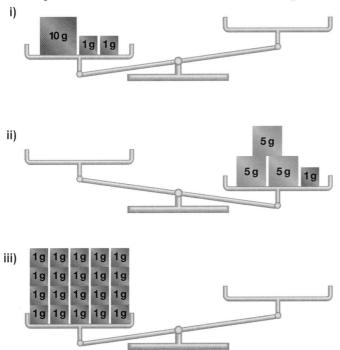

2. Compare your number sentences with those of your classmates.

   a) Did you all write the same sentence to describe each two-pan balance?

   b) If not, how many different sentences were there to describe each two-pan balance?

ACTIVITY 4

1. Compare the results of *Activities 1, 2,* and *3.* Describe the meaning of *equal.*

2. Describe the role of the = sign in a number sentence.

▷▷ *Through Instruction*

A mathematical statement that two expressions are equal is called an *equation.*

These are equations.

$5 \times 5 = 1 + 3 + 5 + 7 + 9$

$18 + 8 = 2 \times 13$

$\left. \begin{array}{l} 125 = 100 + 20 + 5 \\ 125 = 25 \times 5 \end{array} \right\}$ We can use these two equations to write another equation:

                                     $100 + 20 + 5 = 25 \times 5$

In *Activities 1, 2,* and *3,* you created an equation when you wrote that one expression represents the same number as another.

$18 + 8 = 13 + 13$ is an equation.

BOGGLEYOUR**MIND**

The number 4 can be expressed as a sum of natural numbers in several ways:

       $4 = 3 + 1, \ 4 = 2 + 2, \ 4 = 2 + 1 + 1, \ 4 = 1 + 1 + 1 + 1$

The number 200 can be expressed as a sum in 3 972 999 029 389 ways! How many different ways can you express the number 6 as a sum of natural numbers?

Working with Mathematics

Something to talk about

1. Which of these are equations?
  a) $2 \times 12 = 18 + 6$
  b) $6 + 7 + 4 = 19 - 2$
  c) $6 \times 8 < 7 \times 7$
  d) $3 \times 2 + 6 = 3 \times 3 + 4$
  e) $4 \times 5 + 7 = 4 \times 7 + 5$
  f) $10 \div 2 - 5 = 15 \div 3 - 5$
  g) $2 + 4 + 6 + 8 + 10 = 2 \times 15$
  h) $3 \times 5 > 2 \times 7$
  i) $4 \times 4 = 1 + 3 + 5 + 7$
  j) $2 + 4 + 3 = 3 + 4 + 2$
  k) $1 + 1 + 1 + 1 = 1 \times 1 \times 1 \times 4$
  l) $18 + 8 = 52 \div 2$
  m) $10 + 6 + 2 = 3 \times 7$

Practice

2. Match each picture with the appropriate number sentence.
  i) $8 + 10 = 18$ **ii)** $14 + 4 = 18$
  iii) $2 \times 9 = 18$ **iv)** $3 \times 6 = 18$
  v) $18 - 2 = 16$ **vi)** $18 - 5 = 13$

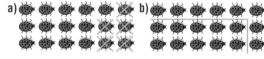

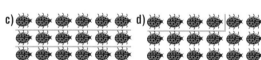

3. Alexander delivers 22 newspapers every day from Monday to Saturday. Write an equation to calculate each answer.
  a) Beni delivers 5 more daily papers than Alexander. How many papers does Beni deliver each day?
  b) Alexander delivers 2 more daily papers than Carlene. How many papers does Carlene deliver each day?
  c) Martin delivers half as many daily papers as Alexander. How many papers does Martin deliver each day?
  d) What is the total number of papers Alexander delivers each week?

Work together

4. a) For each number, think of two different expressions that it is equal to.
    i) 29   **ii)** 49   **iii)** 32
    iv) 50   **v)** 100   **vi)** 78
    vii) 5   **viii)** 77   **ix)** 31
  b) Write each pair of expressions in part a as an equation.
  c) Compare your answers with those of your partner. In each case, did you write the same equation?

5. Each sentence below is followed by a question. Answer each question with a mathematical expression. List the expressions that are equivalent.
  a) Shannon earns \$5/h babysitting. How much does she earn in dollars in 4 h?
  b) A case of pop contains 24 cans. How many cans are there in 4 cases?
  c) Biljit gave 7 baseball cards to her friend and now has 23 left. How many cards did Biljit have to begin with?
  d) Ms Wong divided her class into 3 groups of 10 students. How many students are in her class?
  e) Sincon watched TV for 4 h on Sunday, 2 h on Monday, 3 h on Wednesday, one and a half hours on Thursday, 5 h on Friday, and four and a half hours on Saturday. For how long did Sincon watch TV that week?
  f) Meiko paid \$107 for running shoes; she did not pay provincial sales tax. What was the price of the running shoes before GST was added?

6. Write an equation to calculate each answer.
  a) What is the sum of your age and the age of your mom?
  b) How old will you be in two years' time?
  c) How old were you four years ago?
  d) What is twice your age now?
  e) What is the difference between your mom's age and your age?
  f) What is ten more than twice your age now?

On your own

7. Suppose you have many 1-g, 5-g, and 10-g masses. For each two-pan balance below:
  a) Determine some masses you could put in the empty pan so that it would balance.
  b) Write an equation to describe how the masses on the left side balance the masses on the right side.

  i)
  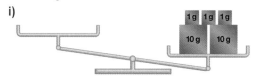

  ii)

  iii)
  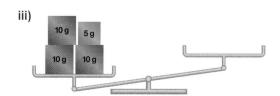

8. Each sentence below is followed by a question. Answer each question with a mathematical expression. List the expressions that are equivalent.
  a) Anita played hockey for 3 h on Sunday, 2 h on Wednesday, 1 h on Friday, and 4 h on Saturday. For how long did Anita play hockey that week?
  b) Hira earns $6.50 an hour pumping gas. How much does she earn in dollars in an 8-h shift?
  c) Thirty people volunteered to clean up the local park. They were divided into 3 equal groups. How many people were in each group?
  d) Mark earned $123.20 in one week, working at his local grocery store. His rate of pay is $5.60 per hour. For how many hours did he work?
  e) Bjorn practised his figure skating routine for 6 h on Saturday, 7 h on Sunday, 4 h on Monday, 3 h on Wednesday, and 2 h on Friday. For how long did Bjorn practise that week?
  f) Gwen had 108 chocolate bars to sell. She sold 56 bars to her family and friends. How many did she have left?

9. Find all the equivalent expressions in the box below.

3×10	$59 - 20$	$90 \div 3$
12×0	13×3	2×15
$36 - 6$	$16 - 16$	$58 \div 2$
$28 + 2$	$7 + 8$	2×7.5
$0 \div 5$	$10 \times 3 + 9$	$39 \div 13 \times 13$

Extend your thinking

10. Use the numbers 2, 3, 5, 7, and 9 and any mathematical symbols to write an equation.

11. What is the sum of the ages of all the students in your class? Write an equation to calculate the answer.

COMMUNICATING

The Ideas

In your journal, describe what an equation is.

More Patterns in a Spreadsheet

Start a new document in a spreadsheet program.

1. Recall from the earlier spreadsheet activity on page 325 how to make the computer count to 10. Type 1 in cell A1. Type =A1+1 in cell A2. Copy this formula from cell A2 down to cell A10.

2. We can use a formula to show the first ten multiples of 3. In cell B1, type a formula that multiplies the number in A1 by 3. This is =A1*3. Copy this formula from cell B1 down to cell B10. What do you see?

TEMPLATE DISK

	A	B	C	D	E	F
1	1	=A1*3				
2	2					
3	3					
4	4					
5	5					
6	6					
7	7					
8	8					
9	9					
10	10					

3. a) Type a formula in cell C1 that will show the multiples of 7. Copy this formula from cell C1 down to cell C10. Do you see the multiples of 7?

b) Type a formula in cell D1 that will show the multiples of 32. Copy this formula from cell D1 down to cell D10. Do you see the multiples of 32?

4. Type this formula in cell E1: =A1*2+5.

a) What number shows in cell E1 after you press Return?

b) Predict what numbers will show in column E if you copy this formula down from cell E2 to cell E10. Do it and check your answer.

c) What will the column of numbers be if the formula in cell E1 is changed to =A1*3−1, and then copied down? Do it and find out.

5. Challenge your friends with this. In column F, type a formula similar to those in exercise 4. Print the spreadsheet. Ask a friend to find the formula you used to get this list of numbers.

6. Delete the entries in the spreadsheet from column B to column F.

a) Type this formula in cell B1: =A1*4+A1*3.

b) Copy this formula down from cell B2 to cell B10.

c) Type this formula in cell C1: =A1*(4+3).

d) Copy this formula down from cell C2 to cell C10.

e) What do you notice about the numbers in column B and column C? Explain.

7. Repeat exercise 6. Replace the plus sign with a minus sign. Explain the results.

Mathematics & Technology

Linking Ideas

How Much Material Do You Require to Frame a Picture?

Aneta runs a picture framing business. Customers bring in pictures and choose different kinds of frames. Develop an expression Aneta can use to determine how much framing material she requires to make a frame for a picture.

Understand the problem

- What are you asked to do?
- Does the amount of framing material required depend on the size of the picture?
- Does it depend on the width of the frame? Why?

Think of a strategy

- Draw a diagram.
- Use an example. Assume a picture has a certain size and the framing material has a certain width. Calculate the amount of framing material required. Repeat for different widths of framing material.
- Try making a table and looking for a pattern.
- Use variables for the length and width of a picture, and for the width of a frame.

Carry out the strategy

- Suppose a customer brings in a picture measuring 20 cm by 16 cm. Suppose the frame is 3 cm wide.

16 cm

20 cm

3 cm

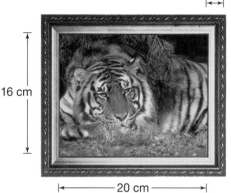

16 cm

20 cm

- Calculate the total length of framing material Aneta requires to frame this picture.
- Suppose the customer considers other frames with different widths. Copy and complete a table like this to show the amount of framing material required.

Length of picture (cm)	Width of picture (cm)	Width of frame (cm)	Total length of framing material required (cm)
20	16	1	
20	16	2	
20	16	3	
20	16	4	

- Repeat this procedure with a different sized picture of your choice.
- Let l and w represent the length and width of a picture, in centimetres. Let f represent the width of the framing material. Write an expression for the length of framing material required to frame the picture.

Look back

- Why doesn't the length of framing material Aneta requires equal the perimeter of the picture?
- Let c represent the cost of one centimetre of framing material, in dollars. Write an expression for the cost of a frame.

Communicating the Ideas

Write a description of this problem and your solution. Include an explanation of how you determined your expression for the total amount of framing material.

7.4 *EQUATIONS INVOLVING VARIABLES*

Developing the Ideas

▶ ▶ *Through Activities*

Work with a partner or in a group.

ACTIVITY 1

The pictures below show two-pan balances. Each balance contains one or more bags. Each bag contains an unknown number of candies. When there is more than one bag in a picture, the bags contain the same number of candies. We can assume that all the candies have the same mass and the bags themselves are light enough not to affect the balance. There are also some loose candies in the pans, which are identical to those in the bags.

Complete exercises 1 to 4 for each picture.

1. How many candies are there in the pan on the right side of the balance?

2. Choose a variable to represent the number of candies in each bag. Write an expression to describe the total number of candies in the pan on the left side of the balance.

3. a) The pans are balanced. What does this tell you about the masses of the objects on each side of the balance? What does this tell you about the number of candies on each side of the balance?

   b) Write an equation that relates the number of candies on each side of the balance.

4. How many candies are in each bag?

i)   ii)

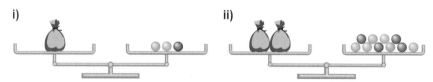

iii)   iv)

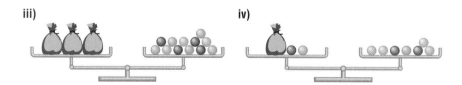

v)   vi)

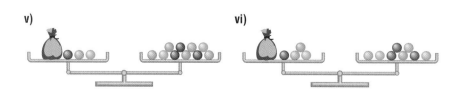

ACTIVITY 2

1. Write an equation to represent each sentence.
   a) 3 more than a number is 41.
   b) 8 less than a number is 19.
   c) Double a number is 23.
   d) A number divided by 9 is 15.
   e) 39 divided by a number is 3.

2. The cost of a CD is $9.00 more than the cost of a cassette tape. Choose a variable to represent the cost of a cassette tape. Suppose a CD costs $17.99. Write an equation to describe the cost of the CD in terms of the cost of a cassette.

3. A pizzeria charges 80¢ for each topping that is ordered. Choose a variable to represent the number of toppings. Suppose a customer is charged $2.40 for toppings. Write an equation to describe the cost of the toppings in terms of the number of toppings.

▶ ▶ *Through Guided Examples*

Example 1

Write an equation to represent each sentence.
a) 4 times a number is 68.
b) 3 less than a number is 25.
c) A number divided by 6 is 7.
d) The cost of 8 hamburgers is $22.32.

Solution

a) Let x represent the number.
   4 times the number is $4 \times x$, or $4x$.
   The equation is $4x = 68$.

b) Let y represent the number.
   3 less than the number is $y - 3$.
   The equation is $y - 3 = 25$.

c) Let n represent the number.
   The number divided by 6 is $\frac{n}{6}$.
   The equation is $\frac{n}{6} = 7$.

d) Let c dollars represent the cost of one hamburger.
   8 hamburgers cost $8 \times c$, or $8c$.
   The equation is $8c = 22.32$.

You can also translate an equation into a sentence.

Example 2

Write each equation in words.
a) $60 - y = 48$
b) $x + 5 = 23$
c) $\frac{n}{3} = 42$

Solution

a) Sixty decreased by a number is 48.
b) A number increased by 5 is 23.
c) A number divided by 3 is 42.

Working with Mathematics

The pictures in exercises 2, 3, and 6 show bags containing unknown numbers of identical candies. When there is more than one bag in a picture, the bags contain the same number of candies.

Something to talk about

1. Look at *Activity 1*. When there was more than one bag on the balance, why was it important to know that the bags contained the same number of candies?

Practice

2. Let n represent the number of candies in each bag. Match each picture with the appropriate expression.

   i) $2n$ **ii)** $3n$ **iii)** $n + 2$

   iv) $n + 3$ **v)** $2n + 3$ **vi)** $3n + 2$

a)    **b)**   **c)**

d)   **e)**   **f)**

3. Let n represent the number of candies in each bag. Write an expression to describe each picture.

a)   **b)**   **c)**

d)   **e)**

4. Draw a picture to represent each expression.

  a) $5n$ **b)** $n + 7$ **c)** $n + 9$

  d) $2n + 4$ **e)** $2n + 7$ **f)** $4n + 3$

5. Choose the correct equation to represent each sentence. Write a sentence to describe each equation you do not choose.

  a) 6 more than a number is 14.

    $n = 14 + 6$ $n + 6 = 14$ $6n = 14$

  b) A number divided by 3 is 8.

    $\dfrac{m}{3} = 8$ $\dfrac{3}{m} = 8$ $3m = 8$

  c) 6 less than a number is 9.

    $p = 9 - 6$ $p - 6 = 9$ $6 - p = 9$

Work together

6. The pictures below show two-pan balances that are balanced. Write an equation relating the number of candies in the pans. How many candies are in each bag?

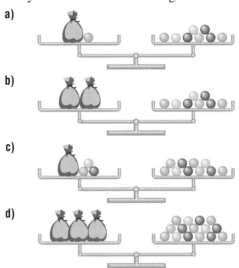

7. Each variable represents a bag with an unknown number of candies and the numbers represent candies. Draw a two-pan balance to represent each equation.

  a) $b + 2 = 5$ **b)** $4 + y = 10$

  c) $3x = 12$ **d)** $2x = 10$

8. Write an equation to represent each sentence.

  a) 8 more than a number is 36.

  b) A number divided by 5 is 13.

  c) Triple a number is 33.

  d) A number increased by 5 is 47.

  e) A number subtracted from 99 is 75.

  f) A number divided by 4 is 3.

  g) 27 divided by a number is 9.

  h) A number decreased by 7 is 14.

9. Write each equation in words.
a) $a + 4 = 11$ b) $9 + b = 13$
c) $4c = 20$ d) $6d = 48$
e) $15 - e = 7$ f) $f - 18 = 22$
g) $\frac{g}{6} = 5$ h) $\frac{h}{3} = 11$
i) $\frac{18}{i} = 3$ j) $\frac{22}{j} = 2$

10. Let n represent the number of customers on Xiaoyuan's paper route.
a) Philipa has 4 fewer customers on her route than Xiaoyuan. Write an expression for the number of customers on Philipa's route.
b) Suppose Philipa's route has 20 customers. Write an equation relating the number of customers on each girl's route.

11. Tarig put his vacation photos in an album. Each page in the album holds 6 photos.
a) Let n represent the number of pages Tarig filled. Write an expression for the number of photos he put in the album.
b) Suppose Tarig had 108 vacation photos. Write an equation that describes the number of pages he filled.

12. Six children are sharing one box of chocolates. Let c represent the number of chocolates in the box. Suppose each child receives 5 chocolates. Write an equation involving c. What does your equation describe?

13. Describe a situation that could be represented by each equation.
a) $x + 4 = 9$ b) $29 - y = 23$
c) $\frac{s}{3} = 18$ d) $1.99x = 19.99$

On your own

14. Write an equation to represent each sentence.
a) 3 less than a number is 19.
b) The product of 8 and a number is 56.
c) 37 decreased by a number is 13.
d) 4 more than a number is 52.
e) The cost of 6 cans of apple juice is $8.94.

15. Write each equation in words.
a) $x + 9 = 101$ b) $5n = 65$
c) $18 - s = 7$ d) $m - 1 = 35$
e) $\frac{d}{5} = 13$ f) $\frac{51}{y} = 17$

16. Let d represent the number of driveways Ovide cleared this week.
a) Jeremy cleared 3 more driveways than Ovide. Write an expression for the number of driveways Jeremy cleared.
b) Suppose Jeremy cleared 12 driveways. Write an equation relating the number of driveways each boy cleared.

17. Let t hours represent the time Zachary spent doing chores.
a) Rhonda spent twice as much time doing chores as Zachary. Write an expression for the time Rhonda spent doing chores.
b) Suppose Rhonda spent 6 h doing chores. Write an equation that relates the time spent doing chores by each person.

Extend your thinking

18. A rectangle has length 10 cm and width w centimetres. Write an equation for w in each case.
a) The width is 2 cm less than the length.
b) The length is 5 cm more than the width.
c) The area of the rectangle is 60 cm^2.
d) The perimeter of the rectangle is 30 cm.

COMMUNICATING

The Ideas

On pages 326 to 331, you worked with expressions. In your journal, describe the difference between an expression and an equation.

7.5 FINDING THE VALUE OF A VARIABLE

Developing the Ideas

▶▶ *Through Activities*

ACTIVITY 1

Work with a partner or in a group.

  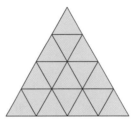

Look at the pattern of figures.

1. Suppose the sides of each small triangle have length 1 unit.
   a) What is the perimeter of the first figure?
   b) What is the length of a side of the second figure?
   c) What is the perimeter of the third figure?

2. Copy and complete this table.

Length of a side (units)	1	2	3	4	5	6
Perimeter of figure (units)						

3. If you know the length of a side of a figure, how can you find its perimeter?

4. For any figure, let *s* represent the length of its side. Let *P* represent its perimeter. Write an equation that you can use to find *P* if you know *s*.

5. Use the equation to find the perimeter of a figure that has a side length of 12 units.

6. If you know the perimeter of a figure, how can you find its side length?

7. Use the equation to find the side length of a figure that has a perimeter of 30 units.

8. Compare your results with those of another group. Did you all write the same equation?

ACTIVITY 2

Work with a partner or in a group.

1. Look at this pattern of rectangles. On grid paper, draw the next three rectangles in this pattern.

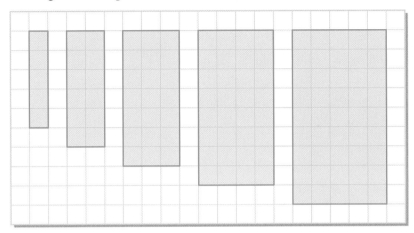

2. The length of one square on the grid is 1 unit. Find the length and width of each of the eight rectangles. Copy and complete this table.

Width of rectangle (units)	1	2	3					
Length of rectangle (units)								

3. For a rectangle in this pattern, if you know its width, how can you find its length?

4. For any rectangle, let *l* represent the length and let *w* represent the width. Write an equation that you can use to find *l* if you know *w*.

5. Use the equation to find the length of a rectangle that has a width of 20 units.

6. For a rectangle in this pattern, if you know its length, how can you find its width?

7. Use the equation to find the width of a rectangle that has a length of 27 units.

8. Compare your results with those of another group. Did you all write the same equation?

In *Activity 1*, for the pattern of figures, the equation you should have written is $P = 3 \times s$, or $P = 3s$. This means that the perimeter is three times the length of a side.

Suppose we know that the perimeter of a figure is 27 units and we want to find its side length. We replace P with 27 in the equation.

We write: $27 = 3s$

This is an equation. For this equation to be a true statement, 27 must equal $3s$.

To find the value of s, we ask: What number multiplied by 3 gives 27?

We know that $27 = 3 \times 9$, so $s = 9$

The side length of the figure is 9 units.

In *Activity 2*, for the pattern of rectangles, the equation that describes the relationship between the length and the width is $l = w + 4$, or $l = 4 + w$.

This means that the length is 4 units more than the width.

Suppose we know that the length of a rectangle is 21 units and we want to find its width. We replace l with 21 in the equation.

We write: $21 = w + 4$

For this equation to be a true statement, 21 must equal $w + 4$.

To find the value of w, we ask: What number added to 4 gives 21?

We know that $21 = 17 + 4$, so $w = 17$

The width of the rectangle is 17 units.

For each equation above, there was only one value of the variable that made the equation a true statement.

A desk calendar consists of two cubes with numbered faces. The cubes can be arranged to show any of the dates 01, 02, 03, ..., 31. How should the faces of the cubes be numbered?

SEPTEMBER

▶▶ Through Guided Examples

Recall that we used a variable to describe any number in a pattern.
We can use an equation to find the position of a number in a pattern.

Example 1

a) A number pattern is represented by the expression $n + 2$. Write the first four numbers in this pattern.

b) What is the 15th number in the pattern?

c) One of the numbers in the pattern is 31. Where does it occur in the pattern?

Solution

The expression describing the pattern is $n + 2$. In this expression, n can represent any of the numbers 1, 2, 3, …. Think of these as being counters for the numbers in the pattern, and make a list like this:

Counter: 1   2   3   4   5   …
Number: 3   4   5   6   7   …

a) The first four numbers are 3, 4, 5, 6.

b) Substitute 15 for n in $n + 2$ to obtain $15 + 2 = 17$.
The 15th number is 17.
This is reasonable because each number is 2 more than the counter.
When the counter is 15, the number is 17.

c) We write the equation $n + 2 = 31$.
We know that $29 + 2 = 31$, so $n = 29$.
The number 31 is the 29th number in the pattern.
This is reasonable because each counter is 2 less than the number.
When the number is 31, the counter is 29.

Example 2

Find the value of the variable that makes each equation a true statement.

a) $23 = x + 5$ **b)** $7p = 77$ **c)** $17 = 22 - a$

Solution

a) $23 = x + 5$
What number do we add to 5 to get 23?
We know that $23 = 18 + 5$, so $x = 18$

b) $7p = 77$
What number do we multiply by 7 to get 77?
We know that $7 \times 11 = 77$, so $p = 11$

c) $17 = 22 - a$
What number do we subtract from 22 to get 17?
We know that $17 = 22 - 5$, so $a = 5$

Working with Mathematics

Something to talk about

1. For *Activity 1*, page 346, the equation that describes the relationship between the perimeter of the figure and the length of its side is $P = 3s$.
   a) If $s = 8$, what is the value of P?
   b) If $P = 60$, what is the value of s?

2. For *Activity 2*, page 347, the equation that describes the relationship between the length and the width of a rectangle is $l = 4 + w$.
   a) If $w = 16$, what is the value of l?
   b) If $l = 16$, what is the value of w?

Practice

3. We often use mental math skills to find the value of a variable. Complete these operations mentally.
   a) $13 - 9$ b) $25 - 8$ c) $17 - 20$
   d) 4×7 e) 8×5 f) $65 \div 5$
   g) $36 \div 4$ h) $72 \div 8$ i) $49 \div 7$
   j) $5 + 28$ k) 9×6 l) $11 - 7$

4. A number pattern is represented by $n + 3$.
   a) Write the first 5 numbers in the pattern.
   b) One of the numbers in the pattern is 10. Where does it occur in the pattern?
   c) Subtract 3 from 10. What do you notice?

5. A number pattern is represented by $4n$.
   a) Write the first 5 numbers in the pattern.
   b) One of the numbers in the pattern is 28. Where does it occur in the pattern?
   c) Divide 28 by 4. What do you notice?

6. What question do you ask to find the value of the variable that makes each equation a true statement? Find this value.
   a) $3n = 24$ b) $p + 2 = 18$
   c) $3 + s = 64$ d) $12 - n = 3$
   e) $k - 3 = 15$ f) $2x = 100$
   g) $\frac{y}{2} = 15$ h) $\frac{w}{3} = 7$
   i) $m + 7 = 22$ j) $50 - r = 31$

Work together

7. Look at the pattern of figures you investigated in exercise 7, page 323. Look at the figures you drew to continue the pattern. Suppose the sides of each triangle have length 1 unit.
   a) Calculate the perimeter of each figure. Copy and complete this table.

Number of triangles	1	2	3	4	5	6
Perimeter of figure (units)						

   b) If you know the number of triangles a figure has, how can you find its perimeter?
   c) For any figure in this pattern, let n represent the number of triangles it has. Let P represent the perimeter. Write an equation you can use to find P if you know n.
   d) Use the equation to find the perimeter of the figure that has 10 triangles.
   e) Use the equation to find the number of triangles in the figure with perimeter 20 units.

8. A number pattern is represented by $10 + n$.
   a) Write the first five numbers in the pattern.
   b) One of the numbers in the pattern is 43. Where does it occur in the pattern?

9. For each number pattern below:
   i) Write the first four numbers in the pattern.
   ii) One of the numbers in each pattern is 36. Where does it occur in the pattern?
   a) $n + 6$ b) $3x$ c) $\frac{m}{3}$ d) $50 - a$
   e) $\frac{t}{2}$ f) $r + 20$ g) $a - 2$ h) $4s$
   i) $9d$ j) $3y$ k) $15 + c$ l) $\frac{p}{10}$

10. Find the value of the variable that makes each equation a true statement.
   a) $x + 3 = 9$ b) $8p = 96$ c) $13 = 43 - x$
   d) $8 = x - 3$ e) $4k = 64$ f) $9 + x = 14$
   g) $\frac{c}{2} = 4$ h) $x + 4 = 12$ i) $75 = 5p$
   j) $9k = 72$ k) $5 = \frac{x}{2}$ l) $12 - x = 5$

11. Which of these equations are true when $x = 3$?

   a) $x + 4 = 7$ **b)** $12 = x + 6$ **c)** $x - 2 = 4$

   d) $2 - x = 1$ **e)** $5x = 18$ **f)** $6 = 3x$

   g) $4x = 12$ **h)** $4 = \frac{x}{2}$ **i)** $\frac{12}{x} = 4$

12. The perimeter of this triangle is 24 cm.

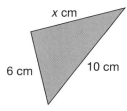

   a) Write an equation that describes the perimeter of the triangle.

   b) Find the value of x that makes the equation a true statement.

13. Draw a triangle. Label two sides with their lengths. Label the third side t. Write an equation that describes the perimeter of your triangle. Exchange equations with your partner. Find the value of t that makes your partner's equation a true statement.

14. The area of this rectangle is 36 cm^2.

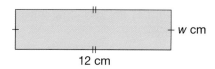

   a) Write an equation that describes the area of the rectangle.

   b) Find the value of w that makes the equation a true statement.

15. Draw a rectangle. Label the longer side with its length. Label the shorter side w. Write an equation that describes the area of your rectangle. Exchange equations with your partner. Find the value of w that makes your partner's equation a true statement.

16. a) For each number given, write a numerical expression that it is equal to.

   b) Write each number and expression in part a as an equation.

c) In each equation you created in part b, replace one number with a variable. Give the three equations with variables to a classmate. Ask her or him to determine the value of each variable.

   i) 15   **ii)** 36   **iii)** 68

On your own

17. Look at this pattern of rectangles.

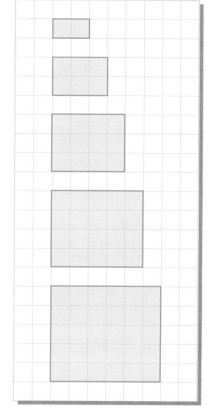

a) Explain the pattern.

b) On grid paper, draw the next three rectangles in this pattern.

c) The length of one square on the grid is 1 unit. Find the length and width of each of the eight rectangles. Copy and complete this table.

Width of rectangle (units)	1	2	3
Length of rectangle (units)			

d) For a rectangle in this pattern, if you know its width, how can you find its length?

e) For any rectangle in this pattern, let l represent the length and let w represent the width. Write an equation you can use to find l if you know w.

f) Use the equation to find the length of the rectangle that has a width of 33 units.

g) Use the equation to find the width of the rectangle with a length of 102 units.

18. A number pattern is represented by $6x$.

   a) Write the first four numbers in the pattern.

   b) One of the numbers in the pattern is 54. Where does it occur in the pattern?

19. For each number pattern below:

   i) Write the first three numbers in the pattern.

   ii) One of the numbers in each pattern is 28. Where does it occur in the pattern?

   a) $7 + x$ **b)** $40 - n$ **c)** $\frac{a}{2}$ **d)** $7m$

20. Which of these equations are true when $x = 4$?

   a) $12 = 3x$ **b)** $\frac{16}{x} = 4$ **c)** $10 = x + 7$

   d) $20 - x = 16$ **e)** $x - 4 = 1$ **f)** $2 = x - 2$

   g) $\frac{20}{x} = 5$ **h)** $5x = 30$ **i)** $1 = \frac{x}{2}$

21. Find the value of the variable that makes each equation a true statement.

   a) $20 = 11 + n$ **b)** $\frac{x}{3} = 6$

   c) $7x = 56$ **d)** $13 - x = 1$

22. The perimeter of this triangle is 30 cm.

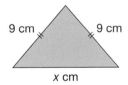

   a) Write an equation that describes the perimeter of the triangle.

   b) Find the value of x that makes the equation a true statement.

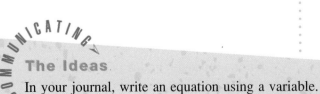

The Ideas

In your journal, write an equation using a variable. Explain how you find the value of the variable.

23. The area of this rectangle is 45 cm².

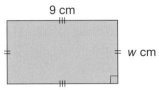

   a) Write an equation that describes the area of the rectangle.

   b) Find the value of w that makes the equation a true statement.

Extend your thinking

24. In *Activity 2*, on page 318, you drew different rectangles all with area 72 cm². Here is one of them.

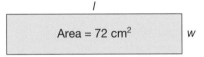

   a) Let l represent the length and w the width. Write an equation that describes the area of the rectangle.

   b) Use the equation in part a to find:

     i) the length of the rectangle when $w = 3.6$ cm

     ii) the width of the rectangle when $l = 40$ cm

25. Also in *Activity 2*, on page 318, you drew different rectangles all with perimeter 72 cm. Here is one of them.

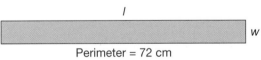

   a) Let l represent the length and w the width. Write an equation that describes the perimeter of the rectangle.

   b) Use the equation in part a to find:

     i) the length of the rectangle when $w = 4.5$ cm

     ii) the width of the rectangle when $l = 25.5$ cm

7.6 REPRESENTING THE STEPS IN THE SOLUTION OF AN EQUATION WITH A TWO-PAN BALANCE

Developing the Ideas

▶▶ *Through Discussion*

All the pictures on pages 353 to 357 show two-pan balances. Each balance contains one or more bags. Each bag contains an unknown number of candies. When there is more than one bag in a picture, the bags contain the same number of candies. We can assume that all the candies have the same mass and the bags themselves are light enough not to affect the balance. There are also some loose candies in the pans, which are identical to those in the bags.

1. Let x represent the number of candies in a bag.
  a) Write an equation relating the number of candies in each pan in the picture below.
  b) What is the value of x? Explain how you know.
  c) How could you check your answer?

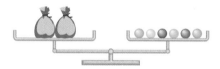

2. Let y represent the number of candies in a bag.
  a) Write an equation relating the number of candies in each pan in the picture below.
  b) Can you say what the value of y is?
  c) How is this equation different from that in exercise 1?

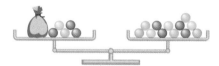

3. To determine the number of candies in the bag in exercise 2, imagine removing the 5 loose candies from the pan on the left.
  a) What must you do to the pan on the right to maintain the balance?
  b) Draw a picture of the balance with the 5 candies removed from each pan. Write an equation relating the number of candies in each pan.
  c) What is the value of y?

4. For each picture below, let x represent the number of candies in a bag.

    a) Write an equation relating the number of candies in each pan.

    b) Imagine removing loose candies or bags, so that the bags are alone in the pan on the left and the loose candies are in the pan on the right. Make sure that you maintain balance. Draw a picture of the balance and write an equation relating the number of candies in each pan.

    c) What is the value of x?

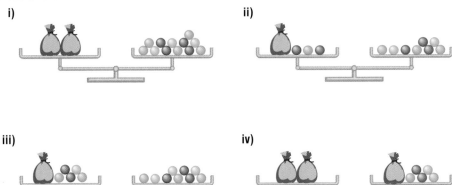

      i)   ii)

      iii)   iv)

▶▶ *Through a Guided Example*

When you found a value for x that made both sides of the equation equal, you *solved* the equation. We say that the value of x *satisfies* the equation.

In some cases, you imagined removing an equal number of loose candies from each pan to make the equation simpler. When all the bags were together on one side and the loose candies were together on the other side, it was easier to think of the number that would satisfy the equation.

To check an answer, you can return to the original picture and replace each bag with the number of candies from the answer. The sides of the scales should be balanced.

Example

Let x represent the number of candies in a bag. Write an equation relating the number of candies in each pan. Solve the equation to find the value of x. Check your answer.

    a)   **b)**

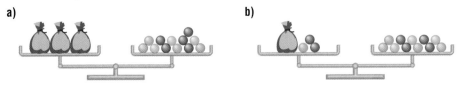

Solution

a) The number of candies in the pan on the left is $x + x + x$, or $3x$.

There are 12 candies in the pan on the right.

The equation is $3x = 12$.

To solve the equation, think:
What number gives 12 when it is multiplied by 3?

We know that $3 \times 4 = 12$, so $x = 4$.

To check this answer, replace each bag in the pan on the left with 4 candies.

Since there are 12 candies in each pan, the pans are balanced.

Therefore, the answer $x = 4$ is correct.

b) The number of candies in the pan on the left is $x + 1 + 1 + 1$, or $x + 3$.

There are 11 candies in the pan on the right.

The equation is $x + 3 = 11$

To make the equation easier to solve, we imagine removing the 3 loose candies from the pan on the left.

To maintain the balance, we must then do the same for the pan on the right. This leaves 8 candies in the pan.

The picture becomes:

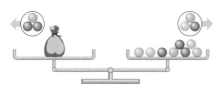

The equation that represents this picture is $x = 8$.

To check this answer, return to the original picture. Replace the bag in the pan on the left with 8 candies.

Since there are 11 candies in each pan, the pans are balanced.
Therefore, the answer $x = 8$ is correct.

Working with Mathematics

Something to talk about

1. Why is it important to maintain the balance each time you imagine removing candies from the two-pan balance?

2. How does a two-pan balance model an equation?

Practice

3. Let x represent the number of candies in each bag. Match each diagram with the appropriate equation. Solve each equation to find the value of x.

   i) $x + 2 = 6$ **ii)** $6 = x + 4$
   iii) $2x = 12$ **iv)** $3x = 6$
   v) $10 = 2x$ **vi)** $4 + x = 10$

   a)
   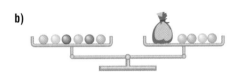

   b)
   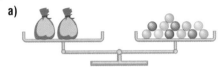

   c)
   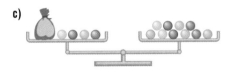

   d)
   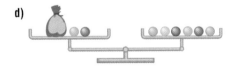

   e)
   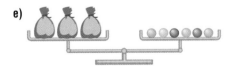

   f)

Work together

Work with a partner to complete exercises 4 to 6. Take turns explaining aloud each step in the solution.

4. Let x represent the number of candies in a bag. Write an equation relating the number of candies in each pan. Solve the equation to find the value of x. Check your answer.

   a)
   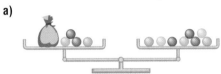

   b)
   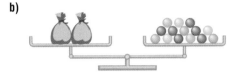

   c)
   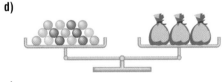

   d)
   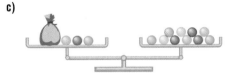

   e)
   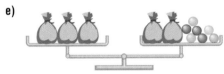

5. Solve the equations from exercise 6 on page 344. Check your answers.

6. Each variable represents a bag with an unknown number of candies and the numbers represent candies. Draw a two-pan balance to represent each equation. Solve the equation. Check your answer.

   a) $a + 8 = 11$ **b)** $7 + b = 12$
   c) $9 = c + 2$ **d)** $10 = 5 + d$
   e) $3e = 21$ **f)** $20 = 5f$
   g) $18 = 2g$ **h)** $4h = 16$
   i) $k + 7 = 2k$ **j)** $3m = 2m + 4$

For exercises 7 to 10, draw a two-pan balance to represent each situation. Use the diagram to find the answer to each question.

7. One week, Angela decides to donate her allowance to a charity. Her mother tells her that she will match Angela's donation. Their combined donation is $10. What is Angela's weekly allowance?

8. Robin has an aquarium. After Brendan gives him 5 new fish, there are 13 fish in the aquarium. How many fish were there before Brendan's gift?

9. Samir has 3 packs of hockey cards. Each pack contains the same number of cards. Samir has 15 cards in total. How many cards are in each pack?

10. Maurice had 7 comic books. After Janeesha gives him some, he has 11. How many comic books did Janeesha give Maurice?

On your own

11. Let x represent the number of candies in a bag. Write an equation relating the number of candies in each pan. Solve the equation to find the value of x. Check your answer.

a)

b)
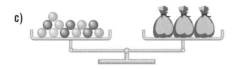

c)

d)

e)
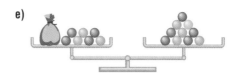

f)
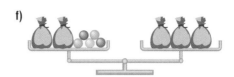

12. Each variable represents a bag with an unknown number of candies and the numbers represent candies. Draw a two-pan balance to represent each equation. Solve the equation. Check your answer.

a) $c + 3 = 9$ b) $w + 6 = 10$
c) $3p = 15$ d) $8 = x + 3$

Extend your thinking

13. In the diagram below, the first scale is balanced. Which block(s) will balance the square block on the second scale? Explain the steps you used to get your answer.

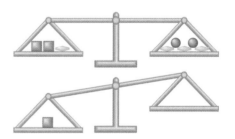

The Ideas

In your journal, describe the procedure for determining the number of candies in each bag in the picture on the right.

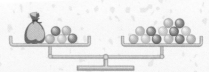

7.7 MODELLING THE STEPS IN THE SOLUTION OF AN EQUATION WITH ALGEBRA TILES

Developing the Ideas

▶▶ *Using Manipulatives*

In the previous section, you used a two-pan balance model to solve equations. This is a good way to model the solutions of equations where all the values are positive, such as $x + 5 = 11$.

You can also use algebra tiles to solve equations. Algebra tiles allow you to model the solutions of equations where some of the numbers are negative.

This tile represents 1.   Flip the tile. ⟶   This tile represents −1.

We call these *unit* tiles.

This tile represents one variable. For example, if you are using x, you can call this a $1x$-tile, or simply an x-tile.   Flip the tile. ⟶   This tile represents the opposite of $1x$, or $-1x$. We simply say it is a $-x$-tile.

We call these *variable* tiles.

To model the algebraic expression $x + 3$, you need one x-tile and three 1-tiles.

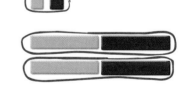

In your integer work, the number zero was modelled by an equal number of tiles of each colour. This is true for both unit tiles and variable tiles.

For example, one 1-tile (+1) and one −1-tile (−1) model zero. Similarly, two x-tiles (+2x) and two $-x$-tiles (−2x) also model 0.

We can write a number sentence for each situation:
$+1 + (-1) = 0$ and $+2x + (-2x) = 0$

We call this the *Zero Principle*.

. . . .

The Zero Principle
Any two opposite tiles add to zero. This means that you can add or remove pairs of opposite tiles without changing an expression.

We can use algebra tiles to determine the value of an expression when the variable has a particular value. We call this *evaluating* the expression.

For example, to evaluate the expression $2x - 1$, when $x = 2$, we first represent the expression with algebra tiles. We use two x-tiles and one -1-tile.

Since $x = 2$, we replace each x-tile with two 1-tiles.

By the Zero Principle, we can remove one pair of opposite tiles. This leaves three 1-tiles.

So, when $x = 2$, the expression $2x - 1$ equals 3

Practise using algebra tiles by completing exercises 1 to 3 with a partner.

1. Write the algebraic expression represented by each group of tiles.

a)

b)

c)

d)

2. Use algebra tiles to determine the value of each expression in exercise 1 when $x = 2$ and when $x = -3$.

3. Use algebra tiles to represent each expression. Determine the value of each expression when $x = 4$ and when $x = -1$.

a) $x + 3$ b) $x - 1$ c) $2x$

d) $1 + 2x$ e) $5 - 2x$ f) $-2x$

The world's largest blanket had a mass of 4 t and covered an area of 17 289.8 m². It was sewn together from pieces knit by thousands of volunteers. The blanket was later cut up into standard blankets and distributed by charities around the world. Estimate the number of standard blankets that were created from this one large blanket.

When we model equations with algebra tiles, we use a *work chart*. A vertical line drawn down the middle of a piece of paper represents the equals sign. You can think of each side of the work chart as a pan on a two-pan balance. This means that if you do something to one side of the work chart, you must do the same thing to the other side. We call this the *Balance Principle*.

● ● ● ● ● ● ● ● ●

The Balance Principle

When you solve an equation using algebra tiles, you can add the same tiles to each side of the work chart and still maintain equality. Similarly, you can remove the same tiles from each side of the work chart and still maintain equality.

For example, in the equation $s + 3 = 7$, $s + 3$ is equal to 7. Make a work chart. Put algebra tiles representing $s + 3$ on the left side of the line. Put tiles representing 7 on the right side of the line.

When we solve the equation, we find the value of s that makes the statement $s + 3 = 7$ true. We can model the steps in the solution with algebra tiles.

▶ ▶ **Through Guided Examples**

Example 1 ···

Use algebra tiles and symbols to solve the equation $s + 3 = 7$.

Solution

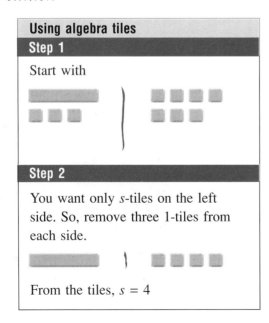

Using algebra tiles	Using symbols
Step 1	**Step 1**
Start with	Start with $$s + 3 = 7$$
Step 2	**Step 2**
You want only s-tiles on the left side. So, remove three 1-tiles from each side.	Subtract 3 from each side. $$s + 3 - 3 = 7 - 3$$ $$s = 4$$
From the tiles, $s = 4$	

Example 2

Use algebra tiles and symbols to solve the equation $x - 7 = 5$.

Solution

Using algebra tiles	Using symbols
Step 1	**Step 1**
Start with	Start with
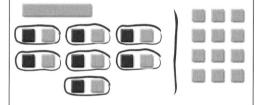	$$x - 7 = 5$$
Step 2	**Step 2**
You want to get all the 1-tiles on the right side. So, add seven 1-tiles to each side.	Add 7 to each side.
	$$x - 7 + 7 = 5 + 7$$ $$x = 12$$
According to the Zero Principle, this is the same as	

From the tiles, $x = 12$	

BOGGLE YOUR **MIND**

Keeping San Francisco's famous Golden Gate Bridge in good repair is a full-time job! In fact, 32 painters work 40 h per week, 50 weeks per year painting the bridge's 757 400 m² of exposed steel. On average, how many square metres does each painter paint in an hour?

There is another principle you will use when you solve equations using algebra tiles. We call it the *Sharing Principle*.

• • • • • • • • •

The Sharing Principle

If two numbers are equal, you can divide each of them by the same number and maintain equality. Similarly, when two sets of tiles are equal, if you can divide both sets into the same number of groups, each of these groups will be equal.

Example 3 ....

Use algebra tiles and symbols to solve the equation $4c = 12$.

Solution

Using algebra tiles	Using symbols
Step 1	**Step 1**
Start with 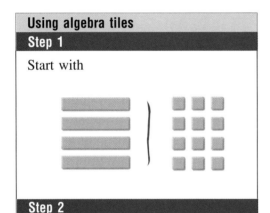	Start with $$4c = 12$$
Step 2	**Step 2**
Each side can be arranged into four equal groups. Each group on the left contains one c-tile and each group on the right contains three 1-tiles. According to the Sharing Principle, you need only use one group from each side and still maintain equality. 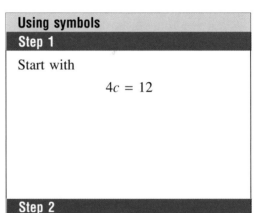 From the tiles, $c = 3$	Since we divided the tiles on each side of the work chart into 4 equal groups, we divide each side of the equation by 4. $$\frac{4c}{4} = \frac{12}{4}$$ $$c = 3$$

Working with Mathematics

Something to talk about

1. Why is it not possible to solve an equation like the one in *Example 2* using a two-pan balance?

2. What does it mean to *solve* an equation?

3. All the numbers that were used in the equations you modelled were integers. Can these models be used to solve an equation like $y + 3.8 = 6.4$? Explain.

4. Describe aloud the steps you would take to model the solution of the equation $k - 12 = 13$.

5. In the previous section, you checked your answer to an equation by replacing each bag in the original picture with the number of candies from your answer. Describe how you could check your answer when you solve an equation using algebra tiles.

Practice

6. What expression does each group of algebra tiles represent? Evaluate each expression when $x = 2$ and when $x = -1$.

   a)

   b)

7. Use algebra tiles to model each expression.
   a) $x + 5$ b) $7 + x$ c) $x - 2$
   d) $3x$ e) $5x$ f) $-3x$
   g) $3x - 4$ h) $7 - 4x$ i) $-2x - 4$

8. Evaluate each expression in exercise 7 when $x = 3$ and when $x = -4$.

9. The pictures model each step in the solution of an equation. Write the symbols that correspond to each step.

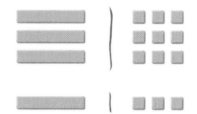

10. The pictures model each step in the solution of an equation. Write the symbols that correspond to each step.

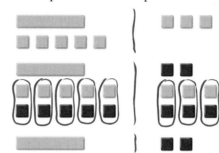

Work together

11. Write the equation represented by each picture.

12. Use algebra tiles to model the solution to each equation in exercise 11. Check your answers.

4. The first diagram shows 1 length of guardrail. The second diagram shows 2 lengths of guardrail.

a) Sketch 3, 4, and 5 lengths of guardrail. Copy and complete this table.

Number of lengths	1	2	3	4	5
Number of posts					
Number of bolts					

b) Describe the relationship between the number of lengths and the number of posts. Use *l* to represent the number of lengths. Write an expression for the number of posts.

c) Repeat part b for the relationship between the number of lengths and the number of bolts.

d) Suppose there are 7 lengths of guardrail. How many post and bolts are there?

e) Suppose you know there are 23 posts. How many lengths of guardrail are there?

f) Suppose there are 52 bolts. How many lengths of guardrail are there?

5. For this number pattern: 6, 7, 8, 9, 10, 11, …
   a) What is the 12th number in the pattern?
   b) What is the 29th number in the pattern?
   c) Use a variable to describe any number in the pattern.

6. For this number pattern:
   7, 14, 21, 28, 35, 42, …
   a) What is the 15th number in the pattern?
   b) What is the 21st number in the pattern?
   c) Use a variable to describe any number in the pattern.

7. Each expression, a to d, represents any number in a pattern. For each pattern:
   i) Write the first five numbers in the pattern.
   ii) One of the numbers in each pattern is 24. Where does it occur in the pattern?
   a) $n + 6$ **b)** $5n - 1$ **c)** $\frac{n}{3}$ **d)** $4n$

8. Every hour, a mechanic can complete 3 oil changes.
   a) Copy and complete the table below.

Number of hours	1	2	3	4
Number of oil changes completed				

   b) Suppose you know the number of hours the mechanic worked. How can you find the number of oil changes she completed?
   c) How many oil changes can she complete in one 7-h work day?
   d) Write an expression for the number of oil changes that can be completed in *n* hours.
   e) Suppose you know the mechanic has completed 18 oil changes. Write and solve an equation to determine the number of hours she worked.

9. Find the pairs of equivalent expressions. Use each pair to write an equation.

   2×3 $8 + 4$ 13×1 6×3
   $9 + 1$ $5 + 1$ $7 + 9$ $1 + 12$
   2×8 $8 + 2$ 2×6 9×2

10. Write an equation to describe each picture.
   a)
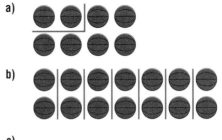
   b)
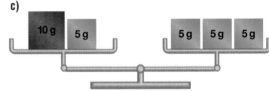
   c)

11. Each sentence below is followed by a question. Answer each question with a mathematical expression.

  a) There are 12 eggs in a carton. How many eggs are there in 7 cartons?

  b) Estelle plants one tree for every 3 m² of her yard. Her yard has an area of 69 m². How many trees does Estelle plant?

  c) On average, there are 4.7 people per home in Talbotville. There are 260 homes in Talbotville. What is the population?

  d) Each turn of a screw sets it 2 mm deeper in the wood. How far will it be set after 3 turns?

  e) Every shovel contains 4 kg of snow. How many shovels are needed to move 36 kg of snow?

  f) A new car comes with 5 tires, including the spare. How many tires are included with 8 new cars?

  g) Rajan had $18.25 when he went to the mall. He spent $13.40. How much money did he have left?

  h) Noah owns 28 CDs. He loans 5 of them to Anita. How many does he have left?

12. Find the value of the variable that makes each equation a true statement.

  a) $30 = 14 + x$ b) $\frac{x}{5} = 3$

  c) $49 = 7x$ d) $5 = 21 - x$

13. Let n represent the number of fish in David's aquarium.

  a) i) Petra's aquarium has 7 more fish than David's. Write an expression for the number of fish in Petra's aquarium.

   ii) Suppose Petra's aquarium contains 13 fish. Write an equation and use it to find the number of fish in David's aquarium.

  b) i) Sophie's aquarium has twice as many fish as David's. Write an expression for the number of fish in Sophie's aquarium.

   ii) Suppose Sophie's aquarium has 18 fish. Write an equation and use it to find the number of fish in David's aquarium.

14. A rectangle has length 12 m and width w metres.

  a) Write an equation that describes the area A of the rectangle.

  b) Suppose you know the area of the rectangle is 60 m². Find the value of w.

15. Each diagram shows loose candies and bags containing unknown numbers of identical candies. Let x represent the number of candies in each bag. Write an equation relating the number of candies in each pan of the balance. Solve each equation.

  a)

  b)
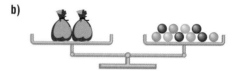

  c)
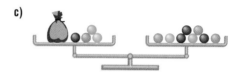

16. A video store rented 6 more game cartridges than game CDs. Fifteen game cartridges were rented. Draw a two-pan balance to represent the situation. Determine the number of game CDs that were rented.

17. Use algebra tiles to model the solution to each equation. Use symbols to record your solutions. Check your answers.

  a) $a + 7 = 11$ b) $9 - b = 5$

  c) $c - 3 = -5$ d) $12 = 2d$

  e) $3e = -12$ f) $7 = 5 - f$

18. One fall evening, the temperature dropped 5°C from 7 p.m. to 10 p.m. The temperature at 10 p.m. was −1°C. What was the temperature at 7 p.m.? Write an equation to describe this situation. Use algebra tiles to model, then solve the equation.

Codes

Do you realize how codes are used in our everyday life? If your television is connected to a satellite dish, a code is used to beam the signal from the satellite to the television. Other examples of codes include the numbers on a bank card, security access codes, voice mail codes, and the UPC symbols on many packaged foods.

In algebra, you substitute numbers for letters. In codes, numbers are substituted for letters, letters are substituted for letters, or letters are substituted for numbers. There are many ways to do this, as the following activities show.

ACTIVITY 1

Telephone Codes

1. Some companies use letters, instead of numbers, for their phone numbers.
   a) Why would a company want to do this?
   b) A computer store asked the phone company for the number 266–7883. Why do you think the store wanted this phone number?
   c) Find another example of a phone number that can be made into a word in this way.

2. Suppose you were creating a 1–800 number for a "homework help line" for *Minds on Math 7*. Create a number that incorporates a message that a student will get help with his homework if he dials the number. Give this number to a classmate. Ask her to identify the message.

3. A company installed a new telephone-answering system. Callers can use the keypad of a touch-tone phone to name the person they are calling. They enter the first three letters of the person's surname.
   a) What digits would you press to speak to a person whose surname is Galloway?
   b) What digits would you press to speak to a person whose surname is Hajee?
   c) Would the answering system be able to tell the difference in your answers to parts a and b?
   d) Suppose you were designing the telephone-answering system. Invent a way that callers could use the keypad to distinguish between the surnames in parts a and b.

Codes are a way to convey a message in a form that no one can read except those who have the key.

ACTIVITY 2

Number Shift Codes

A number shift code relates a number with a letter. Choose a natural number to represent A. In the example below, the number is 7.

Alphabet:	A	B	C	D	E	F	G	...
Key:	07	08	09	10	11	12	13	...

1. Copy and complete this code for all letters.

2. Use the key to code this message:
EARTH IS A HOME FOR ALL OF US

3. Use the key to decode this message:
24 11 10 27 09 11 24 11 27 25 11 24 11 09 31 09 18 11

4. a) Why are zeros written in front of single-digit numbers?
  b) Would there be any confusion if the zeros were omitted?

5. Create a different number shift code. Write a message and use the key to code it. Have a classmate decode your message.

ACTIVITY 3

The Caesar Code

Julius Caesar was a great Roman general. To coordinate his attacks or organize his army's defence, he often sent messages to his generals in a secret code that he himself created. He coded messages as follows:

Step 1. List the alphabet horizontally.

Step 2. Write a name, such as Caesar, below the alphabet but ignore repeated letters (like the second A).

Step 3. Follow the name with the rest of the alphabet in order, but ignore the letters already used.

Alphabet:	A	B	C	D	E	F	G	H	I	J	K	L	M	N	O	P	Q	R	S	T	U	V	W	X	Y	Z
Key:	C	A	E	S	R	B	D	F	G	H	I	J	K	L	M	N	O	P	Q	T	U	V	W	X	Y	Z

1. Use the key to code this message: YOU ARE NOT SAFE, FLY TO MEXICO

2. Use the key to decode this message: SM LMT CQI BMP KMPR KMLRY

3. Use your name to create a Caesar code. Write a message and code it. Have a classmate decode your message.

COMMUNICATING

The Ideas

Make a poster to show some codes and sample coded messages.
Include some coded messages without the codes.

THREE-DIMENSIONAL GEOMETRY

Quests

Minds on Math Project

Wrapping Presents
without Wasting Paper 396

Start With What You Know

1. Some structures built by different civilizations are shown below and on page 373.
   a) Describe each picture. State as many things about it as you can.
   b) Suppose you were in an airplane and could see the structures from directly above. What do you think they would look like? Sketch diagrams to illustrate your answer.
   c) What do you think the opposite side of each building would look like? Sketch diagrams to illustrate your answer.

2. a) Look for parallel sides of the structures. Explain how you know they are parallel.
   b) Look for perpendicular sides of the structures. Explain how you know they are perpendicular.

3. The United Nations Secretariat building was one of the first in the world to have outside walls made mostly of glass windows.
   a) Calculate the area of glass in one window.

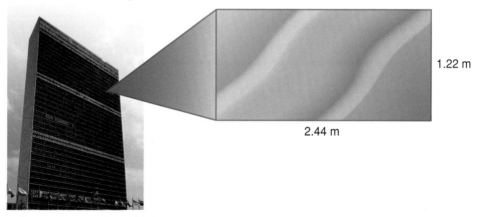

1.22 m

2.44 m

   b) Estimate the number of windows on the wall of this building. Use your answer to part a to estimate the area of the glass in the windows on this wall of the building.

4. Spaceship Earth dominates the horizon at Epcot Center near Orlando, Florida. It is the world's first geodesic sphere. As you can see from the photograph, it is not a sphere. Its surface consists of approximately 11 000 triangular facets made of aluminum. Although these are not all identical, their average area is approximately 0.7 m^2.
   a) Estimate the total area of aluminum in the surface of Spaceship Earth.
   b) If Spaceship Earth were a sphere, what change would there be in the picture?

5. a) Estimate the height and width of each structure.
   b) Explain how you could use features in the photographs to help you estimate.

6. How many years ago was each structure built?

Yingxian Pagoda, China, 11th Century A.D.

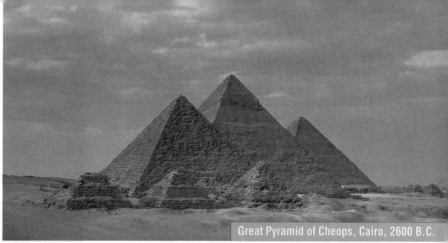

Great Pyramid of Cheops, Cairo, 2600 B.C.

Canadian Mint, Winnipeg, 1974

Spaceship Earth, Orlando, 1982

Flatiron Building, Toronto, 1892

8.2 *SURFACE AREA OF A RECTANGULAR PRISM*

Developing the Ideas

▶ ▶ *Through an Activity*

Work with a partner or in a group. You will need a millimetre ruler and some cardboard boxes like those in the photograph.

The boxes you have are rectangular prisms. Choose one prism. What do you think *surface area* means? Devise a plan for calculating the surface area of this prism. Then use your plan to calculate the surface area.

1. **a)** How many faces does the prism have?
   b) Are any of the faces congruent?
   c) How can you calculate the area of each face? How can you calculate the surface area of the prism?

2. Calculate the surface areas of the other rectangular prisms.

▶▶ *Through Guided Examples*

To calculate the surface area of a prism, you calculate the total area of its faces.

Example 1 ....

A rectangular prism and its net are shown.
Determine the surface area of the rectangular prism.

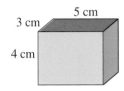

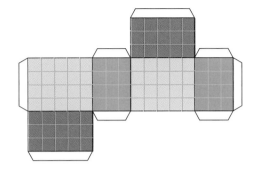

Solution

The area of each blue face is 3 cm × 4 cm = 12 cm².
The total area of the two opposite blue faces is 2 × 12 cm² = 24 cm².
The area of each red face is 3 cm × 5 cm = 15 cm².
The total area of the two opposite red faces is 2 × 15 cm² = 30 cm².
The area of each yellow face is 4 cm × 5 cm = 20 cm².
The total area of the two opposite yellow faces is 2 × 20 cm² = 40 cm².
The surface area is the total area of the three pairs of opposite faces.
The surface area is 24 cm² + 30 cm² + 40 cm² = 94 cm².

• • • • • • • • • •

The surface area of a rectangular prism is given by the formula:
Surface area = the sum of the areas of the faces

Example 2 ....

Two boxes are taped together to make a prop for a play. The smaller box
is a cube with edges 0.4 m. The larger box is a rectangular prism with
the dimensions shown. All faces of the prop except the base are covered
with wallpaper. What is the total area of wallpaper that is visible?

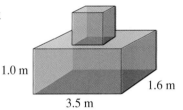

Solution

Five faces of the cube have wallpaper.
The total area of the faces is 5 × 0.4 m × 0.4 m = 0.8 m².
The area of wallpaper visible on the cube is 0.8 m².
Five faces of the rectangular prism have wallpaper. The total area of
these faces is:
(2 × 1.0 m × 1.6 m) + (2 × 3.5 m × 1.0 m) + (1 × 3.5 m × 1.6 m)
= 3.2 m² + 7.0 m² + 5.6 m², or 15.8 m²
The cube covers part of the top face of the rectangular prism.
Subtract the area of a face of the cube from the above area.
The area of wallpaper visible on the rectangular prism is:

15.8 m² − (0.4 m × 0.4 m) = 15.8 m² − 0.16 m²
                          = 15.64 m²

The total area of wallpaper visible on the prop is 15.64 m² + 0.8 m² = 16.44 m².

Working with Mathematics

Something to talk about

1. a) In *Example 1*, which faces of the rectangular prism are congruent?
   b) How could you check the answer to *Example 1*?

2. For *Example 2*, explain a different way to calculate the area of wallpaper that is visible.

3. a) In *Example 2*, does the position of the cube on top of the prism affect the area of wallpaper that is visible? Explain.
   b) Suppose the cube had been attached to a vertical face of the prism. What is the area of wallpaper that is visible? Explain.

Practice

4. Find the area of each figure.

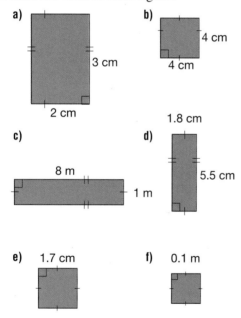

a)

b) 4 cm / 4 cm

c) 8 m / 1 m

d) 1.8 cm / 5.5 cm

e) 1.7 cm

f) 0.1 m

5. Sketch each rectangular prism. Calculate its surface area.
   a) length 10 cm, width 5 cm, height 3 cm
   b) length 6.7 m, width 9.0 m, height 1.8 m
   c) length 14 cm, width 8 cm, height 7 cm
   d) length 6 m, width 6 m, height 6 m

Work together

6. Draw a net for each prism. Estimate its surface area. Calculate its surface area.

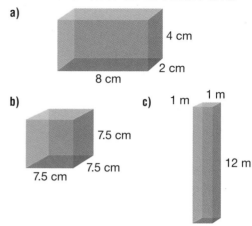

a) 4 cm / 2 cm / 8 cm

b) 7.5 cm / 7.5 cm / 7.5 cm

c) 1 m / 1 m / 12 m

7. a) Calculate the surface area of a cube with each edge length.
   i) 5 cm   ii) 10 cm   iii) 15 cm
   b) Suppose you know the edge length of a cube. Explain how to find its surface area.

8. These skeletons of rectangular prisms were constructed using straws. Each edge is either a whole 19-cm straw or half a straw. What area of paper is needed to cover each prism?

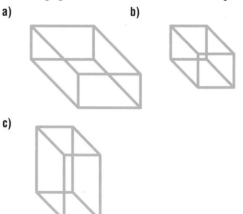

a)   b)

c)

9. Suppose the top of each rectangular prism in exercise 8 is not covered. What area of paper is need for each prism?

On your own

10. Use the cube you constructed in Section 8.1. Estimate its surface area. Take appropriate measurements. Calculate the surface area.

11. What is the surface area of the fridge (below right)?

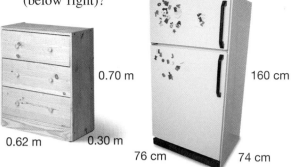 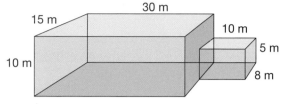

0.70 m   160 cm

0.62 m   0.30 m

76 cm   74 cm

12. The top, front, and both sides of the dresser (above left) are to be painted. What area will be painted?

13. A rectangular sheet of metal is 28 cm long and 18 cm wide. A baking tin is made by cutting a 4-cm square from each corner and turning up the sides. The inside surface is to have a non-stick coating. What area is to be coated?

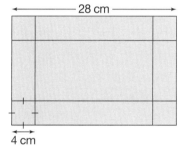

28 cm

4 cm

14. Here is a structure made with 8 cubes.

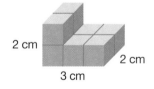

2 cm

2 cm

3 cm

a) What is the surface area of the structure?
b) Suppose other structures are made with 8 cubes. What is the least possible surface area? What is the greatest possible surface area?

15. The diagram represents a warehouse with an adjoining office. The diagram is not to scale.

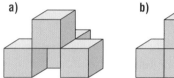 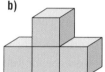

30 m

15 m

10 m

5 m

10 m

8 m

a) Estimate the surface area of the building.
b) Calculate the surface area of the building. How close was your estimate to the actual surface area?
c) One litre of paint covers 10 m^2 and costs $8. What is the cost of painting the outside of the building?

16. Each structure below was constructed from four 1-cm cubes. Calculate the total surface area of each structure.

a)   b)

Extend your thinking

17. How does the surface area of a rectangular prism change if:
    a) one dimension is doubled? Tripled?
    b) two dimensions are doubled? Tripled?
    c) all three dimensions are doubled? Tripled?

18. A rectangular prism has a square base with an area of 16 cm^2. Its surface area is 192 cm^2. What is the height of the prism?

19. The base of a rectangular box has area 50 cm^2. Each front and back face has area 10 cm^2. Each side has area 20 cm^2. Suppose you could fill the box completely with centimetre cubes. How many centimetre cubes would you need?

COMMUNICATING
The Ideas

In your journal, describe how you calculate the surface area of a prism if you know its dimensions. Illustrate your description with some examples.

8.3 VOLUME OF A RECTANGULAR PRISM

Developing the Ideas

▶ ▶ *Through an Activity*

Work in a group. You will need an empty box, some centimetre cubes, and a millimetre ruler.

1. How many centimetre cubes will fit in one layer on the base of the box?

2. a) Describe a way you could use the centimetre cubes to determine the volume of the box.

   b) Estimate the number of centimetre cubes you would need.

3. a) Measure the length and width of the base of the box. How could you use these measurements to determine the number of centimetre cubes that would fit in one layer on the base of the box?

   b) Now measure the height of the box. How could you use this measurement to determine the volume of the box?

▶ ▶ *Through Discussion*

Imagine that a rectangular prism is filled with layers of centimetre cubes. The number of cubes, including part cubes, needed to fill the prism is called its volume. To determine its volume:

• Determine the area of the base by calculating the number of unit cubes in the bottom layer.

• Multiply by the number of layers.

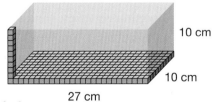

10 cm

10 cm

27 cm

The volume of a rectangular prism is given by the formula:
Volume = area of the base × height

Example 1 ···

Electric fans are rated according to the volume of air they move in a given time. Here is a sketch of a kitchen. Find the volume of air in this kitchen.

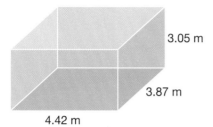

3.05 m

3.87 m

4.42 m

Solution

The kitchen has the shape of a rectangular prism.
The area of the floor is 4.42 m × 3.87 m $\doteq$ 17.11 m^2
Multiply by the height to determine the volume.
The volume is 17.11 m^2 × 3.05 m = 52.19 m^3,
or approximately 52 m^3.

Example 2 ···

Anya wants to buy the suitcase with the greater volume. Which suitcase should she buy?

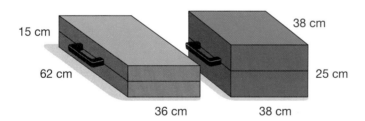

15 cm

62 cm

36 cm

38 cm

25 cm

38 cm

Solution

The volume of the green suitcase is

area of the base × height = 62 cm × 36 cm × 15 cm
$$= 33\ 480\ \text{cm}^3$$

The volume of the blue suitcase is

area of the base × height = 38 cm × 38 cm × 25 cm
$$= 36\ 100\ \text{cm}^3$$

The blue suitcase has the greater volume.

Anya should buy the blue suitcase.

Working with Mathematics

Something to talk about

1. When you determine the volume of a rectangular prism, does it matter which face is taken to be the base? Explain your answer.

2. How would the volume in *Example 1* change if:
   a) the height is doubled? Tripled?
   b) the length and the width are both doubled? Tripled?
   c) the length, width, and height are all doubled? Tripled?

3. **a)** Three rectangular prisms all have a volume of 36 cm³. What are some possible dimensions for these prisms?
   b) Sketch two prisms from part a. Label each prism with its dimensions.

Practice

4. Find the volume of each prism. Round the volumes to 1 decimal place where necessary.

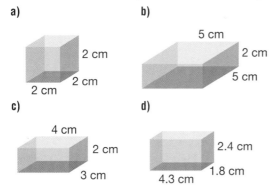

   a) 2 cm, 2 cm, 2 cm

   b) 5 cm, 2 cm, 5 cm

   c) 4 cm, 2 cm, 3 cm

   d) 2.4 cm, 1.8 cm, 4.3 cm

5. Determine the volume of each rectangular prism to the nearest tenth of a cubic centimetre.

Length (cm)	Width (cm)	Height (cm)
9	6	12
7.2	5.8	3.5
1.5	0.9	6.4
1.6	0.6	4.5

Work together

6. Determine the volume of each prism.

a)
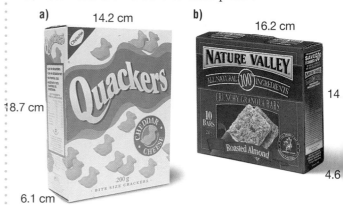
14.2 cm
18.7 cm
6.1 cm

b)
16.2 cm
14
4.6

7. Choose the best estimate of each volume.
   a) the volume of a 9-V battery
   18 cm³
   1.8 cm³
   180 cm³

   b) the volume of a bus
   9 m³
   90 m³
   900 m³

   c) the volume of a textbook
   15 cm³
   150 cm³
   1500 cm³

   d) the volume of a sugar cube
   2 cm³
   20 cm³
   0.2 cm³

8. The fan in the hood of a kitchen range removes air at the rate of 5.66 m³ per minute. About how many minutes would it take to remove the air in the kitchen in *Example 1*?

9. Three rectangular prisms all have a volume of 60 cm³.
   a) Determine some possible dimensions for the prisms.
   b) Do all your prisms in part a have the same surface area? Explain your answer.
   c) Sketch three prisms from part a. Label each prism with its dimensions.

10. There are 4000 $1 U.S. bills in the row of bills under the guard's right hand. Estimate the value of all the money in the photograph.

11. What is the volume of each rectangular prism?
   a) The area of the base is 32 m² and the height is 8 m.
   b) The base is 8 cm long and 4 cm wide. The height is 6 cm.
   c) The base has an area of 16 cm² and the height is 4 cm.
   d) Each face is 3.4 m by 3.4 m.
   e) Each edge length is 0.5 m.

On your own

12. Determine the volume of each prism.

a)

18.0 cm
13.0 cm
21.5 cm

b)

12.5 cm
24.6 cm
23.3 cm

c)

14 cm
19 cm
10 cm

13. Nabisco Shredded Wheat also comes in boxes holding 18 and 24 biscuits. Use your answer to exercise 12c to determine the volumes of these boxes.

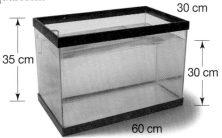

14. Calculate the volume of water in this aquarium.

30 cm
35 cm
30 cm
60 cm

15. These seven polyhedra are from a puzzle called the Soma Cube. It can be quite challenging to put them together to form a cube. Each piece is formed from cubes with edges 2 cm. What is the length of an edge of the Soma Cube?

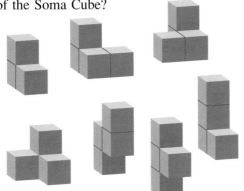

16. The volume of each box is 600 cm³. Determine the missing dimension.

a)
20 cm   10 cm   ?

b)
4 cm
15 cm   ?

c)
2 cm
10 cm   ?

17. Determine the volume of each solid.

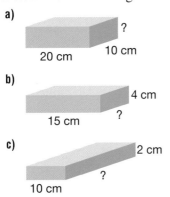

a)
5 cm
9 cm
7 cm   15 cm
6 cm
5 cm   12 cm

b)
4 m   4 m
6 m

18. The bucket on a front-end loader measures 1.2 m by 2.3 m by 1.8 m. The bin of a dump truck measures 4.2 m by 2.5 m by 1.9 m. How many bucket loads will it take to fill the truck?

Extend your thinking

19. This is a graph of volume against height for rectangular prisms with base area 20 cm². Use the graph to complete the exercise.

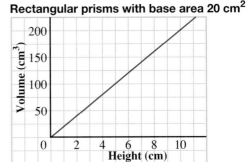

Rectangular prisms with base area 20 cm²

a) What happens to the volume when the height increases? Decreases?
b) Estimate the volume for each height.
   i) 2 cm   ii) 4 cm   iii) 8 cm
c) What happens to the volume when the height is doubled?
d) Estimate the height for each volume.
   i) 60 cm³   ii) 120 cm³   iii) 240 cm³
e) What happens to the height when the volume is doubled?

20. During a snowstorm, 8 cm of snow fell. When snow melts, the volume of the water is about $\frac{1}{10}$ the volume of the snow.
a) What volume of snow fell on a lawn measuring 20 m by 15 m?
b) Suppose the water from the melted snow were collected. How many aquariums like the one in exercise 14 would it fill?

21. A small box measures 2 cm by 3 cm by 5 cm. It is completely filled with tiny cubes with edges 1 mm. Suppose you could stack all these cubes one on top of another. How high would the stack be?

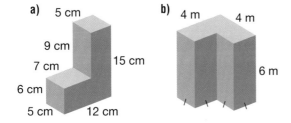

COMMUNICATING
The Ideas

In your journal, explain the difference between surface area and volume.

What Shapes Make Cardboard Cylinders?

Why does a frozen orange juice can have a spiral seam? Nigel Reed of Sunoco Containers Inc. says it's because it's a very efficient way of making cans out of materials other than metal. And Nigel should know: Sunoco Containers manufactures more of these cans than any other company in Canada!

A spiral can is made of 3 layers of material: an inner layer of polymer (plastic), one layer of kraft cardboard, and an outer layer of paper, on which the label is printed. Long strips of these 3 layers are wound onto a long metal rod (called a mantle) at an angle of about 40°. It's much like winding a piece of ribbon around your finger. As the layers are wound, they form a long tube. This tube is cut in 9 places to form 10 cans. An aluminum base is attached and the can is ready to be shipped to juice manufacturers. After the can is filled, the juice manufacturer puts on an aluminum lid.

1. **a)** Suppose you were to cut open a spiral can and unroll the cardboard. What shape do you think it would have?
   b) Check your prediction in part a. You will need a frozen orange juice can, a sharp knife, and a lift-type can opener. Carefully remove the bottom of the can with the can opener. Then cut the cardboard along the seam and flatten it. Was your prediction correct?
   c) Calculate the surface area of the can.

2. **a)** Construct two copies of this parallelogram, and cut them out.
   b) Tape the edges of the parallelogram in two different ways to form two cylinders, with no overlap.
   c) Calculate the base diameter and the height of each cylinder. Give the answers to the nearest millimetre. Check by measuring.

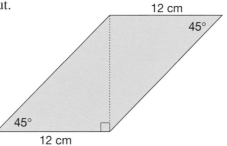

3. Every parallelogram can be used to construct two cylinders in this way. Draw an example of a parallelogram for which the two cylinders would be identical.

How Much Space Do 1.4 Billion Crayons Occupy?

Crayon maker is color-blind

STATE COLLEGE, Pa. (AP)—Crayola company officials might be turning a little red with news that the firm's top crayon maker is color-blind.

Emerson Moser, who is retiring after 35 years, isn't color-blind in the sense that he can't see color at all. It's just that some colors are confusing to him.

That means trying to spot the difference between a cadet blue and a blue green can make him feel, well, like a shrinking violet.

"If you have a serious case of it, you could foul up a lot of materials," said Moser, 63, who has made a record 1.4 billion crayons.

Moser's job is to pour molten wax into a mold that makes 2400 crayons. He does this nearly 100 times a day.

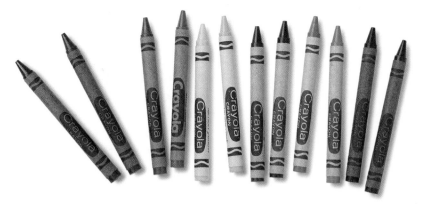

All the crayons Emerson Moser made during his career were packaged in boxes. How much space would all these boxes occupy?

You will need a box of crayons, a centimetre ruler, and a metre stick or tape measure.

Understand the problem

- How many crayons did Emerson Moser make during his career?
- What are you asked to do?

Think of a strategy

- You could find out how many crayons are in one box.
- You could find out how many boxes of crayons could be packed into a room such as your classroom.

Carry out the strategy

- Get a box of crayons and measure its length, width, and height. How many crayons are in the box?
- Measure the length, width, and height of your classroom.
- How many boxes of crayons could be spread out on the floor of your classroom? How many layers of boxes could fit from floor to ceiling? How many boxes would this be in all?
- How many crayons would there be in all these boxes?
- How many rooms full of crayons would you need until you had 1.4 billion crayons?

Look back

- About how many crayons did Emerson Moser make in a year?
- For about how many years do you think Emerson Moser was making crayons?
- About how long would it take him to make enough crayons to fill your classroom?

Communicating the Ideas

In your journal, write a description of this problem and your solution. Include your answers to the questions in *Look back*.

Review

1. Explain each term.
   a) net
   b) face
   c) edge of a polyhedron
   d) vertex of a polyhedron
   e) parallel edges
   f) regular polyhedron
   g) perpendicular edges

2. Use polyhedra you constructed to answer these questions.
   a) How many faces does a cube have?
   b) How many vertices does a square pyramid have?
   c) How many pairs of parallel faces does a rectangular prism have?
   d) How many edges does a triangular pyramid have?

3. Classify each polyhedron as a prism or a pyramid.

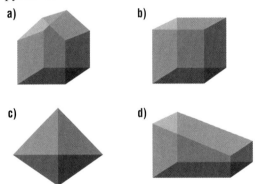

a)   **b)**

c)   **d)**

4. Which of these diagrams are nets for a cube?

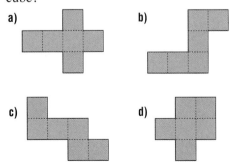

a)   **b)**

c)   **d)**

5. Sketch a net for a triangular prism.

6. The four walls of a bedroom are to be painted. The bedroom is 5.7 m long, 4.1 m wide, and 2.4 m high.
   a) Calculate the total area of the walls.
   b) From the total area, subtract 3.5 m² for the doors and 2.4 m² for the windows. The remaining area will be painted.
   c) One litre of paint covers 10 m². How much paint is needed for two coats?

7. Find the surface area of each solid.

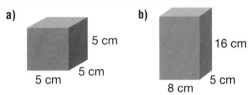

a) 5 cm, 5 cm, 5 cm
b) 16 cm, 8 cm, 5 cm

8. A storage room has length 7.5 m, width 4.0 m, and height 3.0 m.
   a) Find the surface area of the four walls.
   b) One sheet of panelling covers 3 m². How many sheets are needed to cover the walls?

9. This frame for a rectangular prism is constructed with wooden poles.

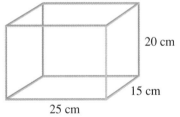

20 cm, 15 cm, 25 cm

   a) What area of cardboard is needed to cover the frame?
   b) How much cardboard is needed for the prism if the top is not covered? If the bottom is not covered?
   c) Suppose all the vertical faces except one are covered. What are two possible areas of cardboard needed?
   d) For a cube with edge length 25 cm, how much cardboard is needed to cover all the faces except one? Explain why there is only one possible answer.

10. **a)** Find the edge length of a cube with each surface area.

   i) 6 cm²   **ii)** 96 cm²   **iii)** 150 cm²

   b) If you know the surface area of a cube, how can you find its edge length?

11. Sketch each rectangular prism. Calculate each surface area and volume.

   a) length 6 cm, width 5 cm, height 7 cm

   b) length 6 cm, width 5 cm, height 14 cm

   c) base area 18 m², width 3 m, height 8 m

   d) base area 18 m², width 3 m, height 16 m

12. Use your calculations from exercise 11 to justify your answers.

   a) Does the surface area of a rectangular prism double when its height is doubled?

   b) Does the volume of a rectangular prism double when its height is doubled?

13. The area of the base and the height of each prism are given. Calculate its volume.

a)
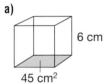
6 cm
45 cm²

b)
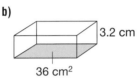
3.2 cm
36 cm²

c)
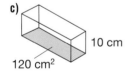
10 cm
120 cm²

d)
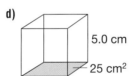
5.0 cm
25 cm²

14. For this exercise you will need 12 cubes.

   a) Arrange your cubes to form a rectangular prism.

   b) Measure the length, width, and height of your prism.

   c) Calculate the volume and the surface area of your prism.

   d) Find some other ways to arrange your cubes to form a rectangular prism, and repeat parts b and c.

   e) **i)** Did all your prisms have the same volume?

       ii) Did they all have the same surface area?

15. Calculate the volume of each prism.

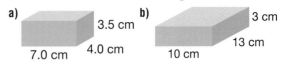

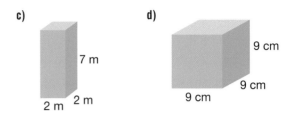

a) 3.5 cm, 7.0 cm, 4.0 cm
b) 3 cm, 13 cm, 10 cm

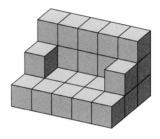

c) 7 m, 2 m, 2 m
d) 9 cm, 9 cm, 9 cm

16. This structure is made from centimetre cubes. What is the volume of the structure?

17. An excavation for the foundation of a building measures 45 m by 30 m by 10 m. How many truckloads of earth must be removed if each truck holds 5.5 m³?

18. Find the volume of each oven.

   a) microwave: 53 cm by 38 cm by 28 cm

   b) toaster: 23 cm by 18 cm by 13 cm

19. Find an object that is a rectangular prism, such as a video, a box, or a book.

   a) Measure the edges to the nearest centimetre.

   b) Calculate the surface area. Round to an amount that is easy to remember.

   c) Calculate the volume. Round to an amount that is easy to remember.

   d) Use the surface area to estimate the surface areas of other objects. Compare your estimates with your classmates' estimates. Explain your method.

Wrapping Presents without Wasting Paper

When you wrap a present you have to decide which way to put it on the paper. Which way is best, or does it matter? What are the dimensions of the largest present you could wrap with a piece of gift wrap? In this project you will determine answers to questions like these.

You will need a box to represent a present that you want to wrap, 2 sheets of gift wrap, and a ruler or tape measure.

ACTIVITY 1

Measure and record the dimensions of the box and the dimensions of the gift wrap. Decide how much to allow for overlapping.

Two ways to put the box on the paper are shown below. For each one, determine the length and width of the smallest piece of gift wrap you need. Also determine the length and width of each piece of gift wrap left over.

Allowing for the overlap, are the dimensions of the gift wrap you need the same in each method? If your answer is no, then which uses less paper? If your answer is yes, then are the pieces left over the same size? If not, does one method leave pieces that are more useful?

ACTIVITY 2

Suppose you decide to allow twice as much for overlapping as before. How would the results in Activity 1 change?

ACTIVITY 3

Determine some possible dimensions of boxes you can wrap without having any pieces of gift wrap left over. Think about the following questions as you do this:

- How much will you allow for overlapping?

- Does it matter which way you put the box on the paper? Investigate some of the possibilities. Are the volumes the same in each case?

ACTIVITY 4

Suppose you decide to allow twice as much as before for overlapping. How would the results in Activity 3 change?

ACTIVITY 5

Sometimes a box is too large to wrap with one sheet of paper. Then you have to tape two pieces of paper together to make a larger sheet. Determine some possible dimensions of boxes you can wrap with two sheets of gift wrap, without having anything left over.

Think about these questions as you do this:

- How much overlap will you need for taping the two sheets together?

- Is there more than one way to combine the sheets? If there is, do the combined sheets have the same dimensions or different dimensions? How will this affect the results?

COMMUNICATING

The Ideas

Write a report summarizing the results of your investigations. Include examples and diagrams in your report.

Cumulative Review

1. What units would you use to measure each item?

   a) the length of a pen

   b) the length of a river

   c) the length of a snake

   d) the distance around a running track

   e) the length of an ant

2. Determine if the figures are congruent. If they are, name the corresponding sides and angles.

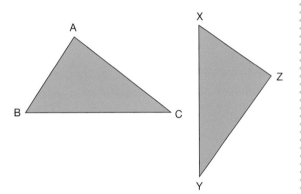

3. Add or subtract.

   a) $\frac{3}{10} + \frac{4}{5}$ **b)** $\frac{7}{8} - \frac{1}{2}$

   c) $1\frac{1}{3} + 2\frac{1}{6}$ **d)** $1 - \frac{1}{4}$

   e) $\frac{3}{5} - \frac{1}{10}$ **f)** $1\frac{1}{8} + \frac{3}{4}$

4. Multiply.

   a) 1.3×4.2 **b)** 0.6×2.3

   c) 3.6×1.5 **d)** 2.7×0.3

5. Write each fraction as a decimal and as a percent.

   a) $\frac{1}{2}$ **b)** $\frac{3}{4}$ **c)** $\frac{4}{5}$ **d)** $\frac{7}{10}$

   e) $\frac{3}{8}$ **f)** $\frac{2}{9}$ **g)** $\frac{8}{15}$ **h)** $\frac{5}{12}$

6. Find each amount to the nearest cent.

   a) 30% of $450.00

   b) 8% of $56.79

   c) 90% of $19.98

   d) 10% of $99.50

   e) 16% of $2.98

   f) 75% of $349.50

7. Simplify. Round each answer to the nearest whole number.

   a) $\frac{1}{2} \times 75$ **b)** $\frac{1}{4} \times 60$

   c) $\frac{1}{3} \times 40$ **d)** $\frac{1}{5} \times 45$

   e) $\frac{1}{7} \times 100$ **f)** $\frac{1}{10} \times 20$

8. Suppose a die is rolled 30 times.

   a) How many times would you expect to roll a 2 or a 3?

   b) How many times would you expect to roll an even number?

   c) How many times would you expect to roll a number that is not greater than 4?

9. The table lists the percent of households in each province that own an air conditioner.

Province	Households with an air conditioner (%)
Newfoundland and Labrador	2
Prince Edward Island	2
Nova Scotia	5
New Brunswick	8
Quebec	15
Ontario	48
Manitoba	48
Saskatchewan	38
Alberta	8
British Columbia	9

   a) Display the information on a graph. Explain how you decided which type of graph to draw.

   b) Describe the shape of your graph.

   c) Based on your graph, predict which parts of Canada have the warmest and the coolest summer temperatures. Do some research on summer temperatures. Were your predictions correct?

10. **a)** Write a set of 5 numbers with a mean of 14 and a median of 11.

   b) Write a set of 6 numbers with a mean of 14 and a median of 11.

   c) Write a set of 7 numbers with a mean of 25 and a mode of 21.

11. Are the following statements correct interpretations of the data in the table?

Age of skier (in years)	Percent of skiing accidents
under 10	10
10 – 19	61
20 – 29	19
30 – 39	5
40 – 49	3
over 50	2

Teenagers are more likely to have skiing accidents than persons in other age groups. People over 50 years of age are the best skiers.

12. Use an integer to describe each situation.
  a) A swimmer dives to a depth of 3 m.
  b) Terry travelled 153 km farther on Tuesday than on Monday.
  c) The temperature was 8°C colder on Saturday than on Friday.
  d) After paying for a CD, Claire has $12 less in her wallet.

13. Use a number line. Write the integer that is:
  a) 7 units to the right of −3
  b) 4 units to the left of +4
  c) 8 units to the right of 0
  d) 12 units to the right of −9
  e) 15 units to the left of −7

14. Determine the area of each parallelogram.

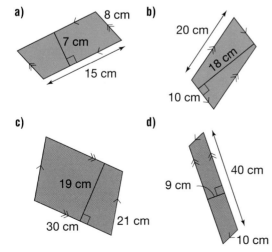

15. For each number pattern below:
  a) Describe the pattern.
  b) What is the 15th number in the pattern?
  c) What is the 20th number in the pattern?
  d) Use a variable to describe any number in the pattern.
    i) 6, 12, 18, 24, 30, 36, …
    ii) 9, 10, 11, 12, 13, 14, …
    iii) 29, 28, 27, 26, 25, 24, …
    iv) 100, 50, $\frac{100}{3}$, 25, 20, $\frac{100}{6}$, …
    v) 180, 90, 60, 45, 36, 30, …

16. Write an equation to represent each sentence. Find the value of the variable that makes each equation true.
  a) 5 more than a number is 21.
  b) A number divided by 3 is 10.
  c) A number subtracted from 8 is −7.
  d) Double a number is 36.
  e) A number increased by 12 is 19.

17. Write each equation in words. Find the value of the variable that makes each equation true.
  a) $a + 7 = 18$ **b)** $3b = -21$
  c) $15 - c = 6$ **d)** $15 = \frac{d}{3}$
  e) $\frac{e}{4} = -2$ **f)** $-8 = f + 4$
  g) $-2 = g - 11$ **h)** $10 = h + 3$

18. Use a two-pan balance or algebra tiles to represent each situation. Find the answer to each question.
  a) Anouk has 5 magazines. After Lesley gives her some, Anouk has 12. How many magazines did Lesley give Anouk?
  b) Michael has some loonies in a piggy-bank. His mother puts 7 more loonies in the bank. Michael then has 11 loonies. How many loonies were in the bank before the 7 loonies were added?
  c) One spring morning, the temperature increased 7°C from 5 a.m. to 10 a.m. The temperature at 10 a.m. was 4°C. What was the temperature at 5 a.m.?

TRANSFORMATIONS

WHAT'S COMING UP?

DEPARTMENTS

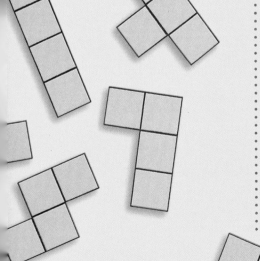

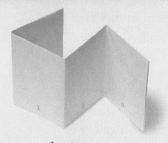

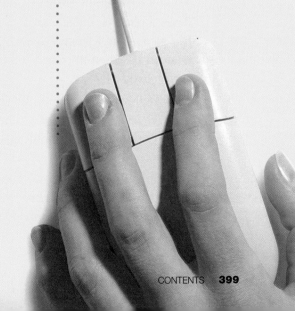

Quests

Minds on Math Project

Start With What You Know

Some computer games and puzzles involve moving pieces so that they fit together. Here are two examples.

Tetris

Tetris is available in many variations. All of them are played using pieces that can be made from four squares. In the basic game, these pieces fall into an empty pit. The object of the game is to fit the pieces together at the bottom of the pit without leaving any gaps.

As each piece falls, the player can move it in three ways — slide left, slide right, or turn 90° clockwise.

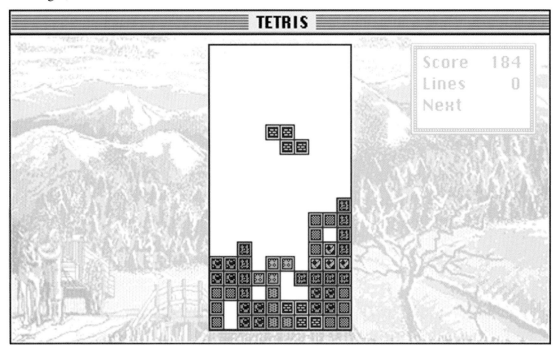

When a piece is aligned properly, the player can drop it into place. The game ends when no room is left for the pieces to drop. Points are awarded based on the number of pieces used, and the time taken to fit them together.

1. Examples of all seven different pieces in *Tetris* are shown in the sample screen above. Draw a diagram to illustrate each piece.

2. Observe that there are two pairs of similar pieces. Why do you think the designers of the game provided these pieces?

An example of a piece sliding left as it falls

An example of a piece sliding right as it falls

An example of a piece turning as it falls

The Ten Tiles Puzzle

In this puzzle, ten tiles are to be put in a rectangular tray. The puzzle has hundreds of different solutions.

In every solution, each tile and its matching tile can be related by a slide, a flip, a turn, or combinations of them.

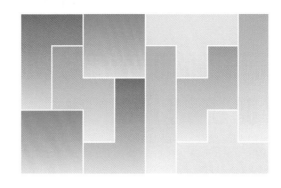

Slide	Flip	Half-turn

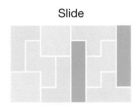  

3. In each solution below, identify how each pair of matching tiles is related. Use a slide, a flip, or a turn; or a combination of two of them.

a) 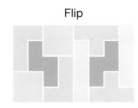 b) c) 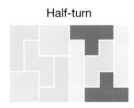 d)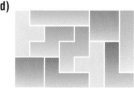

4. a) Glue 1-cm grid paper onto a piece of cardboard. Draw all 10 of the puzzle pieces on the grid paper. Cut them out. Use the pieces to find a solution of the puzzle that is different from those on this page.
   b) Observe that the tiles fit in a rectangle 8 units long and 5 units wide. What other dimensions are possible for this puzzle? Can you find a way to fit the tiles in a rectangle with these dimensions?

5. Compare the tiles in the *Ten Tiles Puzzle* with the *Tetris* pieces. The tiles in the *Ten Tiles Puzzle* are formed by four squares, just as the *Tetris* pieces. Why do you think there are 7 different pieces in *Tetris*, but only 5 different tiles in the *Ten Tiles Puzzle*?

6. We often use a coordinate grid to plot a figure and its image. Plot each set of points on a coordinate grid and join them in the order indicated. Identify the figure formed.
   a) A(6, 1), B(2, −3), C(5, −2); ABCA
   b) P(−1, 1), Q(−6, 1), R(−6, 4), S(−1, 4); PQRSP
   c) K(−1, 2), L(3, −2), M(2, −4), N(−3, 1); KLMNK

In this chapter, we use the word *translation* to describe a slide; *reflection* to describe a flip; and *rotation* to describe a turn. A translation, a reflection, and a rotation are *transformations*.

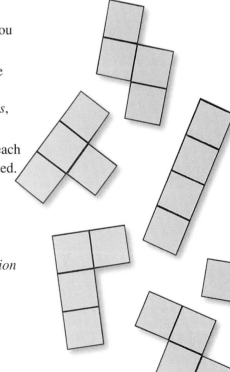

Exploring Transformations with a Paint or Draw Program

Many Paint and Draw programs have tools for transforming letters, words, or pictures. Here are some examples from several programs.

Translations

With most programs you can translate a figure by dragging it with the mouse.

To show the original figure as well as the image figure, make a copy of the figure and drag the copy.

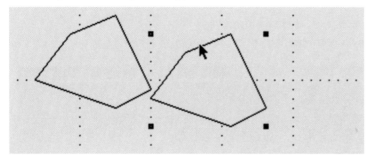

Reflections

Many programs have commands for horizontal or vertical reflections.

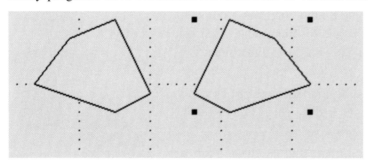

Rotations

Many programs have commands for rotating a figure.

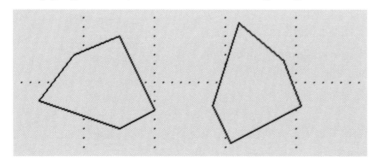

1. Use a Paint or Draw program to make a *Ten Tiles Puzzle* like the one on page 401. Turn on the Autogrid or Snap To Grid. Make four identical small squares. Drag the squares together in the shape of one of the puzzle pieces. Use the Polygon tool to trace the outline of the figure. Move the tracing, rearrange the squares to form another puzzle piece, and trace it. Repeat until you have formed the five puzzle pieces. Duplicate each piece so that you have ten pieces. You can rotate, reflect, and translate the pieces to find a solution of the puzzle that is different from those on page 401.

2. **a)** Start a new Draw or Paint file. Draw a bowling ball like the one on the left.

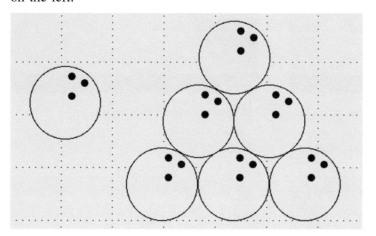

   b) Group all the parts of the bowling ball, then duplicate it six times. Slide the duplicates to form a stack like the one on the right.

3. **a)** Start a new Draw or Paint file. Draw a figure like the one on the left.

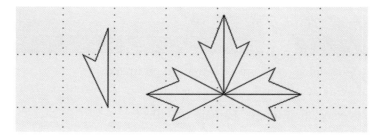

   b) Duplicate the figure six times. Use combinations of translations, reflections, and rotations to re-create the design on the right.
   c) Describe each transformation you used to re-create the design.

4. Create a figure in a new Draw or Paint file. Create a design by duplicating and transforming the figure. Record the transformations you use. Ask a classmate to identify the transformations you used. Is there more than one possible answer for some parts of the design?

5. Are there any other transformations you can apply to figures using your Draw or Paint program? Demonstrate with a diagram.

9.1 TRANSLATIONS

Developing the Ideas

▶▶ Through an Activity

You will need dot paper for this activity.

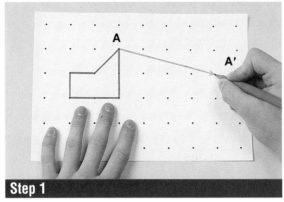

Step 1

Draw any figure on dot paper. Mark a point A on the figure. Draw an arrow from A to any other point on the dot paper. Mark this point A′.

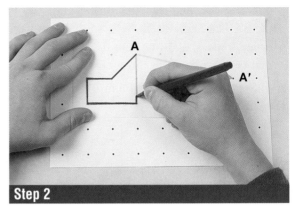

Step 2

Make a tracing of the figure.

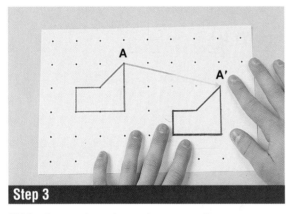

Step 3

Slide the tracing along the arrow. Be sure not to turn the figure.

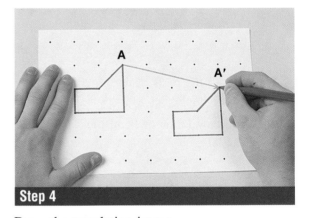

Step 4

Draw the translation image.

1. Compare the original figure and the translation image. Explain how the figures are alike and how they are different.

2. To describe a translation, we say how far the original figure moves left or right, and how far it moves up or down. Describe the translation your figures represent.

Every translation involves these three things:

1. an original figure

2. a description of the translation

3. an image figure

In many problems involving translations, two of these things are given and you are asked to determine the third.

▶ ▶ **Through Guided Examples**

Example 1 ....

A triangle has vertices J(−5, 1), K(−2, −3), and L(4, 2). Draw △JKL and its image after a translation of 4 units right and 5 units up. What are the coordinates of the image triangle? How does the image compare to the original figure?

Solution

On a coordinate grid, draw △JKL. Starting at J, count 4 units to the right and 5 units up to obtain point J'. Locate points K' and L' in the same way. The image triangle has coordinates J'(−1, 6), K'(2, 2), and L'(8, 7).

The image and the original figure have the same size and shape. The figures are congruent.

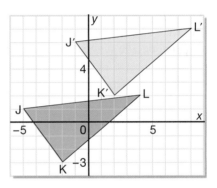

Example 2 ....

A triangle with vertices P'(1, 4), Q'(−4, 5), and R'(−2, −1) is the image of △PQR after a translation of 6 units left and 3 units up. Draw △P'Q'R' and △PQR.

Solution

On a coordinate grid, draw △P'Q'R'.

The original △PQR was translated 6 units to the left and 3 units up to this location.

Thus, we can move △P'Q'R' 6 units to the right and 3 units down to get back to the original triangle.

Starting at P', count 6 units to the right and 3 units down to obtain point P. Locate points Q and R in the same way.

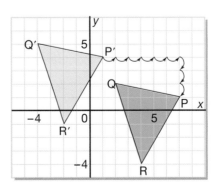

Working with Mathematics

Something to talk about

1. In this drawing by M.C. Escher, the pattern is repeated by a translation. Choose any bird. Describe three translations that would move the bird to another bird of the same colour.

2. For each diagram below, decide whether the pale figure is a translation image of the dark figure. If it is, describe the translation. If it is not, explain how you know.

a)
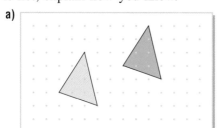

b)
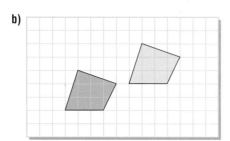

c)
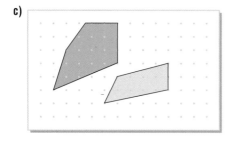

3. Each figure below is divided into four congruent parts. Which parts are related by a translation? Explain your answers.

a) 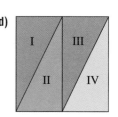   b)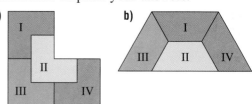

c) 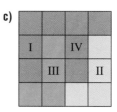   d)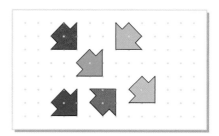

4. Is each statement true or false? Explain.
   a) The translation image of any figure is congruent to the figure.
   b) All translation images of a figure are congruent to each other.

Practice

5. Identify the figures that are translation images of the red figure. Describe each translation.

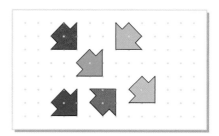

6. Get a set of pattern blocks and a sheet of dot paper. Place one block on the paper, with a vertex on a dot. Trace the block. Translate it so the vertex is on a different dot. Trace the block again. Trade drawings with a classmate. Identify the block and translation used to create the drawing you receive.

7. Copy the figure below onto dot paper. Draw its image after each translation.
   a) 3 units left and 1 unit up
   b) 2 units right and 4 units down
   c) 1 unit right and 3 units up
   d) 4 units left and 5 units down

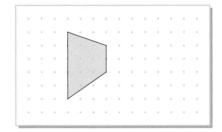

Work together

8. The vertices of a figure and the description of a translation are given. Draw the figure and its image after the translation. What are the coordinates of the vertices of the image? How does the image compare to the original figure?
   a) Triangle: X(−2, 1), Y(0, 5), Z(3, −2)
      Translation: 3 units left and 4 units up
   b) Parallelogram: D(4, −1), E(−1, 3), F(−4, 1), G(1, −3)
      Translation: 2 units right and 5 units down

9. The vertices of a figure and its translation image are given. Draw each figure and its image. Identify each figure. Describe the translation.
   a) Figure: A(2, 5), B(−1, 4), C(−5, −2), D(0, −1)
      Image: A′(5, 1), B′(2, 0), C′(−2, −6), D′(3, −5)
   b) Figure: P(5, 3), Q(6, −2), R(−2, −4)
      Image: P′(1, 8), Q′(2, 3), R′(−6, 1)
   c) Figure: K(−8, 4), L(−5, 7), M(−5, 4), N(−2, 4), P(−6, 0)
      Image: K′(−2, 3), L′(1, 6), M′(1, 3), N′(4, 3), P′(0, −1)
   d) Figure: S(−1, 2), T(3, 0), U(4, 6)
      Image: S′(−6, 0), T′(−2, −2), U′(−1, 4)

10. △A′B′C′ is a translation image of △ABC. One vertex of △ABC is the point (6, 2). Determine as many different translations as you can that satisfy these conditions. For each translation, draw a diagram showing △ABC, △A′B′C′, and the translation arrow.

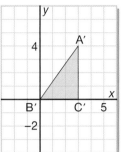

11. Rectangle P′Q′R′S′ is a translation image of rectangle PQRS. One vertex of PQRS is the point (−1, 4). Determine as many different translations as you can that satisfy these conditions. For each translation, draw a diagram showing PQRS, P′Q′R′S′, and the translation arrow.

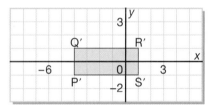

12. Compare your answers to exercises 10 and 11. What do you notice? Suppose you had a similar situation involving a translation image of a pentagon. How many translations would you expect to find? Make up an example of your own using a pentagon and check your prediction.

On your own

13. In the diagram below, identify which triangles are translation images of the blue triangle. Describe the translations.

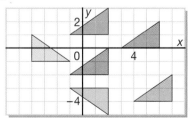

14. Copy the figure below onto dot paper. Draw its image after each translation.
   a) 2 units left
   b) 3 units right and 3 units up
   c) 1 unit left and 3 units down
   d) 2 units left and 4 units up

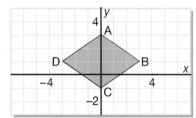

15. The diagram shows a rhombus ABCD.

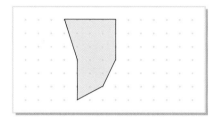

   a) Copy the diagram. Draw the image of the rhombus after a translation of 3 units right and 2 units up.
   b) Name the figure formed by the rhombus and its image.
   c) Describe other translations that would create the same type of figure as in part b.

16. The vertices of a figure and its translation image are given. Draw the figure and its image. Describe the translation.
   a) Triangle: A(2, 2), B(−3, 1), C(−4, −2)
       Image: A′(8, −1), B′(3, −2), C′(2, −5)
   b) Square: D(0, 5), E(−1, 2), F(2, 1), G(3, 4)
       Image: D′(−4, 3), E′(−5, 0), F′(−2, −1), G′(−1, 2)

17. A polygon with vertices P′(−2, 2), Q′(3, 3), R′(3, 8), and S′(1, 4) is the image of polygon PQRS after a translation. Draw the two polygons if the translation is:
   a) 4 units right and 2 units up
   b) 1 unit right and 6 units down
   c) 5 units left and 3 units up

18. Look at a tiled floor. Notice that it is made up of congruent tiles placed in a pattern. There are no gaps between the tiles and they do not overlap. Such a pattern is called a *tiling pattern*. For some figures, you can create a tiling pattern using only translations. Draw each figure below on cardboard. Cut out the figure. Trace around it, slide it, and trace it again. Repeat to create a tiling pattern. Colour parts of your pattern to make a design. Part a is started for you. If you have a computer with a Draw program, use it to complete this exercise.

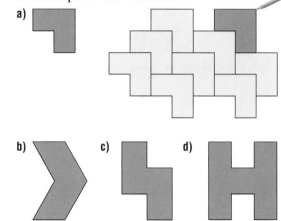

   a)
   b)   **c)**   **d)**

Extend your thinking

19. When a certain geometric object is translated 3 units right and 2 units up, its image appears to be in the same position as the original object. What is the object? Draw a diagram to illustrate your answer.

The Ideas

In your journal, explain how to describe and draw a translation image. State some properties of figures related by a translation. Include drawings.

...9.2 *REFLECTIONS*

Developing the Ideas

▶▶ *Through an Activity*

Suppose you reflect a given figure. Suppose you join matching points
on the figure and its image with line segments. Do you think these line
segments would form any patterns?

You will need dot paper for this activity.

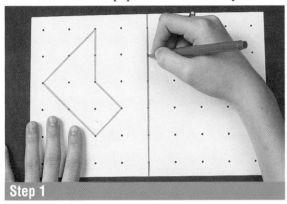
Step 1

Draw any figure on dot paper. Draw a mirror
line.

Step 2

Fold the paper along the mirror line and make
a sharp crease.

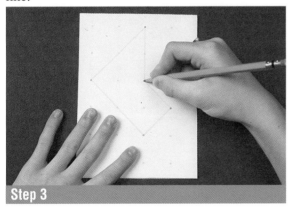
Step 3

Mark the vertices of the figure on the folded
paper.

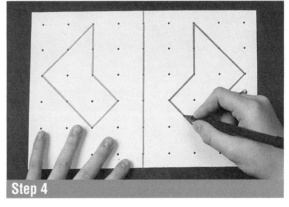
Step 4

Open the paper. Use the vertices you marked
in Step 3. Draw the reflection image.

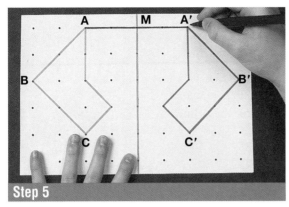
Step 5

Label any three points A, B, and C on the figure and the matching points A′, B′, and C′ on the image. Join A to A′, and label the point M where AA′ intersects the mirror line.

1. How do the lengths of AM and A′M compare?

2. What is the size of the angles formed by AA′ and the mirror line?

3. Repeat, using BB′ and CC′.

4. What did you discover about AA′ and the mirror line? Is this true for BB′ and CC′?

5. Discuss the results of exercise 4 with others in your group. Did everyone get the same results?

6. Compare the original figure with its image. Explain how the figures are the same and how they are different.

▶ ▶ *Through Instruction*

The Dutch artist M.C. Escher made many prints involving transformations. To make this print, he needed to know the basic property of a reflection.

• • • • • • • • •

Basic Property of a Reflection

Line segments joining matching points are perpendicular to the mirror line. The mirror line meets each line segment at its midpoint.

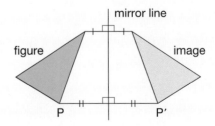

Every reflection in a line involves these three things:

1. an original figure

2. a mirror line

3. an image figure

In many problems involving reflections, two of these things are given and you are asked to determine the third.

You can use the basic property of a reflection to draw a reflection image. For each point A on a figure, draw a line through A perpendicular to the mirror line. Locate a point on this line the same distance from the mirror line as A, but on the other side of the line. Label this point A′. It is the reflection image of A.

You can also use the property to find a mirror line, given a figure and its reflection image. Join a pair of matching points on the figure and its image with a line segment. The mirror line meets this line segment at right angles at its midpoint.

▷▶ *Through a Guided Example*

Example

A triangle with vertices A′(3, 4), B′(−2, 1), and C′(4, −1) is the image of △ABC after a reflection in the *y*-axis. Draw △A′B′C′ and △ABC. What are the coordinates of △ABC? How does the image compare to the original figure?

Solution

On a coordinate grid, draw △A′B′C′.

The original △ABC was reflected in the *y*-axis to become △A′B′C′.

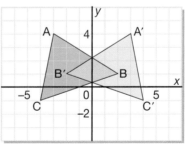

Thus, we can reflect △A′B′C′ in the *y*-axis to return to the original triangle.

Since A′ is 3 units to the right of the *y*-axis, A must be 3 units to the left of the *y*-axis.

That is, the coordinates of A are (−3, 4).

Similarly, the coordinates of B are (2, 1), and the coordinates of C are (−4, −1).

The image and the original figure have the same size and shape. That is, they are congruent.

Working with Mathematics

Something to talk about

1. Would the results of your investigation on pages 409 and 410 still apply if:
   a) one side of the given figure is on the mirror line?
   b) the given figure crosses the mirror line?

2. Refer to the figures in exercise 3 on page 406. Which parts are related by a reflection? Explain your answers.

3. When a figure can be folded such that one half matches the other, the figure has line symmetry. The fold line is the *line of symmetry*. How many lines of symmetry does each figure have? Use a transparent mirror to support your answer.

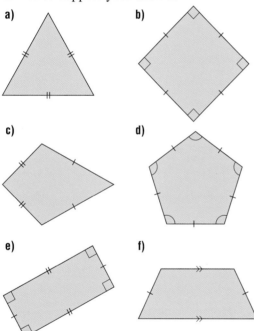

4. Draw a square. Draw one line of symmetry. How could the line of symmetry be described as a mirror line?

5. Does the Escher print on page 410 have a line of symmetry? Explain your answer.

Practice

6. Identify the figures that are reflection images of the red figure. For each reflection image, state whether the mirror line is horizontal, vertical, or slanted.

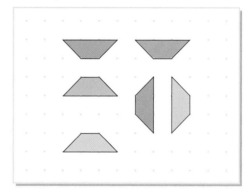

7. Copy each figure onto dot paper. Use paper folding or a transparent mirror to draw each reflection image.

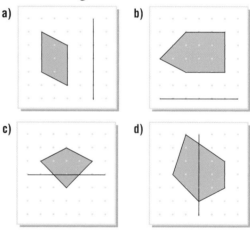

8. Get a set of pattern blocks.
   a) Draw a vertical line on a sheet of paper. Use pattern blocks to copy the design below. Model its reflection image in the vertical line. Trace the blocks that make up the design and its image. Remove the blocks. Use paper folding to verify that your image is correct.

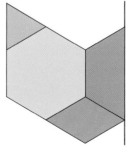

b) Create a design with the pattern blocks. Challenge a classmate to model the reflection image of your design in a vertical or horizontal line. Check her or his solution.

Work together

9. Draw each figure on a coordinate grid. Identify the figure. Draw its image after a reflection in the x-axis. State the coordinates of the vertices of the image.
   a) A(1, 4), B(−2, −3), C(−4, 1), D(−3, 5)
   b) X(−7, 4), Y(−7, 0), Z(−2, 0)
   c) N(2, 5), P(3, 0), Q(7, 2), R(6, 7)
   d) K(3, −4), O(0, 0), M(−4, −7)

10. Repeat exercise 9, but reflect each figure in the y-axis.

11. A quadrilateral has vertices A(2, −1), B(7, −2), C(6, −7), and D(1, −6). Draw this figure on a coordinate grid.
   a) Draw the image after a reflection in the x-axis. State the coordinates of the vertices of the image.
   b) Reflect the image in part a in the y-axis. State the coordinates of the vertices of the image.
   c) Reflect the image in part b in the x-axis. State the coordinates of the vertices of the image.

12. Copy the table. Try to draw an example of a triangle for each space in the table. You may use a transparent mirror to find lines of symmetry. Which triangles do you think cannot be drawn?

Type of triangle	Number of lines of symmetry				
	0	1	2	3	4
acute					
obtuse					
right					
isosceles					
equilateral					

13. **a)** Make a cube with modelling clay. Cut the cube in half. Place a sheet of paper between the pieces. The sheet of paper represents a *plane of symmetry*.

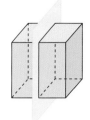

b) How many planes of symmetry like this one does the cube have?

c) Make another cube with modelling clay. Cut the cube in half again, but in a different way. Use a sheet of paper to represent another plane of symmetry. How many planes of symmetry like this one does the cube have?

d) How many planes of symmetry does a cube have altogether?

14. A line of symmetry is a reflection line. How could you describe a plane of symmetry in terms of a reflection?

15. How many planes of symmetry does a sphere have? Use modelling clay to support your answer.

16. Is it possible for a figure to be reflected so that its image coincides with itself? Explain your answer.

17. To do this investigation you will need a small unframed mirror. Use the diagram at the right. Stand the mirror on its edge as shown in the photograph.

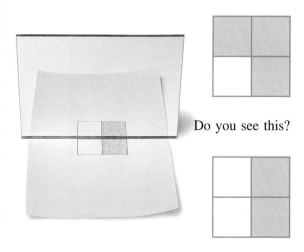

Do you see this?

a) Can you make these figures with the mirror by placing it in different positions?

i)

ii)

iii)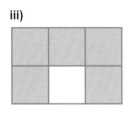

iv)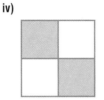

v)

vi)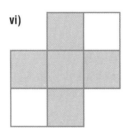

b) What other figures like these can you make with the mirror?

18. At first glance, the building in this photograph may appear symmetrical. On closer inspection, you will see that it is not symmetrical. Find as many examples as you can in the photograph to show that the building is not symmetrical.

19. Many Draw programs contain commands you can use to reflect a figure. However, these commands may not let you indicate where you want the mirror line.

a) Start your Draw program and create any figure. Use the horizontal flip and vertical flip commands. Find out which line the computer uses as the mirror line.

b) Use other commands to check that your answer in part a is correct.

c) Can you find a way to reflect your figure in a different mirror line?

d) Investigate what happens to a figure if you reflect it horizontally then vertically.

On your own

20. The vertices of a figure and its reflection image are given. Draw the figure, its image, and the mirror line.

a) Rectangle: A(0, 7), B(2, 5), C(−2, 1), D(−4, 3)
Image: A′(6, 1), B′(4, 3), C′(0, −1), D′(2, −3)

b) Triangle: P(8, 4), Q(−2, 4), R(−2, 9)
Image: P′(4, −4), Q′(−2, 4), R′(−6, 1)

21. A trapezoid with vertices K′(3, 1), L′(7, 1), M′(7, 3), and N′(5, 3) is the image of trapezoid KLMN after a reflection. Draw the two polygons if the reflection is in:

a) the *x*-axis   **b)** the *y*-axis

c) either of the two lines passing through (0, 0) and inclined at a 45° angle to the *x*-axis

22. Use a Draw program to make a puzzle. Draw a polygon. Make three copies of the polygon. Fill each copy with a different colour or pattern. Flip one copy horizontally, flip one vertically, and flip one both horizontally and vertically. Label the original polygon and print the file. Challenge a classmate to identify which reflection(s) produced each image. To make the problem more challenging, include several polygons and their images on one page.

23. A certain triangle is reflected about one of its sides. The combined figure formed by the triangle and its reflection image is a square. What kind of triangle is it?

24. Copy the table. Try to draw an example of a quadrilateral for each space in the table. You may use a transparent mirror to find lines of symmetry. Which quadrilaterals do you think cannot be drawn?

Figure	Number of lines of symmetry				
	0	1	2	3	4
rectangle					
rhombus					
parallelogram					
trapezoid					

25. Use a coin to draw diagrams like these. Draw and label the lines of symmetry in each diagram.

a)

b)

c)

26. Arrange some coins to form the diagram in exercise 25b. Move only one coin to make a diagram that has:
a) no lines of symmetry
b) only one line of symmetry

27. Arrange some coins to form the diagram in exercise 25c. Move the least number of coins possible to make a diagram with six lines of symmetry. How many coins must be moved?

28. Draw the figure below on a sheet of paper. Use a transparent mirror to make a design by drawing reflection images of the figure.

29. Draw the letter F on a 2-cm square card. Draw the reversed letter on the back of the card.

F Ⅎ

Make an 8 by 8 grid of 2-cm squares. Put the card on one of the squares. You can move the card to any neighbouring square by flipping it about an edge.

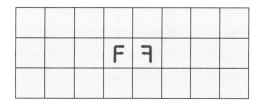

Move the card in this way to other squares and record how the letter F appears in each. Describe the pattern in the results.

Extend your thinking

30. When a certain quadrilateral is reflected in the y-axis, its image appears to be in the same position as the original quadrilateral. What kind of quadrilateral could it be? Draw diagrams to illustrate your answers.

COMMUNICATING

The Ideas

In your journal, explain how to draw the image of a figure reflected in the y-axis. State some properties of figures related by a reflection. Include drawings.

Transformations on the Plane

Work with a partner.

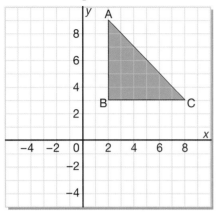

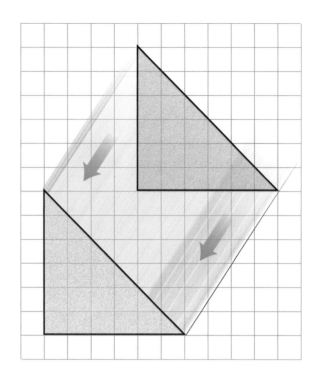

1. Write the coordinates of the points A, B, and C.

We slide △ABC 4 units left and 6 units down.
We draw the triangle in its new position.
We label this image triangle A′B′C′.

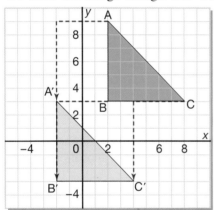

2. Write the coordinates of A′, B′, and C′.

We can describe a translation of 4 units left as −4.
We can describe a translation of 6 units down as −6.
We can use addition expressions to calculate the coordinates
of each image point.
For example, A has coordinates (+2, +9).
A′ has coordinates (+2) + (−4) = −2; and (+9) + (−6) = +3.
The coordinates of A′ are (−2, +3).

3. Use this method to check the coordinates of B′ and C′.

4. a) Write the coordinates
of each vertex of the figure.
Draw the figure on a
coordinate grid.

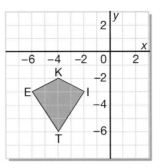

b) Translate figure KITE 6 units
right and 7 units up.
Draw the figure in its
new position. Label the
image figure K′I′T′E′.

c) Write the coordinates of K′, I′, T′, and E′.

d) Write the integer that could describe a translation of 6 units right.

e) Write the integer that could describe a translation of 7 units up.

f) Use addition expressions to calculate the coordinates of the
vertices of K′I′T′E′. Do your results agree with part c?

5. On coordinate axes on grid paper, draw a figure. Label it with the
coordinates of its vertices. Translate your figure. Draw its image.
Exchange figures with your partner. Have your partner write the
addition statements that calculate the coordinates of each vertex of the
image.

6. a) Write the coordinates of
each vertex of the figure.
Draw the figure on a
coordinate grid.

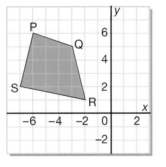

b) Reflect quadrilateral PQRS
in the y-axis. Draw the
figure in its new position.
Label the image figure
P′Q′R′S′.

c) Write the coordinates of P′, Q′, R′, and S′.

d) i) How are the x-coordinates of P and P′ related?

   ii) Is the same relationship true for the x-coordinates of Q and Q′,
   R and R′, and S and S′?

e) How are the y-coordinates of each point and its image related?

7. On coordinate axes on grid paper, draw a figure in the first quadrant.
Reflect the figure in the x-axis. Write the coordinates of the figure and
the coordinates of its image. For each vertex, how are the coordinates
of the point and its image related?

8. On coordinate axes on grid paper, draw a figure in the first quadrant.
Reflect the figure in the y-axis. Then reflect the image in the x-axis.
For each vertex, how are the coordinates of the point and its second
image related?

Designing a Booklet

Maria is preparing an 8-page booklet for printing. When the printed sheet is folded and trimmed, the pages must be right side up and in the correct order. How should she arrange the pages on the printed sheet?

Understand the problem

- Is the sheet printed on both sides?
- How many pages are printed on each side of the sheet?

Think of a strategy

- Use a sheet of paper.

Carry out the strategy

- Fold a sheet of paper two times to form a booklet.
- Without unfolding, number the front and back of the pages in order.
- Unfold the paper to see how the pages should be arranged.

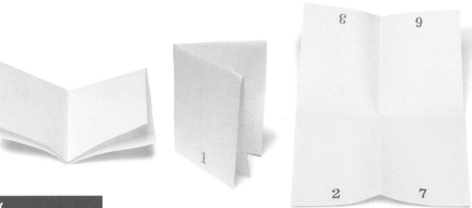

Look back

- Are any of the pages upside down in relation to the others?
- How are the page numbers on opposite sides of the sheet related?
- In the diagrams above, the first fold of the paper is parallel to the short side. Would it make any difference if the first fold were parallel to the long side?
- Determine how to number the pages so that a single sheet of paper can be used to make a booklet with 16 pages.

Communicating the Ideas

In your journal, explain how you can fold a single sheet of paper to create an 8-page booklet. Describe how the pages should be arranged to appear right side up and in the correct order.

....9.3 ROTATIONS

Developing the Ideas

▶▶▶ *Through an Activity*

You will need dot paper for this activity.

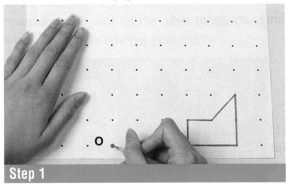

Step 1

Draw any figure on dot paper. Label any point O on the dot paper. This is the rotation centre.

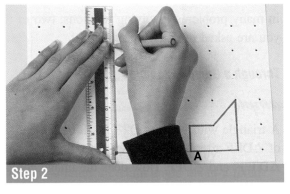

Step 2

Label a point A on the figure and join O to A. Draw a 90° angle at O with one arm OA.

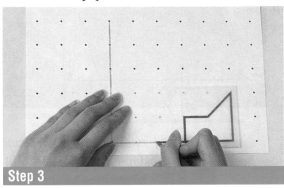

Step 3

Trace the figure.

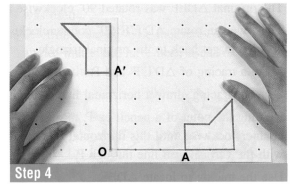

Step 4

With pencil point at O, turn the tracing counterclockwise until the tracing of A lies on the other arm of the angle. Draw the rotation image. Label the image point A′.

1. Compare the original figure with its rotation image. How are the figures alike and how are they different?

BOGGLE YOUR MIND

In an interview, a gardening expert said that the average city housing lot contains about 6 t of earthworms. Estimate the area of lawns and gardens in a city lot. Using the number given, estimate the mass of earthworms in 1 m² of property. The mass of one earthworm is about 5 g. How many earthworms are there in 1 m²?

Splitting Images

Do you think your face is exactly symmetrical? Do you think your pet's face is exactly symmetrical? In this project you will investigate these questions.

ACTIVITY 1

How do you think the above photographs were produced?
Discuss this with a partner.

ACTIVITY 2

Ask your partner to take a photograph of your face.
Do the same for your partner. Take photographs
of some other things that look symmetrical.

27. Get some empty 1-L milk cartons. Their bases are squares. Measure the sides of the square. Draw a line around each carton that is this distance above the base. Cut along the line to form a cube with no top.

Take one of the cubes. Cut along the edges until the faces lie flat to form a net. How many different nets can you make in this way? Do they all require the same number of cuts?

28. The net for a rectangular prism is shown.

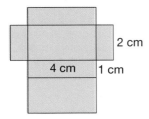

2 cm

4 cm 1 cm

a) Explain why we only need to label the lengths of 3 sides.

b) Find the length of each unmarked side in the figure.

c) Find the total surface area of the rectangular prism.

29. Find the volume of each prism. Round each volume to 1 decimal place where necessary.

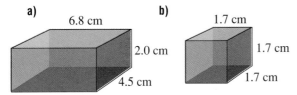

a)
6.8 cm
2.0 cm
4.5 cm

b)
1.7 cm
1.7 cm
1.7 cm

30. a) A room is 4.9 m long, 5.1 m wide, and 3.2 m high. What volume of air is in the room, to the nearest cubic metre?

b) What is the volume of air in the room from part a if the length is doubled? If the length and the width are both doubled?

31. Describe the transformation that maps each figure onto the red figure.

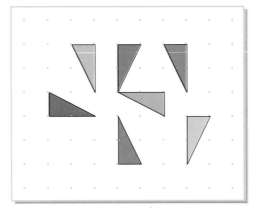

32. The coordinates of the vertices of a figure and its translation image are given. Draw the figure and its image. Identify the figure. Describe the translation.

a) Figure: A(3, 7), B(7, 7), C(7, 3), D(3, 3)
Image: A′(−5, 3), B′(−1, 3), C′(−1, −1), D′(−5, −1)

b) Figure: L(−2, 4), M(−4, −1), N(−1, −4)
Image: L′(5, 7), M′(3, 2), N′(6, −1)

c) Figure: W(−3, 5), X(3, 5), Y(3, 2), Z(−3, 2)
Image: W′(2, −1), X′(8, −1), Y′(8, −4), Z′(2, −4)

33. Draw each figure on a coordinate grid. Identify the figure. Draw its image after a reflection in the y-axis. State the coordinates of the vertices of the image.

a) D(5, 5), E(6, 3), F(1, 1)

b) K(−6, 3), L(−2, 3), M(−2, 2), N(−6, 2)

c) P(2, −2), Q(5, −2), R(5, −5), S(2, −5)

34. Repeat exercise 33, but reflect each figure in the x-axis.

35. Copy each figure onto dot paper. Draw its image after a 90° clockwise rotation about P, and after a 180° rotation about P.

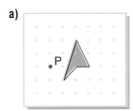

a)
.P

b)
.P

ANSWERS

INTRODUCTION: PATTERN

Start With What You Know, page 24

1. **a)** A: rock strata, B: head of a horsefly, C: honeycomb, D: feather, E: fabric, F: butterfly's wing, G: spider's web, H: interlocking brick, I: broom
   b) Answers may vary.
2. **a)** Baseball scores, football scores, tennis scores, golf scores
   b) Answers may vary.
   c) Answers may vary; yes, there is a time in the year when all sports are played

Patterns in Arithmetic
Developing the Ideas, page 26

1. Answers may vary. You could use multiplication rather than addition to calculate the total cost.
2. Answers may vary. Perhaps an advertising gimmick

Working with Mathematics, page 27

1. **a)** $5.98   **b)** $29.97   **c)** $47.96   **d)** $24.97
2. Answers may vary. Customers think the price is less than it actually is.
3. **a)** 54 000   **b)** 5400   **c)** 540   **d)** 54
   e) 5.4   **f)** 0.54   **g)** 0.054   **h)** 0.0054
4. Answers may vary. The zeros after the 1 tell how many places to move the decimal point to the right. The zeros before the 1 tell how many places to move the decimal point to the left.
5. **a)** 3.5   **b)** 35   **c)** 350
   d) 3500   **e)** 35 000   **f)** 350 000
6. Answers may vary. The zeros after the 1 tell how many places to move the decimal point to the left. The zeros before the 1 tell how many places to move the decimal point to the right.
7. **a)** 2, 20, 200; $8000 \div 4 = 2000$
   b) 3, 33, 333; $9999 \div 3 = 3333$
   c) 6, 600, 60 000; $3000 \times 2000 = 6\ 000\ 000$
   d) 55, 505, 5005; $5 \times 10\ 001 = 50\ 005$
   e) 1001, 2002, 3003; $91 \times 44 = 4004$
   f) 49, 4489, 444 889, $6667 \times 6667 = 44\ 448\ 889$
8. **a)** Answers may vary.
   i) The numbers in the row above are smaller. The difference between each pair of numbers increases by 1.
   ii) The numbers in the row below are greater. The difference between each pair of numbers increases by 1. Explanations may vary.
   b) Each row has a matching column.
9. **a)** Answers may vary. Each number is the product of a number and itself.
   b) Answers may vary.
10. There are more even numbers. Explanations may vary.

11. **a)** The sum of the digits is 9.
    b) Answers may vary. The sums of the digits are all multiples of 9.
    c) Yes, this is true for all multiples of 9.
12. **b)** Patterns will vary.
13. **a)** 24, 2244, 222 444; $6666 \times 3334 = 22\ 224\ 444$
    b) 81, 9801, 998 001; $9999 \times 9999 = 99\ 980\ 001$
    c) 25, 4225, 442 225; $6665 \times 6665 = 44\ 422\ 225$
    d) 10 201, 40 804, 91 809; $404 \times 404 = 163\ 216$
    e) 11, 111, 1111; $1234 \times 9 + 5 = 11\ 111$
    f) 1, 121, 12 321; $1111 \times 1111 = 1\ 234\ 321$
14. **a)** The answer is always 1089.
    b) If the hundreds and ones digits are the same, the answer will be zero at the second step, and you cannot proceed.
15. **a)** **i)** 32, 64, 128   **ii)** 16, 22, 29   **iii)** 11, 13, 14
    b) Answers may vary. For example: 1, 2, 3, 4, 5, 6, ... ; 1, 2, 3, 5, 7, 10, ... ; 1, 2, 3, 1, 2, 3, ...
16. Part d, part e, and part f do not continue for ever. Reasons may vary.

Linking Ideas: Mathematics and Technology
Number Patterns on a Spreadsheet, page 29

1. The formula added 2 to the number in cell A1.
2. Replace the number in cell A1 with 1. Fill Down.
3. Replace the number in cell A1 with 48. Fill Down.
4. Replace the number in cell A1 with 1. Replace the formula in cell A2 with =A1+3. Fill Down.
5. **a)** The formula added 1 to the number in cell A1.
   b) The formula multiplied the number in cell A1 by 2.
6. Replace the formula in cell B1 with =A1*2−1. Fill Down.

Mathematics File: Powers of Ten, page 31

1. **a)** 10^4 **b)** 10^7 **c)** 10^{11}, 10^{14}
2. **a)** 10^3, six hundred forty-nine; 10^7, fourteen million
   b) 10^3, one thousand nine hundred ninety-one; 10^{10}, twenty-four billion five hundred million
   c) 10^{11}, two hundred billion
   d) 10^3, one thousand nine hundred eighty-seven; 10^7, ten million; 10^{18}, one quintillion five hundred quadrillion
   e) 10^{23}, one hundred thirty sextillion
3. **a)** 10^1 **b)** 10^2
   c) Answers may vary. 10^2 or 10^3 **d)** 10^4

Quest: The *One Million* Book, page 32

Between 250 000 and 255 000

Patterns in Measurement

Developing the Ideas, page 35

1. Third column may vary.

Fold	Number of strands	Total length of noodles (m)
0	1	1.6
1	2	3.2
2	4	6.4
3	8	12.8
4	16	25.6
5	32	51.2
6	64	102.4
7	128	204.8
8	256	409.6
9	512	819.2
10	1024	1638.4
11	2048	3276.8

2. a) Answers may vary. Table above assumes 1.6 m.
b) See table above.
c) Yes, it's about 3.3 km. Yes, the claim is reasonable.

3. a) Each number would be 100 times as great.
b) Each number would be 1000 times as small.

Working with Mathematics, page 36

1. a) 4096   **b)** Answers may vary. About 6.6 km

2. a) metre   **b)** metre   **c)** kilometre
d) centimetre   **e)** kilometre

3. a) Divide   **b)** Multiply   **c)** Divide   **d)** Multiply

4. a) centimetres   **b)** metres
c) metres   **d)** centimetres or millimetres
e) metres   **f)** millimetres

5. a) 2000 m   **b)** 0.37 m   **c)** 0.164 m
d) 6.83 m   **e)** 2.649 m   **f)** 500 m

6. a) 500 cm   **b)** 8.4 cm   **c)** 230 000 cm
d) 15.3 cm   **e)** 46 000 cm   **f)** 3620 cm

7. a) 0.25 m   **b)** 1400 m   **c)** 8.4 cm
d) 0.285 m   **e)** 1260 cm   **f)** 0.584 km
g) 5 mm   **h)** 2050 m

8. a) 0.116 km   **b)** 11 160 cm

9. a) 5.951 km   **b)** 595 100 cm

10. Measurements may vary. Each person's height should be similar to her or his arm span.

11. , 12. Answers may vary.

13. a) 3000 cm, 0.03 km
b) , c) Answers may vary.

14. a) 20   **b)** 14 m by 6 m

15. a) Estimates may vary.   **b)** 17 cm, 170 mm

16. a) 533 000 mm   **b)** 2 mm, 26 mm
c) 20 500   **d)** 266 500

17. a) 5.9 cm by 5.4 cm; 59 mm by 54 mm. The measurement in millimetres is 10 times the measurement in centimetres.
b) 31.86 cm^2; 3186 mm^2. The area in square millimetres is 100 times the area in square centimetres.

18. There are four times as many tiles to lay. She should charge four times as much ($2000), assuming that part of the $500 is not a set fee, and independent of the number of tiles laid.

19. 6 cm by 8 cm

Patterns in Geometry

Developing the Ideas, page 38

Activity 1

1. a) Bears and Cardinals, Bears and Hawks, Cardinals and Hawks
b) 3

2. a) Those in exercise 1a, plus Bears and Jays, Cardinals and Jays, Hawks and Jays
b) 6

3. a) Those in exercises 1a and 2a, plus Bears and Lions, Cardinals and Lions, Hawks and Lions, Jays and Lions
b) 10

4. a) Those in exercises 1a, 2a, and 3a, plus Bears and Tigers, Cardinals and Tigers, Hawks and Tigers, Jays and Tigers, Lions and Tigers
b) 15

5.

Number of teams	Number of games
3	3
4	6
5	10
6	15

6. a) 21   **b)** 28

Activity 2

1.

Dots	Lines
3	3
4	6
5	10
6	15
7	21
8	28

2. a) 36   **b)** 45

Activity 3

Answers may vary. They deal with the number of ways in which pairs can be determined.

Working with Mathematics, page 40

1. a) A   **b)** B   **c)** F   **d)** C   **e)** E   **f)** D
2. Answers may vary.
3. 66
4. a) Triangle, trapezoid, rhombus, kite, regular pentagon
b) 5   **c)** 3; multiples of 36° (36°, 72°, 108°)
d) Three acute and two obtuse   **e)** All isosceles
5. a) 6 and 24   **b)** 6 and 18
c) , d) , e) Answers may vary.
6. 60
7. Answers may vary; rotational symmetry

Review, page 42

1. a) 0.0037   **b)** 0.037   **c)** 0.37
d) 3.7   **e)** 37   **f)** 370

2. a) 13 200 000   **b)** 1 320 000   **c)** 132 000
d) 13 200   **e)** 1320   **f)** 132

3. a) 54, 6534, 665 334; 9999 × 6666 = 66 653 334
b) 16, 1156, 111 556; 3334 × 3334 = 11 115 556

c) 9, 98, 987; $1234 \times 8 + 4 = 9876$

d) 49, 4489, 444 889; $6667 \times 6667 = 44\ 448\ 889$

4. a) i) 495 495   ii) 650 650   iii) 286 286   iv) 193 193

b) In each product, the 3 digits repeat.

c) The 4 digits repeat in the product. For example,
$1234 \times 10\ 001 = 12\ 341\ 234$

5. a) 2, 4, 6, 8, 0, 2, 4, 6, 8, 0

b) 4, 8, 2, 6, 0, 4, 8, 2, 6, 0

c) 6, 2, 8, 4, 0, 6, 2, 8, 4, 0

d) Each pattern involves the same 5 digits, but in a different order.

e) You would expect a similar pattern in the row with multiples of 8. The final digits in that row are 8, 6, 4, 2, 0, 8, 6, 4, 2, 0

6. Answers for patterns may vary.

÷	6	5	4	3	2	1
6	1	0.83	0.67	0.5	0.33	0.17
5	1.2	1	0.8	0.6	0.4	0.2
4	1.5	1.25	1	0.75	0.5	0.25
3	2	1.67	1.33	1	0.67	0.33
2	3	2.5	2	1.5	1	0.5
1	6	5	4	3	2	1

7. a) 10^2 b) 10^3 c) 10^6 d) 10^8 e) 10^5 f) 10^4

8. a) 10^2 b) 10^4 c) 10^3 d) 10^4 e) 10^6 f) 10^5 g) 10^5

9. a) centimetre   b) millimetre   c) decimetre   d) metre

10. a) Multiply by 1000.   b) Multiply by 10.
c) Multiply by 100.   d) Divide by 100.

11. a) 150 cm   b) 5 cm   c) 36 cm
d) 50 cm   e) 14 cm   f) 7340 cm

12. a) 3000 m   b) 4 m   c) 0.35 m
d) 100 m   e) 400 m   f) 2.1 m by 0.9 m

13. a) 0.826 km   b) 0.8257 km   c) 0.067 93 km
d) 0.096 km   e) 0.52 km   f) 3.839 km
g) 23.16 km, 14.02 km

14. a) Answers may vary. 8.9 cm   b) About 21.6 m

15. a) 2.5 cm   b) 40   c) 40 000

16. a) 54   b) 24 m by 25 m

17. a) 10 and 16   b) 10 and 6   c) Answers may vary.

CHAPTER 1 TWO-DIMENSIONAL GEOMETRY

Start With What You Know, page 48

Answers may vary.

1.1 Constructing Triangles Using Compasses and Ruler

Developing the Ideas, page 50

Activity 1

1. a) 4 cm; all points on the circle are 4 cm from the centre.
b) No; all points that are 4 cm from P are on the circle.

2. a) 8 cm; the diameter of a circle is twice the radius.

3. Place a string around the circle. Then measure this section of the string.

Activity 2

1. Yes, all the triangles look the same.

Working with Mathematics, page 53

1. No; all points inside the circle are less than 4 cm from A.

2. No; suppose you draw side AB 21 cm long. When you draw arcs with radius 5 cm and 8 cm from A and B, the arcs will not intersect.

3. In a triangle, none of the sides is longer than the sum of the lengths of the other two sides.

4. a) Scalene   b) Equilateral   c) Scalene
d) Isosceles   e) Scalene   f) Equilateral

5. a) Equilateral   b) Isosceles   c) Scalene
d) Scalene   e) Scalene   f) Scalene

6. For a typical sheet of copy paper, the largest equilateral triangle you can draw has side length 25 cm. Answers will vary for how you can tell who drew the largest triangle.

7. For a typical sheet of copy paper, you can draw two large isosceles triangles that have different shapes but the same area. Answers will vary for how you can tell who drew the largest triangle.

8. All triangles with these side lengths have the same shape.

10. Yes; an isosceles triangle has at least 2 sides of equal length. Since an equilateral triangle has 3 sides of equal length, it is also an isosceles triangle.

Linking Ideas: Mathematics and Technology
Investigating the Medians of a Triangle, page 54

For any triangle, the medians intersect at a point inside the triangle.

1.2 Constructing Triangles Using Ruler and Protractor
Developing the Ideas, page 56

Activity 1

1. All the triangles look the same.

Activity 2

1. All the triangles look the same.

Activity 3

2. For each set of measurements, all the triangles look the same.

Working with Mathematics, page 59

1. a) Acute   b) Right   c) Straight
d) Acute   e) Obtuse   f) Right

2. a) Obtuse   b) Acute   c) Right
d) Right   e) Obtuse   f) Acute

3. ∠ABE, ∠FBC, ∠BFC, ∠HFG

4. a) Equilateral   b) Obtuse scalene   c) Acute isosceles
d) Acute isosceles   e) Acute isosceles f) Right scalene

5. a) e   b) b   c) c   d) a   e) f   f) d

6. b) You can draw 2 acute isosceles triangles, 3 right isosceles triangles, 1 right scalene triangle, and 2 obtuse scalene triangles.

7. a) i) Yes   ii) Yes   iii) No   iv) No

8. a) Obtuse
b) Reasons may vary. The side opposite the obtuse angle is the

longest side in a triangle.

c) Reasons may vary. It is impossible to draw a triangle with the length of one side greater than the sum of the other two sides.

d) Estimates will vary. Estimates should be greater than the length of XZ, which is 500 m and greater than the length of YZ, which is 700 m. Estimates should be less than the sum of XZ and YZ which is 1200 m.

9. a) Answers may vary in parts i and iii.
   i) ∠ABD, ∠EBC; ∠ABE, ∠DBC
   ii) ∠JKM; ∠MKL
   iii) ∠PQU, ∠UQT, ∠TQS, ∠SQR; ∠PQS, ∠UQR
   b) Answers may vary.

10. b) Right, scalene

11. Acute

12. The triangle in part d is acute, the triangle in part e is obtuse.

13. b) Each triangle has 2 sides of equal length. Triangles drawn for parts i and ii may vary in size and shape. The right isosceles triangles may vary in size, but will all have the same shape.

14. b) All the triangles may vary in size and shape. The side lengths in each triangle are all different.

15. It is not possible to draw either triangle.

16. a) Scalene, acute
    b) Isosceles; the triangle has two equal angles
    c) Isosceles, obtuse
    d) Isosceles, acute

17. All the angles measure 60°.

18. For each triangle, the angles opposite the equal sides are equal.

20. a) 3
    b) Yes; because the midpoint of a side must be on the side.
    c) No; a side joins two vertices, not a vertex and the midpoint of a side.

Quest: Where Is the Treasure Buried?, page 62

The treasure is buried 15 paces south of the point of intersection of the diagonals of the square.

1.3 Congruent Figures
Developing the Ideas, page 65

Using Manipulatives

1. Matching sides are equal.   2. Matching angles are equal.

3. The figures are identical in size and shape.

5. The figure on dot paper is not the same size as the figures on the geoboard so it is not congruent to the figures on the geoboard, but the figures are similar.

Through an Activity, page 66

1. Each figure is symmetrical about the fold line.

2. 4

Working with Mathematics, page 67

1. a) Yes, if the same size dot paper is used because the figures would be the same size and shape.
   b) Yes, because they would be the same shape

2. a) Yes, when the size of the photocopied figure is the same as the size of the original figure

b) Yes, when the size of the photocopied figure is smaller or larger than the size of the original figure

3. Answers may vary.
   a) So they can be used in and counted by machines
   b) So the axle is the same distance from the ground
   c) So they can filled and packed by machine
   d) So they all travel the same distance when hit with the same force and so they fit into the hole on a green
   e) So stores can organize shoes by size

4. a) Yes, ∠A = ∠F, ∠B = ∠E, ∠C = ∠H, ∠D = ∠G, AB = FE, BC = EH, CD = HG, DA = GF
   b) No, the figures are not the same size
   c) Yes, ∠D = ∠W, ∠E = ∠X, ∠F = ∠Y, ∠G = ∠Z, DE = WX, EF = XY, FG = YZ, GD = ZW

5. Trilliums A, C, D are congruent. Trilliums A, C, D, E, F are similar.

6. a) Yes, the mould determines the size and shape of the statues.
   b) No, the sizes of the gear wheels are different.

8. a) Measure the radii. If these are equal, the circles are congruent.
   b) Yes, all circles have the same shape.

9. a) A and C, B and E, D and F   b) D and F

10. a) Yes   b) Yes
    c) Only if the parts of the key that go into the lock are congruent

11. B and G, E and R, M and F

12. By joining the dots with horizontal or vertical lines, you can draw 4 other pairs of congruent figures different from the figures shown.

13. a) Yes, ∠A = ∠S, ∠B = ∠T, ∠C = ∠Q, ∠D = ∠R, AB = ST, BC = TQ, CD = QR, DA = RS
    b) Yes, ∠U = ∠J, ∠V = ∠K, ∠W = ∠L, ∠X = ∠M, ∠Y = ∠H, ∠Z = ∠I, UV = JK, VW = KL, WX = LM, XY = MH, YZ = HI, ZU = IJ

14. Diagrams or explanations may vary.
    a) True   b) False   c) False   d) True

1.4 Congruent Line Segments, Angles, and Triangles
Developing the Ideas, page 69

Activity 1

1. GH   2. ∠PQR

4. a) Measure the lengths of the line segments.
   b) They have the same length.

5. a) Use a protractor to measure the angles in degrees.
   b) They have the same measures.

Activity 2

1. △DFE

3. a) Measure the lengths of the sides and the measures of the angles.
   b) The sides have the same lengths and the angles have the same measures.

Working with Mathematics, page 71

1. a) AB and CD have the same length.
   b) ∠ABC and ∠DEF have the same measure.
   c) △ABC and △XYZ have the same side lengths and angle measures.

2. Yes, you can place one segment on top of the other so they match.

3. a) Yes
   b) Yes, the measures of the angles determine congruence.

4. a) Yes, since one completely covers the other when they are placed on top of one another, they must have the same area.
   b) No; for example, triangles with base 4 cm and height 3 cm and with base 6 cm and height 2 cm both have an area of 6 cm² but are not congruent.

5. a) Yes; since the side lengths are equal, the perimeters will be equal.
   b) No; for example triangles with side lengths 12 cm, 6 cm, 8 cm, and 10 cm, 9 cm, 7 cm both have perimeter 26 cm, but are not congruent.

6. a) Yes; the two angles have the same measure.
   b) No; they only have 1 pair of equal sides.

7. ∠PQR and ∠STU are congruent.

8. a) ∠BAC = ∠QPR, ∠ACB = ∠PRQ, ∠CAB = ∠RQP, AB = PQ, AC = PR, BC = QR
   b) ∠JKL = ∠XYZ, ∠KLJ = ∠YZX, ∠LJK = ∠ZXY, JK = XY, KL = YZ, JL = XZ

9. CD = LM

11. a) Yes; ∠A = ∠D, ∠B = ∠E, ∠C = ∠F, AB = DE, BC = EF, CA = FD
   b) Yes; ∠A = ∠P, ∠B = ∠Q, ∠C = ∠R, AB = PQ, BC = QR, CA = RP
   c) The triangles are not congruent.
   d) Yes; ∠R = ∠X, ∠S = ∠Z, ∠T = ∠Y, RS = XZ, ST = ZY, TR = YX

12. A and D are congruent.

13. b) △AEB and △DEC, △AED and △BEC, △ABC and △DCB and △CDA and △BAD
   c) △AEB and △DEC: AB = DC, AE = BE = DE = CE
   △AED and △BEC: AD = BC, AE = DE = BE = CE
   △ABC, △DCB, △CDA, △BAD: AC = BD, AB = DC, AD = BC
   d) △AEB and △DEC: ∠AEB = ∠DEC, ∠BAE = ∠ABE = ∠CDE = ∠DCE
   △AED and △BEC: ∠AED = ∠BEC, ∠DAE = ∠ADE = ∠CBE = ∠BCE
   △ABC, △DCB, △CDA, △BAD: ∠ABC = ∠ADC = ∠BAD = ∠BCD, ∠BAC = ∠ACD = ∠ABD = ∠BDC, ∠BCA = ∠DAC = ∠ADB = ∠CBD

14. Answers may include more angles.
   a) ∠AEB = ∠DEC, ∠AED = ∠BEC
   b) ∠EJF = ∠HJG, ∠EJH = ∠FJG
   c) ∠QVT = ∠TVS = ∠SVR = ∠RVQ
   d) ∠UTV = ∠YTX, ∠VTW = ∠YTZ, ∠WTX = ∠UTZ

15. Answers will vary.

16. △MNP and △QSR: ∠MPN = ∠QRS, ∠PMN = ∠RSP, ∠MNP = ∠QSR, MN = QS, PM = RQ, PN = RS; △DEF and △JKL: ∠FDE = ∠LJK, ∠DEF = ∠JKL, ∠EFD = ∠KLJ, DE = JK, EF = KL, DF = JL; △ABC = △YWX: ∠ABC = ∠YWX, ∠ACB = ∠YXW, ∠ACB = ∠YXW, AB = YW, AC = YX, BC = WX

17. a) The angles opposite the congruent sides have equal measures.
   b) The two figures are congruent. Each figure is a right triangle.
   c) The two figures formed by the line of symmetry are

congruent, so corresponding angles in these figures have the same measure. This shows that the third angle of the isosceles triangle is bisected by the line of symmetry.

18. a) △ABC and △AFE, △ACD and △AED, △ABD and △AFD, △AEB and △ACF
   b) △QUR and △TUS, △PTR and △PQS, △RQS and △STR

Linking Ideas: Mathematics and Science
Fingerprints, page 75
Answers may vary.

Review, page 76

1. Explanations may vary.

3. a) Scalene; no equal sides
   b) Isosceles; two equal sides
   c) Isosceles; two equal sides
   d) Equilateral; three equal sides

4. Yes

6. Explanations may vary.
   a) Obtuse   b) Right

8. a) Right   b) Obtuse   c) Acute   d) Right

9. Answers may vary.

10. a) The figures are not congruent because corresponding angles are not equal and corresponding sides are not equal.
   b) The figures are congruent. ∠R = ∠B, ∠S = ∠C, ∠T = ∠D, ∠U = ∠A, RS = BC, ST = CD, TU = DA, UR = AB

11. a) Flags A and D are congruent.
   b) All the flags are similar.
   c) All Canadian flags are similar because they have the same shape and each part of the design of one flag matches the corresponding parts of all the other Canadian flags.

12. a) 6   b) 2   c) 3

13. a) ∠AEB = ∠CED, ∠AED = ∠BEC
   b) ∠KPL = ∠NPM, ∠KPN = ∠LPM

14. EF, IJ   15. Triangle Z

16. a) ∠A = ∠D, ∠B = ∠E, ∠C = ∠F, AB = DE, BC = EF, AC = DF
   b) ∠P = ∠X, ∠Q = ∠Z, ∠R = ∠Y, PQ = XZ, QR = ZY, RP = YX

17. a) ∠W = ∠H, ∠X = ∠I, ∠Y = ∠J, WX = HI, XY = IJ, WY = HJ
   b) ∠L = ∠P, ∠M = ∠R, ∠N = ∠Q, LN = PQ, LM = PR, MN = RQ

Cumulative Review, page 80

1. a) 28 000   b) 2800   c) 280   d) 28
   e) 2.8   f) 0.28   g) 0.028   h) 0.0028

2. a) 0.149   b) 1.49   c) 14.9
   d) 149   e) 1490   f) 14 900

3. a) 45, 5445, 554 445; 5555 × 9999 = 55 544 445
   b) 9, 1089, 110 889; 3333 × 3333 = 11 108 889
   c) 10, 110, 1110; 1234 × 9 + 4 = 11 110
   d) 72, 8712, 887 112; 9999 × 8888 = 88 871 112

4. a) kilometre   b) centimetre   c) metre
   d) kilometre   e) kilometre   f) metre

5. a) centimetres   b) metres
   c) millimetres   d) metres or centimetres

e) metres   f) millimetres

6. a) Divide by 100.   **b)** Divide by 1000.   **c)** Multiply by 1000.

7. a) 2.7 m   **b)** 8000 m   **c)** 950 m
   d) 0.693 m   **e)** 43 m   **f)** 0.85 m

8. a) 150 mm   **b)** 2100 m   **c)** 1450 cm   **d)** 9 cm
   e) 1800 m   **f)** 590 mm   **g)** 0.101 km   **h)** 0.073 m

9. a) 20.7 cm   **b), c)** Estimates will vary.

10. b) 4 and 8, 5 and 10, 6 and 12
   c) 4 and 12, 5 and 15, 6 and 18
   d) 7 and 14, 7 and 21

11. Answers may vary. The answers given here assume Serena allows 1 m from the edge of the garden to the first and the last plants.
   a) 13 m   **b)** 7 m

12. a) $10 \times 10 \times 10 \times 10 \times 10 \times 10$; 1 000 000
   b) $10 \times 10 \times 10 \times 10$; 10 000
   c) $10 \times 10 \times 10 \times 10 \times 10 \times 10 \times 10 \times 10$; 100 000 000
   d) 10
   e) $10 \times 10 \times 10 \times 10 \times 10$; 100 000
   f) $10 \times 10 \times 10 \times 10 \times 10 \times 10 \times 10$; 10 000 000

13. a) 10^4 **b)** 10^6 **c)** 10^3 **d)** 10^6

15. Explanations may vary.
   a) Straight   **b)** Acute

16. a) Right, scalene   **b)** Acute, equilateral   **c)** Obtuse, scalene

17. No; explanations may vary.

18. a) No, yes   **b)** No, yes

20. a) $\angle A = \angle Q$, $\angle B = \angle T$, $\angle C = \angle S$, $\angle D = \angle R$, AB = QT, BC = TS, CD = SR, DA = RQ
   b) $\angle L = \angle Z$, $\angle M = \angle X$, $\angle N = \angle Y$, LM = ZX, MN = XY, NL = YZ

21. Explanations may vary.

22. a) 90°   **b)** 360°   **c)** 360°, 360°

CHAPTER 2 FRACTIONS AND DECIMALS

Start With What You Know, page 84

1. a) 64   **b)** 32   **c)** $\frac{1}{2}$ **d)** $\frac{1}{2}$

2. a) $\frac{1}{2}$ **b)** $\frac{1}{8}$

3. a) $\frac{1}{2}$ **b)** $\frac{1}{4}$

4. a) $\frac{1}{8}$ **b)** $\frac{27}{64}$ **c)** $\frac{7}{32}$ **d)** $\frac{11}{64}$ **e)** $\frac{1}{8}$

5. $\frac{1}{32}$

Linking Ideas: Mathematics and Technology
Constructing Fraction Strips and Number Lines, page 86

1. a) 8 cm   **b)** 5.3 cm, 10.7 cm
   c) 4 cm, 12 cm, 8 cm   **d)** 3.2 cm, 12.8 cm, 6.4 cm, 9.6 cm

2. 3   **3.** 4

2.1 The Concept of a Fraction
Developing the Ideas, page 87

Activity 1

1. a) $\frac{1}{4}$ **b)** $\frac{6}{10}, \frac{3}{5}$ **c)** $1\frac{4}{12}, 1\frac{1}{3}$

2. a) $\frac{3}{4}, \frac{6}{8}$ **b)** $\frac{1}{2}, \frac{3}{6}$ **c)** $\frac{8}{3}, 2\frac{2}{3}$

3. a) $\frac{1}{2}, \frac{1}{2}$ **b)** $\frac{1}{4}, \frac{3}{4}$

Activity 2

1. a) Any four of these: $\frac{1}{2}, \frac{2}{4}, \frac{3}{6}, \frac{4}{8}, \frac{5}{10}$; answers may vary: $\frac{6}{12}, \frac{7}{14}, \frac{8}{16}, \cdots$
   b) Answers may vary; for example, $\frac{2}{6}, \frac{1}{3}$; $\frac{3}{4}, \frac{6}{8}$; $\frac{4}{6}, \frac{2}{3}$.

Activity 3

1. b) Answers may vary. The half strip covers half the distance between 0 and 1 on each number line.
   c) $\frac{2}{4}, \frac{3}{6}, \frac{4}{8}, \frac{5}{10}$

2. Estimates may vary.
   a) $\frac{1}{5}, \frac{3}{4}, 1\frac{2}{3}$ **b)** $\frac{1}{2}, 2\frac{2}{3}, 4\frac{1}{4}$

Working with Mathematics, page 95

1. No, examples may vary.

2. Answers may vary; for example, $\frac{4}{6}$

3. a) $\frac{1}{5}, \frac{2}{10}$ **b)** $\frac{1}{2}, \frac{4}{8}$ **c)** $\frac{3}{4}, \frac{9}{12}$ **d)** $\frac{2}{3}, \frac{6}{9}$

4. a) $\frac{2}{3}$ **d)** $\frac{5}{4}$ **f)** $\frac{7}{16}$
   h) $\frac{11}{8}$ **k)** $\frac{13}{5}$ **l)** $\frac{4}{9}$

5. a) $\frac{4}{6}, \frac{8}{12}, \frac{6}{9}$ **b)** $\frac{6}{8}, \frac{12}{16}, \frac{9}{12}$ **c)** $\frac{8}{10}, \frac{12}{15}$

6. Answers may vary.
   a) $\frac{24}{36}$ **b)** $\frac{6}{9}$ or $\frac{4}{6}$ or $\frac{2}{3}$

7. Answers may vary.
   a) $\frac{4}{6}$ **b)** $\frac{6}{8}$ **c)** $\frac{12}{10}$ **d)** $\frac{14}{4}$
   e) $\frac{6}{20}$ **f)** $\frac{1}{4}$ **g)** $\frac{5}{2}$ **h)** $\frac{6}{22}$

8. a) $\frac{1}{2}, \frac{1}{3}, \frac{1}{6}$ **b)** 6, 3, 2   **c)** 3, $\frac{3}{2}, \frac{1}{2}$ **d)** 2, $\frac{2}{3}, \frac{1}{3}$

9. a) i) $\frac{2}{3}$ **ii)** $\frac{4}{6}$ or $\frac{2}{3}$ **iii)** $1\frac{1}{2}$ or $\frac{3}{2}$ **iv)** 2
   b) i) 4   **ii)** 4   **iii)** 9   **iv)** 12
   c) $\frac{1}{2}, \frac{1}{4}, \frac{1}{6}, \frac{1}{12}$

10. a) You can make $4\frac{1}{2}$ tables.   **b)** $\frac{9}{2} = 4\frac{1}{2}$

11. a) There is enough for each person to have 2 pieces.
   b) There is not enough for each person to have 3 pieces.
   c) $2\frac{2}{6} = \frac{14}{6}$

12. a) i) Quarters   **ii)** Thirds
   b) i) Eighths   **ii)** Sixths
   c) i) Sixteenths   **ii)** Twelfths

13. Diagrams may vary.

14. a) $\frac{2}{3} = \frac{10}{15}$ **b)** $\frac{4}{5} = \frac{16}{20}$ **c)** $\frac{7}{4} = \frac{21}{12}$ **d)** $\frac{9}{15} = \frac{3}{5}$

15. a) $\frac{3}{4}$ **b)** 3   **c)** $\frac{2}{3}$ **d)** $\frac{3}{2}$
   e) $\frac{2}{3}$ **f)** $\frac{1}{3}$ **g)** $\frac{8}{5}$ **h)** $\frac{7}{12}$

16. a) $1\frac{1}{2}$ **b)** $3\frac{1}{5}$ **c)** $4\frac{2}{3}$ **d)** $1\frac{5}{6}$ **e)** $1\frac{5}{9}$

17. a) $\frac{19}{4}$ **b)** $\frac{21}{8}$ **c)** $\frac{16}{9}$ **d)** $\frac{17}{5}$ **e)** $\frac{19}{3}$

18. Answers may vary.

Quest: Dividing a Square into Quarters, page 97

Answers may vary.

2.2 The Concept of a Decimal

Developing the Ideas, page 98

Through Discussion

1. a) Twenty-seven and four tenths; $(2 \times 10) + (7 \times 1) + (4 \times \frac{1}{10})$

b) Two hundredths; $2 \times \frac{1}{100}$

c) One and fifty-two hundredths;
$(1 \times 1) + (5 \times \frac{1}{10}) + (2 \times \frac{1}{100})$

d) Eight thousandths; $8 \times \frac{1}{1000}$

e) Two hundred thirty-three and six hundred fourteen thousandths; $(2 \times 100) + (3 \times 10) + (3 \times 1) + (6 \times \frac{1}{10}) +$
$(1 \times \frac{1}{100}) + (4 \times \frac{1}{1000})$

2. a) 95.54 m **b)** 0.003 cm **c)** 1.75 m^2 **d)** 3.5 cm

Using Manipulatives

1. a) Exchange 10 small cubes for 1 rod.
b) Exchange 10 rods for 1 flat.

2. a) 4.27 **b)** 3.06

3. 0.4 is larger.

4. a) 1.2 **b)** 2.31 **c)** 3.6 **d)** 4.3

Working with Mathematics, page 100

1. a) $\frac{6}{100}$ **b)** $\frac{7}{10}$ **c)** $\frac{4}{1000}$
d) $\frac{9}{100}$ **e)** 500 **f)** $\frac{1}{1000}$
g) $\frac{1}{100}$ **h)** $\frac{6}{10\,000}$ **i)** $\frac{8}{100}$

2. No, what Bryan wrote means five hundredths of a cent. He wanted to write five hundredths of a dollar. Bryan should have written $0.05 or 5¢.

3. a) 2.36 **b)** 1.04

5. a) 3.2 **b)** 1.6 **c)** 4.25 **d)** 2.6

7. a) i) Yes, 4.1 **ii)** No **iii)** Yes, 4.01 **iv)** No
b) Answers may vary. Some examples are: 0.14, 0.41, 1.04, 1.4, 41, 410, 140, 104

8. All the numbers except 4.01, 4.09, and 4.21 can be located on the segment.

9. Answers may vary. On some calculators you can repeat an operation by pressing $\boxed{=}$ again. An answer for part a is shown.
a) 11.1 $\boxed{+}$ 1.1 $\boxed{+}$ 1.1 $\boxed{+}$ .1 $\boxed{+}$ .1 $\boxed{-}$ .01 $\boxed{=}$
This requires 23 keystrokes.
On some calculators, you can enter:
11.1 $\boxed{+}$ 1.1 $\boxed{=}$ $\boxed{=}$ $\boxed{+}$ .1 $\boxed{=}$ $\boxed{=}$ $\boxed{-}$ .01 $\boxed{=}$
This requires 20 keystrokes.

10. a) Twenty-seven and $\frac{49}{100}$ dollars
b) One hundred forty-nine and $\frac{99}{100}$ dollars
c) Twelve and $\frac{89}{100}$ dollars
d) Eighty-eight and $\frac{45}{100}$ dollars

11. a) Seven hundredths; $\frac{7}{100}$
b) One and twenty-two hundredths; $1 + \frac{2}{10} + \frac{2}{100}$
c) Sixty-nine thousandths; $\frac{6}{100} + \frac{9}{1000}$
d) One and eight hundred fifty-two thousandths;
$1 + \frac{8}{10} + \frac{5}{100} + \frac{2}{1000}$
e) Three ten-thousandths; $\frac{3}{10\,000}$

12. a) China, U.S.A., Russia, Canada
b) U.S.A., China, Canada, Russia

13. a) 23.495 **b)** 43.348 **c)** 12.476 **d)** 43.667 **e)** 43.19

14. a) $\boxed{-}$ .2 **b)** $\boxed{-}$ .04 **c)** $\boxed{-}$ .005
d) $\boxed{-}$ .012 **e)** $\boxed{-}$ .11 **f)** $\boxed{-}$ .101

15. b) 23.805

16. a) 0.96 > 0.94 **b)** 0.61 > 0.6 **c)** 0.3 = 0.30
d) 51.887 > 51.878 **e)** 0.0009 < 0.0010 **f)** 304.11 < 304.4

17. b) 721.8204

18. a) 4.66, 5.47, 6.75, 9.65 **b)** 47.94, 35.07, 29.76, 24.13

2.3 Fractions and Decimals

Developing the Ideas, page 102

1. b) 0.4 **c)** 0.40
d) 0.2, 0.4, 0.6, 0.8, 1.0, 1.2, 1.4, 1.6, 1.8, 2.0

2. a) $\frac{6}{8}$, $\frac{9}{12}$, 0.75 **b)** 0.25, 0.50, 0.75, 1.00, 1.25, 1.50, 1.75, 2.00

3. a) $\frac{2}{6}$, $\frac{4}{12}$ **b)** $\frac{4}{6}$, $\frac{8}{12}$ **c)** White 1 strip; 1, 1.0, 1.00
d) 0.33, 0.66, 1.00; first two answers are approximate
e) 0.33, 0.66, 1.00, 1.33, 1.66, 2.00, 2.33, 2.66

Working with Mathematics, page 104

1. a) $\frac{2}{2}$ **b)** $\frac{3}{3}$ **c)** $\frac{4}{4}$ **d)** $\frac{5}{5}$ **e)** $\frac{6}{6}$ **f)** $\frac{8}{8}$ **g)** $\frac{10}{10}$ **h)** $\frac{12}{12}$

2. A thousandths line; it would have 10 times as many divisions as the hundredths line.

3. Answers may vary.
a) Corresponding numbers have the same digit after the decimal point; but different digits in front of the decimal point.
b) On each line, all the numbers have the same denominator; the numerators are different.

4. Answers may vary.
a) They would have the same length, but different labels.
b) 0.40 is $\frac{40}{100}$, which simplifies to $\frac{4}{10}$, which is 0.4.

5. a) 0.3 **b)** 0.81 **c)** 0.7 **d)** 2.7
e) 0.09 **f)** 0.479 **g)** 0.093 **h)** 1.27

6. a) $\frac{26}{100}$, $\frac{13}{50}$ **b)** $\frac{51}{100}$ **c)** $\frac{41}{100}$ **d)** $\frac{65}{100}$, $\frac{13}{20}$
e) $\frac{37}{100}$ **f)** $\frac{74}{100}$, $\frac{37}{50}$ **g)** $\frac{96}{100}$, $\frac{24}{25}$ **h)** $\frac{118}{100}$, $\frac{59}{50}$

7. Answers may vary.
$\frac{1}{2}$, $\frac{2}{4}$, $\frac{3}{6}$, $\frac{4}{8}$, 0.5, $\frac{6}{12}$, 0.50; $\frac{1}{3}$, $\frac{2}{6}$, $\frac{4}{12}$; $\frac{2}{3}$, $\frac{4}{6}$, $\frac{8}{12}$; $\frac{1}{4}$, $\frac{2}{8}$, $\frac{3}{12}$;
$\frac{5}{4}$, $\frac{10}{8}$, $\frac{15}{12}$; $\frac{3}{4}$, $\frac{6}{8}$, $\frac{9}{12}$; they are all sets of equivalent fractions

8. Answers may be approximate.
a) 0.63 **b)** 1.63 **c)** 1.25 **d)** 1.83 **e)** 3.50
f) 0.83 **g)** 1.83 **h)** 1.40 **i)** 1.67 **j)** 2.75

9. Answers may be approximate.
a) 2.625 **b)** 0.22 **c)** 2.22 **d)** 0.428 571
e) 1.428 571 **f)** 2.833 **g)** 0.556 **h)** 0.455
i) 0.909 **j)** 2.142 857

10. Answers may vary.
a) $\frac{8}{10}$ or $\frac{4}{5}$ **b)** $\frac{25}{100}$ or $\frac{1}{4}$ **c)** $1\frac{1}{2}$ or $\frac{3}{2}$ or $1\frac{5}{10}$
d) $2\frac{1}{10}$ or $2\frac{10}{100}$ or $\frac{21}{10}$ **e)** $2\frac{67}{100}$ or $2\frac{2}{3}$ or $\frac{8}{3}$
f) $\frac{75}{100}$ or $\frac{3}{4}$ **g)** $\frac{6}{10}$ or $\frac{3}{5}$ **h)** $\frac{9}{10}$
i) $1\frac{1}{3}$ or $\frac{4}{3}$ **j)** $2\frac{5}{10}$ or $\frac{5}{2}$ or $2\frac{1}{2}$

11. When the denominator is not a divisor or multiple of 10 or 100, you cannot use this method.
a) $\frac{6}{10}$ = 0.6 **c)** $\frac{15}{10}$ = 1.5 **d)** $\frac{52}{100}$ = 0.52
e) $\frac{45}{100}$ = 0.45 **g)** $\frac{9}{10}$ = 0.9 **h)** $\frac{33}{100}$ = 0.33

12. a) 0.333 …

b) Explanations may vary. When you divide each type of block into 3 equal sets, there are always 3 blocks in each set and you always have 1 block left.

13. a) i) 0.1111111   **ii)** 0.2222222   **iii)** 0.3333333

b) They are all repeating decimals. The digit that repeats is the numerator of the fraction.

   i) 0.444...   **ii)** 0.666...   **iii)** 0.888...

c) i) $\frac{5}{9}$ **ii)** $\frac{7}{9}$

14. $\frac{1}{6}, \frac{3}{5}, \frac{7}{8}, 1\frac{1}{3}, 1\frac{4}{9}$

15. $\frac{2}{9}, \frac{3}{8}, \frac{3}{4}, 1\frac{2}{7}, 1\frac{5}{12}$

16. Between 1.3 and 1.4   **17.** Between 0.8 and 0.9

18. Answers may vary.

19. a) $\frac{3}{8} < \frac{2}{5}$ **b)** $\frac{2}{3} < \frac{3}{4}$ **c)** $\frac{3}{8} > \frac{4}{12}$

   d) $0.7 < \frac{9}{12}$ **e)** $\frac{7}{8} < 0.9$ **f)** $\frac{5}{6} > \frac{4}{5}$

20. a) $\frac{5}{6}$ **b)** $\frac{3}{8}$ **c)** $\frac{2}{11}$ **d)** $\frac{6}{7}$ **e)** $\frac{8}{6}$ **f)** $\frac{9}{7}$

21. a) $\frac{4}{5}$ **b)** $\frac{5}{8}$ **c)** $\frac{3}{13}$ **d)** $\frac{7}{9}$ **e)** $\frac{3}{2}$ **f)** $\frac{6}{5}$

22. a) 0.17, 0.33, 0.50, 0.67, 0.83, 1.00

b)

Fraction form	Decimal form
$\frac{1}{6}$	0.17
$\frac{2}{6}$	0.33
$\frac{3}{6}$	0.50
$\frac{4}{6}$	0.67
$\frac{5}{6}$	0.83
$\frac{6}{6}$	1.00

d) Answers may vary. 1.17, 1.33, 1.50, 1.67, 1.83, 2.00

23. 0.08, 0.17, 0.25, 0.33, 0.42, 0.50, 0.58, 0.67, 0.75, 0.83, 0.92, 1.00

24. $\frac{2}{3}$

25. Between 1.7 and 1.8   **26.** Between 0.6 and 0.7

27. a) 0.2   **b)** 0.8   **c)** 7.4   **d)** 4.0   **e)** 0.04

28. a) 6.7   **b)** 67   **c)** 670   **d)** 0.067   **e)** 0.0067

29. Answers may vary.

30. a) $\frac{5}{3} > \frac{3}{2}$ **b)** $\frac{7}{4} < \frac{9}{5}$ **c)** $1.1 < \frac{9}{8}$

   d) $1.7 > \frac{13}{8}$ **e)** $\frac{21}{12} < 1.8$ **f)** $\frac{21}{12} > 1.7$

31. a) i) 0.5, 0.67 or 0.66, 0.83   **ii)** 0.5, 0.33, 0.17

   iii) 0.5, 0.375, 0.3   **iv)** 0.5, 0.6, 0.75

b) i) Increases; decreases   **ii)** Decreases; increases

32. 0.125, 0.25, 0.375, 0.50, 0.625, 0.75, 0.875, 1.00

33. a) $\frac{1.5}{3}$ **b)** $\frac{2.5}{5}$; $\frac{0.75}{3}$, $\frac{1.25}{5}$

Linking Ideas: Mathematics and Technology
Investigating Repeating Decimals, page 107

1. a) Divide the numerator by the denominator.

b) Add one to the numerator.

c) $\frac{1}{99}, \frac{2}{99}, \frac{3}{99}$; 0.0101..., 0.0202..., 0.0303...

2. a) 0.1212..., 0.2828..., 0.5353...., 0.666...

3. a) 0.001001..., 0.002002..., 0.003003...

b) 0.004004..., 0.005005..., 0.014014..., 0.037037..., 0.685685...

4. a) 0.166..., 0.333..., 0.5   **b)** 0.0909..., 0.1818..., 0.2727...

   c) 0.0625, 0.125, 0.1875   **d)** 0.0303..., 0.0606..., 0.0909...

e) 0.027027..., 0.054054..., 0.081081...

f) 0.15625, 0.03125, 0.046875

g) 0.00990099..., 0.01980198..., 0.02970297...

h) 0.0036900369..., 0.0073800738..., 0.0110701107...

5. a) 0.54455445...   **b)** 0.3125

   c) 0.3378378...   **d)** 0.329670329670...

Linking Ideas: Mathematics and Sports
Fractions and Decimals in Baseball and Hockey, page 108

1. a) 0.287   **b)** 0.197   **c)** 0.263   **d)** 0.212   **e)** 0.208

2. a) 3.83   **b)** 1.83   **c)** 3.33   **d)** 0.75

3. a) 0.287, 0.263, 0.212, 0.208, 0.197

b) Helen Callaghan

4. 3.83, 3.33, 1.83, 0.75

b) Joan Westman

5. , 6. , 7. Answers may vary.

2.4 Adding Fractions
Developing the Ideas, page 110

1. a) $\frac{4}{5}$

b) i) $\frac{2}{5}$ **ii)** $\frac{5}{5}$ **iii)** $\frac{7}{5}$

2. b) The quarters line; $\frac{5}{4}$

   c) i) $\frac{3}{4}$ **ii)** $\frac{7}{4}$ **iii)** $\frac{9}{4}$

3. b) The sixths line; $\frac{5}{6}$ **c)** 0.83

   d) i) $\frac{7}{6}$, 1.17   **ii)** $\frac{11}{6}$, 1.83   **iii)** $\frac{11}{6}$, 1.83

4. a) 1.03   **b)** $\frac{5}{8}$, 0.63   **c)** $\frac{9}{10}$, 0.90

   d) $\frac{5}{12}$, 0.42   **e)** $\frac{17}{12}$, 1.42   **f)** $\frac{19}{12}$, 1.58

Working with Mathematics, page 114

1. a) ii   **b)** i

2. It is between 0 and 1.

4. a) $\frac{2}{3}$ **b)** $\frac{3}{3}$, or 1   **c)** $\frac{5}{6}$ **d)** $\frac{7}{12}$ **e)** $\frac{1}{2}$

   f) $\frac{13}{12}$, or $1\frac{1}{12}$ **g)** $\frac{5}{3}$, or $1\frac{2}{3}$ **h)** $\frac{6}{3}$, or 2   **i)** $\frac{5}{4}$, or $1\frac{1}{4}$

5. a) $\frac{7}{6}$, or $1\frac{1}{6}$ **b)** $\frac{7}{10}$ **c)** $\frac{3}{8}$ **d)** $\frac{9}{8}$, or $1\frac{1}{8}$ **e)** $\frac{9}{4}$, or $2\frac{1}{4}$

   f) $\frac{9}{10}$ **g)** $\frac{5}{6}$ **h)** $\frac{19}{12}$, or $1\frac{7}{12}$ **i)** $\frac{3}{2}$, or $1\frac{1}{2}$

6. a) $\frac{7}{6}$, or $1\frac{1}{6}$ **b)** $1\frac{2}{3}$ **c)** $\frac{17}{8}$, or $2\frac{1}{8}$ **d)** $2\frac{1}{4}$

   e) 2   **f)** 2   **g)** 3   **h)** 3   **i)** 2

7. a) $\frac{1}{6} + \frac{1}{6} = \frac{2}{6}$, or $\frac{1}{3}$ **b)** $\frac{1}{6} + \frac{5}{6} = \frac{6}{6}$, or 1

   c) $\frac{1}{6} + \frac{1}{4} = \frac{5}{12}$ **d)** $\frac{1}{6} + \frac{1}{3} = \frac{3}{6}$, or $\frac{1}{2}$

   e) $\frac{1}{6} + \frac{1}{2} = \frac{4}{6}$, or $\frac{2}{3}$ **f)** $\frac{1}{6} + \frac{1}{4} + \frac{1}{3} = \frac{9}{12}$, or $\frac{3}{4}$

   g) $\frac{1}{2} + \frac{1}{4} = \frac{3}{4}$ **h)** $\frac{1}{2} + \frac{1}{3} = \frac{5}{6}$

   i) $\frac{3}{4} + \frac{5}{6} = \frac{19}{12}$, or $1\frac{7}{12}$ **j)** $\frac{3}{5} + \frac{1}{2} = \frac{11}{10}$, or $1\frac{1}{10}$

   k) $\frac{5}{4} + \frac{4}{3} = \frac{31}{12}$, or $2\frac{7}{12}$ **l)** $\frac{2}{3} + \frac{3}{4} + \frac{1}{2} = \frac{23}{12}$, or $1\frac{11}{12}$

8. a) $\frac{2}{8}$ **b)** $\frac{4}{8}$ **c)** $\frac{8}{8}$ **d)** $\frac{6}{6}$ **e)** $\frac{6}{2}$ **f)** $\frac{6}{7}$

9. a) $2\frac{3}{8}$ **b)** $3\frac{3}{8}$ **c)** $4\frac{3}{8}$ **d)** $4\frac{3}{8}$ **e)** $6\frac{3}{8}$ **f)** $11\frac{3}{8}$

10. a) 0.65   **b)** 1.29   **c)** 1.52

11. a) $\frac{22}{35}$ **b)** $\frac{23}{18}$, or $1\frac{5}{18}$ **c)** $\frac{179}{66}$, or $2\frac{47}{66}$

12. Between 0.8 and 0.9   **13.** Between 0.90 and 1.0

14. Forms of fractions may vary.

+	$\frac{1}{4}$	$\frac{1}{2}$	$\frac{3}{4}$	1	$\frac{5}{4}$	$\frac{3}{2}$
$\frac{1}{4}$	$\frac{1}{2}$	$\frac{3}{4}$	1	$1\frac{1}{4}$	$\frac{6}{4}$	$\frac{7}{4}$
$\frac{1}{2}$	$\frac{3}{4}$	1	$\frac{5}{4}$	$1\frac{1}{2}$	$\frac{7}{4}$	$\frac{4}{2}$
$\frac{3}{4}$	1	$\frac{5}{4}$	$\frac{6}{4}$	$1\frac{3}{4}$	$\frac{8}{4}$	$\frac{9}{4}$
1	$1\frac{1}{4}$	$1\frac{1}{2}$	$1\frac{3}{4}$	2	$2\frac{1}{4}$	$2\frac{1}{2}$
$\frac{5}{4}$	$\frac{6}{4}$	$\frac{7}{4}$	$\frac{8}{4}$	$2\frac{1}{4}$	$\frac{10}{4}$	$\frac{11}{4}$
$\frac{3}{2}$	$\frac{7}{4}$	$\frac{4}{2}$	$\frac{9}{4}$	$2\frac{1}{2}$	$\frac{11}{4}$	$\frac{6}{2}$

15. a) $\frac{1}{4} + \frac{1}{2} = \frac{3}{4}$ **b)** $\frac{1}{4} + \frac{1}{3} = \frac{7}{12}$ **c)** $\frac{1}{4} + \frac{1}{4} = \frac{2}{4}$, or $\frac{1}{2}$
d) $\frac{1}{4} + \frac{1}{5} = 0.45$ **e)** $\frac{1}{4} + \frac{1}{6} = \frac{5}{12}$ **f)** $\frac{1}{4} + \frac{1}{8} = \frac{3}{8}$
g) $\frac{5}{8} + \frac{1}{4} = \frac{7}{8}$ **h)** $\frac{3}{2} + \frac{1}{6} = \frac{10}{6}$, or $\frac{5}{3}$, or $1\frac{2}{3}$
i) $\frac{4}{3} + \frac{1}{2} = \frac{11}{6}$, or $1\frac{5}{6}$ **j)** $\frac{2}{5} + \frac{1}{10} = \frac{5}{10}$, or $\frac{1}{2}$
k) $\frac{5}{6} + \frac{3}{4} = \frac{19}{12}$, or $1\frac{7}{12}$ **l)** $\frac{1}{2} + \frac{1}{3} + \frac{1}{4} = \frac{13}{12}$, or $1\frac{1}{12}$

16. a) $1\frac{7}{12}$ **b)** $2\frac{7}{12}$
c) $7\frac{7}{12}$ **d)** $\frac{14}{12}$, or $1\frac{2}{12}$, or $1\frac{1}{6}$
e) $\frac{13}{12}$, or $1\frac{1}{12}$ **f)** $\frac{7}{24}$

17. a) $2\frac{7}{15}$ **b)** $5\frac{7}{15}$ **c)** $8\frac{7}{15}$
18. a) 1.30 **b)** 1.95 **c)** 2.96
19. a) $\frac{43}{30}$, or $1\frac{13}{30}$ **b)** $\frac{19}{24}$ **c)** $\frac{93}{70}$, or $1\frac{23}{70}$
20. Between 1.0 and 1.1 **21.** Between 0.8 and 0.9

22. a) It adds the numbers in cells A1 and B1.
b) Answers may vary.
c) i) Fractions may vary. =A2+B2 **ii)** Answers may vary.
d) i) Fractions may vary. =A3+B3+C3 **ii)** Fractions may vary.

23. $\frac{3}{4}$ of an hour **24.** $\frac{5}{8}$

25. a) No **b)** $\frac{1}{2} + \frac{1}{3} + \frac{1}{6}$ **c)** $\frac{1}{2} + \frac{1}{4} + \frac{1}{6} + \frac{1}{12}$

2.5 Subtracting Fractions
Developing the Ideas, page 116

1. a) $\frac{2}{4}$, or $\frac{1}{2}$ **b)** $\frac{1}{8}$ **c)** $\frac{3}{6}$, or $\frac{1}{2}$
2. a) $\frac{1}{3}$ **b)** $\frac{1}{4}$ **c)** $\frac{3}{4}$
d) $\frac{3}{12}$, or $\frac{1}{4}$ **e)** $\frac{7}{12}$ **f)** $\frac{5}{6}$

Working with Mathematics, page 119

1. a) i and iii **b)** iii
2. a) Answers may vary. **b)** Yes, no
3. Between $\frac{1}{2}$ and $\frac{3}{4}$ **4.** Answers may vary.
5. a) $\frac{2}{4}$, or $\frac{1}{2}$ **b)** $\frac{2}{8}$, or $\frac{1}{4}$ **c)** $\frac{1}{4}$ **d)** $\frac{1}{8}$
e) 0 **f)** $\frac{5}{8}$ **g)** $\frac{1}{4}$ **h)** $\frac{3}{8}$ **i)** $\frac{1}{8}$
6. a) $\frac{7}{10}$ **b)** $\frac{5}{12}$ **c)** $\frac{7}{6}$, or $1\frac{1}{6}$ **d)** $\frac{1}{6}$ **e)** $\frac{2}{10}$, or $\frac{1}{5}$
f) $\frac{1}{12}$ **g)** $\frac{9}{10}$ **h)** $\frac{9}{8}$, or $1\frac{1}{8}$ **i)** $\frac{7}{6}$, or $1\frac{1}{6}$
7. a) $\frac{1}{6}$ **b)** $\frac{2}{8}$, or $\frac{1}{4}$ **c)** $\frac{7}{10}$ **d)** $1\frac{1}{5}$ **e)** $\frac{7}{10}$
f) $1\frac{1}{2}$ **g)** $\frac{3}{10}$ **h)** $\frac{13}{8}$, or $1\frac{5}{8}$ **i)** $\frac{11}{12}$
8. a) $\frac{5}{6} - \frac{1}{3} = \frac{3}{6}$, or $\frac{1}{2}$ **b)** $\frac{7}{6} - \frac{1}{3} = \frac{5}{6}$ **c)** $\frac{9}{6} - \frac{1}{3} = \frac{7}{6}$, or $1\frac{1}{6}$
d) $\frac{5}{6} - \frac{1}{4} = \frac{7}{12}$ **e)** $\frac{5}{6} - \frac{1}{2} = \frac{2}{6}$, or $\frac{1}{3}$ **f)** $\frac{5}{6} - \frac{1}{2} - \frac{1}{4} = \frac{1}{12}$

9. a) $\frac{5}{6}$ **b)** $\frac{3}{6}$, or $\frac{1}{2}$ **c)** $\frac{3}{8}$
d) $\frac{5}{8}$ **e)** $\frac{3}{10}$ **f)** $1\frac{5}{12}$
10. a) $\frac{3}{8}$ **b)** $\frac{2}{8}$, or $\frac{1}{4}$ **c)** $\frac{1}{8}$
11. a) $1\frac{1}{6}$ **b)** $2\frac{1}{6}$ **c)** $4\frac{1}{6}$
12. a) 0.46 **b)** 0.55 **c)** 0.63
13. Between 1.0 and 1.1 **14.** Between 1.6 and 1.7
15. a) $\frac{6}{35}$ **b)** $\frac{5}{18}$ **c)** $\frac{13}{28}$
16. a) $\frac{7}{8} - \frac{1}{8} = \frac{6}{8}$, or $\frac{3}{4}$ **b)** $\frac{7}{8} - \frac{1}{4} = \frac{5}{8}$
c) $\frac{7}{8} - \frac{1}{8} - \frac{1}{8} = \frac{4}{8}$, or $\frac{1}{2}$ **d)** $1 - \frac{5}{8} = \frac{3}{8}$
e) $2 - \frac{7}{8} = \frac{9}{8}$, or $1\frac{1}{8}$ **f)** $1\frac{5}{8} - \frac{3}{4} = \frac{7}{8}$
17. a) $\frac{1}{6}$ **b)** $\frac{1}{12}$ **c)** $\frac{1}{12}$
d) $\frac{4}{3}$, or $1\frac{1}{3}$ **e)** $\frac{3}{6}$, or $\frac{1}{2}$ **f)** $\frac{7}{12}$
18. a) $1\frac{1}{4}$ **b)** $2\frac{1}{4}$ **c)** $3\frac{1}{4}$
19. a) $1\frac{7}{12}$ **b)** $2\frac{7}{12}$ **c)** $\frac{7}{12}$
20. a) $\frac{3}{8}$ **b)** $\frac{8}{6}$, or $\frac{4}{3}$, or $1\frac{1}{3}$
c) $\frac{7}{12}$ **d)** $\frac{13}{12}$, or $1\frac{1}{12}$
21. a) 0.70 **b)** 0.55 **c)** 0.21
22. Between 0.7 and 0.8 **23.** Between 1.9 and 2.0
24. a) $\frac{11}{15}$ **b)** $\frac{5}{28}$ **c)** $\frac{2}{99}$
25. a) =A1−B1 **b)** , **c)** , **d)** Answers may vary.
26. $\frac{1}{2}$ **27.** $\frac{5}{8}$ **28.** Answers may vary.

2.6 Using Place-Value Blocks to Multiply with Decimals
Developing the Ideas, page 121

1. a) 8, 8 **b)** 16, 1.6 **c)** 6, 0.06 **d)** 9.66
e) Answers may vary. **f)** Greater than 8
2. Explanations may vary.

Working with Mathematics, page 122

1. a) 1.5×2.3 **b)** 2.6×3.2
2. a) 7.68 **b)** 4.65 **c)** 5.94 **d)** 12.24
3. a) 3.45 **b)** 8.32
4. a) $1.8 \times 4.3 = 7.74$ **b)** $5.2 \times 3.6 = 18.72$
c) $3.4 \times 4.1 = 13.94$
5. a) 1.56 **b)** 2.94 **c)** 4.32 **d)** 2.24
e) 11.52 **f)** 20.25 **g)** 10.44 **h)** 34.44
6. \$2.00
7. a) 7.75 **b)** 5.12 **c)** 6.44 **d)** 11.96
8. a) 9.03 **b)** 1.95 **c)** 4.42 **d)** 2.48
e) 7.65 **f)** 15.08 **g)** 10.54 **h)** 18.63
9. 40¢
10. Methods may vary.
a) Use the ➕ key to add twelve 35s. The product is 420.
b) Use the ➗ key to calculate $24 \div 10$. Record the result 2.4. Clear the calculator. Use the ➕ key to add four 24s and seven 2.4s. The product is 112.8
c) Since $0.5 = \frac{1}{2}$, use the ➗ key to calculate $29 \div 2$. Without clearing the calculator, use the ➕ key to add six 29s to the result. The product is 188.5
d) Since $0.5 = \frac{1}{2}$, use the ➗ key to calculate $8.3 \div 2$.

Without clearing the calculator, add 8.3 to the result. The product is 12.45.

2.7 Using Place-Value Blocks to Divide with Decimals

Developing the Ideas, page 123

1. a) 8 flats and 1 rod
   b) 5 flats and 7 rods
   c) You can do this 4 times. You are left with 0 flats and 9 rods.
   d) 4 with a remainder of 0.9
   e) She can fix 4 lamps. She has 0.9 m of wire left.
   f) Yes

Working with Mathematics, page 124

1. The digits before the decimal points are equal. The decimal that appears on the calculator display represents the remainder divided by 2.4.

2. a) $6.12 \div 3.6$ b) $3.08 \div 1.4$

3. a) 1.7   b) 2.2

4. a) 1.5   b) 5   c) 2.1   d) 2.4   e) 1.7   f) 3

5. a) 4, remainder 0.9   b) 4, remainder 0.4
   c) 4, remainder 0.8   d) 3, remainder 0.7
   e) 3, remainder 0.2   f) 1, remainder 1.8
   g) 3, remainder 1.4   h) 2, remainder 1.48

6. a) He can make 5 costumes. He will have 1.2 m of fabric left.
   b) The answers are the same, except the calculator expresses the remainder as a fraction of the dividend.

7. a) 3   b) 3.7   c) 3.5   d) 1.4   e) 2.4   f) 2.3

8. a) 3, remainder 1   b) 2, remainder 2
   c) 3, remainder 1   d) 3, remainder 1
   e) 2, remainder 0.3   f) 2, remainder 1.5
   g) 5, remainder 0.2   h) 3, remainder 0.74

9. a) She can make 6 frames. She will have 1 m of framing material left.
   b) See the answer to exercise 6b.

10. a) He can buy 5 fish. He will have 47¢ left.
    b) See the answer to exercise 6b.

11. a) Enter 168, then use the ⬚－ key to subtract 14. Keep subtracting 14 until the result is less than 14. The number of 14s you subtracted is the quotient. The quotient is 12.

    For parts b to d, use a similar technique to that in part a.
    b) The quotient is 31.
    c) The quotient is 23.
    d) The quotient is 6, remainder 1.08.

Quest: Designing a Bookcase, page 125

28.6 cm; 26.7 cm

2.8 Order of Operations

Developing the Ideas, page 126

1. They completed the operations in different orders.
2. Lisa's answer is correct.

Working with Mathematics, page 128

1. So that different people get the same answer when they simplify an expression that involves several operations.

2. a) i) Multiply 2×3.   ii) Multiply 4×5.
   iii) Add $3 + 4$.   iv) Multiply 4×5.
   b) The operation(s) inside the brackets must be completed before any operations outside the brackets.

3. a) i) 49   ii) 99
   b) The addition is completed before the multiplication.

4. a) 32   b) 32   c) 42   d) 16   e) 16   f) 22

5. a) 19   b) 34   c) 23   d) 23   e) 70   f) 38

6. a) You can write 16 different expressions. Since some expressions simplify to the same number, you can get 11 different answers.
   $8 + 4 + 2 = 14$, $8 - 4 - 2 = 2$, $8 + 4 - 2 = 10$ and
   $8 + 4 \div 2 = 10$, $8 - 4 + 2 = 6$ and $8 - 4 \div 2 = 6$,
   $8 + 4 \times 2 = 16$ and $8 \times 4 \div 2 = 16$, $8 \times 4 + 2 = 34$,
   $8 \div 4 + 2 = 4$ and $8 \div 4 \times 2 = 4$, $8 - 4 \times 2 = 0$ and
   $8 \div 4 - 2 = 0$, $8 \times 4 - 2 = 30$, $8 \div 4 \div 2 = 1$,
   $8 \times 4 \times 2 = 64$
   b) You can write 16 different expressions. Since some expressions simplify to the same number, you can get 10 different answers.
   $8 + (4 + 2) = 14$, $8 - (4 - 2) = 6$ and $8 - (4 \div 2) = 6$,
   $8 + (4 - 2) = 10$ and $8 + (4 \div 2) = 10$, $8 - (4 + 2) = 2$,
   $8 \div (4 - 2) = 4$ and $8 \div (4 \div 2) = 4$, $8 \times (4 + 2) = 48$,
   $8 \times (4 - 2) = 16$ and $8 \times (4 \div 2) = 16$ and
   $8 + (4 \times 2) = 16$, $8 \div (4 + 2) = \frac{8}{6}$, $8 - (4 \times 2) = 0$,
   $8 \times (4 \times 2) = 64$, $8 \div (4 \times 2) = 1$

7. a) 55   b) 1   c) 25   d) 4   e) 36   f) 38
   g) 39   h) 30   i) 34   j) 90   k) 27   l) 4

8. a) 17.47   b) 15.75   c) 33.6   d) 14.19   e) 1   f) 4

9. a) $(8 + 2) \times 5 = 50$ b) $6 \times (3 + 1) = 24$
   c) $1 + 6 \times (3 + 1) = 25$ d) $(2 + 8) \times 5 - 1 = 49$
   e) $7 + 14 \div (7 - 5) = 14$ f) $12 \div (2 \times 5 - 4) = 2$

10. Answers to some parts may vary.
    a) $(4 - 2) \times 8 - 6 = 10$ b) $2 + 4 + 6 + 8 = 20$
    c) $4 \times 8 + 2 + 6 = 40$ d) $(8 + 4 \div 2) \times 6 = 60$

11. c) $6 \times 24 \div 3 = 48$

12. b) $2 \times \$7.95 + 3 \times \$4.50 = \$29.40$

13. Answers to some parts may vary.
    a) $(9 - 3) \times 2 = 12$ b) $(9 + 3) \times 2 = 24$
    c) $(9 \times 3) \times 2 = 54$ d) $(9 + 3) \div 2 = 6$
    e) $(9 \times 3) + 2 = 29$ f) $(9 - 3) - 2 = 4$

14. a) 53.6   b) 8.7   c) 15.4   d) 5.2   e) 5.55   f) 2

15. b) $(5 - 3) \times \$47.95 = \$95.90$

16. c) $4 \times 20 + 2 \times 30 = 140$

17. a) $(43 + 7) \times 2 = 100$ b) $4 \times (9 - 2) = 28$
    c) $8 + (9 - 2) \times 4 = 36$ d) $15 - (13 - 8) \times 3 = 0$
    e) $6 + 2 \times (5 - 1) = 14$ f) $8 \times (3 + 2) \times 2 = 80$

18. a) $8 - (3 - 2) + 5 = 12$ b) $3 + (1 + 2) \times 5 = 18$
    c) $(3 + 4) \times (6 + 1) = 49$ d) $2 \times (5 + 3) \times 4 = 64$
    e) $(24 - 4) \div (2 \times 10) = 1$
    f) The equation is true without any brackets.

19. You can write 6 different expressions. Since some of the expressions simplify to the same number, you can get 4 different answers.
    $(1 + 2) \times 3 + 4 = 13$, $1 + 2 \times (3 + 4) = 15$,
    $(1 + 2) \times (3 + 4) = 21$, $(1 + 2 \times 3) + 4 = 11$ and
    $1 + (2 \times 3) + 4 = 11$ and $1 + (2 \times 3 + 4) = 11$

20. Answers may vary.
    $2 \times 3 - 4 - 1 = 1$; $2 \times 3 - 4 \times 1 = 2$; $(4 \times 2 + 1) \div 3 = 3$;

$3 - 2 - 1 + 4 = 4$; $(1 + 2) \times 3 - 4 = 5$; $3 \times 4 \div 2 \times 1 = 6$;
$4 \div 2 \times 3 + 1 = 7$; $(3 - 1) \times 2 + 4 = 8$; $1 \times 4 + 2 \times 3 = 10$

21. a) $(7.4 + 2.1) + 14 = 23.5$ **b)** $(7.4 - 2.1) + 14 = 19.3$
   c) $(7.4 \times 2.1) - 14 = 1.54$ **d)** $(7.4 \times 2.1) \div 14 = 1.11$
   e) $(7.4 - 2.1) \times 14 = 74.2$ **f)** $(7.4 + 2.1) \times 14 = 133$

22. a) $9 \div 3 - 4 + 2 = 1$ **b)** $9 - 3 - 4 - 2 = 0$
   c) $9 + 3 + 4 + 2 = 18$ **d)** $9 \times 3 - 4 \div 2 = 25$
   e) $9 \div 3 \times 4 \times 2 = 24$ **f)** $9 + 3 + 4 \times 2 = 20$

23. a) $4 + 4 + 4 = 12$ **b)** $4 \div 4 \times 4 = 4$
   c) $(4 + 4) \times 4 = 32$ **d)** $(4 + 4) \div 4 = 2$
   e) $4 \times 4 + 4 = 20$

Review, page 130

1. $\frac{2}{5}, \frac{9}{4}, \frac{8}{9}$

2. Answers may vary.
   a) $\frac{4}{6}$ **b)** $\frac{8}{10}$ **c)** $\frac{18}{8}$ **d)** $\frac{2}{3}$
   e) $\frac{3}{4}$ **f)** $\frac{14}{22}$ **g)** $\frac{4}{10}$ **h)** $\frac{10}{12}$

3. Diagrams may vary.

4. a) $\frac{2}{12}$ **b)** $\frac{16}{12}$ **c)** $\frac{30}{12}$ **d)** $\frac{21}{12}$

5. Answers may vary.

6. a) $\frac{1}{2} = \frac{8}{16}$ **b)** $\frac{5}{3} = \frac{25}{15}$ **c)** $\frac{3}{4} = \frac{21}{28}$ **d)** $\frac{24}{36} = \frac{2}{3}$

7. a) $\frac{4}{5}$ **b)** $\frac{2}{3}$ **c)** $\frac{5}{2}$ **d)** $\frac{3}{5}$
   e) $\frac{3}{2}$ **f)** $\frac{7}{11}$ **g)** $\frac{1}{4}$ **h)** $\frac{1}{8}$

8. a) 20 **b)** $\frac{4}{100}$ **c)** $\frac{1}{1000}$ **d)** 60 **e)** $\frac{3}{10\,000}$ **f)** $\frac{6}{10}$

9. The operation to use is described here.
   a) $\boxed{+}$ 6   **b)** $\boxed{-}$ .007   **c)** $\boxed{-}$ 0.11   **d)** $\boxed{+}$ .025

10. a) 1.25 **b)** 1.38 **c)** 5.17 **d)** 7.5
   e) 1.7 **f)** 1.6 **g)** 0.83 **h)** 2.3

11. a) 0.66 **b)** 3.33 **c)** 0.83
   d) $0.714\,285$ **e)** $1.571\,428$ **f)** 0.77

12. a) $\frac{3}{5}$ **b)** $\frac{7}{20}$ **c)** $\frac{49}{10}$, or $4\frac{9}{10}$
   d) $\frac{79}{25}$, or $3\frac{4}{25}$ **e)** $\frac{35}{4}$, or $8\frac{3}{4}$ **f)** $\frac{217}{100}$, or $2\frac{17}{100}$

13. a) $\frac{5}{8} > \frac{3}{5}$ **b)** $\frac{5}{6} > \frac{9}{11}$ **c)** $\frac{7}{3} > \frac{16}{7}$
   d) $\frac{17}{48} > \frac{7}{20}$ **e)** $\frac{17}{48} < \frac{9}{25}$ **f)** $\frac{5}{11} < 0.46$

14. a) $\frac{2}{10}$, or $\frac{1}{5}$ **b)** $\frac{6}{5}$, or $1\frac{1}{5}$ **c)** $\frac{5}{4}$, or $1\frac{1}{4}$
   d) $\frac{7}{12}$ **e)** $\frac{19}{10}$, or $1\frac{9}{10}$ **f)** About 0.78

15. a) 0.7 **b)** 1.625

16. a) $\frac{19}{12}$, or $1\frac{7}{12}$ **b)** $\frac{53}{63}$
   c) $\frac{428}{165}$, or $2\frac{98}{165}$ **d)** $\frac{157}{36}$, or $4\frac{13}{36}$

17. a) $\frac{2}{5}$ **b)** $\frac{1}{8}$ **c)** $\frac{3}{4}$
   d) $\frac{1}{12}$ **e)** $\frac{11}{10}$, or $1\frac{1}{10}$ **f)** $\frac{1}{12}$

18. a) 0.3 **b)** 0.875

19. a) $\frac{7}{12}$ **b)** $\frac{17}{63}$
   c) $\frac{287}{165}$, or $1\frac{122}{165}$ **d)** $\frac{43}{36}$, or $1\frac{7}{36}$

20. a) $3.2 \times 2.3 = 7.36$ **b)** $2.3 \times 2.4 = 5.52$

21. a) 6.72 **b)** 1.95 **c)** 4.73 **d)** 6.56

22. a) 4.32 **b)** 6.86 **c)** 1.75 **d)** 21.93 **e)** 9.62 **f)** 1.86

23. a) $\$11.94$ **b)** $\$23.88$

24. a) 4 **b)** The answers are the same.

25. a) 4 **b)** 3 **c)** 4
   d) 2.2 **e)** 1.3 **f)** 2.3

26. a) 4, remainder 0.4   **b)** 3, remainder 0.6
   c) 3, remainder 0.1   **d)** 2, remainder 1.0

27. $\$2.79$

28. a) 27.2 **b)** 9.8 **c)** 103.68 **d)** 8 **e)** 11.86
   f) 15.3 **g)** 13.9 **h)** 47.6 **i)** 33.6 **j)** 34.9

29. a) $5 \times (9 + 11) = 100$ **b)** $(67 - 24) \times 2 = 86$
   c) $84 \div (7 + 5) = 7$ **d)** $(5 \times 6 + 27) \div 3 = 19$

CHAPTER 3 PERCENT AND PROBABILITY

Start With What You Know, page 136

1. a) $\frac{55}{100} = \frac{11}{20}$ **b)** Yes
   c) $\frac{45}{100} = \frac{9}{20}$
   This represents people surveyed who supported Yes.

2. a) 51 **b)** 49
   c) These people were added to the Yes or No supporters based on their answers to a series of questions.

3. b) The 100-square on page 136 has 4 more red squares.
   c) It decreased by 4%.

4. The No side received 53 498 more votes than the Yes side.

5. a) 50.6%
   b) The October survey provided a more accurate prediction. Reasons may vary.

6. Answers may vary; people may not wish to give their opinions to a survey-taker, or may change their minds.

7. a) $15\ \text{km}^2$ **b)** 25, 75   **c)** 82, 18   **d)** 39 L, 61 L

3.1 Percent

Developing the Ideas, page 138

1. a) $\$25, \$75$ **b)** $\$50, \$150$

2. a) Any amount from $0 to $50; any price from $100 to $50
   b) Any amount from $0 to $100; any price from $200 to $100

3. a) $\$5.75$ **b)** $\$105.75$ **c)** $\$211.50$

Page 140

1. 50   **2.** 10   **3.** 6
4. 1   **5.** 13   **6.** 20

7. Answers may vary; for example, wood, cloth

8. Answers may vary.

Working with Mathematics, page 141

1. Answers may vary. Percent means per hundred or out of one hundred.

2. Sentences may vary.
   a) Jasmine scored $\frac{82}{100}$ on her mathematics test.
   b) The milk in this carton is $\frac{1}{100}$ butter fat by volume.
   c) The sales tax on an item is $\frac{11}{100}$ of the labelled price.
   d) At the end of winter, skis sell for $\frac{30}{100}$ off the labelled price.

3. a) About 14% of Canadians are under 5 years of age.
   b) A furniture salesperson receives about 5% commission on the furniture she sells.
   c) Ian scored 78% on his English examination.
   d) Air contains about 21% oxygen by volume.
   e) The area of Africa is about 20% of the total land area in the world.

4. a) 50%   **b)** 40%   **c)** 25%   **d)** $33\frac{1}{3}$%

5. a) 37%   **b)** 44%   **c)** 40%   **d)** 44%

6. Estimates and explanations may vary.
    a) About 40%   **b)** About 25%   **c)** About 20%   **d)** About 55%

7. a) 21   **b)** 100   **c)** 21   **d)** $\frac{21}{100}$ **e)** 21%

8. a) 0.35; $\frac{7}{20}$ **b)** 0.46; $\frac{23}{50}$ **c)** 0.15; $\frac{3}{20}$ **d)** 0.69; $\frac{69}{100}$
    e) 0.75; $\frac{3}{4}$ **f)** 0.87; $\frac{87}{100}$ **g)** 0.07; $\frac{7}{100}$ **h)** 0.96; $\frac{24}{25}$

9. a) 37%; 0.37   **b)** 4%; 0.04   **c)** 14%; 0.14   **d)** 12%; 0.12
    e) 30%; 0.30   **f)** 20%; 0.20   **g)** 75%; 0.75   **h)** 100%; 1.00

10. a) 45; 45%

11. a) 60; 60%

12. The repeating decimals are rounded to 2 places.
    a) 0.73; 73%   **b)** 0.825; 82.5%
    c) 0.76; 76%   **d)** 0.72; 72%
    e) 0.825; 82.5%   **f)** 0.625; 62.5%
    g) 0.83; 83%   **h)** 0.92; 92%

13. a) i) 21%   **ii)** 32%   **iii)** 47%   **iv)** 53%
    b) 100%

14. Estimates may vary. Pacific: 52%; Atlantic: 23%; Indian: 21%; Arctic: 4%

15. a) i) 34%   **ii)** 11%   **iii)** 8%
    b) 58%   **c)** Questions may vary.

16. a) Summer   **b)** Spring
    c) 26%   **d)** Yes   **e)** 67%

17. a) i) 33%   **ii)** 40%
    b) Answers may vary.   **c)** Answers may vary.

18. b) 93%   **c)** Questions may vary.

19. a) 30 kg   **b)** 30 g   **c)** 3 g   **d)** 300 g

3.2 Visualizing and Estimating Percents
Developing the Ideas, page 144

Estimates may vary.

1. 9 cm   **2.** 60%   **3.** 20 games

Working with Mathematics, page 146

Since most of the exercises involve estimation and visualization, answers may vary. Sample estimates are provided.

1. a) $33\frac{1}{3}$%   **b)** 45%   **c)** 80%

2. a) The regular price would be lower.
    b) The regular price would be higher.

3. 60%   **4.** Just over 2 m

5. Adrian: 25%; Siobhan: 40%; Linda: 80%; Atul: 75%

6. a) 47%   **b)** 24%   **c)** 32%   **d)** 78%

7. 370   **8.** 70%   **9.** 25%   **10.** 35%

11. a) $\frac{7}{8}$ **b)** $\frac{4}{9}$ **c)** $\frac{1}{5}$ **d)** $\frac{1}{10}$

12. 11%

13. Superior: 35%; Huron: 60%; Michigan: 0%; Erie: 50%; Ontario: 53%

3.3 Sales Tax
Developing the Ideas, page 147

1. Percent means per hundred.
    a) $\frac{6}{100}$ **b)** $\frac{7}{100}$ **c)** $\frac{8}{100}$ **d)** $\frac{9}{100}$
    e) $\frac{10}{100}$ **f)** $\frac{11}{100}$ **g)** $\frac{12}{100}$

2. a) Answers may vary.   **b)** $0.07

3. PST will vary. GST:
    a) $0.14   **b)** $0.21   **c)** $0.28   **d)** $0.35

4.

Number of pens	Cost of pens	PST	GST
1	$1.00	will vary	$0.07
2	$2.00		$0.14
3	$3.00		$0.21
4	$4.00		$0.28
5	$5.00		$0.35

Working with Mathematics, page 149

1. Answers may vary. To raise funds for all government-run organizations. The tax rates depend on governments' financial budgets.

2. PST will vary. GST:
    a) $0.35   **b)** $0.84   **c)** $3.15   **d)** $2.80   **e)** $1.68   **f)** $3.50

3. Estimate may vary. Emma's estimates: $5.75, $13.80, $51.75, $46.00, $27.60, $57.50. The calculated costs: $5.70, $13.68, $51.30, $45.59, $27.36, $56.99. Emma's estimates are close to the calculated costs.

4. a) Answers may vary. In 1997, British Columbia and Manitoba—their PST was 7%.
    b) 35¢, 84¢, $3.15, $2.80, $1.68, $3.50

5. PST and total cost will vary. GST:
    a) $2.69   **b)** $0.31   **c)** $14.69   **d)** $35.00   **e)** $1.08   **f)** $3.21

6. a) i) $13.97   **ii)** $14.09
    b) Answers may vary. Calculate the tip before adding the sales tax—you do not tip on sales tax.

7. PST and total cost will vary. GST:
    a) $9.45   **b)** $0.61   **c)** $2.22   **d)** $0.97

8. Answers will vary.

9. a) Answers may vary.
    b) British Columbia, Manitoba, or Saskatchewan

Linking Ideas: Mathematics and the Consumer
Estimating Sales Tax, page 151

1. Estimates may vary. PST will vary. GST:
    a) About $2.10   **b)** About $1.30
    c) About 70¢   **d)** About $10.50

2. , 3. Answers will vary.

3.4 Working with Percent
Developing the Ideas, page 152

Group 1

1. 665   **2.** Estimates may vary.

3. a) 36.2%   **b)** 63.8%

Group 2

1. 484   **2.** Estimates may vary.

3. a) 26.0%   **b)** 74.0%

Group 3

1. a) 1149   **b)** 367   **c)** 782

2. Estimates may vary.

3. a) 31.9%   **b)** 68.1%

Working with Mathematics, page 154

1. a) $6.00   **b)** $4.00

4. Estimation strategies may vary.
   a) 15%   **b)** 25%   **c)** 65%   **d)** 40%   **e)** 65%
   f) 25%   **g)** 65%   **h)** 10%   **i)** 40%   **j)** 75%

5. Estimates may vary.
   a) 16 km   **b)** About $275
   c) About 140 kg   **d)** About 130 h
   e) About $220   **f)** About $250
   g) About 580 g   **h)** About 10 h

6. 13 g   **7.** 31

8. He obtained the same number (45) of correct answers in both the tests.

9. a) About 3054 km   **b)** Answers may vary

10. a) $19.55   **b)** $18.45

11. a) $3.70   **b)** $1.11

12. 400

13. a) 4 cm by 3 cm
   b) 75% horizontal and 75% vertical
   c) Answers may vary.

14. $5.60   **15.** 3 247 920   **16.** 495 000 000

17. a) $15 372.50   **b)** $28 620.00

18. Estimates may vary.
   a) Africa: 20%; Antarctica: 10%; Asia: 20%; Europe: 4%; North and Central America: 15%; Oceania: 6%; South America: 12%; former Soviet Union: 15%
   b) Africa: 12%; Antarctica: 0%; Asia: 60%; Europe: 10%; North and Central America: 7%; Oceania: 0.5%; South America: 5%; former Soviet Union: 5%

19. 109.5 m by 49.2 m

20. Answers will vary depending on the sales tax rate.

21. 20 kg   **22.** 59

23. The area of the new rectangle will be less than the area of the original rectangle.

24. a) 33 L   **b)** 3.64 L

25. a) For a GST rate of 7%: 18.49 ✕ 1.07 =
   b) For a GST rate of 7%, you would key in the final cost followed by this key stroke sequence: ÷ 1.07 =
   c) $74.99

Quest: What Does 2% Mean in 2% Milk?, page 157

About 2% of the 2% milk is fat. About 0.2% of the skim milk is fat.

3.5 Probability Experiments
Working with Mathematics, page 161

1. No

2. a) Not necessarily
   b) Answers may vary.
     i) Point down will be more likely than it was in the experiment.
     ii) Point down will be less likely than it was in the experiment.

3. Explanations may vary. Parts b and d are true.

4. a) 0.16; 16%   **b)** 0.74; 74%   **c)** 0.63; 63%
   d) 0.37; 37%   **e)** 0.85; 85%   **f)** 0.6; 60%

   g) 0.36; 36%   **h)** 0.61; 61%   **i)** 0.77; 77%
   j) 0.57; 57%   **k)** 0.61; 61%   **l)** 0.92; 92%

5. a) The outcomes are Win, Lose, and Tie. They are equally likely because the sectors are equal.
   b) The outcomes are blue, green, and striped. They are not equally likely because there is a different number of each colour of marble.
   c) The outcomes are toffee, mint, chocolate, and licorice. They are equally likely because there is the same number of each type of candy.
   d) The outcomes are 30% discount, 20% discount, and 10% discount. They are not equally likely because different numbers of each type of coupon were distributed.

6. a) 2, 3, 4, 5, 6, 7, 8, 9, 10, J, Q, K, A
   b) All equally likely
   c) , **d)** , **e)** Answers may vary.
   f) The probability should be $\frac{1}{13}$, or about 8%.

7. a) 1, 2, 3, 4, 5, 6   **b)** All equally likely
   c) , **d)** Answers may vary.

8. $\frac{1}{6}$, or about 17%

9. a) Answers may vary. Landing on its side is most likely. Landing top up is least likely.
   b) , **c)** Answers may vary.

10. a) One head and one tail is more likely than two heads or two tails.
   b) , **c)** Answers may vary.
   d) Probabilities are: one head and one tail, $\frac{1}{2}$, or 50%; two heads, $\frac{1}{4}$, or 25%; two tails, $\frac{1}{4}$, or 25%

11. , **12.** Answers may vary.

3.6 Making Predictions
Working with Mathematics, page 165

1. Answers may vary.

2. Explanations may vary. Part b is true.

3. a) 25%   **b)** No

4. a) 20 **b)** 23 **c)** 19 **d)** 3 **e)** 11 **f)** 5 **g)** 5 **h)** 33 **i)** 3

5. a) The probability of each outcome is $\frac{1}{3}$, or $33\frac{1}{3}$%.
   b) Blue: $\frac{1}{3}$, or $33\frac{1}{3}$%; green: $\frac{4}{9}$, or 44%; striped: $\frac{2}{9}$, or 22%
   c) The probability of each outcome is $\frac{1}{4}$, or 25%.
   d) 30% coupon: $\frac{12}{87}$, or about 14%; 20% coupon: $\frac{25}{87}$, or about 29%; 10% coupon: $\frac{50}{87}$, or about 57%

6. a) $\frac{1}{6}$, or about 17%   **b)** $\frac{1}{2}$, or 50%
   c) $\frac{1}{2}$, or 50%   **d)** $\frac{1}{3}$, or about 33%
   e) $\frac{1}{52}$, or about 2%   **f)** $\frac{1}{2}$, or 50%
   g) $\frac{1}{4}$, or 25%   **h)** $\frac{3}{13}$, or about 23%
   i) $\frac{5}{13}$, or about 38%   **j)** $\frac{1}{26}$, or about 4%
   k) $\frac{5}{13}$, or about 38%

7. , **8.** Answers may vary.

9. a) 10   **b)** 30   **c)** 30   **d)** 20

10. e) 1   **f)** 25   **g)** 13   **h)** 12   **i)** 19   **j)** 2   **k)** 19
   We use the word "about" because many of the answers are rounded to the nearest whole number.

11. a) 10   **b)** 30   **c)** 20

12. Answers may vary.

13. Answers may vary.
   a) 250   **b)** 250   **c)** 500

14. Part b is true.   **15.** 20

16. Answers may vary.

17. Answers may vary.
   a) Assume a Canadian population of 30 000 000; 3000 people
   b) Assume a world population of 6 billion; 600 000 people

18. Answers may vary.

Quest: Sharing a Birthday, page 167

Answers may vary.

3.7 Independent Events

Developing the Ideas, page 168

1. $\frac{1}{4}$, or 25%   **2.** $\frac{1}{2}$, or 50%   **3.** $\frac{3}{4}$, or 75%

4. Answers may vary. It helps you check that you have included all the possible outcomes.

Working with Mathematics, page 170

1. Examples may vary.
   a) When the outcome of one experiment does not affect the outcome of another experiment, the outcomes are called "independent events."
   b) Outcomes are equally likely if they have the same probability of occurring.
   c) The probability of an event is the likelihood of the event occurring when an experiment is repeated many times.

2. a) Answers may vary. A game is fair when each player has an equal chance of winning.
   b) Answers may vary. It is a fair game.
   c) Answers may vary.

3. a) Yes; HH, TT, HT, TH
   b) Yes, in both cases the outcome of one toss does not affect the other.

4. a) No. In the first experiment, you may draw the same card twice. This is not possible in the second experiment.
   b) The first experiment involves independent events since the outcome of one draw does not affect the other. The second experiment does not involve independent events since the card that is picked cannot be picked again.

5. a) 10%   **b)** 20%   **c)** About 67%   **d)** 30%
   e) 25%   **f)** 80%   **g)** 0%   **h)** 100%
   i) About 17%   **j)** About 22%   **k)** About 2%   **l)** About 8%

6. a) i) H on both coins, T on both coins, H on the nickel and T on the dime, T on the nickel and H on the dime
     ii) Yes
   b) i) H1, H2, H3, H4, H5, H6, T1, T2, T3, T4, T5, T6
     ii) Yes
   c) i) H1, H2, H3, H4, T1, T2, T3, T4
     ii) Yes
   d) i) HA, HB, HC, HD, HE, TA, TB, TC, TD, TE
     ii) Yes

7. a) Yes, the number that shows up on the die does not affect the coin toss.
   b) i) $\frac{1}{12}$, or about 8%   **ii)** $\frac{1}{4}$, or 25%   **iii)** $\frac{1}{6}$, or about 17%

8. a) Yes, the outcome of the roll of one die does not affect the outcome of the other.

b)

	Die A					
	1	**2**	**3**	**4**	**5**	**6**
Die B **1**	1, 1	1, 2	1, 3	1, 4	1, 5	1, 6
2	2, 1	2, 2	2, 3	2, 4	2, 5	2, 6
3	3, 1	3, 2	3, 3	3, 4	3, 5	3, 6
4	4, 1	4, 2	4, 3	4, 4	4, 5	4, 6
5	5, 1	5, 2	5, 3	5, 4	5, 5	5, 6
6	6, 1	6, 2	6, 3	6, 4	6, 5	6, 6

   c) $\frac{1}{36}$, or about 3%   **d)** $\frac{1}{6}$, or about 17%   **e)** $\frac{1}{4}$, or 25%

9. a)

Sum when 2 dice are rolled

	Die A					
	1	**2**	**3**	**4**	**5**	**6**
Die B **1**	2	3	4	5	6	7
2	3	4	5	6	7	8
3	4	5	6	7	8	9
4	5	6	7	8	9	10
5	6	7	8	9	10	11
6	7	8	9	10	11	12

   b) i) $\frac{1}{6}$, or about 17%   **ii)** $\frac{1}{12}$, or about 8%
   iii) $\frac{1}{9}$, or about 11%   **iv)** $\frac{1}{36}$, or about 3%
   v) $\frac{1}{36}$, or about 3%   **vi)** 0%
   c) $\frac{7}{12}$, or about 58%

10. a)

	Pie		
Sandwich	**Apple**	**Cherry**	**Blueberry**
Cheese	cheese and apple	cheese and cherry	cheese and blueberry
Tuna	tuna and apple	tuna and cherry	tuna and blueberry
Chicken	chicken and apple	chicken and cherry	chicken and blueberry
Peanut butter	peanut butter and apple	peanut butter and cherry	peanut butter and blueberry

   b) Yes, since equal numbers of each sandwich and equal numbers of each pie are available.
   c) i) $\frac{1}{4}$, or 25%   **ii)** $\frac{1}{2}$, or 50%
   iii) $\frac{1}{3}$, or about 33%   **iv)** $\frac{1}{12}$, or about 8%
   v) $\frac{3}{4}$, or about 75%
   d) Once 1 person has chosen, there are no longer equal numbers of the items. This means the outcomes in the table are no longer equally likely.
   e) No, most people would choose the type of sandwich and pie they like best.

11. a) i) $\frac{1}{3}$ **ii)** $\frac{1}{3}$ **iii)** $\frac{1}{9}$
   b) i) $\frac{2}{3}$ **ii)** $\frac{2}{3}$ **iii)** $\frac{4}{9}$
   c) i) $\frac{1}{3}$ **ii)** $\frac{2}{3}$ **iii)** $\frac{2}{9}$

12. a) $\frac{1}{9}$; they are equal. **b)** $\frac{4}{9}$; they are equal.

c) $\frac{2}{9}$; they are equal.

d) The probability of two independent events appears to be equal to the product of the probability of each event.

13. a) Yes, since the result of spinning one pointer does not affect the result of spinning the next pointer.

b)

		Spinner A		
		●	▲	■
Spinner B	1	1, ●	1, ▲	1, ■
	2	2, ●	2, ▲	2, ■
	3	3, ●	3, ▲	3, ■
	4	4, ●	4, ▲	4, ■

The outcomes in the table are all equally likely.

c) i) $\frac{1}{12}$, or about 8% **ii)** $\frac{1}{6}$, or about 17%

iii) $\frac{1}{3}$, or about 33% **iv)** $\frac{1}{3}$, or about 33%

14. a) i) $\frac{1}{3}$ **ii)** $\frac{1}{4}$ **iii)** $\frac{1}{12}$

b) i) $\frac{2}{3}$ **ii)** $\frac{3}{4}$ **iii)** $\frac{1}{2}$

c) i) $\frac{1}{2}$ **ii)** $\frac{1}{3}$ **iii)** $\frac{1}{6}$

d) Yes, in each case the product of the probabilities in parts i and ii is equal to the probability in part iii.

15.

	B	R	G	Y	P
B	B, B	B, R	B, G	B, Y	B, P
R	R, B	R, R	R, G	R, Y	R, P
G	G, B	G, R	G, G	G, Y	G, P
Y	Y, B	Y, R	Y, G	Y, Y	Y, P
P	P, B	P, R	P, G	P, Y	P, P

a) $\frac{1}{25}$, or 4% **b)** $\frac{1}{25}$, or 4% **c)** $\frac{2}{25}$, or 8%

d) $\frac{16}{25}$, or 64% **e)** $\frac{9}{25}$, or 36%

16. a) On each draw, there are 13 outcomes. So, there are $13 \times 13 = 169$ possible outcomes when 2 cards are drawn.

b) i) $\frac{1}{169}$, or about 0.6% **ii)** $\frac{144}{169}$, or about 85%

iii) $\frac{25}{169}$, or about 15%

17. a) You can make 2 columns and 2 rows for Wonder Woman.

		Box A			
		Batman	Superman	Wonder Woman	Wonder Woman
Box B	**Batman**	B, B	B, S	B, W	B, W
	Superman	S, B	S, S	S, W	S, W
	Wonder Woman	W, B	W, S	W, W	W, W
	Wonder Woman	W, B	W, S	W, W	W, W

b) i) $\frac{1}{4}$, or 25% **ii)** $\frac{1}{16}$, or 6.25%

iii) $\frac{1}{4}$, or 25% **iv)** $\frac{3}{4}$, or 75%

c) Yes, each time a figurine is chosen, there is one less figurine

of that type available. But, because of the large number of boxes manufactured, this would not make much of a difference when one calculates the probability.

3.8 Monte Carlo Methods
Working with Mathematics, page 175

1. Spin the arrow 10 times. Count how many times it lands on "correct." Record the number of times if it is 3 or more. Repeat the experiment many times. Divide the number of times that there were 3 or more by the number of experiments.

2. Answers may vary.
a) The representation of one situation through the use of another situation
b) The simulation is easier.
c) Because the simulation imitates the problem

3. a) A coin
b) A coin and a die, or a spinner divided into 12 equal parts
c) A spinner divided into 4 equal parts
d) A coin

4. Answers may vary.
a) Toss 4 coins many times, and record if exactly 3H show.
b) Toss 8 coins many times, and record if 5 or more H show.

5. Answers may vary. Toss 8 coins many times. Record if exactly 5H show. Divide the number of times exactly 5H showed by the number of times the 8 coins were tossed.

6. Answers may vary. Make a spinner with 3 equal sectors. Label one sector "correct." Spin the arrow 10 times. Record if it lands on "correct" 7 or more times. Repeat the experiment many times. Divide the number of recordings of 7 or more by the number of experiments.

7. Make a spinner with 6 equal sectors. Label one sector "defective." Spin the arrow 7 times. Record if it lands on "defective" 2 or more times. Repeat the experiment many times. Divide the number of recordings of 2 or more by the number of experiments.

8. Toss 5 coins many times. Record if 3H or more show. Divide the number of times 3H or more showed by the number of times the 5 coins were tossed.

9. Divide a spinner into regions whose areas are in the ratio 25 : 10 : 25. That is, the sector angles are 150°(green), 60°(yellow), and 150°(red). Spin the arrow 5 times. Record if it lands on green 3 or more times. Repeat the experiment many times. Divide the number of recordings of 3 or more by the number of experiments.

10. Approximately 0.5256

Review, page 176

1. a) 64% **b)** 53% **c)** 17% **d)** 72%
e) 22% **f)** 6% **g)** 93% **h)** 34%

2. a) 40% **b)** 85% **c)** 68% **d)** 10%
e) 64% **f)** 77% **g)** 75% **h)** 75%
i) 83.3% **j)** 53.3% **k)** 73.8% **l)** 72.5%

3. a) 0.24 **b)** 0.726 **c)** 0.28 **d)** 0.18
e) 0.057 **f)** 0.843 **g)** 0.681 **h)** 0.004

4. a) 56% **b)** 37% **c)** 47% **d)** 82.7%
e) 47.1% **f)** 5.7% **g)** 26.5% **h)** 0.1%

5. Estimates may vary.
a) 9% **b)** 62% **c)** 28%

6. a) PST: $4.27; GST: $2.99; total cost: $49.95

b) PST: $100.37; GST: $87.82; total cost: $1442.78

c) Harmonized tax: $20.25; total cost: $155.24

d) GST: $1.18; cost with GST: $18.07; PST: $1.36; total cost: $19.43

e) No PST; GST: $2.56; total cost: $39.15

7. a) i) $19.47 **ii)** $19.72

b) Answers may vary. Calculate the tip on the total before sales tax is added.

8. a) $38.46 **b)** PST: $2.69; GST: $2.69; total cost: $43.84

c) Yes

9. a) $22.93 **b)** $381.35 **c)** $11.12 **d)** $65.74

10. Estimates may vary.

a) 10% **b)** 75% **c)** 35% **d)** 15%

11. a) About 72% **b)** About 28%

12. 324 **13.** About 53 882

14. a) 1, 2, 3, 4, 5, and 6; yes, the probability of each outcome is $\frac{1}{6}$, or about 17%.

b) Yes, No, Probably Yes, Probably No; yes, the probability of each outcome is $\frac{1}{4}$, or 25%.

c) The outcomes are not equally likely — the probabilities are given.
Martha: $\frac{2}{10}$, $\frac{1}{5}$, or 20%; Bryan: $\frac{1}{10}$, or 10%; Connor: $\frac{3}{10}$, or 30%; Edna: $\frac{4}{10}$, $\frac{2}{5}$, or 40%

15. a) $\frac{1}{2}$, or 50% **b)** $\frac{1}{26}$, or about 4% **c)** $\frac{1}{13}$, or about 8%

d) $\frac{3}{13}$, or about 23% **e)** $\frac{2}{13}$, or about 15%

16. a) Yes, since the outcomes of the coin toss does not affect the outcome of the die roll, and vice versa.

b) Yes **c)** $\frac{1}{12}$, or about 8% **d)** $\frac{1}{4}$, or 25%

e) , **f)** Answers may vary.

17. Answers may vary.

Cumulative Review, page 180

1. a) 0.0093 **b)** 0.093 **c)** 0.93

d) 9.3 **e)** 93 **f)** 930

Each product is 10 times as great as the preceding product.

2. a) 2 790 000 **b)** 279 000 **c)** 27 900

d) 2790 **e)** 279 **f)** 27.9

Each quotient is one-tenth as great as the preceding quotient.

3. a) 34 cm **b)** 8.6 m **c)** 1350 cm

d) 1.122 km **e)** 2700 m **f)** 566 mm

5. AB = LK, BC = KJ, CD = JM, DA = ML, ∠A = ∠L, ∠B = ∠K, ∠C = ∠J, ∠D = ∠M

6. Answers may vary.

a) $\frac{1}{3}$ or $\frac{2}{6}$ or $\frac{4}{12}$ **b)** $\frac{2}{3}$ or $\frac{4}{6}$

c) $\frac{6}{8}$ or $\frac{3}{4}$ **d)** $\frac{6}{10}$ or $\frac{3}{5}$

7. a) $\frac{8}{12}$ **b)** $\frac{10}{12}$ **c)** $\frac{9}{12}$ **d)** $\frac{18}{12}$ **e)** $\frac{9}{12}$

8. a) Two and seventy-four hundredths, $(2 \times 1) + \left(7 \times \frac{1}{10}\right) + \left(4 \times \frac{1}{100}\right)$; one hundred fifty-six and five tenths, $(1 \times 100) + (5 \times 10) + (6 \times 1) + \left(5 \times \frac{1}{10}\right)$

b) Five and seven tenths, $(5 \times 1) + \left(7 \times \frac{1}{10}\right)$; one and six tenths, $(1 \times 1) + \left(6 \times \frac{1}{10}\right)$

c) Eleven thousand two hundred seventy-seven, $(1 \times 10\ 000) + (1 \times 1000) + (2 \times 100) + (7 \times 10) + (7 \times 1)$

d) One billion five hundred million, $(1 \times 10^9) + (5 \times 10^8)$

9. a) $\frac{1}{2} > \frac{1}{3}$ **b)** $\frac{5}{7} < \frac{5}{6}$ **c)** $\frac{3}{5} < \frac{2}{3}$

d) $\frac{3}{8} < \frac{2}{5}$ **e)** $0.75 < \frac{7}{9}$ **f)** $\frac{5}{4} = 1.25$

g) $\frac{4}{7} < 0.6$ **h)** $1.2 > 0.8$ **i)** $1.4 > 1.37$

10. a) $\frac{2}{3}$ **b)** $\frac{1}{2}$ **c)** $\frac{11}{10}$, or $1\frac{1}{10}$

d) $\frac{7}{12}$ **e)** $\frac{7}{10}$ **f)** $\frac{9}{8}$, or $1\frac{1}{8}$

11. a) $\frac{19}{20}$ **b)** $\frac{11}{20}$ **c)** $\frac{1}{20}$

12. a) $\frac{1}{12}$ **b)** $\frac{5}{12}$ **c)** $\frac{7}{6}$, or $1\frac{1}{6}$

d) $\frac{1}{8}$ **e)** $\frac{1}{10}$ **f)** $1\frac{1}{6}$

13. a) 7.74 **b)** 17.25 **c)** 18.24 **d)** 2.305

14. a) 106 cm **b)** 742 cm, or 7.42 m

15. a) 3 **b)** 5 **c)** 3.1 **d)** 0.7

16. a) 36.74 **b)** 8.4

17. a) 83%; 0.83 **b)** 7%; 0.07 **c)** 16%; 0.16 **d)** 24%; 0.24

e) 40%; 0.4 **f)** 60%, 0.6 **b)** 50%, 0.5 **h)** 100%, 1

18. PST and total cost will vary. GST:

a) $2.45 **b)** $4.20 **c)** $12.25

d) $3.01 **e)** $1.40 **f)** $2.03

19. a) $29.71 **b)** $50.96 **c)** $148.74

d) $34.39 **e)** $15.96 **f)** $23.19

20. Daily use — toilet: 140 L; showers and baths: 122.5 L; laundry and dishes: 70 L; drinking and cooking: 17.5 L
Yearly use — toilet: 51 100 L; showers and baths: 44 712.5 L; laundry and dishes: 25 550 L; drinking and cooking: 6387.5 L

21. a) $\frac{1}{6}$, or about 17% **b)** $\frac{1}{2}$, or 50%

c) You would expect to roll five 5s and fifteen odd numbers.

d) , **e)** , **f)** Answers may vary.

22. a) Yes, because the outcome of the coin toss does not affect the outcome of the spin, and vice versa.

b)

		Spinner			
		Blue	Yellow	Purple	Green
Coin	Heads	H, B	H, Y	H, P	H, G
	Tails	T, B	T, Y	T, P	T, G

i) $\frac{1}{8}$, or 12.5% **ii)** $\frac{1}{4}$, or 25% **iii)** $\frac{1}{4}$, or 25%

iv) $\frac{3}{4}$, or 75% **v)** $\frac{3}{8}$, or 37.5%

CHAPTER 4 DATA MANAGEMENT

Start With What You Know, page 184

1. a) About 20 000 elephants

b)

Region	Number of elephants
West Africa	20 000
Southern Africa	200 000
East Africa	120 000
Central Africa	280 000

c) West Africa has the fewest elephants and Central Africa has the most elephants.

d) There were about 620 000 elephants in Africa in 1989.

2. a) The mass of ivory in tonnes exported by six African countries in 1986

b) Burundi; about 90 t
c) Zambia; about 10 t
d) About 70 t; no, Sudan exported about 78 t.

3. a) The total mass of ivory in tonnes exported every two years from 1981 to 1989
b) There was an increase from 1981 to 1983, and then a decrease to 1989.

4.1 Interpreting and Constructing Graphs
Developing the Ideas, page 186

1. a) The bar on the left of each pair
b) The bar on the right of each pair

2. a) Central Africa   b) About 280 000

3. West Africa

4. About 1 200 000 elephants; about 600 000

5. a) East Africa   b) About 300 000

6. West Africa

7. How much TV the average Canadian watches in one week, in various age groups

8. a) 25 years and over   b) About 30 h

9. a) 12 – 17 years   b) About 19 h
c) Answers may vary. These are adolescents who have homework to do, and enjoy various sporting activities and/or video games.

10. a) About 20 h   b) Yes, explanations may vary.

11. a) The number of passenger cars produced in Canada every 10 years from 1960 to 1990
b) The number of commercial vehicles produced in Canada every 10 years from 1960 to 1990

12. About 325 000; about 825 000

13. About 60 000; about 800 000

14. Descriptions may vary. For passenger cars, there was an increase between 1960 and 1970, then a gradual decrease to 1990. For commercial vehicles, there was a steady increase in the same period.

15. Estimates may vary. 850 000; 1 300 000

Working with Mathematics, page 189

1. Answers may vary.
a) They both have bars to represent data.
b) For each item along the horizontal axis, the bar graph has one bar and the double-bar graph has two bars.

2. Answers may vary. A double broken-line graph comprises two broken-line graphs. Examples may vary; the numbers of boys and girls in a class each year for a period of several years.

3. a) They both have bars to represent data.
b) Each bar on the bar graph represents a category of data. Each bar on the histogram represents a range of values.

4. Answers and reasons may vary.
a) A bar graph
b) A double-bar graph or double broken-line graph
c) A bar graph
d) A double-bar graph or double broken-line graph

5. a) Both approximately 700 000
b) i) About 1960   ii) 10 years later
c) About 700 000
d) British Columbia; reasons may vary

6. a) 1982 and 1994   b) Engineer   c) Saleswoman

d) i) $23 000   ii) $5000

7. Answers may vary.

8. a) A bar graph; reasons may vary.
b) 20 to 44 years   c) 15 to 19 years   d) About 3 400 000
e) Answers may vary. Many people have seen the error of their ways and for health reasons have given up smoking.
f) Answers may vary. Many chronic smokers die before the age of 65 from heart disease or lung cancer.
g) About 5 500 000
h) Answers may vary. They may think they are invincible and will not suffer bad effects.

9. a) 73 000, 27 000, 73 000, 22 000
b) The blue whale and the humpback whale

10. a) 19 100 000   c) At school
d) Answers may vary; for example, on vacation

11. b) Newfoundland   c) Nova Scotia

12. Graphs may vary.

13. a), b)

Position	Frequency
Pitcher	
Catcher	
Outfield	⫫⫫ ⫫⫫ ⫫⫫ ⏐
First base	⫫⫫ ⏐
Second base	⫫⫫ ⏐⏐
Third base	⫫⫫
Shortstop	⏐

d) Reasons may vary.

14. a) i) 76%   ii) 74%   iii) Answers may vary.
b) Answers may vary. Other relatives, such as children or parents, or hired help

15. b) About 1959, 1974, 1987
c) About 1998   d) About 34 years
e) i) About 15 years   ii) About 13 years
f) About 2009, assuming the population continues to increase at the same rate

Linking Ideas: Mathematics and Technology
Drawing Circle Graphs, page 192

1. 9351   2. 2630   3. 0.281   4. 473   5. 95   6. 412

7. The formula subtracts doubles, triples, and home runs from hits, which leaves singles.

8. Answers may vary.

4.2 Circle Graphs
Developing the Ideas, page 194

Answers may vary.

1. a) 50%   b) $\frac{1}{2}$ c) 5 m^3

2. a) 6%   b) $\frac{6}{100}$ c) 1.2 m^3

3. a) 13 m^3 b) 1 m^3 c) 10 m^3

4. It depends on whether the garbage dumps contain household garbage and/or industrial or commercial garbage.

Working with Mathematics, page 197

1. Explanations may vary.
a) Yes   b) Yes

2. a) Reasons may vary.   i) and iv) because the percents total 100%

b) Answers may vary. **ii)** and **iii)** could be bar graphs

3. a) 50%   **b)** 75%   **c)** 40%   **d)** 70%
e) 15%   **f)** $66\frac{2}{3}$%   **g)** About 11%   **h)** $83\frac{1}{3}$%

4. a) $\frac{1}{4}$ **b)** $\frac{1}{2}$ **c)** $\frac{1}{5}$ **d)** $\frac{1}{20}$
e) $\frac{3}{20}$ **f)** $\frac{7}{100}$ **g)** $\frac{1}{3}$ **h)** $\frac{1}{100}$

5. Estimates may vary. The calculated answers are as follows:
a) 30   **b)** $480   **c)** 1440 kg
d) 18 750   **e)** $1000   **f)** 250 L

6. Estimates may vary. The calculated answers are as follows:
a) $8100   **b)** $4180   **c)** 2000 t
d) 19 200 kg   **e)** 216 L   **f)** 84 000

8. a) The land area of each continent as a sector of a circle
b) About 20%   **c)** $\frac{1}{5}$ **d)** About $\frac{1}{4}$
e) About $\frac{1}{6}$ **f)** About $\frac{2}{5}$ **g)** 1

9. a) Huron   **b)** Superior
c) Superior, Huron, Michigan, Erie, Ontario
d) Answers may vary.

10. a) The number of students in Megan's class with each eye colour, as a sector of a circle
b) i) 12   **ii)** 6   **iii)** 3   **iv)** 3

11. Estimates may vary.
a) About 928 000 000   **b)** About 450 000 000
c) About 390 000 000   **d)** About 340 000 000
e) About 3 125 000 000

12. a) Other, clothing, entertainment, savings, transportation, food, rent
b) About 30%   **c)** Food
d) Answers may vary. Transportation and entertainment
e) About $\frac{55}{100}$ **f)** About $22 000

13. a) Each source of a province's electricity as a sector of a circle
b) Answers may vary.
i) They both use coal and water.
ii) The main source for New Brunswick is oil. The main source for Alberta is coal.
c) Coal
d) Nuclear and oil
e) Answers may vary. In Alberta, it could be oil and/or nuclear. In New Brunswick, it could be natural gas.

14. a) How African elephants were distributed throughout the African continent in 1981 and in 1989
b) About 35%; about 20%
c) Answers may vary. The elephants were killed for their tusks.
d) About 35%; about 45%; the percent increased, explanations may vary
e) We cannot tell, unless we know the numbers in the African continent for those years.
f) The approximate number of elephants in each region

15. a) About 36 000 m^3
b) Answers may vary. The mass of the newspaper will be less than 18% of the total mass because paper has a mass that is less than metal or glass of the same volume.

Quest: Can You Construct a Circle Graph from a Bale of Garbage?, page 200

Graphs may vary in size.

4.3 Median

Developing the Ideas, page 202

1. Seating capacity is how many spectators the stadium can accommodate.

2. a) Commonwealth Stadium   **b)** 60 081

3. Answers may vary. A seating capacity that represents all the capacities listed

4. Answers may vary. No, because it is the largest

5. Answers may vary. No, because it is the smallest

6. Answers may vary.

Working with Mathematics, page 204

1. Answers may vary. The middle value when the numbers are arranged in order.

2. Answers may vary.

3. Answers may vary. Arrange the data in order from smallest to largest.
a) The smallest number is the first number.
b) The largest number is the last number.
c) The median is the middle number, unless there is an even number of numbers, in which case the median is the mean of the two middle numbers.

4. a) 9   **b)** 10   **c)** 24   **d)** 56

5. a) 140   **b)** 104.5   **c)** 37   **d)** 40   **e)** 32.4   **f)** 1095

6. a) 28 kg, 54 kg   **b)** 37 kg

7. a) Answers may vary; any set containing 2 numbers less than 12, 2 numbers greater than 12, and the number 12.
b) Answers may vary; any set of numbers in which the 4th and 5th numbers have a sum of 40 when the numbers are arranged in order from least to greatest.
c) The median will increase by 2.

8. Answers may vary.   **9.** 50 715

10. Answers may vary.   **11.** Answers may vary.

12. 23.5   **13.** Answers may vary.

14. a) 92 years, 31 years   **b)** 65.5 years   **c)** 56 years

15. a) 4.75 kg   **b)** About 718 700

16. a) The 13th number   **b)** The 18th number; the 27th number
c) Answers may vary. Add 1 to the number of numbers, and divide by 2, to get the position of the median.
d) Answers may vary. Divide the number of numbers by 2. The result is the position of the first number to be considered. Add the number in this position to the next number, then divide by 2.

Mathematics File: Stem-and-Leaf Diagram, page 206

1. Pauline Johnson

2. a) 104 years   **b)** Victoria Callihoo

3. a) The mean of the 16th and 17th ages
b) Leaf with stem 8
c) 1, 1, 1, 2, 2, 4, 4, 7, 8, 8, 9; 82 years
d) No

4. a) The pioneer women had a greater median life span than women today.
b) Answers may vary. The median life span today is greater than it was a century ago.
c) Yes, explanations may vary.

5.

Stem	Leaf
5	2
6	
7	9 3 4 9
8	8 2 2 8 1 1
9	1 1 5 5
10	4

a) 104 years and 52 years   **b)** 82 years

6. The median is 63.5 years.

7.

Stem	Leaf
29	7
17	7
16	8 6 1
14	6 1 0
13	6 4 1
12	6 5
11	2
10	9 0
9	8 6 5 4 1 0
8	6 5 3

Linking Ideas: Mathematics and Technology
Exploring Mode, page 208

1. 25   **2.** 20   **3.** Answers may vary.

4. Answers may vary. The mode(s) and median for each other occupation are listed here. Bus driver: modes are 20 and 30, median is 21; primary school teacher: modes are 15, 65, and 75, median is 56; electrical engineer: mode is 30, median is 22; auto mechanic: modes are 15 and 25, median is 20; secretary: mode is 30, median is 20.

4.4 Mean
Working with Mathematics, page 211

1. Answers may vary.
  a) The sum of the hand spans is the same length as the four adjacent spans.
  b) Because we wanted one-fourth of it
  c) Dividing by 4 gives us four equal portions and so does folding the string in half twice.

2. Answers may vary. Only if the quantities whose mean is required are measurable, and the method is practical.

3. 1.3 kg

4. a) 27 mm   **b)** 4.65 mm   **c)** 26.5 mm

5. a) Mean: 6; median: 6; modes: 5 and 7
  b) Mean: 70; median: 70; modes: 60 and 80
  c) Mean: 56; median: 68; no mode
  d) Mean: 45; median: 48.6; no mode
  e) Mean: 172.29; median: 186; no mode
  f) Mean: 48.4; median: 53.45; no mode

6. a) Reasons may vary. Weather and traffic conditions will affect the time the trip takes.
  b) Mean: 20.75 min; median: 18 min; mode: 14 min
  c) Answers may vary; the mode or the median.

7. a) Mean: 49.325 kg; median: 3 kg; mode: 0.1 kg

b) Answers may vary. There is no one typical package size.

8. Answers may vary. Mean: any 7 numbers with a sum of 700; median: a set of 3 numbers less than or equal to 100, 3 numbers greater than or equal to 100, and the number 100; mode: any 7 numbers, as long as 100 occurs more often than the other numbers.

9. , 10. , 11. , 12. Answers may vary.

13. Answers may vary.
  a) Median   **b)** Median   **c)** Mean

14. a) The mean: $51 200   **b)** The mode: $18 000

15. a) ii) $(400 \times 15 + 390 \times 3 + 380 \times 2) \div 20 = 396.5$
  b) Yes

16. The number of pairs sold at each price

17. Answers may vary.
  a) Any 5 numbers with a sum of 100
  b) A set of 5 numbers with a sum of 50, that contains 2 numbers less than or equal to 12, 2 numbers greater than or equal to 12, and the number 12
  c) A set of 6 numbers with a sum of 60, in which the 3rd and 4th numbers when arranged from least to greatest have a sum of 24.
  d) A set of 5 numbers with a sum of 150, in which 25 occurs more often than any other number.

18. a) 1412 pages   **b)** 706 pages   **c)** About 235 pages

19. About 32 tins

20. a) Mean   **b)** $4278.50

21. Mean   **22.** About 11 kg

23. a) How much energy is burned in an hour for each of four activities
  b) 1400 kJ   **c)** 1400 kJ
  d) Divide each energy by 4 and add the results.

24. 1280 kJ

25. a) i) 5.5   **ii)** 5.5
  b) i) 50.5   **ii)** 50.5
  c) Yes, explanations may vary
  d) i) The mean increases by 7.   **ii)** The mean doubles.

4.5 Measures of Data Distribution
Working with Mathematics, page 217

1. a) The extremes are the least and greatest numbers in a set of data.
  b) The range is the difference between the greatest and least numbers in a set of data.
  c) The number at the one-quarter point when a set of data is arranged from least to greatest
  d) The number at the three-quarters point when a set of data is arranged from least to greatest

2. The range would not change. Each of the extremes would increase by 3.

3. Most of the data are very similar. There are only a few exceptional points that lie outside the cluster.

4. a) 11   **b)** 42   **c)** 33

5. a) Extremes: 2 and 30; range: 28   **b)** 25
  c) 11   **d)** 7   **e)** 25

6. a) Extremes: 21 and 55; range: 34   **b)** There is no mode.
  c) 35   **d)** 26   **e)** 47.5

7. i) a) Extremes: 9 and 46; range: 37   **b)** There is no mode.

c) Median: 28; lower quartile: 13.5; upper quartile: 39.5

ii) a) Extremes: 63 and 89; range: 26   b) There is no mode.
c) Median: 75; lower quartile: 67; upper quartile: 88

iii) a) Extremes: 12 and 87; range: 75   b) There is no mode.
c) Median: 35; lower quartile: 15.5; upper quartile: 70

iv) a) Extremes: 0.4 and 50.0; range 49.6   b) There is no mode.
c) Median: 11.2; lower quartile: 5.05; upper quartile: 28.85

v) a) Extremes: 37 and 112; range: 75   b) There is no mode.
c) Median: 78; lower quartile: 53.5; upper quartile: 99.5

vi) a) Extremes: 60 and 100; range: 40   b) 100
c) Median: 88; lower quartile: 66; upper quartile: 100

8. a) The 8th number b) The 4th number c) The 12th number

9. a) Add the 8th and 9th numbers, then divide the sum by 2.
b) Add the 4th and 5th numbers, then divide the sum by 2.
c) Add the 12th and 13th numbers, then divide the sum by 2.

10. a) Extremes: 52 and 104; range: 52
c) Lower quartile: 74.5 years; median: 82 years; upper quartile: 91 years
d) Descriptions may vary. There is a gap between 52 and 63, and between 65 and 71. There is a cluster between 78 and 84.
e) 81 years

11. a) Bermuda, Las Vegas, Palm Springs, Nassau and Tampa, Orlando, Miami Beach, and Daytona Beach, Barbados, Honolulu, Acapulco
b) Extremes: 22°C and 34°C; range: 12°C
c) Median: 29°C; lower quartile: 27°C; upper quartile: 30°C
d) Answers may vary. The data are fairly evenly distributed. Since these are all tropical resort cities, there are no low temperatures.

12. Answers may vary.
b) The resort temperatures are more likely to be evenly distributed since they all have a tropical climate.

14. a) Extremes: 31 years and 92 years; range: 61 years
c) Lower quartile: 51 years; median: 65.5 years; upper quartile: 77 years
d) Descriptions may vary. There are large gaps between 39 and 46, and between 46 and 56.
e) 77 years

15. Answers may vary.

16. If every number in a set of data were doubled, each measure that is listed would double. This would not affect the shape of the line plot: the only change would be that each number on the line would double.

Linking Ideas: Mathematics and Technology
Creating a Database, page 219

1. Answers may vary.
a) Some possible fields are title, artist, playing time, songs included, favourite song, and type of music.

2. Answers may vary.
b) Some possible fields are cost, quantity on hand, record company or distributor.

4.6 Sampling and Reporting
Working with Mathematics, page 222

1. Answers may vary.

2. Answers may vary.

a) A sample whose characteristics do not reflect those of the population
b) The conclusion drawn from an analysis of data

3. Answers may vary.
a) People from all age groups who listen to the radio station
b) People who never listen to the radio station

4. Reasons may vary.
a) Sample A b) Sample B c) Sample A d) Sample B

5. Answers may vary.

6. Answers may vary.
a) People whose first language is not English may find it easier to respond to a personal or telephone interview, rather than to fill out a questionnaire.
b) A personal interview or a questionnaire that accompanies a sample of the product
c) A questionnaire allows people to remain anonymous when they answer questions about their incomes.
d) A questionnaire allows employees to express dissatisfaction anonymously.
e) A questionnaire allows people to respond to this personal question without feeling embarrassed.

7. Answers and reasons may vary.
a) Question 2 b) Question 1 c) Question 2

8. , 9. , 10. Answers may vary.

Quest: How Many Letters Are There in 100 Words?, page 224

Approximately 500 letters in 100 words

4.7 Researching and Reporting
Working with Mathematics, page 228

1. First-hand data are collected through questionnaires and surveys from a sample of the population. Second-hand data are obtained from books, magazines, and databases. Examples may vary.

2. Answers may vary.
a) A telephone book
b) *The Guinness Book of Records*
c) A newspaper
d) *Billboard Magazine*
e) *The World Almanac*
f) *The Guinness Book of Records*
g) E-STAT

3. Answers may vary. The references may not be the most recent, and may perhaps contain data from different years.

4. References may vary.
a) *The Guinness Book of Records* — Beauvais, France
b) A telephone book — St. John's is 4.5 h ahead of Vancouver
c) *Canadian Encyclopedia* — James Naismith in 1891
d) *The Complete Book of the Olympics* — Edith McGuire

5. Questions may vary.

6. Data and graphs may vary.

7. a) , b) Data and graphs may vary.
c) Pacific, Atlantic, Indian, Arctic

8. , 9. Data and graphs may vary.

10. In 1981: boys: 984 740; girls: 936 130

11. Answers may vary.

12. Saturn: 1 427 000 000 km; Uranus: 2 869 600 000 km;

Neptune: 4 496 700 000 km; Pluto: 5 900 000 000 km

13. a) Primary school teacher in Zurich
   b) i) Abu Dhabi   **ii)** No, Luxembourg   **iii)** $14 375.70
   c) i) Chicago   **ii)** No, Zurich

15. a) How the Canadian dollar compared to the U.S. dollar from 1976 to 1992
   c) Answers may vary. When one graph has a peak, the other graph has a valley, and vice versa.
   d) Graphs may vary.
   e) Answers may vary. There are many economic and political factors that affect the value of the Canadian dollar.

4.8 Assessing Reported Data
Working with Mathematics, page 232

1. Answers may vary.
   a) The graph suggests an increase but, for 6 out of the past 7 years, the numbers have been decreasing.
   b) The bars are not aligned horizontally and the unemployment rate appears to be greater than it is.

2. Answers may vary.
   a) It does not say what percent of people who ski do not take lessons. There could be many more people who don't take lessons who have accidents, but the percent would be smaller.
   b) This is not misleading.
   c) We need to know what percent of drivers 1775 is, and what percent of cyclists 102 is, before we can say which is the safer mode of transport.

3. Graphs may vary.

4. to 7. Answers may vary.

8. Answers may vary. There are few accidents because there is little traffic on the road at this time, drivers reduce their speeds in fog, and very few drivers travel at 150 km/h.

9. , 10. Answers may vary.

Review, page 234

1. a) 25 to 29 years   **b)** 384 909
   c) Answers may vary. The range of values is so great that the smallest value would not show on a histogram. You would have to decide what to do with the group "age not stated."

2. a) i) Of or belonging to a city
   ii) Of or belonging to the country
   c) 1921   **d)** 1921, 1951, 1971
   e) Between 1951 and 1961   **f)** Predictions may vary.

3. a) The countries in the world that produced the most rice in 1990
   b) Answers may vary between $\frac{1}{3}$ and $\frac{2}{5}$
   c) Thailand and Vietnam
   d) Japan
   e) Indonesia, Bangladesh, Thailand, Vietnam
   f) Answers may vary.
   i) Between 170 million tonnes and 200 million tonnes
   ii) Between 17 million tonnes and 20 million tonnes

4. a) 9   **b)** 6   **c)** 51   **d)** 46

5. a) $138   **b)** $27.60   **c)** $7176
   d) $1435.20   **e)** $598   **f)** $119.60

6. Answers may vary.

7. a) Extremes: 28 kg and 54 kg; range: 26 kg

c) Descriptions may vary. There are gaps between 44 kg and 47 kg, and between 48 kg and 52 kg.
   d) Lower quartile: 34 kg; median: 37 kg; upper quartile: 43 kg

8. Answers will vary depending on the cities selected.

9. a) 5 469 000, 4 934 000   **b)** 7 847 000, 4 656 000

10. , 11. Answers may vary.

CHAPTER 5 INTEGERS

Start With What You Know, page 240
Activity 1

1. There are 2 more basketball uniforms than softball uniforms.

2. Answers may vary.

Activity 2

1. Answers may vary.

2. a) 8 o'clock   **b) i)** Ahead   **ii)** 120 min

3. a) 120 min behind   **b)** 180 min ahead   **c)** 210 min ahead

4. a) 10 a.m.   **b)** 120 min

5. Answers may vary.

5.1 What Is an Integer?
Developing the Ideas, page 243

1. a) i) There is 1 more yellow tile than red tile.   **ii)** +1
   b) i) There are 3 more yellow tiles than red tiles.   **ii)** +3
   c) i) There is no difference between the number of yellow tiles and the number of red tiles.
   ii) 0
   d) i) There are 3 fewer yellow tiles than red tiles.   **ii)** −3
   e) i) There are 2 fewer yellow tiles than red tiles.   **ii)** −2

2. a), b), c) i) There are 2 more yellow tiles than red tiles.
   ii) +2

3. a), b), c) i) There are 5 fewer yellow tiles than red tiles.
   ii) −5

Working with Mathematics, page 245

1. Answers may vary. A number that represents the difference between the numbers of elements in two groups.

2. There are more yellow tiles than red tiles.

3. There are fewer yellow tiles than red tiles.

4. a) Positive three   **b)** Positive eighteen   **c)** Negative two
   d) Negative fourteen   **e)** Zero

5. a) Move back 10 spaces.   **b)** Ride up 3 floors.
   c) Hike 1500 m down a trail.   **d)** Walk down 10 stairs.
   e) Cycle 7 km north.

6. 3 red tiles   **7.** 0 red tiles   **8.** Answers may vary.

9. a) −1   **b)** +1   **c)** −1   **d)** +1

10. Answers may vary.   **11.** Answers may vary.

12. a) Sea level at 0 m   **b)** 0°C   **c)** Sea level at 0 m

13. a) +24   **b)** −5   **c)** +110   **d)** −10   **e)** −$50 billion

14. a) Vancouver: 1 602 502 − 320 501;
   Edmonton: 839 924 − 320 501;
   Regina: 191 692 − 320 501;
   Winnipeg: 652 354 − 320 501;
   Whitehorse: 17 925 − 320 501;
   Yellowknife: 15 179 − 320 501;
   Toronto: 3 893 046 − 320 501;

Montreal: 3 127 242 − 320 501;
Saint John: 124 981 − 320 501;
Charlottetown: 15 396 − 320 501;
St. John's: 171 859 − 320 501

b) Vancouver: +1 282 001; Edmonton: +519 423;
Regina: −128 809; Winnipeg: +331 853;
Whitehorse: −302 576; Yellowknife: −305 322;
Toronto: +3 572 545; Montreal: +2 806 741;
Saint John: −195 520; Charlottetown: −305 105;
St. John's: −148 642

c) Vancouver : −762 578; Regina: +648 232;
Winnipeg: +187 570; Whitehorse: +821 999;
Yellowknife: +824 745; Toronto: −3 053 122;
Montreal: −2 287 318; Saint John: +714 943;
Halifax: +519 423; Charlottetown: +824 528;
St. John's: +668 065

15. a) 8   **b)** 98   **c)** $n − 2$ **d)** $n + 5$

Linking Ideas: Integers and Data Management
Comparing Provincial Populations, page 247

1. a) 926 200 is subtracted from each population. The positive integers result from populations larger than 926 200. The negative integers result from populations smaller than 926 200.

b) The difference between each province's population and the population of Saskatchewan

2. a) New Brunswick, Nova Scotia

b) Alberta, British Columbia, Manitoba, Newfoundland and Labrador, Ontario, Prince Edward Island, Quebec

c) All provinces except Prince Edward Island

Mathematics File: Representing Integers, page 248

1. −2   **2.** −2   **3.** −2   **4. a)** −2   **b)** −2   **5.** −2

6. Answers may vary.

a) Assume there are 10 yellow tiles and 5 red tiles. The difference between the yellow and red tiles is +5. Add 5 tiles to each set. We have 15 yellow tiles and 10 red tiles. The difference is still +5.

b) Assume there are 10 yellow tiles and 8 red tiles. The difference between the yellow and red tiles is +2. Take away 3 tiles from each set. We have 7 yellow tiles and 5 red tiles. The difference is still +2.

5.2 Ordering Integers
Developing the Ideas, page 250

1. a) From zero, the numbers go up in 10s and down in 10s.
b) i) We use a negative integer.
ii) We use a positive integer.

2. b) −22°C, −15°C, −10°C, −5°C, −4°C, −2°C, −1°C, 0°C, +1°C, +2°C, +5°C, +7°C

c) Aklavik, Whitehorse, Winnipeg, Saskatoon, St. John's, Edmonton, Moncton, Charlottetown, Halifax, Toronto, Montreal, Vancouver

Activity 1

1. −10, −9, −8, −7, −6, −5, −4, −3, −2, −1, 0, +1, +2, +3, +4, +5, +6, +7, +8, +9, +10

2. Answers may vary. Each red column has 1 fewer tile than the preceding column; the yellow column remains the same,

until you reach zero. Then, each red column remains the same, while each yellow column has 1 more tile than the preceding column.

3. +7 is 8 yellow tiles and 1 red tile.
−7 is 1 yellow tile and 8 red tiles.

4. a) No   **b)** No   **c)** No

Working with Mathematics, page 254

1. Opposite integers have the same digits, but opposite signs. They are the same distance from 0, and on opposite sides of 0 on a number line.

2. Answers may vary. It is the integer with which all other integers are compared.

3. They are listed from least to greatest.

4. They are listed from greatest to least.

5. Answers may vary. +3 is to the right of −2 on a number line.

6. a) +2   **b)** −2   **c)** +3   **d)** 0

7. a) −4   **b)** −5   **c)** −2   **d)** −9

8. Yes, −4 is to the left of +2 on a number line.

9. a) −7, −6, +1, +4, +5   **b)** −13, −1, 0, +3, +10
c) −15, −5, +1, +4, +11   **d)** −20, −12, 0, +4, +7, +18
e) −17, −16, +4, +5, +17

10. a) +9   **b)** +7   **c)** +7   **d)** −5   **e)** −11   **f)** −10

11. Answers may vary.

12. a) Calgary, Regina, Winnipeg
b) +3°C, −6°C, −12°C, −18°C, −19°C

13. a) +5 > +2   **b)** +7 > 0   **c)** −4 < −1   **d)** −11 > −14
e) +8 > −3   **f)** −15 < +9   **g)** +14 > −14   **h)** −10 < +10

14. a) +5   **b)** −5   **c)** −3   **d)** +2   **e)** +4   **f)** −4

15. Answers may vary.
a) +4, +5; +2, +1   **b)** −1, 0; −3, −4
c) −3, −2; −5, −6   **d)** +6, +5; +2, +3

16. a) Edmonton   **b)** Toronto   **c)** Dawson
d) Yellowknife   **e)** Winnipeg   **f)** Churchill

17. a) Each integer is 2 less than the preceding integer: −2, −4, −6
b) Each integer is 2 more than the preceding integer: +1, +3, +5
c) The numbers increase by 1 but the signs alternate: +5, −6, +7
d) Each integer is 3 less than the preceding integer: −5, −8, −11

18. a) −5   **b)** +3   **c)** +3
d) −5   **e)** +10   **f)** −10

19. Diagrams may vary.

20. a) +2   **b)** −3   **c)** 0

Linking Ideas: Integers and Graphing
The Coordinate Plane, page 256

1. A distance of 3 units to the left of 0 in a horizontal number line

2. A distance of 5 units below 0 in a vertical line

3. a) 1   **b)** 2   **c)** 4   **d)** 3   **e)** 4   **f)** 2

4. a) Quadrants 1 and 3   **b)** Quadrants 2 and 4

5. Points may vary. They lie in a vertical line.

6. Points may vary. They lie in a horizontal line.

7. B(+2, −3), C(−5, +3), D(+2, +5), E(0, +3), F(−4, −2),

G(−3, 0), H(+5, 0), J(0, −5)

8. a) Square   **b)** Parallelogram   **c)** Trapezoid

9. 8-pointed star

10. , 11. Answers may vary.

12. (−2, −2), (+2, −2); (−2, +6), (+2, +6); (0, +4), (0, 0)

5.3 Using Tiles to Add Integers

Developing the Ideas, page 259

1. (+3) + (−5) = −2   **2.** (−2) + (+6) = +4   **3.** (+4) + (+7) = +11

4. (−2) + (−8) = −10   **5.** (−4) + (+4) = 0

Working with Mathematics, page 260

1. Zero; the result is always true.

2. a) (+2) + (−4) = −2   **b)** (+4) + (−1) = +3   **c)** (−1) + (+6) = +5
   d) (+2) + (−7) = −5   **e)** (−3) + (+3) = 0   **f)** (−5) + (+3) = −2
   g) (+2) + (−5) = −3   **h)** (−1) + (+3) = +2   **i)** (+1) + (−6) = −5

3. −5, −5, −3, −2, −2, 0, +2, +3, +5

4. a) 0   **b)** 0   **c)** 0   **d)** 0   **e)** −13   **f)** +12   **g)** −2   **h)** +5   **i)** −11   **j)** −4

6. a) (+12) + (−10) = +2   **b)** (+10) + (−15) = −5
   c) (+8) + (−13) = −5   **d)** (+14) + (−17) = −3
   e) (+20) + (−11) = +9   **f)** (+19) + (−8) = +11

7. a) (+3) + (−5) = −2   **b)** (+10) + (+7) = +17
   c) (−9) + (−2) = −11   **d)** (−11) + (+4) = −7
   e) (+13) + (−1) = +12   **f)** (−3) + (+20) = +17
   g) (+2) + (−3) = −1   **h)** (−3) + (+8) = +5
   i) (−7) + (+5) = −2   **j)** (−2) + (−4) = −6

8. a) +4   **b)** −5   **c)** −6   **d)** −9   **e)** −2   **f)** −3
   g) +5   **h)** −11   **i)** +7   **j)** +10   **k)** −4   **l)** −9

9. a) +3   **b)** −5   **c)** −9   **d)** +14   **e)** −3   **f)** +5

10. a) +9   **b)** +7   **c)** +10   **d)** +10   **e)** −8
   f) −4   **g)** −9   **h)** −18   **i)** −7   **j)** −6

11. a) +2   **b)** +7   **c)** +5   **d)** +4   **e)** −5
   f) −3   **g)** −2   **h)** 0   **i)** −10   **j)** +9

12. Examples may vary.
   a) True   **b)** False   **c)** True   **d)** True

13. a) −2   **b)** +21   **c)** +5   **d)** −9   **e)** −21
   f) −11   **g)** −8   **h)** +6   **i)** +1

14. Explanations may vary.

15. a)   **b)**

16. a) Yes   **b)** Yes
   c) Answers may vary. The order in which integers are added
     does not affect their sum.

17. −3   **18.** −9

5.4 Using Tiles to Subtract Integers

Developing the Ideas, page 263

1. +4   **2.** −4   **3.** −4   **4.** +8   **5.** +8   **6.** +4   **7.** −8   **8.** −8

Working with Mathematics, page 265

1. a) No tiles, a group of yellow tiles, or a group of red tiles
   b) No tiles, a group of yellow tiles, or a group of red tiles

---

   c) A group of red tiles
   d) A group of yellow tiles

2. Answers may vary. Subtracting an integer is the same as
adding its opposite. Groups of tiles are combined to get the
result.

3. a) +6   **b)** −7   **c)** +5   **d)** +8   **e)** +7   **f)** −3   **g)** −5   **h)** +2   **i)** 0   **j)** +2

4. −7, −5, −3, 0, +2, +2, +5, +6, +7, +8

5. a) −2   **b)** −4   **c)** +3   **d)** +5   **e)** +1   **f)** −5
   g) −1   **h)** −7   **i)** +3   **j)** −3   **k)** −1   **l)** +7

6. Answers may vary.

7. a) −7   **b)** +5   **c)** +14   **d)** +12   **e)** −5   **f)** +12
   g) +8   **h)** +1   **i)** +3   **j)** −7   **k)** +2   **l)** −2

8. Examples may vary.
   a) True: (+7) − (+2) = +5; false: (+7) − (+10) = −3
   b) True: (−3) − (−1) = −2; false: (−3) − (−5) = +2

9. a) (−4) − (+5) = −9   **b)** (−7) − (−8) = +1
   c) (+5) − (+12) = −7   **d)** (−8) − (−6) = −2
   e) 0 − (+5) = −5   **f)** (+3) − (−3) = +6
   g) (+12) − (+1) = +11   **h)** (−4) − (−4) = 0

10. a) +5°C   **b)** +35°C   **c)** +20°C

11. a) +9   **b)** +9   **c)** −7   **d)** −8   **e)** +7   **f)** −8
   g) −1   **h)** −5   **i)** −6   **j)** +5   **k)** −5   **l)** +3

12. Explanations and examples may vary.
   a) True   **b)** True

13. a) +103°C, +103°C, +91°C, +100°C, +74°C, +104°C
   b) Saskatchewan
   c) Prince Edward Island
   d) Alberta and British Columbia

14. a) (+7) − (+2) = +5   **b)** (+11) − (−3) = +14
   c) (+1) − (+6) = −5   **d)** (+4) − (−13) = +17
   e) (−17) − (−5) = −12   **f)** (−13) − (+8) = −21
   g) (+6) − (+14) = −8   **h)** (−2) − (−21) = +19
   i) (−5) − (+17) = −22

15. a) +6   **b)** −1   **c)** −8   **d)** +14

16. Explanations may vary.

17. a) +10   **b)** −9   **c)** −4   **d)** −8   **e)** +3   **f)** +4

18. 357°C

Mathematics File: Time Zones, page 267

2. a) 5 a.m.   **b)** 2 a.m.   **c)** 10 a.m.   **d)** 6 p.m.

3. a) 10 a.m.   **b)** 6 a.m.   **c)** 9 p.m.   **d)** 3 p.m.

4. a) Noon   **b)** 7 a.m.   **c)** 5 p.m.   **d)** 11 p.m.

Quest: Travelling Time, page 268

Severn leaves Vancouver on Tuesday June 2. She returns to
Vancouver on Saturday June 6. Severn misses 4 days from
school.

Review, page 270

1. a) You travel 1000 km south; +1000, −1000
   b) You swim up 3 m to the surface. −3, +3
   c) You descend 100 m in a hot-air balloon. +100, −100
   d) You go back to Grade 7. +1, −1

2. Models may vary.

3. a) +11   **b)** −19   **c)** +45   **d)** +8
   e) +5   **f)** −2   **g)** +10

4. a) +1 **b)** −3 **c)** −6 **d)** 0

5. a) −1 **b)** −3 **c)** −9 **d)** −103 **e)** −8 **f)** −7

6. a) +3 > −1 **b)** −6 < −2 **c)** −7 > −32 **d)** 0 > −3

7. a) True, +3 is to the right of −3 on a number line.
  b) True, 0 is to the right of −1 on a number line.
  c) False, +2 is to the right of −4 on a number line.

8. a) +6, −3, +5, +8, +4, +3, −7, −4, 0, +8
  b) Zhen Yuan and Marianne **c)** Emile **d)** +20
  e) +20
  f) +2; answers may vary.

9. a) +3 **b)** −4 **c)** −10 **d)** −4 **e)** +6 **f)** −8

10. a) −5 **b)** +7 **c)** −5 **d)** −5 **e)** +1

11. a) −4, −2, 0, +1, +5 **b)** −5, −1, +2, +3, +6 **c)** −4, −3, 0, +4, +7
  d) −10, −8, −7, +9, +11 **e)** −12, −6, −4, +2, +15

12. a) Each integer is 2 less than the preceding integer: −5, −7, −9
  b) Each integer is 2 more than the preceding integer: +4, +6, +8
  c) Each integer is 3 less than the preceding integer: −12, −15, −18

13. a) (+3) + (−1) = +2 **b)** (−4) + (+2) = −2 **c)** (+5) + (−5) = 0
  d) (−3) + (−2) = −5 **e)** (+4) + (−3) = +1

14. a) +7 **b)** −7 **c)** −9 **d)** 0 **e)** −13 **f)** +3 **g)** +5 **h)** −24
  i) −2 **j)** +11 **k)** +3 **l)** −21 **m)** −3 **n)** −29 **o)** +2 **p)** −2

15. a) −2 **b)** −6 **c)** −4 **d)** +4

16. Examples may vary. **a)** False **b)** False

17. a) +3 **b)** −1 **c)** −8

18. a) (−3) − (−1) = −2 **b)** (−4) − (+2) = −6 **c)** 0 − (+3) = −3

19. a) +2 **b)** +4 **c)** +5 **d)** +9 **e)** −5 **f)** +1 **g)** −5 **h)** −1
  i) −12 **j)** −12 **k)** +16 **l)** +16 **m)** −4 **n)** −7 **o)** +14 **p)** +7

20. a) +12°C, +8°C, +9°C, +13°C, +5°C, +2°C, +7°C
  b) Thursday **c)** Saturday

21. Examples may vary. **a)** False **b)** False

Cumulative Review, page 274

2. Explanations may vary.
  a) △ABC, △EDF; AB = DE, BC = DF, CA = FE; ∠A = ∠E, ∠B = ∠D, ∠C = ∠F
  b) △ABC, △HIG; AB = HI, BC = IG, AC = GH; ∠A = ∠H, ∠B = ∠I, ∠C = ∠G

3. a) $\frac{2}{3}$ **b)** $\frac{3}{4}$ **c)** $\frac{1}{4}$ **d)** $\frac{3}{10}$ **e)** $\frac{1}{4}$
  f) $\frac{3}{4}$ **g)** $\frac{1}{2}$ **h)** $\frac{1}{4}$ **i)** $\frac{1}{5}$ **j)** $\frac{1}{3}$

4. a) 0.1 **b)** 0.8 **c)** 0.15 **d)** 0.32 **e)** 0.83
  f) 0.47 **g)** 0.48 **h)** 0.53 **i)** 0.37 **j)** 0.57

  From least to greatest, the fractions are: $\frac{1}{10}$, $\frac{3}{20}$, $\frac{8}{25}$, $\frac{11}{30}$, $\frac{7}{15}$, $\frac{29}{60}$, $\frac{21}{40}$, $\frac{4}{7}$, $\frac{4}{5}$, $\frac{5}{6}$

5. a) 10% **b)** 80% **c)** 15% **d)** 32% **e)** 83%
  f) 47% **g)** 48% **h)** 53% **i)** 37% **j)** 57%

6. a) $\frac{7}{8}$ **b)** $\frac{8}{9}$ **c)** $\frac{1}{4}$
  d) $\frac{3}{12}$, or $\frac{1}{4}$ **e)** $\frac{15}{10}$, or $1\frac{1}{2}$ **f)** $\frac{3}{5}$

7. a) 40% **b)** 70% **c)** 100% **d)** 75%

8. a) $494.25 **b)** PST and total cost will vary. GST: $34.60
  c) Answers will vary.

9. a) i) $\frac{1}{6}$, or about 17% **ii)** $\frac{1}{3}$, or about 33%
  iii) $\frac{1}{2}$, or 50% **iv)** $\frac{1}{2}$, or 50%
  v) $\frac{5}{6}$, or about 83%
  b) i) 10 **ii)** 20 **iii)** 30 **iv)** 30 **v)** 50

10. a) 22 588 **b)** 31 623 **c)** 1129

11. a) A bar graph or broken-line graph may be drawn.
  b) Answers may vary. **c)** Answers may vary.

12. a) Mean: 169.2 cm; median: 166 cm; modes: 162 cm, 166 cm, 173 cm
  b) Mean: 67.8 kg; median: 65 kg; mode: 65 kg
  c) Mean: 68.4%; median: 67%; modes: 65%, 67%, 73%

13. Answers may vary. Mean: any 7 numbers with a sum of 350; median: 3 numbers less than or equal to 50, the number 50, and 3 numbers greater than or equal to 50; mode: any 7 numbers as long as 50 occurs more often than any other number

14. a) −2 **b)** +6 **c)** 0 **d)** −1 **e)** +7 **f)** −5

15. a) +4 **b)** −5 **c)** −1 **d)** +100
  e) 0 **f)** −19 **g)** +26 **h)** −10

16. a) −18 **b)** +6 **c)** −43 **d)** 0
  e) −5 **f)** +1 **g)** +32 **h)** −50

17. a) The extreme values are −13°C and 15°C. The range is 28°C.
  b) 14°C
  d) Descriptions may vary. There is a cluster near each extreme value. There are gaps between −9°C and −5°C, −5°C and 0°C, and +3°C and +12°C.
  e) The median is +2°C, the lower quartile is −9°C, and the upper quartile is +13°C.

18. Answers may vary.

CHAPTER 6 MEASUREMENT

Start With What You Know, page 278

1. Estimates may vary.

2. Objects may vary. **3.** At C

4. a) 4000 **b)** 60 000 **c)** 3000 **d)** 210 000 **e)** 540
  f) 10 000 **g)** 1000 **h)** 8 **i)** 1

5. Estimates may vary. For example:
  a) 4000 **b)** 60 000 **c)** 3000 **d)** 210 000 **e)** 540
  f) 10 000 **g)** 1000 **h)** 8 **i)** 1

6. Explanations may vary.

7. a) 16 cm² **b)** 3.24 m² **c)** 8100 cm² **d)** 490 000 mm²
  e) 625 m² **f)** 3600 cm² **g)** 1.44 m² **h)** 0.36 m²

8. 1 m² **9.** Answers may vary.

10. a) 4 m² **b)** 1.5 cm² **c)** 180 cm²
  d) 8 cm² **e)** 2.2 m² **f)** 18 m²

Linking Ideas: Measurement and Data Management
The Long and the Short of Canadian Mammals, page 280

1. Field names may vary, depending on the program used.
  a), **b)** Average mass, kg; average total length, cm; average tail length, cm; average gestation period, days

2. a) 11 **b)** 1

3. a) 16 **b)** 6 **c)** Greater by 5 young

4. Most seals and sea lions live between 17 and 40 years. Most insectivores live about 1.25 years.

5. a) Answers may vary.
  b) Answers may vary. The percents will generally be greater than those in part a.
  c) Answers may vary. Rodents use their tails primarily for balance.

6. Whales, dolphins, and porpoises, and seals and sea lions; answers may vary. These mammals have tails but it is difficult to determine where the body ends and the tail begins. Therefore, the tail length cannot be measured.

6.1 Working with Perimeter and Area

Developing the Ideas, page 281

Activity 1

1. a) Answers may vary.   **b)** 36 square units
   c), **d)** Answers may vary.

2. a) i) Yes   **ii)** Yes   **iii)** No
   b)

Length (units)	Width (units)	Area (square units)	Perimeter (units)
36	1	36	74
18	2	36	40
12	3	36	30
9	4	36	26
6	6	36	24

   c) i) Yes   **ii)** No   **d)** Square

3. a) 36 m^2
   b) i) 6 m, 24 m   **ii)** 4 m, 26 m   **iii)** 3 m, 30 m
   iv) 2 m, 40 m   **v)** 1.5 m, 51 m   **vi)** 1 m, 74 m
   c) i) Yes   **ii)** No

4. a)

Length (m)	Width (m)	Area (m^2)	Perimeter (m)
6	6	36	24
9	4	36	26
12	3	36	30
18	2	36	40
24	1.5	36	51
36	1	36	74

   b) Answers may vary.

5. b) i) Yes   **ii)** Join the points with a smooth curve.
   iii) Include more values of length and perimeter.

6. a) The width decreases.   **b)** The perimeter increases.

7. 6 m by 6 m

Activity 2

1. Answers may vary.

2. a) i) Yes   **ii)** No
   b)

Length (units)	Width (units)	Area (square units)	Perimeter (units)
11	1	11	24
10	2	20	24
9	3	27	24
8	4	32	24
7	5	35	24
6	6	36	24

   c) i) Yes   **ii)** No   **d)** Square

3. a) 24 m
   b) i) 6 m, 36 m^2 **ii)** 5 m, 35 m^2 **iii)** 4 m, 32 m^2
   iv) 3 m, 27 m^2 **v)** 2 m, 20 m^2 **vi)** 1 m, 11 m^2
   c) i) Yes   **ii)** No

4. a)

Length (m)	Width (m)	Area (m^2)	Perimeter (m)
6	6	36	24
7	5	35	24
8	4	32	24
9	3	27	24
10	2	20	24
11	1	11	24

   b) Answers may vary.

5. b) i) Yes   **ii)** Join the points with a smooth curve.
   iii) Include more values of length and area.

6. a) The width decreases.   **b)** The area decreases.

7. 6 m by 6 m

Working with Mathematics, page 286

1. a) 30 m   **b)** 9 m by 4 m   **c)** It is a square.

2. a) 32 m^2 **b)** 10 m by 2 m   **c)** It is a square.

3. a) 5 cm   **b)** 9 cm   **c)** 5 cm   **d)** 5 cm   **e)** 8 cm   **f)** 7 cm

4. a) 24 m, 35 m^2 **b)** 10.2 km, 2.7 km^2
   c) 12 cm, 8.36 cm^2 **d)** 27.6 mm, 33.17 mm^2

5. a) 4.6 cm   **b)** 2.4 cm   **c)** 201.4 km   **d)** 55 cm

6. Answers may vary.
   a) In each case, the numbers in the tables were the same.
   b) In each case, the units in the tables were different.

7. a) 11 cm^2, 16 cm   **b)** Figures may vary.
   c) 16 cm^2 **d)** 7 cm^2

8. a) 16 cm^2, 26 cm   **b)** Figures may vary.
   c) 34 cm   **d)** 16 cm

9. a) 32 cm   **b)** 96 cm^2

10. a) 10.6 cm   **b)** 7 cm^2

11. a) The same marks are drawn on the sides.
   b) 480 m^2 **c)** Answers may vary.

12. a) 12.6 cm   **b)** 10 cm^2

13. Bedroom 1 is $452.00, bedroom 2 is $381.10, and living room is $1049.50.

14. a) 220 cm^2; 50 cm   **b)** 20 m^2; 22 m

15. 2100 m^2

16. a) Measurements may vary. The first 4 formulas calculate the area of each wall. The last formula adds the 4 areas.
   b) Measurements may vary. The first 4 formulas calculate the area of each door and window. The last formula adds the 4 areas.
   c) Answers may vary.
   d) Answers may vary.

17. a) 11.25 cm^2, 16 cm   **b)** 156 cm^2, 68 cm

18. a) 140.4 m   **b)** 1122 m^2 **c)** 36

19. a) $64.80   **b)** $97.20

20. a) Swimming pool: 65 m^2, wading pool: 18 m^2
   b) 62 m^2

21. a) 100 cm^2 **b)** 32 cm

23. Answers may vary

6.2 Area of a Parallelogram

Developing the Ideas, page 290

Step 1 — The areas are 21 cm^2, 15 cm^2, 16 cm^2.

Step 6 — The area of the rectangle is equal to the area of the parallelogram.

3. The area of a parallelogram is the product of its base and its height.

Working with Mathematics, page 292

1. a) No   **b)** No
   c) The height is perpendicular to the base.

2. a) Answers may vary. 6.0 cm^2
   b) If the answers are different, the measurements might not have been accurate.

3. Answers may vary.

4. a) 6 cm^2 **b)** 9 cm^2 **c)** 8 cm^2 **d)** 4 cm^2 **e)** 15 cm^2

5. a) 6 m^2 **b)** 37.8 cm^2 **c)** 220 cm^2 **d)** 4.0 m^2

6. a) 35 cm^2 **b)** 7 cm   **c)** 5 cm   **d)** 64 cm^2

7. Parallelograms may vary.

8. a) 4 cm   **b)** 6 cm

9. Answers may vary.   **10.** 13.5 m^2

11. Answers may vary.
   a) 5.4 cm^2 **b)** 4.6 cm^2 **c)** 5.6 cm^2 **d)** 6.4 cm^2 **e)** 10.5 cm^2

12. a) 1600 cm^2 **b)** 2030 cm^2

13. Answers may vary.   **14.** About 17 cm^2

Linking Ideas: Mathematics and Technology

Triangle-Square Puzzle, page 294

Answers may vary.

The area of the square is equal to the sum of the areas of the triangles.

6.3 Area of a Triangle

Developing the Ideas, page 295

Step 1 — The areas are 22.5 cm^2, 32 cm^2, 16 cm^2.

Step 5 — The area of the triangle is one-half of the area of the parallelogram.

Step 6 — Calculate the area of the parallelogram, then divide by 2.

3. The area of a triangle is one-half the product of its base and height.

Working with Mathematics, page 297

1. Examples may vary.
   a) No   **b)** No
   c) The height is perpendicular to the base.

2. Examples may vary. No

3. Answers may vary. After Step 4, cut the parallelogram and tape the parts to form a rectangle, as in Step 3 on page 290.

4. Yes, the triangles have equal areas, because they have equal bases and the same height.

5. a) 6 cm^2 **b)** 7.5 cm^2 **c)** 8 cm^2
   d) 4.5 cm^2 **e)** 3 cm^2 **f)** 6 cm^2

6. a) 12 m^2 **b)** 20 cm^2 **c)** 60 cm^2
   d) 10.85 m^2 **e)** 42.33 cm^2 **f)** 23.805 cm^2

7. a) 12.6 cm   **b)** 12 cm   **c)** 20 cm
   d) 20.4 m   **e)** 29.2 cm   **f)** 44.6 m

8. Triangles may vary.

9. a) =B3*B4/2   **b)** =C5*2/C3   **c)** =D5*2/D4
   d) i) 204   **ii)** 25   **iii)** 1.5

10. a) 6 cm   **b)** 12 cm

11. Answers may vary.

12. a) 26 cm^2 **b)** 6.75 cm^2

13. 8.4 m^2 **14.** 5.6 m^2

15. a) 5.1 cm^2 **b)** 6.8 cm^2 **c)** Results may vary.

16. 4500 cm^2 **17.** 24 cm^2

18. a) 12 cm

19. a, b, d

20. Whole pane: 202.5 cm^2; half pane: 101.25 cm^2

21. a) 3 pairs
   b) i) No   **ii)** No
   c) Explanations may vary.
   d) Yes; explanations may vary.

Quest: Do Triangles with Longer Sides Have Greater Areas than Triangles with Shorter Sides?, page 300

It is possible to have a triangle with all three sides longer than another triangle, and the area of the first triangle is less than the area of the second triangle.

Mathematics File: Area of a Trapezoid, page 302

1. a, c

2. A trapezoid is a figure with 4 sides such that only 1 pair of sides is parallel.

4. b) Draw a diagonal to cut the trapezoid in two triangles. Find the area of each triangle. Add the areas to find the area of the trapezoid, which is 18 cm^2.

5. Multiply each length by the height. Divide each area by 2. Add the results.

6. a) 45 cm^2 **b)** 42 cm^2 **c)** 5.04 cm^2

7. c) The area of one trapezoid is half the area of the parallelogram.
   d) 36 cm^2; 18 cm^2

8. Answers may vary.

9. Add the lengths of the parallel sides. Multiply by the height. Divide by 2.

10. a) 14 cm^2 **b)** 10.5 cm^2 **c)** 4.62 cm^2

Quest: What is the Area of a Newspaper?, page 304

Answers may vary.

Mathematics File: Regular Polygons, page 306

1. Explanations may vary.
   a) Octagon, yes; rectangle, no
   b) Square, yes; pentagon, yes
   c) Pentagon, yes; triangle, no

2. a) Dollar and cent
   b) The dollar has 11 sides and angles. The cent has 12 sides and angles.
   c) Answers may vary. The vertices are rounded.

4. Triangle: 7.2 cm; square: 8.0 cm; pentagon: 7.5 cm; hexagon: 7.8 cm; octagon: 6.4 cm

5. Multiply the number of sides by the length of one side.

6. Hexagon; explanations may vary.

7. **a)** 4.0 cm^2 **b)** 5.9 cm^2 **c)** 8.8 cm^2 **d)** 10.8 cm^2

8. Halve the product of the number of sides, the length of one side, and the distance to the centre.

9. **a)** 27.0 cm   **b)** 18.3 m   **c)** 63.2 km
   d) 3.6 cm   **e)** 10 m   **f)** 35.6 km

6.4 Working with Square Units

Developing the Ideas, page 308

1. **a)** 100   **b)** 10 000

2. **a)** 100 cm   **b)** 10 000 cm^2

Working with Mathematics, page 309

1. **a)** 10 000   **b)** A square with sides 10 m

2. 1 000 000   3. 1 000 000

4. **a)** 10   **b)** 100   **c)** 100
   d) Multiply by 100.   **e)** Divide by 100.

5. **a)** Multiply by 1000. **b)** Multiply by 1 000 000.
   c) Divide by 1000.   **d)** Divide by 1 000 000.

6. **a)** Larger   **b)** Smaller   **c)** Larger   **d)** Larger   **e)** Smaller
   f) Larger   **g)** Larger   **h)** Smaller   **i)** Smaller   **j)** Smaller

7. **a)** 500 cm   **b)** 80 000 cm   **c)** 6 cm
   d) 90 cm   **e)** 4500 cm   **f)** 70 cm
   g) 300 000 cm   **h)** 0.65 cm   **i)** 4820 cm

8. **a)** 2 500 000 cm^2 **b)** 250 000 cm^2 **c)** 25 000 cm^2
   d) 2500 cm^2 **e)** 8 000 000 cm^2 **f)** 0.6 cm^2
   g) 9000 cm^2 **h)** 450 000 cm^2 **i)** 7 cm^2

9. **a)** 2 m   **b)** 3000 m   **c)** 8 m
   d) 900 m   **e)** 5000 m   **f)** 50 000 m
   g) 0.08 m   **h)** 25 000 m   **i)** 0.902 m

10. **a)** 7 m^2 **b)** 0.7 m^2 **c)** 0.07 m^2
    d) 0.02 m^2 **e)** 3 000 000 m^2 **f)** 0.008 m^2
    g) 9 m^2 **h)** 50 m^2 **i)** 50 000 000 m^2

11. **a)** 100 m^2 **b)** 2025 cm^2 **c)** About 530

12. **a) i)** 250 000 m^2 **ii)** 2 500 000 m^2
    b) i) 0.46 ha   **ii)** 0.046 ha

13. **a)** About 5976 m^2 **b)** 0.5976 ha

15. **a)** 5 000 000 mm^2 **b)** 50 000 cm^2 **c)** 0.000 005 km^2

17. **a)** 25 000 m^2 **b)** 2500 m^2 **c)** 25 000 000 m^2

18. **a)** 6.4 ha   **b)** 64 ha

19. **a)** About 8696 m^2 **b)** 0.8696 ha

20. Answers may vary.
    a) No; 23 football fields have an area of 20.0 ha.
    b) Between the goal lines, 23 football fields have an area of 13.7 ha so this value is closer.

21. **a)** 56 304 000 m^2 **b)** 56.304 km^2 **c)** 5630.4 ha

Review, page 311

1. **a)** 3 cm   **b)** 5 cm   **c)** 7 cm   **d)** 9 cm

2. **a)** 36 cm, 45 cm^2 **b)** 3.8 km, 0.6 km^2 **c)** 98 m, 598 m^2
   d) 30 mm, 50 mm^2 **e)** 29.4 cm, 52.7 cm^2 **f)** 7.8 m, 3.6 m^2

3. 32 m^2, 24 m

4. **a)** 6 m   **b)** 36 m^2
   c) The area of the square is greater than the area of the rectangle.

d) When rectangles and a square have the same perimeter, the square always has the greatest area.

5. **a)** 188 m^2 **b)** 68 m

6. **a)** Corn: 88 000 m^2; barley: 50 000 m^2; wheat: 40 000 m^2; oats: 92 000 m^2
   b) 2200 m   **c)** 1250 m   **d)** 3450 m

7. **a)** 56.25 cm^2 **b)** 24 cm

8. **a)** 86 m   **b)** $1892

9. **a)** 16 cm   **b)** 11.5 cm^2

10. **a)** 750.76 m^2 **b)** 109.6 m

11. **a)** Perimeter   **b)** Area   **c)** Perimeter

12. **a)** 15 cm^2 **b)** 16 cm^2 **c)** 6 cm^2 **d)** 3 cm^2

13. Diagrams may vary.

14. **a)** 54 cm^2 **b)** 26.1 m^2 **c)** 324 mm^2

15. **a)** 10 cm^2 **b)** 12 cm^2 **c)** 6 cm^2 **d)** 7.5 cm^2

16. **a)** 14.6 cm^2 **b)** 10.5 m^2

17. **a)** 27 cm^2 **b)** 13.05 m^2 **c)** 162 mm^2

18. **a)** 4.6 cm   **b)** 8 m   **c)** 0.5 km   **d)** 6.4 m   **e)** 4.0 cm

19. Diagrams may vary.

20. Answers may vary.
    a) Base 10 cm, height 7 cm   **b)** Side length 12 m
    c) Length 8 km, width 6 km   **d)** Base 8 m, height 7 m
    e) Base 6 cm, height 6 cm   **f)** Side length 8 m
    g) Length 12 cm, width 2 cm   **h)** Base 12 cm, height 2 cm

21. Areas are:
    i) 33.62 m^2 **ii)** 42.25 m^2 **iii)** 36.66 m^2
    iv) 21.56 m^2 **v)** 37.76 m^2 **vi)** 38.48 m^2
    a) The square   **b)** The trapezoid

22. **a) i)** 24.6 m **ii)** 26 m   **iii)** 28.8 m **iv)** 19.2 m **v)** 26.4 m **vi)** 25.2 m
    b) No   **c)** Yes

23. **a)** 11.4 m^2 **b)** 799 m^2

24. Diagrams may vary.

25. Answers may vary. The product of base and height in exercise 13 is one-half the same product in exercise 24.

26. **a)** More   **b)** Fewer   **c)** Fewer   **d)** More

27. **a)** 120 000 cm^2 **b)** 2.5 cm^2 **c)** 6000 cm^2 **d)** 0.1 cm^2

28. **a)** 1.5 m^2 **b)** 2 000 000 m^2 **c)** 140 000 m^2 **d)** 0.3 m^2

29. **a)** 0.27 ha   **b)** 2.8 ha

30. **a)** 40 000 cm^2 **b)** 0.000 004 km^2 **c)** 4 000 000 mm^2

31. **a)** 20 cm   **b)** 400 cm^2 **c)** 20 cm
    d) 20 cm   **e)** 200 cm^2 **f)** 200 cm^2
    g) The area for part b is the sum of the areas for parts e and f.

32. **a)** False   **b)** False   **c)** True

33. **a)** 1   **b)** 2   **c)** 4   **d)** 3   **e)** 4

CHAPTER 7 FROM ARITHMETIC TO ALGEBRA

Start With What You Know, page 318
Activity 1

Descriptions may vary.

1. Add 2: 11, 13, 15, 17, 19

2. Add 10: 140, 150, 160, 170, 180

3. Add 20: 113, 133, 153, 173, 193

4. Add 5: 325, 330, 335, 340, 345

5. Subtract 4: 40, 36, 32, 28, 24

6. Multiply by 2: 32, 64, 128, 256, 512

Activity 2

3. Answers may vary, 6 if natural number dimensions

4. Answers may vary.

7. Answers may vary, 18 if natural number dimensions

8. Answers may vary.

Activity 3

1. , 2. See student's text, page 326.

3. Descriptions may vary.
  a) Add the first number of the row to the previous number, to get the next number.
  b) Subtract the first number of the row from the previous number, to get the next number.
  c) Add the first number of the column to the previous number, to get the next number.
  d) Subtract the first number of the column from the previous number, to get the next number.

4. The numbers in each row and column are: 11, 22, 33, 44, 55, 66, 77, 88, 99, 110, 121; start with 11, then keep adding 11 to get the following numbers.

5. a) Descriptions may vary. Each number is 7 more than the preceding number.
  b) They are multiples of 7.   **c)** Yes

6. a) 1, 4, 9, 16, 25, 36, 49, 64, 81, 100, 121
  b) Each number is the product of a number and itself.
  c) 144, 169, 196, 225, 256
  d) Answers may vary. 12×12, 13×13, 14×14, 15×15, 16×16

7. Answers may vary.

7.1 Extending Geometric Patterns

Developing the Ideas, page 320

Activity 1

1. a) The side length is equal to its position. All triangles have two equal sides. They are made up of the same small triangles. Each triangle's base equals its height.
  b) They contain different numbers of small triangles.

3.

Length of base of large triangle (units)	1	2	3	4	5	6	7
Number of small triangles	1	4	9	16	25	36	49

4. a) Descriptions may vary.
  b) The number of small triangles is equal to the length of a side of the large triangle, multiplied by itself.

5. 100   **6.** 225

Activity 2

1. Equilateral triangle, square, regular pentagon
  a) They have the same side length.
  b) They have different numbers of sides.

2. Regular hexagon, regular heptagon, regular octagon

3.

Number of sides	3	4	5	6	7	8
Perimeter (cm)	9	12	15	18	21	24

4. b) The perimeter is the product of 3 cm and the number of sides.

5. 300 cm

Working with Mathematics, page 323

1. Find which number, multiplied by itself, has the product that is the number of small triangles.

2. Divide the perimeter by 3 cm.

3. Subtract 2 from the perimeter of the figure.

4. a) $2p$ **b)** $5p$ **c)** $\frac{p}{2}$ **d)** $p + 3$ **e)** $p - 2$ **f)** $p - 5$

5. a) $n + 1$ **b)** $n + 4$ **c)** $n - 2$ **d)** $5n$ **e)** $\frac{n}{3}$

6. a)

Number of lengths	1	2	3	4	5
Number of posts	2	3	4	5	6
Number of rails	2	4	6	8	10
Number of pickets	5	9	13	17	21

  b) The number of posts is 1 more than the number of lengths. $n + 1$
  c) The number of rails is twice the number of lengths. $2n$
  d) The number of pickets is 1 greater than 4 times the number of lengths. $4n + 1$

7. a) Each figure has 1 more triangle and 1 more dot than the preceding figure.
  b)

Number of triangles	1	2	3	4	5	6
Number of dots	3	4	5	6	7	8

  d) I would add 2 to 100.   **e)** 102; 202
  f) The number of dots is 2 more than the number of triangles.
  g) $n + 2$

8. a) Each figure has 1 more row, which contains 2 more squares than the largest row of the preceding figure.
  b)

Number of layers	1	2	3	4	5	6
Number of squares	1	4	9	16	25	36

  c) 81; 400
  d) The number of squares is the number of layers multiplied by itself.
  e) Variables may differ. $s \times s$

9. a) Each figure has 1 more dot, and 1 more square than the preceding figure.
  b)

Number of dots	1	2	3	4	5	6
Number of squares	2	3	4	5	6	7

  c) I would subtract 1 from 35.   **d)** 49
  e) The number of dots is 1 less than the number of squares.
  f) $s - 1$

10. a) Each figure has 3 more toothpicks than the preceding figure.

b)

Number of vertical toothpicks	1	2	3	4	5	6	7
Total number of toothpicks	3	6	9	12	15	18	21

d) 36; 180

e) The total number of toothpicks is 3 times the number of vertical toothpicks.

f) $3v$

11. $d - 2$

12. Find the number which when multiplied by itself produced the number of squares in the figure.

Linking Ideas: Mathematics and Technology
Creating a Pattern in a Spreadsheet, page 325

1. 2; the formula adds 1 to the number in cell A1.

2. The numbers 1 to 10 show in cells A1 to A10.

3. a) Each number is 4 more than the preceding number.
b) Add 4. The formula is =B4+4.
c) The numbers 2, 6, 10, 14, 18, 22, 26, 30, 34, 38 should show in cells B1 to B10.

4. The formula is =C3+5.
Five is added to each previous number.
The numbers 5, 10, 15, 20, 25, 30, 35, 40, 45, 50 should show in cells C1 to C10.

5. The formula is =A4*5.
The numbers should be the same as in exercise 4.

6. The formula is =D3−5.
Five is subtracted from each previous number.
The numbers 100, 95, 90, 85, 80, 75, 70, 65, 60, 55 should show in cells D1 to D10.

7.2 Extending Number Patterns
Developing the Ideas, page 326

Activity 1

1. $2 = 2 \times 1$; $4 = 2 \times 2$; $6 = 2 \times 3$; $8 = 2 \times 4$; $10 = 2 \times 5$;
$12 = 2 \times 6$; $14 = 2 \times 7$; $16 = 2 \times 8$; $18 = 2 \times 9$; $20 = 2 \times 10$

2. $40 = 2 \times 20$ **3.** $200 = 2 \times 100$

4. $2 \times n$ **5.** Answers may vary.

6. Explanations may vary. $15 \times n$

Activity 2

1. a) 7 **b)** 7 **c)** 7

2. a) Add 7 to the number in the 18th cell.
b) Add 7 to the number in the 99th cell.
c) i) $n + 7$ **ii)** $n - 7$

3. Answers may vary.

Activity 3

1. 40, 36, 32, 28, 24, 20, 16, 12, 8, 4

2. It decreases by 4.

3. a) i) 12 **ii)** $12 = 16 - 4$
b) i) 12 **ii)** $12 = 16 - 4$

4. a) $n - 4$ **b)** $n - 4$

Working with Mathematics, page 330

1. a) $3n$ **b)** $5n$ **c)** $8n$ **d)** $10n$

2. a) The position of any cell **b)** The number in any cell

3. a) 14 **b)** 104 **c)** Variables may differ. $4 + n$

4. a) 80 **b)** 400 **c)** Variables may differ. $4n$

5. a) 3, 4, 5, 6 **b)** 5, 4, 3, 2 **c)** 7, 8, 9, 10 **d)** 7, 14, 21, 28
e) 3, 6, 9, 12 **f)** 12, 6, 4, 3 **g)** $\frac{1}{4}$, $\frac{1}{2}$, $\frac{3}{4}$, 1 **h)** 3, $\frac{3}{2}$, 1, $\frac{3}{4}$

6. a) $2n$ **b)** $10n$ **c)** $n + 7$
d) $100 - n$ **e)** $\frac{60}{n}$

7. a) 4, 5, 6, 7 **b)** 21, 20, 19, 18 **c)** 8, 16, 24, 32
d) 3, 5, 7, 9 **e)** $\frac{1}{2}$, 1, $\frac{3}{2}$, 2 **f)** 3, $\frac{3}{2}$, 1, $\frac{3}{4}$

8. Answers may vary.

9. a)

Regular price ($)	75	90	125	160
Sale price ($)	55	70	105	140

b) The sale price is $20 less than the regular price.
c) $r - 20$

10. a)

Number of hours	1	2	3	4	5
Earnings ($)	4	8	12	16	20

b) Multiply by the number of hours worked by $4.
c) $48 **d)** $4h$

11. Answers may vary. An example is given for each expression.
a) The number of cookies left after 4 are eaten
b) The number of cookies after 12 are added
c) The number of cookies each person would get if 6 people shared the cookies equally

12. Answers may vary. An example is given for each expression.
a) The number of ice-cream bars sold on the next day
b) The number of ice-cream bars sold in 1 week
c) The amount of money received for the ice-cream bars

13. a) 4, 5, 6, 7, 8 **b)** 9, 8, 7, 6, 5 **c)** 5, 9, 13, 17, 21
d) 10, 20, 30, 40, 50 **e)** $\frac{1}{3}$, $\frac{2}{3}$, 1, $\frac{4}{3}$, $\frac{5}{3}$ **f)** 2, 1, $\frac{2}{3}$, $\frac{2}{4}$, $\frac{2}{5}$

14. a)

Cost of cassette ($)	7	8	9	10
Cost of CD ($)	16	17	18	19

b) Add $9 to the cost of the cassette.
d) $c + 9$

15. a)

Number of hours	1	2	3	4	5	6	7
Earnings ($)	5.60	11.20	16.80	22.40	28.00	33.60	39.20

b) Multiply the numbers of hours by $5.60.
c) $67.20 **e)** $5.60h$

16. a)

Number of beats in 15 s	18	19	20	21	22	23
Number of beats in 1 min	72	76	80	84	88	92

b) 168 beats/min **c)** $4p$ beats/min

17. a)

Number of pencils	1	2	3	4	5
Cost ($)	0.55	1.10	1.65	2.20	2.75

b) Multiply the number of pencils by $0.55.
c) $8.25   **d)** $0.55n

18. a) 19   **b)** 39   **c)** Variables may differ. $2x - 1$

Quest: Help Dorothy Get to the Wizard, page 332

There are 70 different ways for Dorothy to travel to the wizard.

7.3 What Is an Equation?

Developing the Ideas, page 334

Activity 1

1. 12

2. Answers may vary. For example, $1 + 11 = 12$

3. $2 + 10 = 12, 3 + 9 = 12, 4 + 8 = 12, 5 + 7 = 12, 6 + 6 = 12$

4. They all have the same sum, 12.

5. Answers may vary.

Activity 2

1. a) i) 37   **ii)** 42   **iii)** 39   **iv)** 12
    b) Answers may vary.
    i) $40 - 3$, 1×37, $37 \div 1$ **ii)** $40 + 2$, 7×6, $84 \div 2$
    iii) $40 - 1$, $30 + 9$, $78 \div 2$ **iv)** 3×4, $10 + 2$, $14 - 2$

2. Answers may vary.   **3.** There is an infinite number.

Activity 3

1. Number sentences may vary.
    a) i) 12 g   **ii)** 16 g   **iii)** 20 g
    b) i) $10 + 1 + 1 = 12$ **ii)** $5 + 5 + 5 + 1 = 16$
    iii) $1 + 1 + 1 + 1 + 1 + 1 + 1 + 1 + 1 + 1 + 1 + 1 + 1 + 1 + 1 + 1 + 1 + 1 + 1 + 1 = 20$
    c) Answers may vary.
    i) $5 + 5 + 1 + 1 = 5 + 1 + 1 + 1 + 1 + 1 + 1 + 1$
    ii) $10 + 5 + 1 = 5 + 5 + 1 + 1 + 1 + 1 + 1 + 1$
    iii) $10 + 10 = 5 + 5 + 5 + 5$

2. Answers may vary.

Activity 4

1. Answers may vary. When two quantities are *equal*, they represent the same amount.

2. The = sign shows that the numbers on the left side represent the same amount as the numbers on the right side.

Working with Mathematics, page 337

1. a, b, f, g, i, j, k, and l

2. a) vi) $18 - 5 = 13$ **b) i)** $8 + 10 = 18$
    c) iv) $3 \times 6 = 18$ **d) ii)** $14 + 4 = 18$
    e) iii) $2 \times 9 = 18$ **f) v)** $18 - 2 = 16$

3. a) $22 + 5 = 27$; Beni delivers 27 papers each day.
    b) $22 - 2 = 20$; Carlene delivers 20 papers each day.
    c) $22 \div 2 = 11$; Martin delivers 11 papers each day.
    d) $6 \times 22 = 132$; Alexander delivers 132 papers each week.

4. Expressions may vary.
    b) i) $28 + 1 = 30 - 1$ **ii)** $7 \times 7 = 50 - 1$ **iii)** $2 \times 16 = 4 \times 8$
    iv) $2 \times 25 = 100 \div 2$ **v)** $10 \times 10 = 90 + 10$
    vi) $80 - 2 = 79 - 1$ **vii)** $5 \times 1 = 6 - 1$
    viii) $7 \times 11 = 80 - 3$ **ix)** $31 \times 1 = 32 - 1$
    c) Answers may vary.

5. a) 5×4 **b)** 24×4 **c)** $23 + 7$ **d)** 3×10
    e) $4 + 2 + 3 + 1.5 + 5 + 4.5$ **f)** $107 - 100$
    $5 \times 4 = 4 + 2 + 3 + 1.5 + 5 + 4.5$; $23 + 7 = 3 \times 10$

6. Answers may vary.
    a) $13 + 13 = 26$ **b)** $13 + 2 = 15$ **c)** $13 - 4 = 9$
    d) $13 \times 2 = 26$ **e)** $35 - 13 = 22$ **f)** $2 \times 13 + 10 = 36$

7. Equations may vary.
    i) a) 23 g   **b)** $5 + 5 + 5 + 5 + 1 + 1 + 1 = 10 + 10 + 1 + 1 + 1$
    ii) a) 16 g   **b)** $10 + 5 + 1 = 5 + 5 + 5 + 1$
    iii) a) 35 g   **b)** $10 + 10 + 10 + 5 = 5 + 5 + 5 + 5 + 5 + 5 + 5$

8. a) $3 + 2 + 1 + 4$ **b)** 8×6.50
    c) $30 \div 3$ **d)** $123.20 \div 5.60$
    e) $6 + 7 + 4 + 3 + 2$ **f)** $108 - 36$
    $3 + 2 + 1 + 4 = 30 \div 3$; $8 \times 6.50 = 108 - 56$;
    $6 + 7 + 4 + 3 + 2 = 123.20 \div 5.60$

9. 3×10, $36 - 6$, $90 \div 3$, 2×15, $28 + 2$; 12×0, $0 \div 5$, $16 - 16$;
    $59 - 20$, 13×3, $39 \div 13 \times 13$, $10 \times 3 + 9$; $7 + 8$, 2×7.5

10. Answers may vary; for example, $2 \times 5 - 7 = 9 \div 3$

11. Equations may vary.
    For example, $12 \times 2 + 13 \times 20 + 14 \times 3 = 326$

Linking Ideas: Mathematics and Technology

More Patterns in a Spreadsheet, page 339

2. The multiples of 3: 3, 6, 9, 12, 15, 18, 21, 24, 27, 30

3. a) The formula is =A1*7.   **b)** The formula is =A1*32.

4. a) 7   **b)** 9, 11, 13, 15, 17, 19, 21, 23, 25
    c) 2, 5, 8, 11, 14, 17, 20, 23, 26, 29

5. Answers may vary.

6. b) The numbers are the multiples of 7.
    d) The numbers are the multiples of 7.
    e) The numbers are equal because the formulas are equivalent.

7. a) The formula is =A1*4–A1*3.
    b) The numbers are 1, 2, 3, 4, 5, 6, 7, 8, 9, 10.
    c) The formula is =A1*(4–3).
    d) The numbers are 1, 2, 3, 4, 5, 6, 7, 8, 9, 10.
    e) The numbers are the same because the formulas are equivalent.

Quest: How Much Material Do You Require to Frame a Picture?, page 340

The length of framing material needed is $2l + 2w + 8f$. The cost is $c(2l + 2w + 8f)$ dollars.

7.4 Equations Involving Variables

Developing the Ideas, page 342

Activity 1

1. i) 3   **ii)** 10   **iii)** 12   **iv)** 7   **v)** 10   **vi)** 8

2. Variables may differ.
    i) x **ii)** $2x$ **iii)** $3x$ **iv)** $x + 2$ **v)** $x + 3$ **vi)** $x + 4$

3. a) The masses of the objects on each side of the balance are equal. So, the numbers of candies on each side of the balance are equal.
    b) i) $x = 3$ **ii)** $2x = 10$ **iii)** $3x = 12$
    iv) $x + 2 = 7$ **v)** $x + 3 = 10$ **vi)** $x + 4 = 8$

4. i) 3   **ii)** 5   **iii)** 4   **iv)** 5   **v)** 7   **vi)** 4

Activity 2

Variables may differ.

1. a) $x + 3 = 41$ **b)** $y - 8 = 19$

c) $2z = 23$ d) $\frac{k}{9} = 15$ e) $\frac{39}{m} = 3$

2. Let c represent the cost of a cassette tape. $17.99 = c + 9.00$

3. Let n represent the number of toppings. $2.40 = 0.80n$

Working with Mathematics, page 344

1. So that you can use the same variable to describe the number of candies in each bag

2. a) iii) $n + 2$ b) v) $2n + 3$ c) ii) $3n$
   d) vi) $3n + 2$ e) i) $2n$ f) iv) $n + 3$

3. a) $4n$ b) $n + 4$ c) $n + 5$
   d) $2n + 4$ e) $3n + 3$

5. a) $n + 6 = 14$
   $n = 14 + 6$: A number is equal to the sum of 14 and 6.
   $6n = 14$: 6 times a number is 14.
   b) $\frac{m}{3} = 8$
   $\frac{3}{m} = 8$: 3 divided by a number is 8.
   $3m = 8$: 3 times a number is 8.
   c) $p - 6 = 9$
   $p = 9 - 6$; A number is equal to the difference of 9 and 6.
   $6 - p = 9$: 6 decreased by a number is 9.

6. Variables may differ.
   a) $x + 1 = 8$; there are 7 candies in each bag.
   b) $2x = 8$; there are 4 candies in each bag.
   c) $x + 3 = 10$; there are 7 candies in each bag.
   d) $3x = 15$; there are 5 candies in each bag.

8. Variables may differ.
   a) $a + 8 = 36$ b) $\frac{b}{5} = 13$
   c) $3c = 33$ d) $d + 5 = 47$
   e) $99 - e = 75$ f) $\frac{f}{4} = 3$
   g) $\frac{27}{g} = 9$ h) $h - 7 = 14$

9. Some sentences may vary.
   a) 4 more than a number is 11.
   b) 9 increased by a number is 13.
   c) 4 times a number is 20.
   d) 6 times a number is 48.
   e) 15 decreased by a number is 7.
   f) A number decreased by 18 is 22.
   g) A number divided by 6 is 5.
   h) A number divided by 3 is 11.
   i) 18 divided by a number is 3.
   j) 22 divided by a number is 2.

10. a) $n - 4$ b) $n - 4 = 20$

11. a) $6n$ b) $108 = 6n$

12. Answers may vary; $\frac{c}{6} = 5$, or $c = 5 \times 6$

13. Answers may vary. An example is given for each equation.
    a) In 4 years, Shauna will be 9. Her age now is x.
    b) Joshua is 29 years old. y years ago, he was 23.
    c) 3 children are given s dollars to share equally. When they do this, they each get $18.
    d) An item costs $1.99 each. You can buy x for $19.99.

14. Variables may differ.
    a) $x - 3 = 19$ b) $8y = 56$ c) $37 - z = 13$
    d) $k + 4 = 52$ e) $6c = 8.94$

15. Some sentences may vary.
    a) A number increased by 9 is 101.
    b) 5 times a number is 65.
    c) A number subtracted from 18 is 7.
    d) A number decreased by 1 is 35.

e) A number divided by 5 is 13.
f) 51 divided by a number is 17.

16. a) $d + 3$ b) $d + 3 = 12$

17. a) $2t$ b) $2t = 6$

18. a) $w = 10 - 2$, or $w = 8$ b) $w + 5 = 10$
    c) $60 = 10w$ d) $30 = 2w + 20$

7.5 Finding the Value of a Variable

Developing the Ideas, page 346

Activity 1

1. a) 3 units   b) 2 units   c) 9 units

2.

Length of side (units)	1	2	3	4	5	6
Perimeter of figure (units)	3	6	9	12	15	18

3. Multiply the length of a side by 3.

4. $P = 3s$ 5. 36 units

6. Divide the perimeter by 3.   7. 10 units

8. The equations should be the same.

Activity 2

2.

Width of rectangle (units)	1	2	3	4	5	6	7	8
Length of rectangle (units)	5	6	7	8	9	10	11	12

3. Add 4 units to the width.   4. $l = 4 + w$

5. 24 units   6. Subtract 4 units from the length.

7. 23 units   8. The equations should be the same.

Working with Mathematics, page 350

1. a) 24   b) 20

2. a) 20   b) 12

3. a) 4   b) 17   c) -3 d) 28   e) 40
   f) 13   g) 9   h) 9   i) 7

4. a) 4, 5, 6, 7, 8   b) 7th position
   c) 7; it is equal to the position of the number 10 in the pattern.

5. a) 4, 8, 12, 16, 20   b) 7th position
   c) 7; it is equal to the position of the number 28 in the pattern.

6. a) What number do we multiply by 3 to get 24? 8
   b) What number do we add to 2 to get 18? 16
   c) What number do we add to 3 to get 64? 61
   d) What number do we subtract from 12 to get 3? 9
   e) What number is greater than 15 by 3? 18
   f) What number do we multiply by 2 to get 100? 50
   g) What number do we divide by 2 to get 15? 30
   h) What number do we divide by 3 to get 7? 21
   i) What number do we add to 7 to get 22? 15
   j) What number do we subtract from 50 to get 31? 19

7. a)

Number of triangles	1	2	3	4	5	6
Perimeter of figure (units)	3	4	5	6	7	8

b) Add 2 to the number of triangles.
c) $P = n + 2$ d) 12 units   e) 18

8. a) 11, 12, 13, 14, 15   b) 33rd position

9. a) i) 7, 8, 9, 10   **ii)** 30th
b) i) 3, 6, 9, 12   **ii)** 12th
c) i) $\frac{1}{3}, \frac{2}{3}, 1, \frac{4}{3}$ **ii)** 108th
d) i) 49, 48, 47, 46   **ii)** 14th
e) i) $\frac{1}{2}, 1, \frac{3}{2}, 2$ **ii)** 72nd
f) i) 21, 22, 23, 24   **ii)** 16th
g) i) −1, 0, 1, 2   **ii)** 38th
h) i) 4, 8, 12, 16   **ii)** 9th
i) i) 9, 18, 27, 36   **ii)** 4th
j) i) 3, 6, 9, 12   **ii)** 12th
k) i) 16, 17, 18, 19   **ii)** 21st
l) i) $\frac{1}{10}, \frac{1}{5}, \frac{3}{10}, \frac{2}{5}$ **iii)** 360th

10. a) 6   **b)** 12   **c)** 30   **d)** 11   **e)** 16   **f)** 5
    g) 8   **h)** 8   **i)** 15   **j)** 8   **k)** 10   **l)** 7

11. The equations in parts a, g, and i are true when $x = 3$.

12. a) $24 = 10 + 6 + x$ **b)** 8 cm

13. Answers may vary.

14. a) $36 = 12w$ **b)** 3 cm

15. Answers may vary.

16. Expressions may vary. Variables may differ.
   i) a) 3×5 **b)** $15 = 3 \times 5$ **c)** $15 = 3a$
   ii) a) $40 - 4$ **b)** $36 = 40 - 4$ **c)** $36 = 40 - a$
   iii) a) $60 + 8$ **b)** $68 = 60 + 8$ **c)** $68 = a + 8$

17. a) Explanations may vary. The length and width increase by 1 unit each time.
   c)

Width of rectangle (units)	1	2	3	4	5	6	7	8
Length of rectangle (units)	2	3	4	5	6	7	8	9

   d) Add 1 unit to the width.
   e) $l = w + 1$ **f)** 34 units   **g)** 101 units

18. a) 6, 12, 18, 24   **b)** 9th

19. a) i) 8, 9, 10   **ii)** 21st
   b) i) 39, 38, 37   **ii)** 12th
   c) i) $\frac{1}{2}, 1, \frac{3}{2}$ **ii)** 56th
   d) i) 7, 14, 21   **ii)** 4th

20. The equations in parts a, b, d, f, and g are true when $x = 4$.

21. a) 9   **b)** 18   **c)** 8   **d)** 12

22. a) $30 = x + 9 + 9$ **b)** 12 cm

23. a) $45 = 9w$ **b)** 5 cm

24. a) $72 = l \times w$
   b) i) 20 cm   **ii)** 1.8 cm

25. a) $72 = 2 \times l + 2 \times w$
   b) i) 31.5 cm   **ii)** 10.5 cm

7.6 Representing the Steps in the Solution of an Equation with a Two-Pan Balance

Developing the Ideas, page 353

1. a) $2x = 6$ **b)** 3; explanations may vary.
   c) Imagine replacing each bag with 3 candies. Check whether there would be the same number of candies in each pan.

2. a) $y + 5 = 12$ **b)** Answers may vary.
   c) There are numbers on both sides of the equation.

3. a) Remove 5 candies.
   b) $y = 7$ **c)** 7

4. i) a) $2x + 1 = 13$ **b)** $2x = 12$ **c)** 6

ii) a) $x + 3 = 8$ **b)** $x = 5$ **c)** 5
iii) a) $x + 5 = 9$ **b)** $x = 4$ **c)** 4
iv) a) $2x = x + 5$ **b)** $x = 5$ **c)** 5

Working with Mathematics, page 356

1. So that you can write an equation relating both sides of the balance

2. Just as the two sides of an equation are equal, when the two pans of the scale are balanced, the objects in each pan have equal mass.

3. a) iii) $2x = 12$; $x = 6$ **b) ii)** $6 = x + 4$; $x = 2$
   c) vi) $4 + x = 10$; $x = 6$ **d) i)** $x + 2 = 6$; $x = 4$
   e) iv) $3x = 6$; $x = 2$ **f) v)** $10 = 2x$; $x = 5$

4. a) $x + 4 = 8$; $x = 4$ **b)** $2x = 14$; $x = 7$
   c) $x + 3 = 10$; $x = 7$ **d)** $15 = 3x$; $x = 5$
   e) $3x = 2x + 7$; $x = 7$

5. a) 3   **b)** 6   **c)** 4   **d)** 5

6. a) $a = 3$ **b)** $b = 5$ **c)** $c = 7$ **d)** $d = 5$ **e)** $e = 7$
   f) $f = 4$ **g)** $g = 9$ **h)** $h = 4$ **i)** $k = 7$ **j)** $m = 4$

7. $2x = 10$; Angela's weekly allowance is $5.

8. $n + 5 = 13$; there were 8 fish in the aquarium.

9. $3p = 15$; there are 5 cards in each pack.

10. $7 + c = 11$; Janeesha gave Maurice 4 comic books.

11. a) $x + 2 = 7$; $x = 5$ **b)** $2x = 8$; $x = 4$
   c) $12 = 3x$; $x = 4$ **d)** $5 = x + 1$; $x = 4$
   e) $x + 7 = 10$; $x = 3$ **f)** $2x + 5 = 3x$; $x = 5$

12. a) $c = 6$ **b)** $w = 4$ **c)** $p = 5$ **d)** $x = 5$

13. 1 circle and 1 diamond; You can remove 1 diamond from each pan and still maintain the balance. Each square then balances 1 circle and 1 diamond. You can remove 1 square from the left and 1 circle and 1 diamond from the right and still maintain the balance.

7.7 Modelling the Steps in the Solution of an Equation with Algebra Tiles

Developing the Ideas, page 358

1. a) $3x + 4$ **b)** $2x - 2$ **c)** $2x + 5$ **d)** $x - 3$

2. When $x = 2$:
   a) 10   **b)** 2   **c)** 9   **d)** −1
   When $x = -3$:
   a) −5   **b)** −8   **c)** −1   **d)** −6

3. When $x = 4$:
   a) 7   **b)** 3   **c)** 8   **d)** 9   **e)** −3   **f)** −8
   When $x = -1$:
   a) 2   **b)** −2   **c)** −2   **d)** −1   **e)** 7   **f)** 2

Working with Mathematics, page 363

1. Because we cannot show negative numbers on the two-pan balance.

2. To solve an equation is to find the value(s) of the variable for which the equation is true.

3. No, we do not have a way of showing decimals using the tiles or the two-pan balance.

5. Replace each x-tile with the number of unit tiles from your answer.

6. a) $5 - 3x$; −1; 8   **b)** $2x + 8$; 12; 6

8. When $x = 3$:
   a) 8   **b)** 10   **c)** 1   **d)** 9   **e)** 15

f) −9   **g)** 5   **h)** −5   **i)** −10

When $x = -4$:

a) 1   **b)** 3   **c)** −6   **d)** −12   **e)** −20

f) 12   **g)** −16   **h)** 23   **i)** 4

9. $3x = 9$; $\frac{3x}{3} = \frac{9}{3}$; $x = 3$

10. $x + 5 = 3$; $x + 5 - 5 = 3 - 5$; $x = -2$

11. a) $x + 2 = 5$ **b)** $5 = x + 1$ **c)** $x - 1 = 2$
d) $4 = x - 1$ **e)** $2x = 4$ **f)** $-6 = -3x$

12. a) $x = 3$ **b)** $x = 4$ **c)** $x = 3$
d) $x = 5$ **e)** $x = 2$ **f)** $x = 2$

13. a) $a = 5$ **b)** $b = 3$ **c)** $c = -1$
d) $d = 7$ **e)** $e = 2$ **f)** $f = -1$

14. a) $k = 5$ **b)** $w = 13$ **c)** $s = -3$
d) $p = 10$ **e)** $d = -5$ **f)** $b = 5$

15. a) $g = 12$ **b)** $y = 8$ **c)** $k = -1$
d) $x = 2$ **e)** $d = 3$ **f)** $x = -2$

Variables may differ in exercises 16 to 19.

16. $3x - 15$; each sister should receive 5 pogs.

17. $12 - y = 7$; Amanda lent 5 CDs to Melissa.

18. $s - 2 = -5$; the temperature on Saturday was −3°C.

19. $4b = 8$; two students went with Mr. Bernstein.

20. a) $3 = x - 3$ **b)** $-6 = 3x$
c) $-2x = 4$ **d)** $x - 2 = -3$

21. a) $a = 7$ **b)** $b = -4$ **c)** $c = 6$
d) $d = -12$ **e)** $e = 7$ **f)** $f = 10$
g) $g = -2$ **h)** $h = -5$ **i)** $i = 2$
j) $j = 3$ **k)** $k = -1$ **l)** $l = 7$

22. a) $x + 3 = 11$; Shaulin is 8.   **b)** $x - 5 = 9$; Shaulin is 14.
c) $x = \frac{14}{2}$; Shaulin is 7.   **d)** $3x = 12$; Shaulin is 4.

23. a) $x = 3$ **b)** $x = 1$ **c)** $x = 2$
d) $x = -2$ **e)** $x = 2$ **f)** $x = -3$

Review, page 365

1. a) Each square has a side length 1 unit greater than the preceding square. Each unshaded region is a square with side length 1 unit greater than the preceding unshaded region.

c)

Position in pattern	1	2	3	4	5	6	7
Number of shaded squares	1	3	5	7	9	11	13

f) 15   **g)** 53

h) The number of shaded squares is 1 less than two times the position of the figure.

i) $2n - 1$

2. a)

Position in pattern	1	2	3	4	5	6	7	8
Number of small squares	1	4	9	16	25	36	49	64

d) Multiply 20 by itself to get 400.

e) Variables may differ. $n \times n$ **f)** 1369

3. a) 5; 10; 15   **b)** $5r$ **c)** 40

d) $5r = 65$; there are 13 rows in the wall.

e) 1; 2; 3   **f)** $\frac{r}{2}$, where r is an even number

g) 12   **h)** $\frac{r}{2} = 15$; there are 30 rows in the wall.

4. a)

Number of lengths	1	2	3	4	5
Number of posts	3	5	7	9	11
Number of bolts	10	16	22	28	34

b) The number of posts is 1 greater than twice the number of lengths; $2l + 1$

c) The number of bolts is 4 greater than 6 times the number of lengths. $6l + 4$

d) 15 posts and 46 posts

e) 11 lengths

f) 8 lengths

5. a) 17   **b)** 34   **c)** Variables may differ. $n + 5$

6. a) 105   **b)** 147   **c)** Variables may differ. $7n$

7. a) i) 7, 8, 9, 10, 11   **ii)** 18th
b) i) 4, 9, 14, 19, 24   **ii)** 5th
c) i) $\frac{1}{3}, \frac{2}{3}, \frac{3}{3}, \frac{4}{3}, \frac{5}{3}$ **ii)** 72nd
d) i) 4, 8, 12, 16, 20   **ii)** 6th

8. a)

Number of hours	1	2	3	4
Number of oil changes completed	3	6	9	12

b) Multiply the number of hours by 3.

c) 21

d) $3n$

e) $3n = 18$; she has worked 6 h.

9. $2 \times 3 = 5 + 1$; $9 + 1 = 8 + 2$; $2 \times 8 = 7 + 9$; $8 + 4 = 2 \times 6$; $13 \times 1 = 1 + 12$; $6 \times 3 = 9 \times 2$

10. a) $6 + 2 = 8$
b) $7 \times 2 = 14$, or $14 \div 7 = 2$, or $14 \div 2 = 7$
c) $10 + 5 = 5 + 5 + 5$

11. a) 12×7 **b)** $69 \div 3$ **c)** 4.7×260
d) 3×2 **e)** $36 \div 4$ **f)** 8×5
g) $18.25 - 13.40$ **h)** $28 - 5$

12. a) 16   **b)** 15   **c)** 7   **d)** 16

13. a) i) $n + 7$
ii) $n + 7 = 13$; there are 6 fish in David's aquarium.
b) i) $2n$
ii) $2n = 18$; there are 9 fish in David's aquarium.

14. a) $A = 12w$ **b)** $w = 5$

15. a) $x + 3 = 5$; $x = 2$ **b)** $2x = 10$; $x = 5$
c) $x + 4 = 9$; $x = 5$

16. $n + 6 = 15$; 9 game CDs were rented.

17. a) $a = 4$ **b)** $b = 4$ **c)** $c = -2$
d) $d = 6$ **e)** $e = -4$ **f)** $f = -2$

18. $t - 5 = -1$; the temperature at 7 p.m. was 4°C.

CHAPTER 8 THREE-DIMENSIONAL GEOMETRY

Start With What You Know, page 372

1. a) Answers may vary.

2. Answers may vary.

3. a) About 3.0 m²   **b)** About 2000 m²

4. a) About 7700 m²   **b)** The surface would be smooth.

5. Answers may vary.

6. Answers will vary, depending on the current year.

8.1 Constructing Polyhedra

Working with Mathematics, page 378

1. a) Tetrahedron **b)** Rectangular prism
c) Cube **d)** Triangular prism

2. a) In the rectangular prism and the cube: AD ∥ BC ∥ FG ∥ EH;
AB ∥ DC ∥ HG ∥ EF; AE ∥ BF ∥ CG ∥ DH
In the triangular prism: AB ∥ DE; BC ∥ EF; AD ∥ BE ∥ CF;
AC ∥ DF
In the square pyramid: BE ∥ CD; BC ∥ ED
In the triangular pyramid, no edges are parallel.
In the rectangular pyramid: BE ∥ CD; BC ∥ ED

b) In the rectangular prism and the cube:
AB ⊥ AD ⊥ AE; BC ⊥ BF ⊥ BA; CD ⊥ CG ⊥ CB;
DA ⊥ DC ⊥ DH; EA ⊥ EF ⊥ EH; FB ⊥ FG ⊥ FE;
GC ⊥ GH ⊥ GF; HD ⊥ HG ⊥ HE
In the triangular prism:
AD ⊥ AC; DF ⊥ AD; CF ⊥ CA; EF ⊥ BE;
AB ⊥ AD; DE ⊥ AD; BC ⊥ BE; BE ⊥ DE;
AB ⊥ BE; CF ⊥ CB; CF ⊥ DF; CF ⊥ FE
In the square pyramid and the rectangular pyramid:
BC ⊥ BE; CD ⊥ BC; DE ⊥ CD; BE ⊥ DE
In the triangular pyramid, no edges are perpendicular.

c) In the rectangular prism: AE = DH = BF = CG;
AB = DC = GH = FE; AD = BC = FG = EH
In the cube, all edges have the same length.
In the triangular prism: AC = CB = BA = DE = EF = FD;
AD = BE = CF
In the square pyramid: AB = AC = AD = AE;
BC = CD = DE = EB
In the triangular pyramid, all edges have the same length.
In the rectangular pyramid: CD = BE; BC = DE

3. a) In the rectangular prism and the cube: ABCD ∥ EFGH;
BCGF ∥ ADHE; ABFE ∥ DCGH
In the triangular prism: ABC ∥ DEF
In the square, triangular, and rectangular pyramids, there are
no parallel faces.

b) In the rectangular prism and the cube:
ABCD ⊥ BFGC, CGHD, ADHE, ABFE;
BCGF ⊥ ABCD, EFGH, ABFE, CGHD;
EFGH ⊥ BCGF, ADHE, ABFE, CGHD;
ADHE ⊥ ABCD, EFGH, ABFE, CGHD;
ABFE ⊥ ABCD, EFGH, BCGF, ADHE;
DCGH ⊥ ABCD, EFGH, BCGF, ADHE
In the triangular prism: ABC ⊥ ACFD, ABED, BCFE;
DEF ⊥ ACFD, ABED, BCFE
In the square, rectangular, and triangular pyramids, no faces
are perpendicular.

c) In the rectangular prism: ABCD, EFGH; ABFE, DCGH;
ADHE, BCGF
In the cube, all faces have the same size and shape.
In the triangular prism: ABC, DEF; ABED, BCFE, ACFD
In the square pyramid: ABC, ACD, ADE, ABE
In the triangular pyramid, all faces have the same size and
shape.
In the rectangular pyramid, no faces have the same size and
shape.

4. a) Triangular prism
b) Square pyramid, triangular pyramid, rectangular pyramid
c) Rectangular prism, cube
d) Cube, triangular pyramid

5. Cube, tetrahedron

6. a) Rectangular prism, cube, triangular prism, triangular
pyramid
b) Rectangular prism, cube, triangular prism, triangular
pyramid

8. Yes

9. a) i, iv, v **b)** Answers may vary.

10. Answers may vary. Spaceship Earth, Great Pyramid, and
Canadian Mint

11. Answers may vary.

12. a) Rectangle **b)** Scalene right triangle
c) Equilateral triangle

15. a) Number of sides + 2 **b)** 3 × number of sides
c) 2 × number of sides

16. a) Number of sides + 1 **b)** 2 × number of sides
c) Number of sides + 1

Quest: Relating Faces, Vertices, and Edges of Polyhedra, page 380

The number of edges is 2 less than the sum of the numbers of
faces and vertices.

8.2 Surface Area of a Rectangular Prism

Developing the Ideas, page 382

1. a) 6 **b)** Yes, opposite faces
c) Answers may vary. Calculate the area of each face that is
different. Add the three areas and multiply by 2.

2. Answers may vary.

Working with Mathematics, page 384

1. a) Opposite faces
b) Answers may vary. Count the squares on each face.

2. Answers may vary. Calculate the area of 5 faces of the cube.
Calculate the areas of pairs of opposite vertical faces of the
larger prism. Calculate the area of the top face of the larger
prism less the area of one face of the cube. Add these areas.

3. a) No. The cube would cover the same area of wallpaper.
b) 16.44 m^2; the cube would cover the same area of wallpaper
on any face.

4. a) 6 cm^2 **b)** 16 cm^2 **c)** 8 m^2
d) 9.9 cm^2 **e)** 2.89 cm^2 **f)** 0.01 m^2

5. a) 190 cm^2 **b)** 177.12 m^2 **c)** 532 cm^2 **d)** 216 m^2

6. a) 112 cm^2 **b)** 337.5 cm^2 **c)** 50 m^2

7. a) i) 150 cm^2 **ii)** 600 cm^2 **iii)** 1350 cm^2
b) Multiply the edge length by itself, then multiply the answer
by 6.

8. a) 1444 cm^2 **b)** 541.5 cm^2 **c)** 902.5 cm^2

9. 1083 cm^2, 451.25 cm^2, 812.25 cm^2

10. 64 cm^2 **11.** 5.92 m^2 **12.** 1.04 m^2 **13.** 440 cm^2

14. a) 28 cm^2 **b)** 24 cm^2, 34 cm^2

15. a) Estimates may vary.
b) 1530 m^2; not including the base **c)** $1224

16. a) 24 cm^2 **b)** 18 cm^2

17. a) Surface area increases. **b)** Surface area increases.
c) Surface area is multiplied by 4 and multiplied by 9.

18. 10 cm **19.** 100

8.3 Volume of a Rectangular Prism

Developing the Ideas, page 386

1. Answers may vary.

2. a) Fill the box with centimetre cubes, then count the cubes.
   b) Answers may vary.

3. a) Multiply the length by the width. The result is the number of cubes.
   b) Multiply the product of length and width in part a by the height. The result is the number of centimetre cubes, and also the volume in cubic centimetres.

Working with Mathematics, page 388

1. No; explanations may vary.

2. a) Doubled; tripled
   b) Quadrupled; multiplied by a factor of 9
   c) Multiplied by a factor of 8; multiplied by a factor of 27

3. a) Answers may vary; for example: 1 cm by 1 cm by 36 cm, 1 cm by 3 cm by 12 cm, 1 cm by 4 cm by 9 cm, 1 cm by 6 cm by 6 cm, 2 cm by 2 cm by 9 cm, 2 cm by 4 cm by 4.5 cm, 2 cm by 5 cm by 3.6 cm, 6 cm by 2 cm by 3 cm, 3 cm by 3 cm by 4 cm, 18 cm by 2 cm by 1 cm

4. a) 8 cm^3 **b)** 50 cm^3 **c)** 24 cm^3 **d)** 18.6 cm^3

5. 648 cm^3, 146.2 cm^3, 8.6 cm^3, 4.3 cm^3

6. a) 1620 cm^3 **b)** 1066 cm^3

7. a) 18 cm^3 **b)** 90 m^3 **c)** 1500 cm^3 **d)** 2 cm^3

8. About 9 min

9. a) Answers may vary; for example, 1 cm by 1 cm by 60 cm, 1 cm by 3 cm by 20 cm, 1 cm by 4 cm by 15 cm, 1 cm by 6 cm by 10 cm, 1 cm by 8 cm by 7.5 cm, 2 cm by 2 cm by 15 cm, 2 cm by 4 cm by 7.5 cm, 10 cm by 3 cm by 2 cm, 5 cm by 6 cm by 2 cm, 12 cm by 5 cm by 1 cm, 4 cm by 5 cm by 3 cm, 30 cm by 2 cm by 1 cm
   b) No; explanations may vary.

10. Answers may vary; about $1 000 000 U.S.

11. a) 256 m^3 **b)** 192 cm^3 **c)** 64 cm^3
   d) 11.56 m^3 **e)** 0.125 m^3

12. a) 5031 cm^3 **b)** 7165 cm^3 **c)** 2660 cm^3

13. 3990 cm^3, 5320 cm^3

14. 54 000 cm^3

15. 6 cm

16. a) 3 cm **b)** 10 cm **c)** 30 cm

17. a) 585 cm^3 **b)** 72 m^3

18. About 4

19. a) The volume increases. The volume decreases.
   b) Estimates may vary.
      i) 40 cm^3 **ii)** 80 cm^3 **iii)** 160 cm^3
   c) The volume doubles.
   d) Estimates may vary.
      i) 3 cm **ii)** 6 cm **iii)** 12 cm
   e) The height doubles.

20. a) 24 000 000 cm^3, or 24 m^3 **b)** About 38

21. 30 m

Mathematics File: What Shapes Make Cardboard Cylinders?, page 391

1. a) Parallelogram **c)** Answers may vary.

2. c) 3.8 cm, 12.0 cm; 5.4 cm, 8.5 cm

3. The parallelogram is a rhombus.

Quest: How Much Space Do 1.4 Billion Crayons Occupy?, page 392

Answers may vary.

Review, page 394

1. Explanations may vary.

2. a) 6 **b)** 5 **c)** 3 **d)** 6

3. a) Prism **b)** Prism **c)** Pyramid **d)** Prism

4. a, c **5.** Diagrams will vary.

6. a) About 47 m^2 **b)** About 41 m^2 remain **c)** About 8 L

7. a) 150 cm^2 **b)** 496 cm^2

8. a) About 69 m^2 **b)** 23 sheets

9. a) 2350 cm^2 **b)** 1975 cm^2, 1975 cm^2
   c) 2050 cm^2, 1850 cm^2
   d) 3125 cm^2; all faces of a cube are congruent.

10. a) i) 1 cm **ii)** 4 cm **iii)** 5 cm
   b) Divide the surface area by 6, then find which number multiplied by itself is equal to the quotient.

11. a) 214 cm^2, 210 cm^3 **b)** 368 cm^2, 420 cm^3
   c) 180 m^2, 144 m^3 **d)** 324 m^2, 288 m^3

12. a) No **b)** Yes

13. a) 270 cm^3 **b)** 115.2 cm^3 **c)** 1200 cm^3 **d)** 125 cm^3

14. a), b), c), d) Answers will vary.
   e) i) Yes **ii)** No

15. a) 98 cm^3 **b)** 390 cm^3 **c)** 28 m^3 **d)** 729 m^3

16. 27 cm^3 **17.** About 2455 truckloads

18. a) 56 392 cm^3 **b)** 5382 cm^3

19. Answers may vary.

Cumulative Review, page 396A

1. a) centimetres **b)** kilometres **c)** centimetres
   d) metres **e)** millimetres

2. The figures are congruent. $\angle$A = $\angle$Z, $\angle$B = $\angle$X, $\angle$C = $\angle$Y, AB = ZX, BC = XY, CA = YZ

3. a) $\frac{11}{10}$, or $1\frac{1}{10}$ **b)** $\frac{3}{8}$ **c)** $3\frac{3}{6}$, or $3\frac{1}{2}$
   d) $\frac{3}{4}$ **e)** $\frac{5}{10}$ **f)** $1\frac{7}{8}$

4. a) 5.46 **b)** 1.38 **c)** 5.4 **d)** 0.81

5. The repeating decimals are rounded to 2 decimal places.
   a) 0.5; 50% **b)** 0.75; 75%
   c) 0.8; 80% **d)** 0.7; 70%
   e) 0.375; 37.5% **f)** 0.22; 22%
   g) 0.53; 53% **h)** 0.42; 42%

6. a) $135.00 **b)** $4.54 **c)** $17.98
   d) $9.95 **e)** $0.48 **f)** $262.13

7. a) 38 **b)** 15 **c)** 13 **d)** 9 **e)** 14 **f)** 2

8. a) 10 **b)** 15 **c)** 20

9. a) Graphs may vary. A bar graph would be suitable.
   b) Descriptions may vary. The graph is bell-shaped.
   c) Based on the shape of the graph, one would predict that the Maritime provinces have the coolest summer temperatures, and Ontario and Manitoba have the warmest summer temperatures.

10. Answers may vary.

a) A set of 2 numbers less than or equal to 11, 2 numbers greater than or equal to 11, and the number 11, such that the sum of all 5 numbers is 70

b) A set of 6 numbers, such that when arranged in order from least to greatest, the 3rd and 4th numbers have a sum of 22, and the sum of all 6 numbers is 84

c) A set of 7 numbers with a sum of 175, such that the number that occurs most often is 21

11. Answers may vary. It could be that many more teenagers ski than any other age group. Similarly, it could be that very few people over the age of 50 ski.

12. a) -3 **b)** $+153$ **c)** -8 **d)** -12

13. a) $+4$ **b)** 0 **c)** $+8$ **d)** $+3$ **e)** -22 **f)** $+21$

14. a) 105 cm^2 **b)** 180 cm^2 **c)** 570 cm^2 **d)** 360 cm^2

15. i) a) Each number is a multiple of 6.

b) 90 **c)** 120 **d)** $6n$

ii) a) Each number is 1 more than the preceding number. Each is the sum of 8 and a number.

b) 23 **c)** 28 **d)** $8 + n$

iii) a) Each number is 1 less than the preceding number. Each is the difference between 30 and a number.

b) 15 **c)** 10 **d)** $30 - n$

iv) a) Each number is equal to 100 divided by a number.

b) $\frac{100}{15}$, or $\frac{20}{3}$ **c)** 5 **d)** $\frac{100}{n}$

v) a) Each number is equal to 180 divided by a number.

b) 12 **c)** 9 **d)** $\frac{180}{n}$

16. a) $a + 5 = 21$; $a = 16$ **b)** $\frac{b}{3} = 10$; $b = 30$

c) $8 - c = -7$; $c = 15$ **d)** $2d = 36$; $d = 18$

e) $e + 12 = 19$; $e = 7$

17. Some sentences may vary.

a) A number increased by 7 is 18; $a = 11$

b) 3 times a number is -21; $b = -7$

c) 15 decreased by a number is 6; $c = 9$

d) A number divided by 3 is 15; $d = 45$

e) A number divided by 4 is -2; $e = -8$

f) A number increased by 4 is -8; $f = -12$

g) A number decreased by 11 is -2; $g = 9$

h) A number increased by 3 is 10; $h = 7$

18. a) 7 **b)** 4 **c)** $-3°C$

CHAPTER 9 TRANSFORMATIONS

Start With What You Know, page 400

2. The pieces in each pair are flips. It is helpful to have both pieces because you cannot transform one piece to get the other using the three commands available to you.

4. Answers may vary.

5. You do not need the matching pairs described in exercise 2 since you can flip pieces in the *Ten Tiles* puzzle by turning them over.

6. a) Triangle   **b)** Rectangle   **c)** Trapezoid

Linking Ideas: Mathematics and Technology
Exploring Transformations with a Paint or Draw Program, page 402

1. Answers may vary.

3. c) The centre figure is created using a translation and a reflection. Each of the other figures is a rotation image of the centre figure.

4. , 5. Answers may vary.

9.1 Translations
Developing the Ideas, page 404

1. The figures have the same size and shape and face the same direction.

2. Answers may vary.

Working with Mathematics, page 406

1. Answers may vary.

2. a) Yes; 5 units left, 2 units down

b) Yes; 5 units right, 2 units up

c) No; the figures are not congruent.

3. a) II and III

b) None of the parts are related by a translation.

c) I and IV, II and III   **d)** I and III, II and IV

4. Explainations may vary.

a) True   **b)** True

5. Green: 2 units right, 2 units down; yellow: 6 units right, 4 units down; purple: 5 units down

6. Drawings may vary.

8. Each image is congruent to the original figure.

a) X′(−5, 5), Y′(−3, 9), Z′(0, 2)

b) D′(6, −6), E′(1, 2), F′(−2, −4), G′(3, −8)

9. a) Quadrilateral; 3 units right, 4 units down

b) Triangle; 4 units left, 5 units up

c) Pentagon; 6 units right, 1 unit down

d) Triangle; 5 units left, 2 units down

10. There are three possible translations.

i) 3 units left and 2 units up; the coordinates are A(6, 2), B(3, −2), and C(6, −2)

ii) 3 units left and 2 units down; the coordinates are A(6, 6), B(3, 2), and C(6, 2)

iii) 6 units left and 2 units down; the coordinates are A(9, 6), B(6, 2), and C(9, 2)

11. There are four possible translations.

i) 3 units left and 5 units down; the coordinates are P(−1, 4), Q(−1, 6), R(4, 6), S(4, 4)

ii) 3 units left and 3 units down; the coordinates are P(−1, 2), Q(−1, 4), R(4, 4), S(4, 2)

iii) 2 units right and 5 units down; the coordinates are P(−6, 4), Q(−6, 6), R(−1, 6), S(−1, 4)

iv) 2 units right and 3 units down; the coordinates are P(−6, 2), Q(−6, 4), R(−1, 4), S(−1, 2)

12. The number of possible translations is equal to the number vertices the figure has. For a pentagon, there would be five possible translations. Examples may vary.

13. Red: 3 units down; purple: 4 units right and 1 unit down; grey: 5 units right and 5 units down

15. b) Parallelogram

c) 3 units left and 2 units down; 3 units right and 2 units down; 3 units left and 2 units up

16. a) 6 units right and 3 units down

b) 4 units left and 2 units down

17. a) The coordinates are P(−6, 0), Q(−1, 1), R(−1, 6), S(−3, 2).

b) The coordinates are P(–3, 8), Q(2, 9), R(2, 14), S(0, 10).

c) The coordinates are P(3, –1), Q(8, 0), R(8, 5), S(6, 1).

19. Any line for which you move 3 units right and 2 units up to get to another point on the line

9.2 Reflections
Developing the Ideas, page 409

1. AA′, BB′, and CC′ are all perpendicular to the mirror line.

3. The figures are the same size and shape, but face different directions.

Working with Mathematics, page 412

1. a) Yes **b)** Yes

2. a) I and III, III and IV, I and IV
b) I and II, III and IV
c) , **d)** None of the parts are related to one another by a reflection.

3. a) 3 **b)** 4 **c)** 1 **d)** 5 **e)** 2 **f)** 1

4. Answers may vary. Each point on the square on one side of the line of symmetry has a matching point on the other side of the line.

5. No, explanations may vary. The black and white are reversed; the patchwork pattern in the fields and the birds in the sky are not symmetric.

6. Green: horizontal; blue: vertical; orange: horizontal; purple: slanted

8. b) Designs may vary.

9. a) Quadrilateral; A′(1, –4), B′(–2, 3), C′(–4, –1), D′(–3, –5)
b) Right triangle; X′(–7, –4), Y′(–7, 0), Z′(–2, 0)
c) Parallelogram; N′(2, –5), P′(3, 0), Q′(7, –2), R′(6, –7)
d) Triangle; K′(3, 4), O′(0, 0), M′(–4, 7)

10. a) A′(–1, 4), B′(2, –3), C′(4, 1), D′(3, 5)
b) X′(7, 4), Y′(7, 0), Z′(2, 0)
c) N′(–2, 5), P′(–3, 0), Q′(–7, 2), R′(–6, 7)
d) K′(–3, –4), O′(0, 0), M′(4, –7)

11. a) A′(2, 1), B′(7, 2), C′(6, 7), D′(1, 6)
b) A″(–2, 1), B″(–7, 2), C″(–6, 7), D″(–1, 6)
c) A‴(–2, –1), B‴(–7, –2), C‴(–6, –7), D‴(–1, –6)

12. Examples may vary. The triangles that cannot be drawn are: an acute triangle with 2 or 4 lines of symmetry; an obtuse triangle with 2, 3, or 4 lines of symmetry; a right triangle with 2, 3, or 4 lines of symmetry, an isosceles triangle with 0, 2, or 4 lines of symmetry; an equilateral triangle with 0, 1, 2, or 4 lines of symmetry.

13. b) 3
c) Cut the cube in half along the diagonal of a face. There are 6 planes of symmetry like this.
d) 9

14. Answers may vary. Each point on a figure on one side of the plane of symmetry has a matching point on the other side of the plane.

15. A sphere has an infinite number of planes of symmetry.

16. Yes, it is possible. If the triangle has a line of symmetry, reflect the triangle in this line.

17. b) Answers may vary.

18. Answers may vary. On the ground floor, there is a window on the left, but a door on the right. The words written across the building are not symmetrical.

19. a) In ClarisWorks and Microsoft Works, horizontal flips use a vertical line through the centre of the figure as the mirror line. Vertical flips use a horizontal line through the centre of the figure as the mirror line.
c) Answers may vary. **d)** Answers may vary.

20. a) The mirror line is the line through (0, 1) and (2, 3).
b) The mirror line is the line through (–2, 4) and (6, 0).

21. a) The coordinates are K(3, –1), L(7, –1), M(7, –3), N(5, –3).
b) The coordinates are K(–3, 1), L(–7, 1), M(–7, 3), M(–5, 3).
c) For the line through (1, 1), the coordinates are K(1, 1), L(1, 7), M(3, 7), N(3, 5). For the line through (1, –1), the coordinates are K(–1, –3), L(–1, –7), M(–3, –7), N(–3, –5).

23. The triangle is an isosceles right-angled triangle.

24. Examples may vary. The quadrilaterals that cannot be drawn are: a rectangle with 0, 1, or 3 lines of symmetry; a rhombus with 0, 1, or 3 lines of symmetry; a parallelogram with 1 or 3 lines of symmetry; a trapezoid with 2, 3, or 4 lines of symmetry.

25. a) 2 lines of symmetry **b)** 3 lines of symmetry
c) 1 line of symmetry

27. Two coins must be moved.

29. Descriptions may vary.

30. Any quadrilateral that has at least one line of symmetry, drawn so that the y-axis is a line of symmetry

Linking Ideas: Geometry and Integers
Transformations on the Plane, page 416

1. A(+2, +9), B(+2, +3), C(+8, +3)

2. A′(–2, +3), B′(–2, –3), C′(+4, –3)

4. a) K(–4, –2), I(–2, –3), T(–4, –6), E(–6, –3)
c) K′(+2, +5), I′(+4, +4), T′(+2, +1), E′(0, +4)
d) +6 **e)** +7 **f)** Results should agree.

5. Answers may vary.

6. a) P(–6, +6), Q(–3, +5), R(–2, +1), S(–7, +2)
c) P′(+6, +6), Q′(+3, +5), R′(+2, +1), S′(+7, +2)
d) i) They are opposite integers. **ii)** Yes
e) They are equal.

7. Figures may vary. The first coordinates of the image and the figure are the same. The second coordinate of the image is the opposite of the second coordinate of the figure.

8. The coordinates of the image are the opposites of the coordinates of the figure.

Quest: Designing a Booklet, page 418

Yes, some of the pages are upside down.
The numbers on the front and back of each page differ by 1.
If the first fold were parallel to the long side the pattern in the page numbers would not change, but the numbers would appear in different corners of the sheet. The final booklet would be short and wide rather than tall and narrow.

9.3 Rotations
Developing the Ideas, page 419

1. The figures are the same size and shape, but face different directions.

Working with Mathematics, page 421

1. You can rotate the green reptile so it coincides with each other reptile except for the other green ones.

2. **a)** I and III, I and IV, III and IV
   b) I and II, I and III, I and IV, II and III, II and IV, III and IV
   c) I and II, I and III, II and IV, III and IV
   d) I and II, I and IV, II and III, III and IV

4. The centre of rotation could be the point at the top, middle, or bottom of their common side.

5. Answers to part b may vary.
   i) a) S   **b)** 60°   **ii) a)** R   **b)** 72°
   iii) a) B   **b)** 45°   **iv) a)** Q   **b)** 30°

7. **a)** In Microsoft Works, the object is rotated about its centre. In ClarisWorks, the computer creates an invisible rectangular box around the object and rotates the object about the centre of this box.
   c) Answers may vary.

8. **a)** A′(−8, 5), B′(−5, 9), C′(−5, 5)
   b) A′(11, −2), B′(7, 1), C′(11, 1)
   c) A′(−4, 7), B′(−7, 3), C′(−7, 7)
   d) A′(−1, −10), B′(−5, −7), C′(−1, −7)

9. The coordinates of the original figures are as follows:
   a) K(−3, 6), L(−3, 2), M(−1, 2), N(−1, 6)
   b) K(6, −3), L(6, 1), M(4, 1), N(4, −3)
   c) K(−10, 5), L(−6, 5), M(−6, 7), N(−10, 7)

10. An isosceles right triangle

11. Descriptions may vary.

12. You need to know whether the rotations are clockwise or counterclockwise.

13. Answers may vary. The first player should turn her or his page so its sides are not parallel to the sides of the table.

Quest: Identifying Transformations, page 423

Answers may vary.

For the horizontal images: a rotation of 180°; reflection in a horizontal line; reflection in a vertical line; each word has been reflected in a vertical line through its centre; each letter has been reflected in a vertical line through its centre

For the vertical images: a reflection in a line at 45° to the horizontal; a rotation of 90° counterclockwise

Review, page 424

1. **a)** I and II, I and IV, II and IV
   b) I and III, II and IV
   c) I and III, II and III, III and IV

2. Orange: translation 3 units right, 3 units down; brown: 180° rotation; purple: reflection in a horizontal line; yellow: reflection in a vertical line; pink: 90° counterclockwise rotation; green: reflection in a horizontal line; blue: reflection in a horizontal line followed by a translation 5 units right; brown: 180° rotation

3. **b)** The design is a large triangle made from 4 small, congruent triangles. You can continue the design for another row by translating the original triangle 3 times: 2 units left, 4 units down; 4 units down; 2 units right, 4 units down.

4. **a)** A′(4, 6), B′(8, 4) C′(2, 1)
   b) D′(−6, 3), E′(−4, 5) F′(1, 0), G′(−1, −2)

5. There are three such translations. Their descriptions and the coordinates of the vertices of the original are as follows:
   2 units left and 1 unit up: A(0, −2), B(2, 3), C(5, 0)
   1 unit right and 2 units down: A(−3, 1), B(−1, 6), C(2, 3)
   4 units left and 4 units down: A(2, 3), B(4, 8) C(7, 5)

6. There are four such translations. Their descriptions and the coordinates of the vertices of the original are as follows:
   1 unit right and 2 units up: D(−4, 3), E(3, 3), F(3, 0), G(−4, 0)
   1 unit right and 5 units up: D(−4, 0), E(3, 0), F(3, −3), G(−4, 3)
   6 units left and 5 units up: D(3, 0), E(10, 0), F(10, −3), G(3, −3)
   6 units left and 2 units up: D(3, 3), E(10, 3), F(10, 0), G(3, 0)

7. No, the image of a translation must be congruent to the original.

8. **a) i)** P′(3, −4)   **ii)** Q′(−2, −5)
   iii) R′(−3, 1)   **iv)** S′(4, 2)
   b) i) P′(−3, 4)   **ii)** Q′(2, 5)
   iii) R′(3, −1)   **iv)** S′(−4, −2)

9. **a) i)** A′(2, −1), B′(5, −3), C′(1, −4)
   ii) D′(1, −1), E′(2, 3), F′(0, 5), G′(−2, 1)
   b) i) A′(−2, 1), B′(−5, 3), C′(−1, 4)
   ii) D′(−1, 1), E′(−2, −3), F′(0, −5), G′(2, −1)

10. **a)** The mirror line is the vertical line through (−1, 0).
    b) The mirror line is the slanted line through (−1, 1) and (1, −1).

11. **a)** 1   **b)** 4

12. **a)** X   **c)** Both
    d) The letters A, H, I, M, O, T, U, V, W, and Y can all be drawn so they are identical to their reflection image in a vertical line. The letters B, C, D, H, I, K, M, and O can all be drawn so they are identical to their reflection image in a horizontal line.

14. Figures **1** and **2** have rotational symmetry.

15. **a)** W(−2, 1), X(−2, 7), Y(3, 7), Z(3, 1)
    b) W(2, −1), X(2, −7), Y(−3, −7), Z(−3, −1)
    c) W(7, −2), X(1, −2), Y(1, 3), Z(7, 3)

16. Designs may vary.

17. **a)** Answers may vary. Possible coordinates of P are: (6, 6), (−6, −6), (6, −6), (−6, 6), (3, 12), (−3, −12), (3, −12), (−3, 12), (12, 3), (−12, −3), (12, −3), (−12, 3), (4, 9), (−4, −9), (4, −9), (−4, 9), (9, 4), (−9, −4), (9, −4), (−9, 4), (2, 18), (−2, −18), (2, −18), (−2, 18), (18, 2), (−18, −2), (18, −2), (−18, 2), (1, 36), (−1, −36), (1, −36), (−1, 36), (36, 1), (−36, −1), (36, −1), (−36, 1)
    b) You can move P to any coordinate in part a and the rectangle will still have an area of 36 square units.
    c) Only if you moved P so that both rectangles are congruent

Cumulative Review, page 428

2. **a)** $\frac{2}{7} < \frac{1}{2}$ **b)** $\frac{3}{4} < \frac{8}{9}$ **c)** $\frac{4}{5} > \frac{7}{12}$
   d) $\frac{2}{3} = \frac{10}{15}$ **e)** 0.55 > $\frac{4}{9}$ **f)** $\frac{8}{6} < 1.5$
   g) $\frac{3}{10} > 0.28$ **h)** 5.8 < 6.1   **i)** 10.05 > 4.95

3. **a)** $\frac{3}{8}$ **b)** $\frac{7}{6}$, or $1\frac{1}{6}$ **c)** $\frac{5}{10}$, or $\frac{1}{2}$

4. **a)** 60   **b)** 60%

5. **a)** 18; 14   **b)** 30; 2   **c)** About 9%   **d)** About 41%

6. Answers will vary, depending on the sales tax rate.

7. a) 0.15   **b)** 0.08   **c)** 0.035   **d)** 0.7
e) 0.909   **f)** 0.047   **g)** 0.002   **h)** 0.016

8. a) Yes, the outcome of the die roll does not affect the outcome of the coin toss, and vice versa.

b)

		Die roll			
		1	2	3	4
Coin toss	Heads	H1	H2	H3	H4
	Tails	T1	T2	T3	T4

c) i) $\frac{1}{4}$, or 25%   **ii)** $\frac{1}{8}$, or 12.5%
iii) $\frac{1}{4}$, or 25%   **iv)** $\frac{3}{8}$, or 37.5%

9. a) Extremes: 3 and 10; range: 7   **b)** 7
d) Descriptions may vary. There is a cluster between 7 and 8.
e) Median: $7\frac{1}{2}$; lower quartile: $6\frac{1}{2}$; upper quartile: 8
f) Answers may vary.
g) Answers may vary. The information would help you decide how many of each size of shoe to order.

10. a) Rome, New York, Ho Chi Minh City, Prague, Taipei, Singapore, Frankfurt, Hanoi, Central London, Guangzhou, Mexico City, Paris, Tokyo, West London, New Delhi, Shanghai, Beijing, Hong Kong, Central Tokyo, Bombay
b) £372.5; Guangzhou and Mexico City
c) £460.05; New Delhi

11. a) The order of the cities is the same as in exercise 10a. The cities with rental costs closest to the median and mean cost are the same as in exercise 10.
b) Answers will vary.

12. a) +5, +2, 0, −1, −6   **b)** +10, +4, +1, −4, −8
c) +12, +8, −3, −7, −10   **d)** +11, +7, 0, −9, −20

13. a) +11   **b)** +10   **c)** 0   **d)** +6   **e)** +4
f) +12   **g)** −1   **h)** +9   **i)** +5

14. a) +11   **b)** −1   **c)** −6   **d)** −4   **e)** +1
f) −13   **g)** −5   **h)** +12

15. a) −14   **b)** −1   **c)** +9   **d)** −4   **e)** −5
f) +13   **g)** −6   **h)** +6

16. a) 3 p.m.   **b)** 5 a.m.   **c)** 11 p.m.
d) 8 a.m.   **e)** 3 p.m.   **f)** 1 p.m.

17. a) 15.6 cm, 14.4 cm^2 **b)** 31.8 m, 57.2 m^2 **c)** 21.4 km, 18.7 km^2

18. a) 133 cm^2 **b)** 15 cm^2

19. a) 16 m   **b)** 8 cm   **c)** 6.4 km
20. 2600 cm^2 **21.** 925 m^2

22. b)

Width	1	2	3	4
Length	2	4	6	8
Perimeter	6	12	18	24

c) The length is twice the width. $2w$
d) $2w = 16$; $w = 8$
e) The perimeter is 6 times the width. $6w$
f) $6w = 36$; $w = 6$

23. a) v) $n + 7$ **b) iii)** $n - 7$ **c) vi)** $7n$
d) iv) $\frac{n}{7}$ **e) ii)** $\frac{7}{n}$ **f) i)** $7 - n$

24. a) i) $a + 2$ **ii)** $3a$ **iii)** $a - 7$
a) i) 12   **ii)** 30   **iii)** 3

25. The equations in parts a, b, and e are true when $x = 5$.

26. a) $2 = x + 3$; $x = -1$
b) $x - 2 = -5$; $x = -3$
c) $x + 3 = -4$; $x = -7$

27. 8; yes

28. a) Explanations may vary. We know the lengths of the other sides because the edges of a prism are formed by joining sides of a net.
b) The four longest sides are each 4 cm; the five middle-length sides are each 2 cm; the seven shortest sides are each 1 cm.
c) 28 cm^2

29. a) 61.2 cm^3 **b)** 4.9 cm^3

30. a) 80.0 m^3 **b)** 160.0 m^3, 320.0 m^3

31. Green: reflection in a vertical line; blue: reflection in a vertical line; orange: 90° clockwise rotation; pink: translation 3 units right, 3 units down; purple: 90° counterclockwise rotation; black: reflection in a horizontal line

32. a) Square; 8 units left, 4 units down
b) Triangle; 7 units right, 3 units up
c) Rectangle; 5 units right, 6 units down

33. a) Triangle; D′(−5, 5), E′(−6, 3), F′(−1, 1)
b) Rectangle; K′(6, 3), L′(2, 3), M′(2, 2), N′(6, 2)
c) Square; P′(−2, −2), Q′(−5, −2), R′(−5, −5), S′(−2, −5)

34. a) Triangle; D′(5, −5), E′(6, −3), F′(1, −1)
b) Rectangle; K′(−6, −3), L′(−2, −3), M′(−2, −2), N′(−6, −2)
c) Square; P′(2, 2), Q′(5, 2), R′(5, 5), S′(2, 5)

acute angle: an angle measuring less than 90°

acute triangle: a triangle with three acute angles

algebraic expression: a mathematical expression containing a variable; for example, $6x - 4$ is an algebraic expression

angle: the figure formed by two rays from the same end point

approximate: close to the exact value; the symbol $\doteq$ means "is approximately equal to"

arc: part of a circle
        AB is an arc of the circle, centre O.

area: the number of square units needed to cover a region

assumption: something that is accepted as true, but has not been proved

average: a single number that represents a set of numbers; in common usage often the same as the *mean*

balance: a scale that uses two pans on the ends of a pivoting rod to measure mass

Balance Principle: when the same number is added to or subtracted from two equal expressions, the results will be equal

bar graph: a graph that displays data by using horizontal or vertical bars whose lengths are proportional to the numbers they represent

base: the side of a polygon or the face of a solid from which the height is measured; the factor repeated in a power

bias: an emphasis on characteristics that are not typical of the entire population

box graph: a graph that displays data by using shaded parts of a 100-square

broken-line graph: a graph that displays data by using points joined by line segments

centimetre cube: a cube 1 cm long, 1 cm wide, and 1 cm high

circle: a closed curve, all of whose points are the same distance from a point within called the centre

circle graph: a diagram that uses parts of a circle to display data

circumference: the distance around a circle, and sometimes the circle itself

cluster: a section of a line plot in which there is at least one piece of data at each point on the number line

common factor: a number that is a factor of each of the given numbers; for example, 3 is a common factor of 15, 9, and 21

commutative property: the property stating that two numbers can be added or multiplied in any order; for example, $6 + 8 = 8 + 6$ and $4 \times 7 = 7 \times 4$

compasses: an instrument for drawing circles

congruent: figures that have the same size and shape, but not necessarily the same position

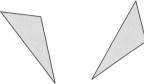

coordinate axes: the *x*- and *y*-axes on a grid that represents a plane

coordinate plane: a two-dimensional surface on which a coordinate system has been set up

coordinates: the numbers in an ordered pair that locate a point on a grid by telling the distance and direction of the point from the *x*-axis and the *y*-axis

cube: a solid with six congruent, square faces

data: facts or information

database: an organized collection of facts or information, often stored on a computer

decimal: a numeral that shows fractional amounts by using digits to the right of a dot called the decimal point; for example, 0.7 is a decimal for $\frac{7}{10}$

denominator: the bottom numeral in a fraction; the denominator tells the number of parts into which the whole has been divided

descending order: arranged in order from greatest to least

diagonal: a line segment that joins two vertices of a figure, but is not a side

diameter: the distance across a circle, measured through the centre; a line segment through the centre of a circle whose endpoints are on the circle

difference: the result when one number is subtracted from another

digit: any of the symbols 0, 1, 2, 3, 4, 5, 6, 7, 8, 9 used to write numbers

dimensions: measurements, such as length, width, and height

discount: the amount by which a price is reduced

dividend: a number to be divided by another number

divisor: the number by which another number is to be divided; a number that divides another without a remainder

double-bar graph: a bar graph that shows two sets of data

double broken-line graph: a broken-line graph that shows two sets of data

edge: the line segment where two faces of a solid meet

equation: a mathematical statement that two expressions are equal

equilateral triangle: a triangle with three equal sides

equivalent: having the same value; for example, $\frac{2}{3}$ and $\frac{6}{9}$ are equivalent fractions

estimate: a careful guess that is close to the actual value, without calculating it exactly

even number: an integer that has 2 as a factor; for example, 2, 4, −2, and −4 are even numbers

event: any set of outcomes of an experiment

expanded form: a way of writing a number so that the place value of each digit is shown; for example, 4679 in expanded form is $(4 \times 1000) + (6 \times 100) + (7 \times 10) + 9$

experimental probability: the probability of an event calculated from experimental results; another name for the *relative frequency* of an outcome

exponent: a number, shown in a smaller size and raised, that tells how many times the number before it is used as a factor; for example, 2 is the exponent in 6^2

expression: a mathematical phrase made up of numbers and/or variables connected by operations

extremes: the highest and lowest values in a set of numbers

face: a flat surface of a solid

factor: any of the natural numbers used to form a product; for example, 2 and 4 are factors of 8

factor tree: a way to find the prime factors of a composite number

first-hand data: data gathered by oneself

formula: a rule that is expressed as an equation

fraction: a number that represents part of a whole or part of a set

frequency: the number of times a particular number occurs in a set of data; the number of times an outcome occurs

gap: a region on a line plot where no data points are plotted

geodesic sphere: a ball-like construction whose framework is made up of triangular sections

greatest common factor (GCF): the greatest natural number that divides into each number in a set; for example, 5 is the greatest common factor of 10 and 15

Greek cross: a geometric figure that resembles an addition sign

hand span: the distance between the tips of the outstretched thumb and little finger of one hand

hectare: a unit of area represented by a square with sides 100 m

height: the perpendicular distance from the base of a figure to the opposite vertex or side (if it is parallel to the base); the perpendicular distance from the base of a pyramid to the opposite vertex; the perpendicular distance between congruent faces in a prism

hexagon: a six-sided polygon

histogram: a graph that uses bars, where each bar represents a range of values, and the data are continuous

image: the figure that results from a transformation

improper fraction: a fraction with a numerator greater than the denominator; for example, both $\frac{6}{5}$ and $\frac{5}{3}$ are improper fractions

independent events: when the outcome of one event does not affect the outcome of another event

inference: a conclusion drawn from factual evidence or data

integer: any of the numbers $\dots -3, -2, -1, 0, +1, +2, +3, \dots$

intersecting lines: lines that meet or cross; lines that have one point in common

intersection: a point where lines or curves meet or cross

irregular polygon: a polygon that is not a regular polygon

isosceles triangle: a triangle with two equal sides

kilojoule: a measure of energy

line: a set of points in a straight path extending infinitely in both directions

line plot: a number line on which each number in a set of data is plotted by making a mark above the number line

line segment: a part of a line between two points on the line

line symmetry: a figure that maps onto itself when it is reflected in a line is said to have line symmetry; for example, line *l* is the line of symmetry for figure ABCD

lower quartile: the number at the one-quarter point when data are arranged in increasing order

mass: the amount of matter in an object

mean: the middle value found by adding the numbers in a set, then dividing the sum by how many are in the set; for example, 38 is the mean for the set of numbers 30, 40, 44

median: the middle number or value when data are arranged in numerical order; for example, 11 is the median for the set of numbers 6, 10, 11, 20, 42

median of a triangle: a line segment from one vertex to the midpoint of the opposite side

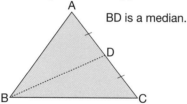

BD is a median.

metric system: a system of measurement based on the decimal system in which units are related by 10, 100, 1000, and so on

midpoint: the point that divides a line segment into two equal parts

minimum: the least value or amount

mixed number: a number consisting of a whole number and a fraction

mode: the number that occurs most often in a set of numbers

Monte Carlo method: the procedure of performing an experiment whose outcomes have the same probability as the outcomes in another experiment that is more difficult to perform

multiple: the product of a given number and a natural number; for example, some multiples of 8 are 8, 16, 24, …

natural numbers: the set of numbers 1, 2, 3, 4, 5, …

negative integer: any of the numbers −1, −2, −3, −4, …

numeral: the written form of a number

numerator: the top numeral in a fraction; the numerator tells how many parts are being considered

obtuse angle: an angle greater than 90° and less than 180°

obtuse triangle: a triangle with one angle greater than 90°

octagon: an eight-sided polygon

odd number: an integer that does not have 2 as a factor; for example, 1, 3, and −7 are odd numbers

operation: a mathematical process or action such as addition, subtraction, multiplication, or division

opposite integers: two integers whose sum is 0; for example, +3 and −3 are opposite integers

order of operations: the rules about which operations to do first when simplifying or evaluating an expression

origin: the point where the *x*-axis and the *y*-axis intersect

outcome: a possible result or answer of an experiment or survey question

parallel lines: lines in the same plane that do not intersect

parallelogram: a quadrilateral with both pairs of opposite sides parallel

pentagon: a five-sided polygon

pentagram: a design showing a five-pointed star with all five points connected by line segments

per capita: for each person

percent: the number of parts per 100; the numerator of a fraction with denominator 100

perimeter: the distance around a closed figure

perpendicular: lines intersecting at right angles

pictograph: a graph that uses a symbol to represent a certain amount, and repetitions of the symbol illustrate the data

pie graph: see *circle graph*

plot: to place in the correct location on a coordinate grid

polygon: a closed figure that consists of line segments; for example, triangles, squares, and quadrilaterals are polygons

population: the set of all the things or people being considered

positive integer: any of the numbers +1, +2, +3, +4, …

power: a representation of a number as the product of equal factors; for example, 64, or $4 \times 4 \times 4$, can be expressed as the power 4^3

power of 10: a product in which all the factors are 10; for example, 10^2 and 10^3 are powers of 10

prediction: a statement of what you think will happen

probability: the likelihood of a particular outcome; the ratio of the number of times a particular outcome occurs to the total number of outcomes

product: the result when two or more numbers are multiplied

protractor: an instrument for measuring angles in degrees

pyramid: a solid whose base is a polygon and whose other faces are triangles that meet at a common vertex

quadrant: one of the four regions into which coordinate axes divide a plane

quadrilateral: a four-sided polygon

quartiles: quarters of the data when they are arranged in order

quotient: the result when one number is divided by another

radius (plural, **radii**): the distance from the centre of a circle to any point on the circumference; a line segment joining the centre of a circle to any point on the circumference

random sample: a sample in which all members of the population have an equal chance of being selected

range: the difference between the highest and lowest values (the *extremes*) in a set of data

rectangle: a quadrilateral that has four right angles

rectangular prism: a prism whose faces are rectangles

reflection: a transformation that maps every point P onto an image point P′ such that P and P′ are equidistant from the mirror line, and line PP′ is perpendicular to the mirror line

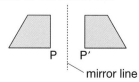

regular hexagon: a polygon that has six equal sides and six equal angles

regular octagon: a polygon that has eight equal sides and eight equal angles

regular polygon: a polygon whose sides are equal and whose angles are equal

regular polyhedron: a polyhedron with faces that are congruent regular polygons

relative frequency: the ratio of the number of times a particular outcome occurred to the total number of times the experiment was conducted

repeating decimal: a decimal in which one or more digits repeat endlessly

rhombus: a parallelogram with four equal sides

right angle: an angle of 90°

right triangle: a triangle that has one right angle

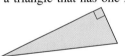

rotation: a transformation in which a figure is turned about a fixed point

rotational symmetry: a figure that maps onto itself in less than one full turn is said to have rotational symmetry; for example a square has rotational symmetry about its centre O

sample/sampling: a representative portion of a population

scalene triangle: a triangle with no two sides equal

second-hand data: data not collected by oneself, but by others; data found in sources such as books, databases, newspapers, encyclopedias, and atlases

sequence: a set of numbers or objects arranged in a certain order

sharing principle: when two equal expressions are divided by the same number, the results will be equal

similar: figures that have the same shape, but not necessarily the same size

simplest form: a fraction is in simplest form when the only common factor of the numerator and denominator is 1

skeleton: a model showing only the edges and vertices of a solid

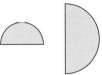

solid: a three-dimensional object whose interior is completely filled; for example, a sphere, a cube, and a pyramid are solids

spreadsheet: a computer-generated arrangement of data in rows and columns, where a change in one value can result in appropriate changes in the other values

square: a rectangle with four equal sides

stem-and-leaf diagram: an arrangement of a set of data showing the concentration of the values; for two-digit values, the tens digits are shown as the "stems" and the ones digits as the "leaves"

straight angle: an angle measuring 180°

sum: the result when two or more numbers are added

surface area: the total area of the surface of an object

symmetrical: possessing symmetry; see *line symmetry* and *rotational symmetry*

tally chart: a chart that uses stroke marks to record the frequency of data

terminating decimal: a decimal with a limited number of digits; a decimal that is complete after a certain number of digits, with no repetition

tetrahedron: a solid with four triangular faces

tiling pattern: a pattern made up of congruent tiles that do not overlap and that leave no gaps

transformation: a reproduction of a figure that results in a change in position, shape, or size of the figure; for example, slides, flips, and turns are transformations

translation: a transformation that moves a point or a figure in a straight line to another position in the same plane

trapezium: a quadrilateral with no parallel sides

trapezoid: a quadrilateral that has only one pair of parallel sides

triangle: a three-sided polygon

triangular prism: a prism whose bases are triangles

triangular pyramid: a pyramid whose base is a triangle

two-dimensional: having length and width, but no thickness, height, or depth

upper quartile: the number at the three-quarter point when data are arranged in increasing order

variable: a letter or symbol that represents a quantity that can vary

vertex (plural, **vertices**)**:** the corner of a figure or a solid

volume: the amount of space occupied by an object

whole numbers: the set of numbers 0, 1, 2, 3, 4, …

x-axis: the horizontal number line on a coordinate grid

x-coordinate: the first number of an ordered pair; the x-coordinate represents the distance and direction from zero along the horizontal number line

y-axis: the vertical number line on a coordinate grid

y-coordinate: the second number of an ordered pair; the y-coordinate represents the distance and direction from zero along the vertical number line

Zero Principle: the sum of opposites is zero

INDEX

Rook, 84, 85
Rotation, 401–403, 419–423
Rotation centre, 419–423
Rotation image, 419–422
Rotational symmetry, 425

St. Lawrence River, 154
Sales tax, 147–151
Sample 220, 223
    biased, 220
    unbiased, 220
Sampling, 220
Satisfies the equation, 354
Scalene triangle, 52
Seating capacity, 202
Second-hand data, 226, 228
Sector, 170, 196, 201
Segment, see *Line Segment*
Septillion, 30
Sequence, 325
Sextillion, 30
Sharing Principle, 362
Similar, 64–66
Simplest form, 94
Simulations, 175
Sixths, 88–92, 110, 116, 117
Slide, 400, 401
Snowfall, 315
Solar system, 31
Solving equations, 346–364
Soma Cube, 392
Spreadsheets, 29, 103, 106, 107, 115, 120, 174, 192, 193, 197, 213, 222, 247, 261, 288, 298, 325, 339
Square, 44, 306, 307, 321
Square centimetres, 279, 308–310
Square kilometres, 308–310
Square metres, 279, 308–310
Square millimetres, 308–310
Square pyramid, 376–381
Statistics Canada, 187, 207, 213, 246
Stem, 206
Stem-and-leaf diagram, 206–207
Straight angle, 58

Subtracting
    fractions, 116–120
    integers, 262–266
Subtraction expression, 262, 263
Subtraction statement, 119, 264
Supernova, 31
Surface area, 382–385
    of a rectangular prism, 382–385
Suzuki, Severn, 268, 269
Symmetry, 412–415, 426, 427

Tally chart, 142, 158–166
Tangram, 78
Temperature, 218, 246, 250, 254, 255, 265, 266, 273, 314, 364
Ten Tiles puzzle, 401, 403
Tenths, 88–92, 98, 102, 103
Terminate, 103
Tetrahedral die, 186
Tetrahedron, 377
Tetris, 400, 401
Thermometer, 250, 255, 256, 266, 314
Thirds, 88–92, 110, 112, 113, 116–118
Thousand Islands, 152
Thousandth, 98, 108
Tiling pattern, 408
Time zones, 241, 267–269
Transformations, 401–403, 416, 417, 423
Translation, 401–408, 416, 417, 423
Translation arrow, 404
Translation image, 404–408
Trapezium, 79
Trapezoid, 40, 44, 302, 303, 414, 415
Trend, 226
Triangle, 40, 51–61, 294–301, 306, 307, 321
Triangular prism, 376–381
Triangular pyramid, 377–381
Trillion, 30
Twelfths, 88–92, 112, 116, 118
Two-pan balance, see *Balance*
Turn, 400, 401

Unit fractions, 115
Unit tile, 358
Upper quartile, 216

Valid, 231
Valley folds, 96
Variable, 321, 340–352
Variable tile, 358
Vertex, vertices, 44, 45, 54, 257, 376–381, 405–409, 411, 413–417, 420, 422
Vertical axis, 256
Volume, 386–393
    of a cube, 387–390
    of a rectangular prism, 386–390

Water use, 236, 237
Women's professional baseball, 108
Word processing, 221, 225
Work chart, 360

x-axis, 256, 257
x-coordinate, 256, 257
x-tile, 358

y-axis, 256, 257
y-coordinate, 256, 257

Zero, 243, 249, 250, 252, 256, 258, 259, 273
Zero Principle, 358, 361

PHOTO CREDITS AND ACKNOWLEDGMENTS

The publisher wishes to thank the following sources for photographs, illustrations, articles, and other materials used in this book. Care has been taken to determine and locate ownership of copyright material used in this text. We will gladly receive information enabling us to rectify any errors or omissions in credits.

p.24 (top) Tom Till/Tony Stone Images/p.24 (middle left) Geoff Dore/Tony Stone Images/p.24 (middle right) Art Wolfe/Tony Stone Images/p.24 (bottom left) David Paterson/Tony Stone Images/p.24 (bottom right) S.P.L./Photo Researchers/p.25 (top left) Peter Timmermans/Tony Stone Images/p.25 (top right) Charles Krebs/Tony Stone Images/p.25 (bottom left) J.R. Williams/Earth Scenes/p.25 (bottom right) Joe Lepiano/p.26 Pronk&Associates/p.29 David Michael Allen/p.30 (left) Doug Pensinger/Allsport/p.30 (top right) Courtesy of Mr. Douglas Mawson/p.30 (bottom right) David Madison/Tony Stone Images/p.31 (top left) Rafael Macia/Photo Researchers/p.31 (top right) Reuters/Corbis-Bettmann/p.31 (middle right) S.P.L./Photo Researchers/p.31 (bottom right) NASA/p.32–33 From *One Million* by Hendrik Hertzberg. Copyright © 1993 by Hendrik Hertzberg. Reprinted by permission from Times Books, a division of Random House, Inc./David Michael Allen/p.34 Ian Crysler/p.35 Ian Crysler/p.38 David Madison/Tony Stone Images/p.39 Joe Lepiano/p.40 exercise 1a) CF is a registered trademark of the Cadillac Fairview Corporation Limited b) Clarkson Gordon, Woods Gordon c) The Imperial Life Assurance Company of Canada d) © Mercedes Benz e) Bell Mobility Cellular f) Acorn Structures Inc./p.44 Ian Crysler/p.48 Vic Thomasson/Tony Stone Images/p.49 (top left) Peter Miller/Photo Researchers/p.49 (top right) Paolo Koch/Photo Researchers/p.49 (bottom) Hilarie Kavanagh/Tony Stone Images/p.50 (top) Corbis-Bettmann/p.50 (bottom) Ian Crysler/p.51 Ian Crysler/p.54 *The Geometer's Sketchpad*, Key Curriculum Press, P.O. Box 2304, Berkeley, CA 94702, 1-800-995-MATH/p.55 David Michael Allen/p.56 Ian Crysler/p.57 Ian Crysler/p.61 Guy Motil/First Light/p.62 Dave Starrett/p.64 Ian Crysler/p.84 David Michael Allen/p.85 David Michael Allen/p.93 David Michael Allen/p.98 (left) Nathan Bilow/Allsport/p.98 (right) Bernard Asset/Allsport/p.108 (top) All-American Girls Professional Baseball League/p.108 (bottom left) All-American Girls Professional Baseball League/p.108 (bottom right) Saskatchewan Sports Hall of Fame & Museum photograph/p.109 (left) Peter J. Thompson/p.109 (right) A.D. Percival/p.110 Ian Crysler/p.113 David Michael Allen/p.116 Ian Crysler/p.120 Joe Lepiano/p.123 Ian Crysler/p.126 (top and bottom) Canapress/p.132 (top left) David Young Wolff/Tony Stone Images/p.132 (top right) Jon Gray/Tony Stone Images/p.132 (middle) Jeff Kaufman-F.P.G./Masterfile/p.132 (bottom left) Walter Hodges/Tony Stone Images/p.132 (bottom right) John Riley/Tony Stone Images/p.133 (left) Bruce Ayers/Tony Stone Images/p.133 (right) David Ximeno Tejada/Tony Stone Images/p.136–137 (all) Canapress/p.138 David Michael Allen/p.140 David Woodfall/Tony Stone Images/p.143 David Michael Allen/p.144 (left) Ian Crysler/p.144 (right) David Michael Allen/p.145 David Michael Allen/p.152 Ken Straiton/First Light/p.153 Stephen Homer/First Light/p.157 David Michael Allen/p.158 David Michael Allen/p.159 David Michael Allen/p.160 Excerpted from the article "Viva Italia! Olé, Olâ, Brasil!" in the *Toronto Star*, July 16, 1994/p.163 David Michael Allen/p.164 David Michael Allen/p.165 "Animal Crackers" cartoon reprinted by permission: *Tribune Media Services*/p.166 "One in 10,000 Chance You'll Live to be 100" reprinted with permission—The Toronto Star Syndicate/p.167 David Michael Allen/p.168 Dave Starrett/p.169 Ian Crysler/p.174 David Michael Allen/p.178 David Michael Allen/p.179 Rate card courtesy of the *Winnipeg Free Press* advertising department/p.184 Frans Lanting/First Light/p.185 (top) Louise Gubb/JB Pictures/p.185 (bottom) Patrick Morrow/First Light/p.186 Art Wolff/Tony Stone Images/p.187 Adaptation of graphs by Stephen Fink/*Canadian Geographic*/p.188 Ron Watts/First Light/p.193 Stephen Dunn/Allsport/p.194 (top) Adaptation of graph by Pierre Mion © National Geographic Society/p.194 (bottom) Joe Lepiano/p.196 Joe Lepiano/p.200 David Michael Allen/p.202 (top) John Sutton/Photo Search/p.202 (bottom) Walter Schmidt/Tony Stone Images/p.203 Canapress/p.206 Canapress/p.207 (left) The Provincial Archives of Alberta/p.207 (middle left) Canapress/p.207 (middle right) Anahareo, Acc. 9164 S14412; Archives of Ontario/p.207 (right) Canapress/p.209 Ian Crysler/p.210 Ian Crysler/p.214 Everett Collection/p.215 (all) Everett Collection/p.221 David Michael Allen/p.224 John Sutton/Photo Search/p.224 Excerpt from "The Future of Poetry in Canada" by Elizabeth Brewster from *Selected Poems* by permission of Oberon Press/p.226 (top) Joe Lepiano/p.226 (bottom) David Michael Allen/p.227 (top) Mike Powell/Allsport/p.227 (bottom) Gray Mortimore/Allsport/p.230 (top) "Hi & Lois" reprinted with special permission of King Features Syndicate/p.231 Used by permission of Ann Landers and Creators Syndicate/p.232 "Winter Resort Industry Takes Off" reprinted from *200% of Nothing* by A.K. Dewdney. Copyright © 1993 A.K. Dewdney. Reprinted by permission of John Wiley & Sons, Inc./p.233 Corbis-Bettman/p.236 "Canada's Garbage Is Piling Up" reprinted with permission—The Toronto Star Syndicate/p.240 Ian Crysler/p.241 Pronk&Associates/p.242 Ian Crysler/p.243 Ian Crysler/p.245 Ian Crysler/p.247 (top) Ken Straiton/First Light/p.247 (bottom) Melanie Rockett/Photo Search/p.250 (top) David Michael Allen/p.250 (left) Greg Locke/First Light/p.250 (middle) Richard Hartmier/First Light/p.250 (right) Dave Reede/First Light/p.256 David Michael Allen/p.268 (top) *Vancouver Sun*/p.268 (bottom) Barry Rowland/Tony Stone Images/p.269 Lawrence Migdale/Photo Researchers/p.272 (left) Courtesy of Dr. Katherine Heinrich/p.272 (right) Courtesy of Dr. Alvin Baragar/p.278 exercise 1 a)-e) Joe Lepiano f) Ian Crysler; exercise 3 David Michael Allen/p.284 Bill Ross/First Light/p.285 David Michael Allen/p.290 Ian Crysler/p.295 Ian Crysler/p.297 Bob Alexander/p.298 (top) Ron Watts/First Light/p.298 (bottom) Joe Lepiano/p.299 David Michael Allen/p.304 "What Is the Area of a Newspaper?" reprinted with permission—The Toronto Star Syndicate/p.304 (top and bottom) The *Toronto Star*/p.305 David Michael Allen/p.306 (top) Bob Alexander/p.306 (bottom left) Joe Lepiano/p.306 (bottom middle) David Michael Allen/p.306 (bottom right) Joe Lepiano/p.308 Ian Crysler/p.310 "It's Alive!" reprinted with permission—The Toronto Star Syndicate/p.314 David Michael Allen/p.315 Ian Crysler/p.332 Everett Collection/p.333 Everett Collection/p.340 David Michael Allen/p.341 Pronk&Associates/p.343 David Michael Allen/p.353 David Michael Allen/p.355 David Michael Allen/p.359 Courtesy of Mrs. Gloria Buckley/p.361 Glen Allison/Tony Stone Images/p.368 David Michael Allen/p.372 Ed Pritchard/Tony Stone Images/p.373 (top left) Dean Conger © National Geographic Society/p.373 (top right) Stephen Studd/Tony Stone Images/p.373 (middle right) Dave Reede/First Light/p.373 (bottom left) Alan Smith/Tony Stone Images/p.373 (bottom right) Ron Watts/First Light/p.374 (top) Stephen Evans (photo), Richard Sinclair (model)/Kuwabara Payne McKenna Blumberg/p.374 (bottom) Ian Crysler/p.382 David Michael Allen/p.382 (inset) Ian Crysler/p.385 Joe Lepiano/p.386 (left) Ian Crysler/p.388 exercise 6 David Michael Allen; exercise 7a) David Michael Allen b) and c) Joe Lepiano/p.389 (bottom left) Canapress/p.389 David Michael Allen/p.392 "Crayon Maker Color-blind" reprinted with permission from

Associated Press/p. **392** Greg Holman/p. **392** (insets) Courtesy of Binney & Smith Canada/p. **393** David Michael Allen/p. **396** David Michael Allen/p. **397** David Michael Allen/p. **402** David Michael Allen/p. **404** Ian Crysler/p. **409** Ian Crysler/p. **410** Ian Crysler/p. **413** David Michael Allen/p. **414** Bob Alexander/p. **418** David Michael Allen/p. **419** Ian Crysler/p. **420** Corbis-Bettmann/p. **426** (top) Ian Crysler/p. **426** (bottom) First Light/p. **427** David Michael Allen

ILLUSTRATIONS

Steve Attoe **160, 173, 253, 264, 326, 327, 328, 421**
Graham Bardell **151**
Mike Herman **30, 87, 272, 273, 320, 321**
Brian Hughes **38, 149, 150, 192, 194, 216, 236, 279**
Bernadette Lau **280, 282, 283**
Steve MacEachern **78, 79, 117, 148, 237, 248, 249, 291, 346, 347, 366, 368, 369**
Martha Newbigging **27, 241**
Jun Park **88, 89, 125, 251, 252, 258, 268, 281, 300, 318–319**
Ian Phillips **380**
Steve Quinlan **195**
Brian Ritchie **220**
Kent Smith **334, 335, 336, 342, 348**
Margo Stahl **147**
Technical art by Pronk&Associates unless otherwise stated.